CHILDREN'S LITERATURE
IN
HITLER'S GERMANY

The Cultural Policy
of National Socialism

CHRISTA KAMENETSKY

Ohio University Press
Athens, Ohio
London

Library of Congress Cataloging in Publication Data

Kamenetsky, Christa, 1934-
  Children's literature in Hitler's Germany.

  Bibliography: p.
  Includes index.
  1. Children's literature, German—History and criticism. 2. National
socialism and literature. 3. National socialism in literature. I. Title.
PT1021.K35 1984   830'.9'9287   83-8220
ISBN 0-8214-0699-X

To Ihor
and Andrey
for their love
and patience.

Contents

Acknowledgments

I wish to thank the following publishers whose illustrations I used with their formal or implied consent:

ARS edition (formerly: Verlag ARS sacra Josef Müller); Deutsche Verlags-Anstalt; Verlag Moritz Diesterweg (and Otto Salle), G.m.b.H.; Alfred Hahn's Verlag, Walter Dietrich K.G.: Hanseatische Verlagsanstalt (formerly Aktiengesellschaft Hanseatische Verlagsanstalt); Harper and Row, Publishers (on behalf of Lippincott); Verlag Ferdinand Hirt; Informationen Jugendliteratur und Medien; Gerhard Stalling Verlag; Thienemanns Verlag; Cornelsen-Velhagen & Klasing G.m.b.H.; Voggenreiter Verlag. In addition, I thank the staff of the Hoover Institution on War, Revolution, and Peace (Stanford) for having made accessible to me illustrated materials that were originally published by the National Socialist Party, the Reich Youth Leadership Organization, the National Socialist Teachers Association, and other official agencies of the Third Reich.

I also wish to express my appreciation to the German Information Office (New York), the Börsenverein des Deutschen Buchhandels (Frankfurt), the Deutsche Bibliothek (Frankfurt), and the Library of Congress for having aided me in locating some of the sources and publishers.

Illustrations

Plate Number	Source	Page Number

Plate Number   Source   Page Number

Preface

In children's literature the Nazis perceived one of their most important tools for re-educating children in the spirit of National Socialism. They were not satisfied with controlling their behavior merely by drill and discipline but aimed through children's books at promoting such values that would induce them to internalize the National Socialist ideology and to defend it enthusiastically.

In order to achieve a total control over the minds of children, the Nazis tried to convey through children's books the spirit of their Volkish ideology. To that end, they engaged thousands of censors, drafted mainly from the members of the National Socialist Teachers Association and the Reich Youth Leadership Organization, who would systematically screen every book that was published, sold, loaned, purchased, circulated, or discussed. Through school reforms and a reorganization of libraries throughout the nation they further institutionalized censorship measures that would separate the books they preferred from those that were to be discarded. By abolishing all civil liberties and the possibilities of open dissent, and by centralizing the vast network of the censorship apparatus within the general power structure of Party and State, they hoped to reach their goal not within a year or two but certainly in the decades to come. They generally referred to their long-range goals in this regard as the *Volkserziehungsprogramm* (folk education program).

The Nazis' censorship procedure followed a "negative" as well as a "positive" direction. The "negative" censorship received its first orientation from Goebbels' so-called "black lists" containing the titles of works that were to be removed from the schools, libraries, and bookstores because they fell under the category of "folk alien" or "decadent" literature. This process began rather dramatically with rallies and book burning ceremonies in public squares, yet it evolved into a less visible continuous process when the centralized censorship apparatus had been mobilized to take action.

The "positive" censorship was systematically applied after the bulk of the books that were deemed offensive had been discarded. There was nothing truly "positive" about it, except that it helped to fill the empty shelf spaces. The kinds of books that took the place of those which had been removed, however, were just as carefully screened as the rest, perhaps even more so, as they were thought to be the basic tools for forming the "young team" of the future that obediently and loyally would fight for the German folk community and the *Führer*. The Nazis considered this censorship to be "positive," as it was supposed to single out everything that would contribute first of all to a positive image of Ger-

many's past and the National Socialist present. To these ends, they gave particular attention to German and Nordic Germanic folklore, because in the inherited values of the past they discovered ideals and traits that they adjusted to
their own political purposes. Such remodelled values they hoped to develop
into a mythos appealing to romantic, idealistic, and patriotic sentiments, thus
creating the impression that Hitler's "folk state" was firmly rooted in the traditions of the Nordic Germanic "ancestors."

The time of the Nazis' seizure of power coincided with an era in the Weimar
Republic when various Volkish groups were promoting the idea of strengthening German unity and national consciousness by emphasizing pride in the German and Nordic Germanic folk heritage. While some of these were already
racially oriented, many other circles merely pursued some nationalistic goals.
The Nazis cleverly simulated the romantic aspects of Volkish thought, while
approaching them selectively and adding weight to racial tendencies. With increasing political control, however, they gradually eliminated all liberal, democratic, and international ideas that used to characterize not only the orientation
of some early German writers of the Romantic movement but also various
nationalistic circles that by 1933 were not yet entirely integrated within the
framework of the National Socialist ideology.

In regard to children's literature, the Nazis' cultural policy led to a biased and
didactic view of the inherited folk tradition, as well as to an ethnocentric perspective of literary criticism. Through an abundance of books dealing exclusively with the German and "Nordic" spheres of interest, children were exposed
to a distorted view of German and Nordic Germanic folklore. At the same time,
this policy consciously kept them away from books promoting world understanding across racial and national boundary lines.

I have dedicated a major portion of this work to an investigation of the
Nazis' Volkish-racial bias and its implications for such genres of children's literature as folktales, myths, sagas, fiction, the classics, and picture books. In the
Nazis' uses and adaptations of children's literature, whether in regard to reading primers, dramatic activities, or Volkish rituals, I have tried to trace the
pattern which emerged from their manipulation of traditional values for the
purpose of ideological indoctrination. The analysis of the role which children's
literature and folklore played in the curricular reforms and the reorganization
of libraries is intended to give further insight into the Nazis' relatively consistent
practice of institutionalizing their Volkish ideology within the educational system on a more permanent basis.

The full impact of the Nazis' cultural policy on children's literature may be
estimated only in view of trends that preceded it. For this reason I have devoted
the opening chapter to a close investigation of the background pertaining to
children's literature within the context of the broader cultural and political
context of pre-Nazi Germany. This analysis will reveal certain weaknesses in
Romantic nationalistic ideas that were already evident among some Volkish

groups in pre-Nazi days, but it will also reveal how the Nazis distorted other Romantic concepts while imposing upon them their own interpretation. Among the most admirable aspects of Romantic thought which became subject to the Nazis' abusive policy were those that gave rise to the German and international folklore revival and to the creative and professional development of children's literature as a respectable discipline.

When Hitler came to power in 1933, literary standards, along with pedagogical, psychological, and universal human perspectives of children's literature had to be sacrificed to the "one and only goal," the folk state of the *Führer*. In the name of the German "folk community," the Nazis made children's books into the means toward another end that would perpetuate the power of the Third Reich both at the time and in the future.

I am grateful to the staff of a number of libraries in Germany and in the United States for having made accessible to me the resources that pertained to my research on this topic. I acknowledge with great appreciation the help I received in Munich from the Bavarian State Library, the International Youth Library, and the Institute for Contemporary History, and in Frankfurt from the Youth Book Research Institute of the Johann Wolfgang von Goethe University. In the United States I am very much indebted to the University of Illinois Library (Urbana), the University of California Library (Berkeley), the Stanford University Library, the Hoover Institution on War, Revolution, and Peace (both at Stanford), and the Library of Congress. I wish especially to thank Mrs. Agnes Petersen, Miss Mary Schofield, Mr. Adorjan I. de Gaffy, and Mr. Milodrad M. Drachkovitch at the Hoover Institution and Archives for assisting me in locating some valuable research materials pertaining to my topic. Also, I sincerely thank Mr. H. Shields from the Children's Book Division of the Library of Congress for guiding me through a maze of relevant literature.

A Research Professorship Grant from Central Michigan University enabled me to travel to various libraries in connection with this project, while it provided me for one semester with released time from teaching responsibilities. I have deeply appreciated this unique opportunity and thank President Harold Abel, Vice Provost Ernest Minelli, Dr. Hans Fetting, and the Committee on Research and Creative Endeavors for their encouragement on this behalf. Thanks are also due to the staff of the Park Library at Central Michigan University, to Mary Moses (Smith), to Carol Swan, and Carol Pasch for some technical assistance.

Finally, I wish to extend a word of gratitude to my husband, Ihor Kamenetsky, for having alerted me to the ideological schemes of totalitarian states that undermine individual moral responsibility and critical judgment. To my sister, Alice Breyer, and to Jürgen, her husband, I acknowledge with thanks their warm interest in this work throughout its creation, and also their loan of some rare books from a private collection.

PART I

Literary Theory and Cultural Policy

1

The Roots of Children's Folk Literature in Pre-Nazi Germany

During the eighteenth and nineteenth centuries, children's literature in Germany in many respects resembled that of other countries in Europe. First, there were didactic books that were specifically written for children with the intent of teaching them religious lessons along with secular morals and manners. Secondly, there were the "classics," many of which were originally written for adults but were later adapted for children. Finally, there was folklore in various forms: ballads, folk songs, myths, legends, and folktales of many lands, which German children enjoyed both in the oral tradition and in the printed versions.

In didactic literature for children, stories usually served as a means to another end, and the sermons were often longer than the plot—if plots were present at all. Some of these books contained tales about the saints, including religious legends, but others were merely illustrated catechisms or children's sermons. The secular literature included ABC books, works on geography, history, and science, as well as handbooks on manners and morals designed to instruct "young ladies" and "young gentlemen." The style of such works was often stilted and artificial, or else, dry and rather factual. In both cases, children could count on a moralistic ending.

In the eighteenth century, children particularly enjoyed those works that were richly illustrated, regardless of whether they were didactic in nature or of even older origin. Thus, Goethe in his childhood read Comenius' *Orbis Pictus* (*The World of Pictures*), and Raff's *Naturgeschichte* (*Natural History*).[1] At that time Bodmer's works, too, enjoyed great popularity, in spite of their didactic tendencies, as did Weisse's first German children's journal, *Der Kinderfreund* (*The Children's Friend*).[2] In 1787 Friedrich Gedike observed that, for his taste, there were too many types of books for children on the market, such as almanacs, story anthologies, poetry books, sermons for children, novels, comedies, tragedies, books of history, geography, biography, letters, and instructional conversations. Unfortunately, he wrote, most of these had been composed by "scribblers" with limited skills in writing. Children's book publishers, too, had cared more for their own financial profits than for good quality.[3] It

2

appears from the context of Gedike's complaint that he objected primarily to stylistic flaws and the shabby paper on which these works had been printed— not to the didactic tendencies present in most of them. Obviously, both the didactic content and the moralistic tone of books for children was taken for granted in those days. Humor, imagination, and adventure were rare commodities in children's literature of the eighteenth century, as the authors placed instruction far above entertainment.

Therefore, it does not come as a surprise that children in Germany and elsewhere turned to the "classics." Here, at last, they found what their own books denied them: above all, a good story with a convincing plot. Some of the most popular works among the classics were the *Odyssey* and the *Iliad* by Homer, including the myths and hero tales of classical mythology. Further, they enjoyed reading Aesop's *Fables*, the tales of the *Arabian Nights* including *Sinbad the Sailor*, the epic tales of *Roland* and *Siegfried*, the romance of King Arthur and his knights of the Round Table, Cervantes' *Don Quixote*, Swift's *Gulliver's Travels*, and, of course, the Bible. They either read these works in an unabridged form, skipping whatever they didn't like or didn't understand, or their parents read aloud to them at family gatherings. The case was different with Defoe's *Robinson Crusoe*, as an all-time favorite with children, as Campe had successfully prepared the first German children's edition of this work as early as 1720. During the course of the eighteenth century four more adaptations of the book appeared in Germany, but Campe's remained the most popular one until the twentieth century.[4] Goethe read it in his childhood—alongside with other works not written for children: *Insel von Felsenburg* (*Island of Rock Castle*), Lord Anson's *Reise um die Welt* (*Journey Around the World*) and most of the other classics.[5]

In the nineteenth century, German children very much enjoyed reading, in addition, Hoffmann's *Struwwelpeter* (*Slovenly Peter*), and the jolly picture stories in verse by Wilhelm Busch, *Max und Moritz* (*Max and Moritz*) and *Hans Huckebein* (the story of a mischievous raven). Even though these stories were still "moralistic," they presented, in a tongue-in-cheek fashion, a grotesque kind of humor that appealed to children. In the last decades of the nineteenth century children also became acquainted with some of the finest newer books from abroad. In German translation they read Cooper's *Leatherstocking Tales*, Mark Twain's *Tom Sawyer* and *Huckleberry Finn*, Kipling's *Jungle Book*, Dickens' *Oliver Twist*, Dumas' *The Three Musketeers*, Verne's *Twenty Thousand Leagues under the Sea*, and Lewis Carroll's *Alice's Adventures in Wonderland*. These were works that appealed to their sense of imagination and adventure, as they had plots, themes, and characters with whom they could identify. One of the most popular works with children and adults alike was Harriet Beecher Stowe's *Uncle Tom's Cabin*. Even though literary critics had reservations about it on account of its sentimental style, they did not deny its humanitarian spirit. Children liked it, above all, not because it "taught" them the principles of brotherhood and Christian love, but simply because it moved them to warm compassion, particularly for "Uncle Tom."[6] Here and in the other classics there were *concrete* stories, not *abstract* lessons.

A third category of books available to German children in earlier centuries dealt with folklore. In this genre, German children were especially well supplied with works appealing to their sense of adventure and imagination at a relatively early date when moralistic trends in England, for example, still dominated the scene. Herder and the Brothers Grimm initiated an interest in native as well as international folklore collections that eventually would fascinate all of Europe. Even before the Brothers Grimm printed their *Kinder- und Hausmärchen* in 1812, German children had enjoyed, in addition to the oral tradition, the German *Volksbücher* (folk books or chapbooks) dating back to the Middle Ages. Among them were the tales of Dr. Faustus, Magelone, Till Eulenspiegel, Siegfried, Genoveva, and Reynard the Fox.[7] Goethe rewrote a number of these chapbooks which even Musäus, Brentano and the Brothers Grimm read with pleasure in their childhood.[8] In the wake of Romanticism Görres published *Die Teutschen Volksbücher* (*The German Chapbooks*) and thus made the bulk of them available to young people in an anthologized form.

When the Brothers Grimm first began to record the oral tradition of German folktales, these stories still circulated freely among the more conservative peasant folk in the countryside. By this time, however, the Grimms noted that many of the city folk and the educated elite looked down upon them as "superstitious stuff" not worthy of the printer's ink. With their publication of the folktales, and especially with their prefaces to the various editions, the Brothers Grimm contributed much to the acceptance of folktales as literature, for they built up a new understanding for the grace and poetry contained in their simple language, vivid imagery and sense of justice.[9] The very fact that the work became an instant success in Germany and was reedited several times in expanded editions shows that the German readers warmed to their folktales to an unexpected degree.

Nevertheless, some parents remained sceptical toward the folktale. In 1828, the literary historian Wolfgang Menzel observed: "They are afraid that folktales might implant into their children's souls some superstitions, or, at any rate, that reading folktales might lead them to be preoccupied with realms of fancy—something that would be detrimental to their schoolwork."[10] Evidently, these sceptics overrated the role of factual instruction as much as they underrated the role of the creative imagination. Menzel felt that their views reflected a certain narrow-minded attitude and also bad taste. It was a pity, he wrote, that in many cases children were given such moralistic and prosaic stories to read as "Poky Little Franzi" and "Curious Little Lotti," while their parents kept them away from the rich world of poetry and imagination that lay waiting for them in the world of folktales. We know that similar attitudes prevailed in Great Britain at approximately the same time. In both cases, parents tended to rate "useful" information, explanatory remarks, and a character's "reasonable" behavior—at least at the end of a given story—far above the "fanciful" adventures of the mind.[11]

In Germany, the acceptance of folk literature as an integral part of children's literature, and simultaneously, a greater appreciation of the literary fairy tale, began in the era of Romanticism. Writers such as Tieck, Arnim, and Brentano, for example, not only warmed the general public to collected folktales but also to fantasies, many of which were read by both children and adults.[12] To that era also belonged such writers as Novalis (Friedrich von Hardenberg), de la Motte-Fouqué, von Chamisso, E.T.A. Hoffmann, and Mörike, all of whom, in their own unique ways, explored the fairy tale for their literary purposes while contributing to the creative growth of children's literature. The undercurrent of didactic trends was not strong enough to halt the new wave of interest in folklore and works of the creative imagination.[13]

The Nazis glorified Herder, the Brothers Grimm, and the Romantic movement as a whole, but mainly for their contributions to the discovery of the "healthy folk reality"—not for their discovery of free imagination. Consequently, they would pay tribute to the collectors of German folklore, yet they would largely ignore the writers of fantasy. Even in singling out Herder and the Brothers Grimm for their "positive" contributions to the growth of the German nation, as they put it, they would selectively emphasize their collections of *national* folklore while they would ignore their contributions to comparative folklore and literature as well as to international understanding.[14]

And yet, it was Herder who, with his first international folk song collection toward the end of the eighteenth century, stimulated German interest in the *Urpoesie* (primeval poetry) of many lands. His *Stimme der Völker* (*Voice of the Nations*) contained authentic folk songs from a great number of nations, including the American Indians, and its preface supported the idea that, originally, all nations had sung with "one voice" to honor God who had endowed each one of them with an equal share of love. As a true Christian, Herder believed that each nation, like every individual, was equal and unique before God and that it was equipped with a "folk soul." To recapture this soul, he said, which civilization had partially buried, it was necessary that each nation should collect the folk songs, myths, folktales and legends of the past, for in these was still living the naïve and pure spirit of ancient times.[15]

The Brothers Grimm shared Herder's concept of the *Urpoesie*, which they renamed *Naturpoesie* (nature poetry). In respecting this theory of its common origin, they kept alive their vital interest in the folktales of other lands. Folklorists from the Scandinavian countries, among them Asbjörnsen and Moe, corresponded with them over many years, and so did folklore scholars from England, Scotland, Ireland, Russia, and Serbia, to name just a few. The Brothers traveled to various foreign countries, and in turn, they received many visitors from foreign lands.[16]

The poetic and scholarly contributions of the Brothers Grimm to international and cross-cultural studies are quite remarkable by themselves. Wilhelm translated old Danish and old Scottish ballads while studying their background, and in 1823, just one year after its original publication, he translated, together with Jacob, the *Fairy Legends of the South of Ireland*, to which he added an original essay about the fairies of Ireland, Scotland and Wales.[17] Jacob published in 1835 the first study of comparative mythology, the *Deutsche Mythologie (Teutonic Mythology)* that contained a systematic arrangement and analysis of parallel myths and folk beliefs in all of the "Teutonic" countries. This work is too scholarly to be counted as children's literature, but like his comparative grammar, the *Deutsche Grammatik (German Grammar)*, and his translation of the monumental Serbian grammar, it gives evidence of his international (rather than merely national) orientation in folklore, language and linguistics.

What Herder and the Brothers Grimm told the other nations on behalf of the search for their "folk soul" through native folklore, they applied also to themselves. Undoubtedly, they had strong sentiments for their own fatherland and hoped to strengthen Germany's self-awareness by reviving her national folk traditions. In this context they considered the Nordic Germanic folk heritage as an integral part of the native German tradition. Their "forefathers" had not been "savages," they said, but peasants and warriors worthy of respect. As they encouraged their compatriots at home to shake off the fetters of foreign imitations, they called for the development of national pride, hoping that a revival of native folklore would help in promoting this goal.[18]

A closer analysis of the changing role of German and Nordic Germanic folklore in German culture of the nineteenth century is important for our background study of children's literature in Nazi Germany, as the Nazis willfully distorted it. Whereas officially they took pride in having initiated a cultural revolution with the establishment of a "New Order" in the Third Reich, in effect, they spent much energy on "documenting" the "evolution" of Nazism from pre-Romantic and Romantic thought. The Nazi writer Dahmen, for example, in his work *Die nationale Idee von Herder bis Hitler* (The *Idea of Nationalism from Herder to Hitler*) claimed that Nazism was rooted in the heritage of Herder and the German Romantic movement. Julius Petersen went so far as to expound the idea that in their "Nostalgia for the Third Reich in German Legend and Literature," the Nordic Germanic tribes had, more than a thousand years ago, foreseen the coming of the "savior," Adolf Hitler;[19] that the Romantic writers had continued this dream, and that the Nazi Regime had finally brought a fulfillment of this prophecy. In their text selections the Nazis consistently gave preference to political Romanticism over cultural Romanticism, while even in this case quoting passages out of context.

Among the early Romantic writers there were some indeed whose interest in folklore and poetry was secondary to a concern with politics.[20] They were patriots at heart and strongly nationalistic, although not radically exclusive as far as other nations, races, or traditions were concerned. Among these were Friedrich Ludwig Jahn and Ernst Moritz Arndt. In 1810, Jahn published his book *Deutsches Volkstum* (*German Ethnicity*) in which he expressed his longing for a renewal of Germandom from its "source." He shared some ideas with Grimm but had his own plan. Folklore played a definite role in his program, especially folk songs, but in the final analysis, it represented only a minor aspect of his physical fitness program based on the principles of patriotism.[21] Yet, folklore fused with nationalistic ideas was to have a very strong impact on the German Youth movement in the years to come, which considered Jahn as one of their spiritual fathers.[22] Ernst Moritz Arndt, too, was better known for his political contributions than for his folklore research or his volumes of fairy tales.[23] In his work *Volk und Staat* (Folk *and State*), published between 1802 and 1815, he praised the solid and safe possession of the soil inherited from generation to generation. Like Langbehn and de Lagarde after him, he saw the peasant as guardian not only of folklore but of the soil, thus praising him as the protector of the German state. He deserved to be called "the first of the fatherland," and Arndt, as he had best preserved the original native concepts of custom, law, honor, loyalty and closeness to tradition and the land. He set the peasant up as a sharp contrast to the *Bürger* (bourgeois) of the cities who had lost interest in both tradition and land while chasing after superficial entertainment.[24] While Jahn used German folk songs for his youth programs, thus hoping to revive German national consciousness among the young, Arndt became more engaged in political theory which made substantial use of the Nordic Germanic folk heritage.

The idea that the simple peasant held the key to certain intuitive powers of knowledge which were lacking in civilized man was not the invention of the early Romanticists nor of Herder, but originally came from Rousseau. New to the German interpretation of the "noble savage" concept was its association of the "golden age" with that of the Nordic Germanic past within the context of an "organic" folk state.[25] It was mainly due to the influence of Heinrich Wilhelm Riehl that by the middle of the nineteenth century the study of folklore in Germany developed as a science, with close affinities to the field of sociology. In the idyllic and peaceful peasant community Riehl saw the basis for a new society built according to the pattern of medieval estates. For the industrial worker he developed a plan that was to transform him into a member of the folk community: he was to receive a small piece of land that he was expected to cultivate in his free time. Riehl thought that in this way he would not only strengthen his communion with the soil but also with the people of the peasant community. Within this community, he would recapture what he had lost as a result of civilization: his creative self, his individuality.[26] Tönnies later developed the sociological contrast between the *Gemeinschaft* (community) and the *Gesellschaft* (society), both of which the Nazis adopted for their own purposes while denying the role of the individual within the community.[27]

We may identify two reasons why the German Romantic writers placed so much emphasis on folklore and folk community. Aside from Schelling's nature philosophy which influenced many of their thoughts pertaining to the mystical power of the landscape, they faced some real problems with regard to the state of the nation, as well as the German cultural situation at large. Both of these they hoped to remedy. After Napoleon's conquest, the three hundred diverse little dukedoms and kingdoms that made up Germany were reduced to forty-eight, which still did not bring about political or cultural unity. Officially, Germany did not reach statehood until 1871, and even then there were diverse systems, customs, and traditions that seemed to work against the ideal of the folk community. Nordic Germanic folklore, and peasant folklore in general, were at least a bond in history that was thought to work in favor of national unity.

A general dissatisfaction with the state of German culture motivated many German writers in the second part of the nineteenth century to diagnose the "disease" and to propose some remedies. As a cultural critic, Friedrich Nietzsche attacked German philistinism prevalent at his time in all spheres of life and art, along with rationalism and an extreme type of aestheticism. Other critics, although of lesser intellectual status than he, shared this diagnosis, but instead of advocating the contemplative power of the spiritual "superman" gaining wisdom from social isolation, they strongly urged for a return to the folk community and the "roots" of German ethnicity. Among them, particularly Paul de Lagarde and Julius Langbehn had a strong influence on the development of Volkish thought that would influence children's literature a few decades later.

De Lagarde bemoaned the fact that there was no *German* history, no *German* education, and no *German* folklore in the cultural life of the nation. People had forgotten their heritage; they trampled thoughtlessly upon the ruins of old monasteries and landmarks and hardly remembered Siegfried, the treasure of the *Nibelungen*, or the old German folktales. Education paid homage to classical ideals of Greece and Rome while neglecting native folklore, history, and literature. Nevertheless, Lagarde thought it was not too late to revitalize the idea of German ethnicity: "The old Germany is not yet dead . . ." he wrote in his *Deutsche Schriften* (*German Writings*). Even though life in the cities resembled that of wilting hothouse plants taken out of their natural environment, there was still hope for the German peasantry "rooted" in German traditions: "Behind the plow and in the forest, at the anvil of the lonely smithy, there we will find it. It helps us to fight our battles and grow the corn in our fields."[29] De Lagarde proposed a Nordic Germanic "Volkish" orientation within an "organic" folk community concerned with native religion, art, science, and literature—*albeit* under a "God-inspired *Kaiser*."

Julius Langbehn, too, advocated a return to the Germanic North. Although he wrote his doctoral dissertation on Greek sculpture and spent much of his time in the South, he idealized the Nordic Germanic peasants and men of the North in general as the "true symbols of Volkish strength." Like de Lagarde he glorified the German peasant, but more as the true representative of the German *Volk* who might save the nation from cultural despair. To him, the Germans were a peasant folk at heart, an *Urvolk* (primeval folk), endowed with native intelligence, a sense of independence and creativity. Rembrandt was his model of the *Urvolk*, of Nordic Germanic man himself. In his work *Rembrandt als Erzieher* (*Rembrandt as an Educator*) he proposed that Germans had to become true to their character and origin, just as Rembrandt had always been. Only in this way would they be able to unfold their mystical creative powers from within and once more rise as a nation. Langbehn strongly recommended a national art policy that would build up German self-confidence through a contemplation of German history and folklore. His book went through eight editions within the first two years following its publication and turned out to be the "Germanic Gospel" for hundreds of educators. Leaders of the German Youth movement reportedly carried it along on hiking trips, where it helped them to formulate their program.[30]

De Lagarde and Langbehn were strongly anti-semitic. For the Nazis, however, who very much admired both of them, their anti-semitism wasn't strong enough, as they both believed in the "assimilated Jewry" determined by the degree of conversion to Nordic Germanic and conservative thought, rather than by blood.[31] On the other hand, we have in the writings of these "Conservatives" already the idea of a cultural policy based on the concept of German ethnicity. In a more radical way Adolf Bartels and Josef Nadler applied this idea to literature around 1900, thus introducing a racially oriented literary policy[32] pursued on an unprecedented scale by the Nazis after 1933. While Bartels and Nadler were the first ones to use the term "decadent literature" in association with "undesirable" cosmopolitan, liberal and Jewish influences, the Nazis later added to it the term "heroic literature" in an effort to promote a "positive" censorship policy based on Nordic Germanic heroic ideals and their own ideology.

This is not to say that all Volkish thought was racist or political, or that Nazism was the inevitable result of a historical evolution. On the contrary, trends in the nineteenth and twentieth centuries give evidence of a great variety of ideas and concepts existing side by side. The Volkish writers themselves were full of inconsistencies and paradoxes—a fact that the Nazis preferred to ignore. De Lagarde and Langbehn, like Jahn, Arndt, and Riehl, also still believed in the unique individual and his organic role within the folk state—a thought from which the Nazis extracted only the latter part. In selecting passages from their works, National Socialist textbook writers and anthologists worried little about possible misrepresentation of Volkish thought, as long as it helped to support their ideological orientation.[33]

Plate 1
THE PEASANT AND THE NORDIC PAST
"Either we will be a peasant Reich, or we will not be at all!"

(Adolf Hitler)

Toward the end of the nineteenth century, a neo-Romantic wave inspired the writing of a number of regional and historical novels concerned with German ethnicity, the German peasant, and the Nordic Germanic past. Among the historical novels were those of Dahn and Freytag, and among the peasant novels, the works of Keller, Raabe, and Storm. Whereas the first focused on the peasant and warrior of Germanic times, the second glorified the mysterious powers of the landscape and the life of the sturdy German peasant. At the same time there emerged a number of regional novels concerned with the theme of man's kinship with the soil and his home, namely by Löns, Sohnrey and von Polenz.[34] These works were "Volkish," yet unpolitical in the sense that they served no political interest groups and advocated no national policy for Germany's cultural reform. Still, the Nazis felt they were well suited for the promotion of their Volkish ideology.

According to Martin Broszat, the word "Volkish" involved a conglomerate of divergent meanings. "Hardly another word, due to its glittering power of association has so well paved the way for National Socialism as the word 'Volkish.' Indeed, under this term we find all kinds of ideologies from anti-semitism to ideas about the folk community; from blood-and-soil theories to the new Germanic mythos."[35]

The history of the children's literature reform movement around the turn of the century well illustrates the diverse directions which the Volkish movement itself had inspired in this area. In response to the writings of Langbehn and to their own professional conscience as educators, Lichtwark and Avenarius in Hamburg were instrumental in founding the German Art Education movement, the so-called *Kunsterziehungsbewegung*. They also founded the journal *Der Kunstwart* (The Art Guardian), and through its pages advocated the revival of art and folklore within the school curriculum and in German cultural life in general, so as to help the nation in its realization of becoming a genuine folk community. Through art and folklore they hoped to cure German civilization from insensitivities and a superficial and fragmented life style developed under the stress of a purely prosaic life. Heinrich Wolgast was a member of this movement and adopted its aesthetic principles for the field of children's literature, while appealing to educators, writers, illustrators and publishers of children's books in order to implement his reform suggestions.[36]

In 1896 Wolgast published *Das Elend unserer Jugendliteratur* (*The Troubled State of Our Children's Literature*),[37] in which he deplored the declining quality of children's books while setting up new literary and artistic standards for their possible improvement. Wolgast was not alone in his plight. The German *Jugendschriften-Bewegung* (Youth Book movement or Childrens' Literature Association) was formed by educators a few years earlier, and in 1893, the various branches of this Association in Augsburg, Berlin, Coburg, Bremen, Frankfurt a.M., Hamburg, Hildesheim, Königsberg, Nördlingen, Wiesbaden and Zerbst jointly issued the first professional children's literature journal, the *Jugendschriften-Warte* (*Youth Literature Guardian*). At the beginning, it was published as a supplement to a major pedagogical newspaper, but then became independent under Wolgast's editorship. Throughout its existence, until the time when the Nazis took it over for their own ideological purposes in 1933, it maintained its position beyond political interest groups while fighting for standards in children's literature.[38] Wolgast's work set the major guidelines for the editorial committee, at least for the first decade or two. Later, an inner struggle of different reform ideas developed, in the course of which Wolgast came under attack and was partially overruled, but even today it is recognized that he laid the cornerstone of a literary criticism that elevated children's literature from a subservient position to a well respected genre.[39]

The first target of Wolgast's criticism were publishers, writers and illustrators who for the sake of improving their income had lowered their standards to the degree that they had produced what he called *Schundliteratur* (trash). Under this term he grouped a great variety of books that he considered to be in poor taste by being overly sentimental, overly didactic, too trite, too "incredible" as far as their plots and characters were concerned, or merely shabby in their style and illustrations. Among these he counted not only works cheaply printed for "mass consumption" (often given away in department stores as advertisements) but also mystery, adventure and detective stories characterized by sensationalism and clichés, as well as the popular girls' books patterned in a sentimental style after Richardson's *Pamela* but within a German upper-class setting. Children would fare much better without reading these "trivia," said Wolgast, as they were quite unrelated to good taste.

Wolgast was the first critic who called for quality control in children's literature on the basis of literary, and artistic standards. He appealed to writers, illustrators and publishers to show their respect for the child by producing their very best. Writers should abstain from "talking down" to the child, artists should not "scribble," and publishers should not look for business first. Significantly, Wolgast was also the first critic to voice his objection against didacticism in childrens' literature. Gedike, Menzel, and others, in spite of their critical views, had taken for granted that childrens' books were primarily there to teach certain things. Wolgast called the didactic trend an "abuse" of children's literature. Whenever an interest group, be it religious, educational, political, or economic in nature, used the child's book as a means to another end, thus reducing the story itself to a carrier of his message, it showed little respect for literature and less for the child. Children deserved respect, insisted Wolgast, and therefore, he demanded for them the best that national literature and world literature had to offer. Good quality books were meant to develop good taste in the child and to bring him in touch with humanity as a whole.[40]

Wolgast made a particular point of attacking children's books that taught chauvinism. In one of his reviews he pointed out that one story character had been eager to forgive his friend the sins of lying, cheating, and stealing, but that he had been pitiless in his judgment when he found out that he had faltered in his loyalty to the fatherland. Wolgast expressed his dismay at the discovery that a writer should have placed the value of loyalty to the nation above that of respect for the Ten Commandments. This was pure chauvinism, he wrote, which was as misplaced in children's literature as were religious and secular didacticism, business interests, or political ideologies.[41]

Due to Wolgast's initiative, children's book authors, publishers and illustrators worked together to produce several series of inexpensive paperback editions with tasteful designs and in attractive formats. These were intended to bring to young people the very best of national and world literature, thus providing a bridge for human understanding through literature. Among others, he published *Schöne Kinderreime* (*Beautiful Children's Rhymes*), the folktales by the Brothers Grimm, a new edition of the *Nibelungenlied* (*Song of the Nibelungs*), tales by Hebel and Hauff, medieval chapbooks, memoirs of the Napoleonic wars and a children's book version of *Wilhelm Tell* (*William Tell*), in addition to a number of children's classics from other lands. In 1909 the Hillger Publishing Company brought out a series entitled *Deutsche Jugendbücherei* (*German Youth Book Library*), and between 1903 and 1910 the Kunstwart Publishing House, representing the Art Education movement, issued the series *Der deutsche Spielmann* (*The German Organ Grinder*), all of which contributed much to raise the quality and respectability of children's literature in Germany. Above all, these publications showed that it was perfectly possible to combine an emphasis on national literature and folklore with a genuine interest in world literature. Wolgast's various writings were pioneering also in regard to the development of children's book illustrations in Germany, for in the wake of the Children's Literature movement such famous illustrators as Ernst Kreidolf, Fritz Kredel, Else Wenz-Viëtor, Elsa Eisgruber and others produced the very best of their works.[42]

On several accounts Wolgast was strongly challenged, however. One of the major criticisms was voiced by Lichtenberger, on the basis that Wolgast had gone "overboard" by advocating "art for art's sake" in children's literature. It was wrong, he said, to apply the same aesthetic and literary criteria to children's books as to books written for adults. Such an approach ignored all the insights gained through theories of education and psychology pertaining to child development. In the first place, it was necessary to recognize that books for children had to have "childlike" qualities (without being childish or condescending in tone or simplistic in regard to the illustrations). This meant that it would have to recognize children's needs while appealing to the child's way of thinking and the child's imagination. Such an approach to criticism found strong support among the members of the Children's Literature Association, most of whom represented teachers who were informed about child development, and it is still widely accepted today.[43]

The second challenge came from the Socialist Party, the SPD, claiming that Wolgast, in his over-emphasis on aesthetic criteria, had not given enough attention to the needs of workers' children. On the contrary, his sharp criticism of so-called "tendentious literature" had come into direct conflict with the promotional efforts of the SPD and its ideology and should be retracted or amended.

During an official meeting of the National Children's Literature Association, this criticism gained a hearing, but it was not recognized as valid. Upon a long discussion of the matter, the leader of the Socialist Party retracted his own letter of complaint while in principle acknowledging the validity of the Association's concern with quality control based on Wolgast's ideas.[44] For Wolgast himself this was a real victory.

A third and more serious challenge came from Severin Rüttgers, an educator who had well established his reputation in children's literature circles by his publications on the literary education of elementary school children. He attacked Wolgast, and with him the entire Art Education movement, for having been too "bookish" and too "aesthetic" in their evaluation of art and literature for children. In particular, he accused Wolgast of having labelled sound patriotism in children's books as "chauvinistic trends." Such an approach to criticism revealed nothing less than that Wolgast himself lacked warm feelings for the fatherland, possibly because he simply lacked patriotism. As early as 1913 Rüttgers had previously denounced some trends in German education as "unpatriotic" and "sterile" on a similar basis, while coming to the conclusion that aestheticism was derived from an unhealthy overemphasis on a humanistic-classical education. Rüttgers reasoned, then and now, that as an antidote to such a trend teachers should place a greater emphasis on German and Nordic Germanic folklore in their reading curricula at all levels, so as to build up in children a love of home and country. In fact, it was quite sufficient, he wrote, if elementary school children read nothing else but German and Nordic Germanic folktales, myths, and legends, in addition to some medieval chapbooks, and, perhaps, some regional ballads.[45]

Much of the discussion on this issue was carried on in various issues of the *Jugendschriften-Warte*, especially after World War I. The editors gave equal space to Wolgast and Rüttgers, but it appeared that Wolgast was in a defensive position throughout. Nevertheless, he stated quite clearly that, while he had never denied the value of a German and Nordic Germanic folklore emphasis, he had consistently rejected chauvinism in children's books like any other type of didacticism, be it of a religious or secular nature. Children's books should never be used as a means to another end, he concluded emphatically.[46]

During the following years it became evident that Rüttgers had won the argument as far as the majority of the teachers were concerned. Although opinions were still divided among them as a professional group, the Volkish-political orientation gradually took the upper hand, and with it also the nationalistic folklore trend. Many publishing houses by the mid-twenties were printing an abundance of German and Nordic Germanic folklore for children and youth, which, in turn, made this reading material more readily available to teachers. Rüttgers himself edited the series *Blaue Bändchen* (*Little Blue Volumes*) and *Quellen* (*Sources*) and also contributed to folklore publications creatively by rewriting a number of myths and legends of the Nordic Germanic tradition for children and youth. Among these, his *Nordische Heldensagen* (*Nordic Hero Tales*) was well received by the younger generation.[47]

By 1922 Rüttgers had underscored the significance of national literature and folklore at a national children's literature convention, while calling them representative of "German blood and German fate."[48] The literary critics Josef Prestel[49] and Irene Graebsch[50] early during the Nazi period still commended him for his strong stand on behalf of a renewal of the German national identity from the sources of German and Nordic Germanic folklore. Graebsch at that time expressed her admiration for his deep faith in "the one and only future" (*die ganze und einzige Zukunft*). In her view, Severin Rüttgers' publications, along with Leopold Weber's children's books on Norse mythology and the Nordic sagas, Theodor Seidenfaden's *Heldenbuch* (*Book of Heroes*), Will Vesper's version of the *Nibelungenlied*, but also the regional "Volkish" tales of Blunck, Matthiessen, and Watzlik, had well prepared the ground for the new orientation under National Socialism. As the National Socialists did not yet have their own writers, she explained, it was only "natural" that they should turn to those older works that corresponded to their line of thinking.[51] Prestel and Graebsch were remarkably uncritical in their evaluation of National Socialism and its uses of folklore, while presenting the case as if the Nazis were merely continuing a well established "natural" and innocent trend.

A closer examination of trends in children's literature during the twenties will reveal, however, that they were still characterized by variety rather than uniformity, and that in the educational policy of the Weimar Republic some reform movements were underway that might have paved the way to democracy and a true concept of freedom. The folklore emphasis in the twenties was characterized by nationalistic tendencies, yet it was not yet exclusive of other cultures and traditions. A number of works appeared for children that introduced them to other lands as well. Rüttgers himself did not only publish works on Norse mythology but also on the legends of the saints, for example. His *Gottesfreunde* (*The Friends of God*) certainly did not correspond to "Volkish thought" of Nazism, and neither did Weismantel's *Blumenlegende* (*Flower Legends*) or Arntzen's *Vom Heiland und seinen Freunden* (*The Savior and His Friends*). Further, there was a movement toward contemporary themes in children's books. Erich Kästner's *Emil und die Detektive* (*Emil and the Detectives*) focused on self-reliant street boys in Berlin who in superb coordination tried to solve their own case problems. The Children's Literature Association in Hamburg recommended this book in 1930,[52] along with others that were concerned with modern problems, such as Scharrelmann's *Piddl Hundertmark* (*Piddl One-Hundred-Marks*), Newerow's *Taschkent, die brotreiche Stadt* (*Tashkent, the Corn-Rich City*), Beumelberg's *Sperrfeuer um Deutschland* (*Fire Surrounding Germany*) and Remarque's *Im Westen Nichts Neues* (*All's Quiet on the Western Front*). It is remarkable that the last book was still recommended at this date, for three years later it was one of the first ones to be thrown onto the public bonfires and—on account of its pacifist theme—to be banished from all school and public libraries.

Translations from other languages, too, enriched the field of children's literature during the twenties. Particularly at this time, Mark Twain's *Tom Sawyer* and *Huckleberry Finn* met with a great success, and also Kipling's books for young people were very popular. Quite a number of books were translated from the Danish, Norwegian, and Swedish, too, among them Marie Hamsun's *Langerrudkinder* (*The Langerrud Children*), Westergaard's *Per von der Düne* (*Peter of the Dunes*) and Floden's *Harald und Ingrid* (*Harald and Ingrid*), although we may speculate that these works corresponded again to the Nordic orientation of the "Volkish" trend. Nevertheless, the trend was still well balanced by the classics from many lands available to children and youth in various editions. In spite of nationalistic tendencies there were no restrictions placed on international literature, as far as the public schools or libraries were concerned.[53]

Between 1924 and 1925 the Prussian Ministry of Education published curricular guidelines for elementary and high schools in Germany, which had been worked out in cooperation with representatives of the teaching profession. These guidelines were not mandatory, however, and left each school enough freedom to work out variations. Great emphasis was placed on cooperative planning with students. For the first time in the history of German education the use of source materials was encouraged over the use of textbooks, and students were taught to enjoy discussions and debates. This was quite a welcome change in comparison with the previous emphasis on lectures, memorizing, and drill. There was also the introduction of so-called *Wandertage* (hiking days) and of camps and school houses in the country meant to accommodate youngsters on field trips arranged by teachers. Both of these innovations represented an inspiration of the German Youth movement.[54]

Side by side there existed in the Weimar Republic liberal and Volkish-conservative thoughts, and in that sense, the era may well be called one of experimentation. The Volkish thinkers, however, slowly gained the upper hand, in education too. Next to Rüttgers there were Otto von Greyerz and Martin Havenstein who not only emphasized the use of regional literature, German and Nordic Germanic folklore, along with German history, but who also rejected "foreign" influences on German culture and education, thus trying to confine children's reading to national literature and folklore exclusively.[55]

To answer the question of why these educators gained such mass support in Germany, we would have to examine the emergence of various Volkish groups in the twentieth century that favored such an attitude. First, there was the *Alldeutscher Verband* (*Pan-Germanic League*), founded as early as 1894, which stated as its main platform the introduction of German folk culture into education and all spheres of life. Its constitution defined as one of its major objectives the promotion of education on the basis of German ethnicity and a simultane-

Plate 2
The Wandervogel Mood Still Prevailed . . .

ous suppression of all factors deemed contrary to German national development. Among other things, this meant the prohibition of using foreign languages at club meetings, a rejection of "foreign" influences, and a replacement of foreign place names by German ones. The League consisted of 44,000 members in 1917 and had a strong impact on the "Volkish interpretation" of Gobineau's principles of race and culture in Germany.[56]

Another Volkish group that strongly influenced the "Nordic" orientation of German literature and culture in the twenties was the *Thule Gesellschaft* (Thule Society), founded in 1917 by Count Sebottendorf. It was designated as a German order of medieval knighthood in the Nordic Germanic style. Its symbol was the swastika, and its values combined nationalism with the Norseman's code of honor. Particularly in their rituals and festivals the members of the Thule Society paid homage to the Nordic gods, while they practiced Nordic customs and traditions, including solstice celebrations in honor of Balder. The renowned publisher of folklore for young people, Eugen Diederichs, was an active member, and so were a number of prominent intellectuals who later formulated the Nazi Party program. The Society's journal, the *Völkischer Beobachter* (*The Volkish Observer*)[57], like Stapel's journal *Deutsches Volkstum* (*German Ethnicity*), at this time made substantial use of Nordic folklore and Volkish thought for political purposes.[58]

In 1924, F. K. Günther published his work *Ritter, Tod und Teufel* (*Knight, Death, and Devil*) which later became the German bible of anti-semitism and was also instrumental in developing the so-called "Nordic Renaissance" in Germany that influenced the Reich Peasant Leader Walther Darré and National Socialist thought in general. The work was sponsored by the *Deutsche Nationale Volkstums-Partei* (German National People's Party) which called for "a German rulership by German blood" and "a protection from foreign invaders" by censorship measures that would "purify" law, science, literature, art, and the press from "folk-alien" elements.[59] Günther borrowed his symbol of the knight from Dürer, but in his theory it came to represent a mixture of Nietzsche's ideal hero and the saga hero of the Germanic North, of racial "Volkish" strength and Odin-Wotan's spirit of defiance.

Class, President of the Pan-Germanic League, managed to join the various Volkish-political groups in an alliance early in the twenties.[60] Many of them expressed their thoughts in Bartels' journal, *Deutsches Schrifttum* (*German Writings*).[61] These various Volkish groups were neither consistent nor uniform in their racial orientation, yet they believed in promoting nationalism through native folklore and Volkish thought.

The longing for community was also a characteristic trend of the German Youth movement. It included left wing and right wing groups, Christian groups and sports organizations, young workers groups and even the German Boy Scouts. Even the most prominent group among them, the *Wandervogel Bewegung* (Wandering Birds movement) was split up into different ideological groups, although all of them shared with the rest a love of nature and a desire to sing, to hike, and to work *together* for the unity of the fatherland. The movement which began in 1901, found a common goal during the renowned meeting of all members in 1913 on Mt. Hohen Messner (near Darmstadt), and it flourished vigorously even after the First World War had taken from their midst a

Ritter St. Georg   Albrecht Dürer

Plate 3
St. George or the Norse God Odin?
(Illustration from a German School Reader of 1937:
An Echo of F. K. Günther's Thoughts)

great number of volunteers who fell in battle. The *Wandervogel Bewegung* never developed into a political group or party, yet its ideological convictions exercised a strong influence on German youth, and it left its mark also on the orientation of many teacher training colleges in Germany. Being dissatisfied with the growing atomization and alienation of urban life, its egotism, and liberalism, these young people yearned to find "youth among youth" within a classless community of equals. They symbolized a kind of non-political rebellion against the stagnant life pattern of the *"petit bourgeois"* in society. On the other hand, the movement as a whole also contributed to conservative thought and a growing nationalism in Germany, and even though it was non-political, its racial exclusiveness (at least in some groups) coincided with some of the Nazi trends.[62]

The folklore revival of the German Youth movement resembled that of the German Romantic movement, although there was a stronger emphasis here on the actual uses of folklore in outdoor activities and celebrations. On hiking trips and around campfires the young Germans would sing and strum their guitars as they enjoyed their togetherness in the small communities. Nationalism was only a part of their program, although they tended to associate the bonds that united them within their groups with the bonds of the larger folk community. Walter Flex, who also wrote a popular book about the involvement of the members of the German Youth movement in World War I in *Der Wanderer zwischen zwei Welten* (*The Wanderer between Two Worlds*), composed the leading theme for them:

> To remain pure
> And to grow mature:
> This is the most beautiful
> And most difficult art of life.[63]

Even more popular with German youth at that time was Hans Breuer's *Der Zupfgeigenhansel* (*Jack, the Guitar Strummer*) that was first published in 1908.[64] Many of these apparently innocent interests in nature and the outdoors, in storytelling, folk singing, and solstice celebrations (in the old Nordic Germanic style) we shall rediscover a few decades later in the Hitler Youth program.

One of the more radical of the various groups of the German Youth movement was the *Artamanen* movement. It was a utopian type of community founded by Willibald Hentschel in 1923, which pursued not only nature and group activities of the *Wandervogel* type but also some Volkish-political objectives. Officially it stood for the "fight for German ethnicity"—a theme which we encounter again in many variations in the Nazis' reading primers for young people. Like the Nazis at a later date, the *Artamanen* made active use of Nordic Germanic folklore, particularly in rituals and festivals designed to arouse their members to a feeling of "unity" for their common cause. Part of their program was to settle young Germans as peasants in the Eastern Provinces, particularly where they thought that German ethnic identity was endangered by foreign cultural influences. In 1925 the initial group of the *Artamanen* had only 140 members, but the idea for which they stood evidently caught on, for two years later their membership had grown to 1,800. Much of what we consider an integral part of the Nazi ideology, including the Nordic Germanic orientation and the emphasis on the peasant cult, was derived from the influence of the *Artamanen* on the Nazi leaders. Walther Darré, Reich Peasant Leader and also Agricultural Minister under Hitler, was a member of this movement,[65] and Heinrich Himmler, Reich Leader of the SS, was for some time a leader of the Bavarian *Artamanen* group. After 1933, the Nazis formally integrated the *Artamanen* into the *Reichssiedlungsamt* (Reich Settlement Office), and from their settlement program and community service the Nazis developed the *Reichsarbeiterdienst* (Reich Workers Service). Rödiger, Eisenbeck, and Kretschmer of the Reich Workers Service, were all former members of the *Artamanen*, thus providing a direct line of continuity.[66] Robert Proksch, Head of the *Reichsamt für Deutsche Bauernbevölkerung* (Reich Office for the German Peasant Population) was also a former member of the *Artamanen* and continued to appraise its history even after Hitler's seizure of power. Proksch saw a direct influence of the *Artamanen* on the Nazis' determination to conquer the "living space areas" (*Lebensraumgebiete*) in Eastern Europe.[67] The *Artamanen*, he said, believed in strength based on culture and race, as well as on God's deepest knowledge. Their "blood-and-soil" concept motivated young people to become peasants and to move across the German frontiers into the Eastern Provinces, so as to "*fight for German ethnicity*" (it.), thus helping the nation as a whole. To achieve their objectives, the *Artamanen* felt that it was necessary to cultivate German and Nordic Germanic folklore within dramatic settings, so as to build up a "sense of community" among Germans at home and abroad.[68] In that sense they considered folklore as a "weapon" in the struggle toward national unity.

The Nazis were quick to seize upon these ideas for their own purposes. In the *Wandervogel* movement and the *Artamanen* movement they perceived perfect examples of how German and Nordic Germanic folklore could be applied to festivals and rituals in such a way as to enhance the "feeling for community"— something toward which they aspired through their "folk education" program. Undoubtedly, they received some of their ideas from Severin Rüttgers, too, who, in various contexts, had emphasized the need to place folklore into "action," in order to develop in children a strong emotional identifiction with the community of the nation. In earlier publications on literary education for elementary school children Rüttgers had begun to defend the idea that it was not enough to *read* folktales, myths, and legends but that children should *experience* (it.) them in the context of festivals and celebrations. His 1933 edition of *Erweckung des Volkes durch seine Dichtung* (*The Awakening of the Nation through Its Literature*) essentially underscored the need to employ children's literature and folklore for Volkish-political purposes.[69]

The very fact that the Nazis did borrow a substantial number of ideas and customs from earlier Volkish groups and individuals, however, does not necessarily imply that these may be held responsible for their misuses within the Nazi Regime. Undoubtedly, some of the "roots" of Volkish thought came rather close to the Nazi ideology, and in extreme cases were identical with some of its aspects. Still, in pre-Nazi times, none of the writers or groups had ever attempted to adopt its ideology exclusively for the entire nation and to implement it by force, while making children's literature and folklore their instrument of Volkish propaganda. Nevertheless, it appears clear that the Nazis did not invent ethnocentric and racial ideas based on the concept of German ethnicity.

In 1933, the German Youth movement was formally dissolved to make room for the Hitler Youth Organization under the leadership of Baldur von Schirach. Many of its members joined the ranks of the Hitler Youth in the hope that Hitler was the destined "leader" of the people as their poet, Heinrich George, had prophesied it. Scholars today differ in their views of whether the leadership cult and some anti-democratic tendencies of the Youth movement in pre-Nazi days may be held responsible for the rise of Nazism. Pross maintains that its "blue flower of longing" contained its own poison, whereas Sontheimer believes in its innocence, while he characterizes it as a "movement beyond politics."[70] The truth probably lies somewhere in between.

The Nazis disapproved of the German Youth movement as a whole, mainly because it served a variety of groups with different orientations. Significantly, however, they did try to keep alive all of its activities that had a romantic appeal, including the emphasis on folk songs, storytelling, and such sports as cross-country hiking, along with nature crafts, campfires, and even the solstice celebrations.[71] All of these they merged with their own ideology, while superimposing upon them the stamp of uniformity. By 1939, the Hitler Youth Organization was the only youth organization left, and about seven million children and youths were forced to march, sing, and celebrate according to the same blueprints. By that time, some of the activities had already lost their popularity, mainly because they were no longer based on a freedom of choice and because attendance had become mandatory nation-wide.

Given the amount of freedom and the diversity of movements that had still existed in the Weimar Republic, totalitarianism cannot be considered a predestined fate of the German nation or an inevitable evolution of history. In earlier days, the Volkish-political groups still used to be balanced by others representing liberal and international ideas along with the peaceful goal of world understanding. All of these countervailing forces were abolished by force, along with the opposition, when Hitler seized power in 1933.

With the rise of Nazism a didacticism was imposed upon children's literature for which there was also no equivalent in the past. The didactic trends of earlier

Plate 4
Young Hero of the Reich

times had served at least the moral and religious instruction of the individual child, but now literature and the child were both placed at the service of the State. One of the main reasons why such a radical change in the literary and ideological orientation was not immediately evident to all involved was because the Nazis so cleverly emphasized the Romantic folklore revival[72] and pre-Nazi Volkish trends. Many former members of the German Youth movement and others, too, who had been steeped in Volkish thought, came to believe that censorship was a necessary temporary measure to bring to fruition the German dream of national unity. The following analysis will show how step-by-step the Nazis utilized such misconceptions to their own advantage by promoting a "Volkish literature" to strengthen the ideological goals of the Third Reich.

NOTES

1. Johann Wolfgang von Goethe, *Dichtung und Wahrheit* in Bernt von Heiseler, ed., *Goethe, Gesammelte Werke*, Vol. 6 (Gütersloh, Bertelsmann Verlag, 1954), Part I.

2. Christian Felix Weisse published in 1766 *Lieder für Kinder*, a volume of children's songs, that went through five different editions within the span of ten years. His *Kinderfreund* appeared between 1775 and 1882 in twenty-eight volumes and was translated into French and Dutch. Kunze refers to it as the typical journal of the enlightenment, as it emphasizes morality and the power of reason. See Horst, Kunze, *Schatzbehalter: Vom Besten aus der alten Deutschen Kinderliteratur* (Hanau, Werner Dausien Verlag, 1965), p. 124.

3. Friedrich Gedike, *Gesammelte Schulschriften*, Vol. I (Berlin, 1789), pp. 422-423. Cited by Kunze.

4. Bettina Hürlimann, *Three Centuries of Children's Books in Europe* (Cleveland, The World Publishing Co., 1968), pp. 99-113.

5. Goethe, in reference to the year 1760. See Kunze, pp. 37-38. He further mentioned Fénelon's *Telemacchus* and the German chapbooks.

6. Kunze, pp. 293-295. An excerpt from *Uncle Tom's Cabin* is the only sample of "foreign children's books" popular with German children that Kunze includes in his anthology, the *Schatzbehalter*. See also Hürlimann, pp. 173-174.

7. *Ibid.*, pp. 39-40. See also: Joseph Prestel, *Handbuch der Jugendliteratur*, Vol. 3. (Freiburg, Herder Verlag, 1933), pp. 53-56. A new edition of the German chapbooks is available in two volumes under the title *Die Deutschen Volksbücher* (Retold by Gustav Schwab). (Vienna, Verlag Lothar Borowsky, 1975). Originally, the *Volksbücher* were not anthologized but were sold individually as slim (and inexpensive) paperbacks.

8. *Ibid.*, pp. 37-38.

9. See Wilhelm Grimm, "Vorrede" *Kinder- und Hausmärchen* (based on the Oelenberg manuscript) (Heidelberg, J. Lefftz, 1927). In this preface Wilhelm Grimm explained that in rewriting the folktales he followed as closely as possible the *spirit* of the original language. This intention frequently has been confused with the original recording of the tales that was done in complete loyalty to the oral tradition. See Christa Kamenetsky, "The Brothers Grimm: Folktale Style and Romantic Theories" *Elementary English* (March, 1974), 379-383.

10. Wolfgang Menzel, *Die deutsche Literatur*, Part I (Stuttgart, 1828), pp. 270-273. Cited by Kunze, p. 43.

11. Harvey Darton, *Children's Books in England: Five Centuries of Social Life* Cambridge, Cambridge University Press, 1932), pp. 163-168. Darton explores in these pages the reasons why some British writers at that time did hold

folktales in a rather low esteem. See Samuel F. Pickering, Jr., *John Locke and Children's Books in Eighteenth-Century England* (Knoxville, The University of Tennessee Press, 1981), pp. 40-69, and Cornelia Meigs, et al., *A Critical History of Children's Literature* (New York, Macmillan Co., 1953), pp. 97-98.

12. Tieck and Brentano were less concerned about loyalty to the spirit of the oral tradition than were the Brothers Grimm, and thus did not care too much about making a distinction between the folktale (*Volksmärchen*) based on the inherited oral tradition and the literary fairy tale or fantasy (*Kunstmärchen*) based largely on the writer's imagination. Yet, in taking certain liberties and mixing the genres, they created a number of delightful fairy tales that appealed to all ages. See also: Jens Tisner, *Kunstmärchen* (Stuttgart, Metzler, 1977), pp. 4-5.

13. Hürlimann, pp. 1-41.

14. The very extensive preface of the Grimms' longer combined folktale edition of 1950 includes an extensive bibliographical listing of all fairy tale editions that had appeared in other countries since 1812. See *Kinder- und Hausmärchen gesammelt durch die Brüder Grimm*. Erster Band, Grosse Ausgabe. (Göttingen, Verlag der Dieterichschen Buchhandlung, 1850) pp. i-iviii.

15. Herder always emphasized each nation's obligation to realize from the outset its own potentialities and then to turn to humanity at large. Nobody could constructively contribute to humanity if he neglected to cultivate his own garden. See Johann Gottfried Herder, "Briefe zur Beförderung der Humanität" in *Herders Sämmtliche Werke XVII, ed. Bernhard Suphan (Berlin, 1894), pp. 153-155. See also Oscar Walzel, German Romanticism* (New York: Putnam's Sons, 1967), Chapter I, and Robert Clark, Jr. *Herder: His Life and Thought* (Berkeley, University of California Press, 1965), chapters 3 and 5.

16. The correspondence of the Brothers Grimm gives us a good idea about the international connections. See, for example, Wilhelm Schoof, ed., *Unbekannte Briefe der Brüder Grimm. Unter Ausnutzung des Grimmschen Nachlasses* (Bonn, Athenäum, 1960). As an example of Jacob Grimm's influence on Sir Walter Scott consult Sir Walter Scott, *Letters on Demonology and Witchcraft* (Wakefield, Yorkshire, S. R. Publishers, Ltd., 1968). In various notes Scott acknowledged the Grimms' contributions to the study of folklore and mythology.

17. *Irische Elfenmärchen* (Leipzig, Fleischer Verlag, 1826). Croker was so delighted with Wilhelm Grimm's essay "About the Fairies" that he himself translated it into English and affixed it to the second English edition of *Fairy Legends*. Thomas Keightley used it for his books on comparative mythology, and so did others after him. One of the finest essay collections pertaining to the Grimm Brothers' contributions to international folklore research is Wilhelm v. Steinitz Fraenzer, ed., *Jacob Grimm zur 100. Wiederkehr seines Todestages. Festschrift*. (Berlin, Akademischer Verlag, 1968). For a treatment of The Grimm Brothers' literary influence in Great Britain consult Violet A. Stockley,

German Literature as Known in England: 1750 - 1830 (London: Routledge and Sons, 1929).

18. Hermann Gerstner, *Die Brüder Grimm: Biographie mit 48 Bildern*. (Gerabonn, Crailsheim, Hohenloher Verlag, 1970), pp. 203-220. For a comprehensive analysis of the relationship between the Grimms' study of folklore and linguistics see also Carl Zuckmayer, *Die Brüder Grimm: Ein deutscher Beitrag zur Humanität* (Frankfurt, Suhrkamp, 1948) Zuckmayer showed that poetic and scientific theories were the strongest motivating factors in the work of the Brothers Grimm, although he did not deny some of their nationalistic inclinations and sentiments.

19. Hans Dahmen, *Die nationale Idee von Herder bis Hitler* (Cologne, Hermann Schaffstein Verlag, 1934) and Julius Petersen, "Die Sehnsucht nach dem Dritten Reich in deutscher Sage und Dichtung" *Dichtung und Volkstum*, Vol. 35, I (1934) pp. 18-40. (Two parts). This line of interpretation was representative of most critics during the Nazi Regime, as it corresponded to the official Party policy. See also: Heinz Kindermann, *Dichtung und Volkheit: Grundzüge einer neuen Literaturwissenschaft* (Berlin, Volksverlag, 1937).

20. Even during the time of the Romantic movement itself we may observe a movement from literature to politics. The Jena group is usually associated with the first, the Heidelberg group with the second type. See Walzel, pp. 140-144.

21. Friedrich Ludwig Jahn indicated in his earliest *Deutsches Volkstum* (*German Ethnicity*) which appeared in 1810, that the German folk community was a reality within the German folk state. Like Arndt, however, he rejected a centralized control. See Hans Kohn, *The Mind of Germany: The Education of a Nation* (New York, Scribner's, 1960), pp.124-126. See also: Friedrich Meinecke, *The German Catastrophe: Reflections and Recollections* (Cambridge, Harvard University Press, 1950), p. 215.

22. Georg Mosse, *The Crisis of German Ideology: Intellectual Origins of the Third Reich* (New York, Grosset and Dunlap, 1964), p. 153.

23. Ernst Moritz Arndt, *Märchen und Jugenderinnerungen* in *Werke* ed. by Leffson and W. Steffens, Vols. I and III (Berlin, Bony, 1913). Other references to Arndt's fairy tales in Tismar, p. 32.

24. Kohn, pp. 69-78, and Paul Kluckhorn, *Das Ideengut der deutschen Romantik* (Tübingen, Wunderlich Verlag, 1961), pp. 60-101.

25. Mosse, pp. 14-30.

26. Wilhelm Heinrich Riehl, *Die Naturgeschichte des deutschen Volkes*, ed. by Dr. Hans Naumann and Dr. Rolf Haller (Leipzig, Reclam, 1934.) See in particular the preface pointing out the "relevance" of Riehl to the Nazi ideology. Also: Julius Petersen, *Die Wesensbestimmung der deutschen Romantik* (Leipzig, Dürr, 1926), pp. 9-10. Petersen explains the more recent preference for Jahn, Arndt, and Goerres over German Romantic writers that were more concerned with literature and poetry *per se*. This preference foreshadows the

selective approach of Nazism to the Romantic period and Volkish writers in general.

27. Ferdinand Tönnies, *Gemeinschaft und Gesellschaft: Grundbegriffe der reinen Soziologie* (Berlin, Volks-Verlag, 1926). See also: Rolf Dahrendorf, "Soziologie und Nationalsozialismus" in Andreas Flitner, ed., *Deutsches Geistesleben und Nationalsozialismus. Eine Vortragsreihe der Universität Tübingen* (Tübingen, Rainer Wunderlich Verlag, 1965), pp. 117-119.

28. Friedrich Nietzsche, *The Birth of Tragedy from the Spirit of Music* (New York, Anchor, 1965), Introduction. Nietzsche associates here the powerful spirit of Wagner with that of Dionysus. In both he perceives an inspiration by the irrational forces of life that he considers the necessary complements to rational and aesthetic concepts.

29. Paul de Lagarde, *Deutsche Schriften* (originally published in 1874) (Munich, Dürr, 1924), pp. 276-277. Alfred Rosenberg cited him in *Mythos of the Twentieth Century*. See Henry Hatfield, "The Myth of Nazism" in Henry Murray, ed., *Myth and Mythmaking* (New York, Putnam's Sons 1960), pp. 199-239. One of the most authoritative studies on de Lagarde and his influences is Fritz Stern, *The Politics of Cultural Despair* (Berkeley, University of California Press, 1961). See also Mosse, pp. 31-51.

30. Julius Langbehn, *Rembrandt als Erzieher* (Leipzig, Selbstverlag, 1927). (Originally, the work was published anonymously and merely bore the reference: "*Von einem Deutschen*" (By a German).

31. In a Nazi-oriented analysis, Hippler excuses de Lagarde in that, unfortunately, in his time racial theories had only partially been developed. See Fritz Hippler, *Staat und Gesellschaft bei Mill, Marx, Lagarde. Ein Beitrag zum soziologischen Denken der Gegenwart* (Berlin, Junker und Dünnhaupt, 1937), p. 161 and p. 230.

32. Bartels was a student of Professor Sauer who taught a "Volkish approach" to literature in Prague. Nadler, in turn, was Bartels' student. See Josef Nadler, *Literaturgeschichte des deutschen Volkes: Dichtung der deutschen Stämme und Landschaften* (Berlin, Junker und Dünnhaupt, 1941.)

33. On behalf of Jahn's and Arndt's concept of the individual consult Kohn, p. 215, and also: Wolfgang Emmerich, *Zur Kritik der Volkstumsideologie* (Frankfurt, Suhrkamp, 1961), pp. 24-26. According to de Lagarde himself, the German character was distinguished by his originality and his quest for independence and solitude. See de Lagarde, p. 278. It should be noted, however, that the Romantic and "Volkish" writers did recognize the individual's "organic links" with ethnic groups based on language, culture, and tradition.

34. See Horst Geissler, *Dekadenz und Heroismus. Zeitroman und nationalsozialistische Literaturkritik* (Stuttgart, Deutsche Verlagsanstalt, 1964), p. 50 and pp. 250-257.

35. Martin Broszat, *Die nationalsozialistische Weltanschauung: Programm*

und Wirklichkeit (Series: Schriftenreihe der niedersächsischen Landeszentrale für politische Bildung. Heft No. 8) (Stuttgart, Deutsche Verlagsanstalt, 1960), pp. 1-5.

36. Irene Graebsch, *Geschichte des deutschen Jugendbuches* (Leipzig, A. Harrassowitz, 1942), pp. 193-196. See also: Franz Schonauer, Deutsche Literatur im Dritten Reich (Freiburg im Breisgau, Walter Verlag, 1961), pp. 28-30. Schonauer made the distinction between the Aesthetic movement and the Volkish movement within the Art Education movement.

37. Heinrich Wolgast, *Das Elend unserer Jugendliteratur. Beiträge und künstlerische Erziehung unserer Jugend* (Hamburg, Selbstverlag, 1950). The work was first published in 1896.

38. "Was Wir Wollen" (Editorial) *Jugendschriften-Warte* I (1893), pp. 1-7.

39. Graebsch, pp. 116-124 and Prestel, pp. 90-98.

40. Wolgast became the Chief Editor of the *Jugendschriften-Warte* and was supported in his ideals and endeavors by the German Children's Literature Association for more than a decade—until Rüttgers challenged him. Kunze, pp. 66-69.

41. *Ibid.* Reprinted on pp. 80-81. The review originally appeared in 1894.

42. Graebsch, pp. 201-220.

43. *Ibid.*

44. Clara Zetkin, SPD Protokoll vom Parteitag der SPD 1916, Mannheim. For a documentation consult Kunze, p. 74 and p. 80.

45. Severin Rüttgers, *Deutsche Dichtung in der Volksschule* (Leipzig, Dürr'sche Buchhandlung, 1914) and *Erweckung des Volkes durch seine Dichtung* (Leipzig, Dürr'sche Buchhandlung, 1919). The second work was reprinted by Dürr in 1933, after the Nazis' seizure of power.

46. Graebsch, pp. 195-210 and Kunze, pp. 67-70.

47. The series *Blaue Bändchen* and *Grüne Bändchen* included not only folktales, chapbooks and regional legends, as well as Nordic Germanic myths and hero tales, but regional novels (*Heimatbücher*), too. Other series were inspired by Rüttgers but not edited by him, such as the *Wiesbadener Volksbücher* and *Bunte Jugendbücher.* See also Georg Lukácz, *Die Zerstörung der Vernunft* Berlin, Luchterhand, 1955), pp. 551-552.

48. This refers to a comment made by John Barfaut. See Peter Aley, *Jugendliteratur im Dritten Reich: Dokumente und Kommentare* (Hamburg, Verlag für Buchmarktforschung, 1969), p. 215.

49. Prestel, pp. 91-95.

50. Graebsch, p. 225.

51. *Ibid.* See also H.L. Köster, *Geschichte der deutschen Jugendliteratur* (Munich-Pullach, Verlag Dokumentation, 1968) 4th ed.

52. *Hamburger Prüfungsausschüsse*, (Hamburg Committee on the Evaluation of Children's Literature) "Liste gegenwartsbetonter Bücher" (1933) cited in Graebsch, pp. 226-227.

53. *Ibid.*, pp. 228-230.

54. Susanne Charlotte Engelmann, *German Education and Re-Education* (New York, International University Press, 1945), Chapter 2.

55. Peter Hasubek, *Das Deutsche Lesebuch in der Zeit des Nationalsozialismus. Ein Beitrag zur Literaturpädagogik zwischen 1933 und 1945* (Hannover, Hermann Schroedel Verlag, 1972), Introduction.

56. Mosse, pp. 218-225. The citation stems from Lewis Hertzmann, *DNVP. Right Wing Opposition in the Weimar Republic, 1918-1924* (Lincoln, University of Nebraska Press, 1963), p. 162. See also: Werner Maser, *Die Frühgeschichte der N.S.D.A.P.: Hitlers Weg bis 1924* (Frankfurt, Athenaeum), pp. 258-259.

57. Hans Joachim Gamm, *Der braune Kult: Das Dritte Reich und seine Ersatzreligion. Ein Beitrag zur politischen Bildung* (Hamburg, Rütten und Loening, 1962), pp. 188-206.

58. Mosse, p. 229. Other Volkish-political groups were: *Völkischer Schutz- und Trutzbund; Reichskammerbund; Hochschulring deutscher Art.* The last one especially influenced higher education in regard to the "Nordic Renaissance."

59. *Ibid.*, pp. 302-303.

60. *Ibid.*, pp. 224-225.

61. Adolf Bartels, *Deutsches Schrifttum: Jüdische Herkunft und Literaturwissenschaft* (Leipzig, H. Haessel Verlag, 1921).

62. For a general discussion consult Werner Klose, *Lebensformen deutscher Jugend: Vom Wandervogel zur Popgeneration* (Munich, Günter Olzog Verlag, 1970), and Harry Pross, *Vor und nach Hitler: Zur deutschen Sozialpathalogie* (Freiburg/Breisgau, Walter Verlag, 1962), Chapter 1. Also: Walter Z. Laqueur, *Young Germany: A History of the German Youth Movement* (New York, Basic Books, 1962).

63. Flex, cited by Laqueur, p. 47. Flex's work was first published in Munich, 1916, and it went through numerous re-editions. During the Nazi period it was among the ten works with the highest number of copies printed, partially because it had retained popularity, and partially because the Nazis promoted it actively within the context of the Hitler Youth Organization. See Dietrich Strothmann, *Nationalsozialistische Literaturpolitik* (Bonn, Bouvier, 1968), pp. 91; 257; 381. For a general discussion of Flex's contributions to the Youth movement, consult Kurt Hohoff, *Dichtung und Dichter der Zeit* (Düsseldorf, August Bage Verlag, 1964), pp. 324-235. The following analysis represents an analysis of the German Youth movement by one of its former members: Friedrich Kayser, "Wandervogel, Idee und Wirklichkeit; Gedanken einer Selbstdarstellung der deutschen Jugendbewegung" (typescript). Sender Freies Berlin, "Kulturelles Wort," June 13, 1962, *Document.* Collection Title: *The German Youth Movement Collection,* No. 956. Hoover Institution Archives, Hoover Institution on War, Revolution, and Peace, Stanford, California.

64. Graebsch, pp. 125-126.

65. *Document*. Collection title: *The German Youth Movement Collection* No. 956, Folder 3, pp. 60-64. Typescript on "Die Artamanen."

66. *Ibid.*, pp. 69-75.

67. *Ibid.*

68. *Ibid.*

69. Severin Rüttgers, *Erweckung des Volkes durch seine Dichtung* (Leipzig, Dürr, 1933). Consult also Aley, pp. 13-18 and p. 215.

70. Pross, pp. 1-30. Consult also: Kurt Sonthheimer, "Das Reich der Unpolitischen. Die Jugendbewegung vor 1933" (typescript). Südwestfunk, Jugendfunk. Program of October 18, 1961, 11 p.m. *Document: The German Youth Movement Collection* No. 956, Folder 6, pp. 10-14.

71. *Ibid.* Consult also: "Wie ich die H.J. sah und erlebte" (anonymous typescript). *Document*. Collection title: *T.S. National Socialism* No. 467. Hoover Institution Archives, Hoover Institution on War, Revolution, and Peace, Stanford, California. The document is mainly concerned with a description of the "Volkish illusion" that originally inspired many of the young followers of the Nazi Regime, particularly those among the older Hitler Youth. In the same folder consult also: "Einfluss der H.J. auf die Jugend" (typescript).

72. Rudolf Hurtfield, "Severin Rüttgers als Erwecker des Sinnes für volkhafte Dichtung" *Jugendschriften-Warte* 44, 1 (January, 1939), 6-10.

2

From Book Burning
Toward *Gleichschaltung*

The first indications of an emerging cultural policy in Germany were barely noticed by the general public. On April 13, 1933 the German Student Association posted a twelve point "Proclamation" at the entrance doors of the University of Berlin, demanding from the universities a greater sense of responsibility toward the German race, the German language, and German literature.[1] This demand essentially corresponded to the direction of the Nazis' cultural policy to be implemented just a few weeks later, yet it appeared to be spontaneous and no more than the usual sign of political unrest among the German student groups. Even when three weeks later the *Frankfurter Zeitung* announced the explicit demand by the German Student Association to remove all "un-German" books from the libraries,[2] the public did not feel alerted to systems of control that soon would permeate all spheres of German cultural and political life.

The book burning ceremonies, that began on May 10, 1933 in the public squares of numerous German cities, were also ascribed to the initiative of some radical students, although the presence of prominent professors and Party and State representatives during these occasions placed the events in a different light. The cities affected included Cologne, Bonn, Frankfurt, Munich, Nuremberg, Würzburg, and Berlin.[3] In Berlin, Josef Goebbels, the German Reich Minister of Propaganda, personally sanctioned the action by a public address while the books were still smoldering in the ashes. "One thing we know for sure," he said, "namely that political revolutions will have to be prepared from a spiritual basis. At their beginning there always stands an idea, and only if the idea has been merged with power, will the historical miracle of a reform movement occur, and only then it will rise and develop."[4]

The "spiritual basis" to which Goebbels referred, was already essentially prepared in a rough outline by the students who dramatically stepped forward toward the bonfires and solemnly recited the "sins" of the authors whose works they committed to the flames. As one after another would state what books were needed in Germany at the present time, they would condemn certain authors while recommending others—both in line with "Volkish" criteria. Thus, they denounced Marx and Kautsky for emphasizing class struggle and Marxism. They would blame Heinrich Mann, Ernst Glaeser, Erich Kästner, Friedrich Wilhelm and Sigmund Freud for having promoted a spirit of "decadence, moral decay, sloppy thinking, political treason, and eroticism," whereas they accused Emil Ludwig and Werner Hegemann of having "falsified German history and degraded the great German heroes of the past," and Theodor Wolff and Georg Bernhard of having created a "folk-alien journalism of the democratic and Jewish type." Erich Maria Remarque they charged with "literary treason" against the German soldiers fighting so bravely in World War I; Alfred Kerr, with having "crippled the German language," and Tucholsky and Ossietzky with having sinned against the German ethnic spirit by showing "a lack of respect for the German folk soul."[5]

The recommendations followed the same order. The first student praised the idea of the German folk community which from then on literature should portray in idealistic terms. The second one demanded that books be faithful to the German people and the state. The third requested of literature that it portray the "nobility of the German soul," and the fourth reminded all German authors that their works should reveal respect for German history, the spirit of the ancestors, and the spirit of the past. Others still referred to the necessity of promoting a type of literature that would show reverence for the German folk spirit by concerning itself with the love of home and nation, a search for the "roots" of German national identity, with native folklore and history, and a respect for "honesty and truth." As such, it should be the goal of all literature to serve the German folk community rather than to express the "selfish" interests of its authors. The ceremonies took place at night, illuminated by dramatic torchlight processions and accompanied by marching bands of the military and police. Singing and cheerleading further dramatized the events which neither the public nor the press could overlook.[6]

For those who were directly affected by the "witch hunt" action, there were not too many alternatives left. Erich Kästner, for example, in an interview a few years ago, commented that in personally witnessing the book burning ceremonies in which his own works were condemned, he would have liked to shout back at "them" through the microphone, yet instead, he only clenched his fists in his pockets.[7] Then during the same night he and his friends had urged the writer Ossietzky to flee the country, yet Ossietzky had decided to stay and "fight back" as well as he might.[8] Others were less optimistic. When Goebbels dissolved the Prussian Academy of Literature and dismissed a substantial portion of its membership while appointing new members to take their places in the *Reichsliteraturkammer* (Reich Literature Chamber), Thomas Mann,[9] and Ricarda Huch resigned voluntarily. As a branch of the *Reichskulturkammer* (Reich Culture Chamber), which Goebbels founded to control art, literature, theater, press, radio, music and film, the Reich Literature Chamber no longer

Plate 5
Traditional Bonfires in Support of the New "Fate Community"

was meant as a place for a free exchange of ideas but as a censorship organization. Huch was especially enraged that Goebbels' "miracle of a reform movement" had resulted in Döblin's dismissal on racial grounds. In her letter of resignation, she wrote among other things:

> It appears quite natural to me that each German citizen should feel as a German. And yet, there are various opinions as to what it means to be a German and how Germandom should assert itself. What the present regime prescribes as "national consciousness" does not correspond to my understanding of Germandom. I consider it as un-German to centralize all power, to use force and brutal methods, and to defame those who think differently.[10]

The defamation of those who thought differently indeed had begun very early. After the burning of the *Reichstag* in Berlin, Göring proceeded to arrest thousands of Communist suspects all over Germany.[11] In the name of the State, he had armed the regular police force, adding to it 25,000 S.A. men and 10,000 SS men, which during the election days in Berlin alone arrested 5,000 persons.[12] Only two days after the *Reichstag* incident, Hitler suspended all normal civil liberties guaranteed by the Constitution while turning the Secret Service into an instrument of terror. This meant that Germans were denied freedom of speech and of the press, the freedom to gather in groups, as well as the freedom of privacy regarding mail, telegrams, and telephone calls. Anyone who acted suspiciously or was overheard saying something against the Nazi Regime could be arrested and detained without trial.[13] Even before this time, the Party would send its agents to public lectures and gatherings of groups, and it was known to have dispersed meetings when speakers uttered even some harmless jokes at the expense of the Party. Intellectuals experienced harrassment if they were suspected of dissent, and early as May, 1933 there were arrests, imprisonments and reported mistreatments of those who disagreed openly with the Party's policy.[14]

During the year 1933 a total of 1,684 academics lost their jobs. Among these were 781 professors, 322 instructors, 42 lecturers, 232 assistants, 133 academic employees at scientific institutions, and 174 persons of academic rank working in schools, libraries, and museums.[15] Among these, undoubtedly, were those who were dismissed on racial grounds, but there were also others who had "shouted back at them" in the way that Kaestner would have liked to do.

Simultaneously with the Nazis' purge of academics and intellectuals there occurred the "cleansing" of the libraries and school libraries. Party and State authorities followed up the public book burning ceremonies so thoroughly that the public no longer was held in doubt who had instigated the "book purge" in the first place. In Bonn alone 20,000 books were thrown into the flames. In Berlin 70,000 tons of books were removed from the libraries. Books were no longer counted but merely measured in terms of estimated weight.[16] By mid-May, 1933 the action had spread to the smaller towns in Germany, where local authorities were placed in charge of removing the "undesirable" literature from the library shelves.[17] It is estimated that in this process about one-third of all library holdings in Germany was destroyed.[18] This affected not only general literature but also children's literature. Whatever the authorities considered "folk-alien" or "decadent," whatever appeared to promote the spirit of Bolshevism, liberalism or internationalism, or whatever had been written by Jewish authors was condemned to go to the incinerator, the public bonfire or the scrap paper collection. While in the beginning the book "purge" was carried out somewhat erratically, following only the general guidelines and "black lists" of Goebbels, eventually it was stabilized within the context of a gigantic censorship apparatus of Party and State authorities that screened every book that was printed, sold, purchased or circulated.

The only consistent factor from the very beginning was the National Socialist ideology. In spite of lapses in the implementation of censorship at various levels, the National Socialist ideology determined a cultural policy in which Volkish-political views prevailed throughout the Nazi Regime. Rooted in the "organic" concepts of folk and community, it selectively emphasized Volkish thought of pre-Nazi times while calling for a new unity of the German Reich

Plate 6
A New Call for Unity and Community

under the swastika flag. The frequent references of the Nazi ideologists and Hitler himself to such concepts as the "folk spirit," the "folk soul," the "folk tradition," and the "folk community" harkened back to earlier times when Herder, Grimm, Jahn, and Arndt, and later Langbehn, de Lagarde, and Moeller van den Bruck had appealed to the German people to unite in their quest for unity and German ethnic identity.[19]

While a number of intellectuals in those early days of the Nazi Regime just "played along" in the hope that one day things would change for the better, while contributing their required amount of "Volkish thought" to literary, educational, and scientific journals, without taking themselves too seriously in this role, others were genuinely enthusiastic about the Party's "Volkish" ideology. Unlike Ricarda Huch who had premonitions about the nightmare of a totalitarian super-power that was only in its childhood stages, others welcomed the rise of a "folk state" as a fulfillment of their pre-Nazi "Volkish" dreams about ethnic identity, unity, and community. Nolte commented that when on February 1st the masses joined the mammoth torchlight processions in honor of the "People's Chancellor," they did not react to mere propaganda but to their heartfelt hope that Hitler would realize their dreams of a unified folk community built on German faith, morality, and honor, and that he would re-establish pride in German history and heroism while making the Germans more idealistic in fighting for a common cause. Many famous philosophers, professors, and writers tended to look at the Nazis' "Volkish" cultural policy in optimistic terms.[20] Whereas on the one hand they perceived in it a continuation of Volkish ideas prevailing in the twenties, they did not think that it was necessarily opposed to Christianity either. Hitler himself had promoted this illusion by stating in *Mein Kampf* that National Socialism not only stood for "neutrality" in regard to the domain of the churches, but that both the Catholic Church and the Protestant Church were needed to build the true community spirit of the German *Volk*.[21] The *Concordat* of July, 1933 further supported the notion that the Catholic Church would be able to pursue its goals and preserve its rights, provided it would agree to a clear separation of State and Church. Little did the public realize that this agreement actually served Hitler personally, as it led to the dissolution of the Catholic Labor Union which he feared as a rival.[22] In his 1934 speech in Marburg, von Papen further gave the appearance that the Nazis were not at all inclined to foster a "Volkish" dictatorship at the expense of the Christian conscience and the concept of a united Christendom in Europe. Whatever might look somewhat "extreme" in regard to the Nazis' practical politics, he assured his audience, was only to be understood as the result of some temporary measures, and it was the Party's goal to achieve the freedom of every member of the German folk community, including his *voluntary* participation in the work of the folk community.[23]

During the National Convention of the German Teachers Association in Magdeburg in June, 1933, Hans Schemm, President of the Association, used similar rhetoric to von Papen by reminding his colleagues that the German folk community under National Socialism actually stood for the "*unity of Christianity*," and that both the Catholic and the Protestant churches now stood united in its cause.[24] Schemm's speech was greeted with strong applause, and then all of the 155 regional delegates, one by one, stepped forward and signed a document committing them formally to the Party's policy of *Gleichschaltung* (coordination), which also implied a submission to censorship. There were no abstentions. In retrospect, we realize that it was dangerous for individuals at that time to express their dissent openly, for in practice the *Gleichschaltung* was already enforced by the power politics of Party and State. Some sources made available after World War II indicate that during the Convention opinions among teachers were actually still divided among those who supported Wolgast's liberal ideas on behalf of education through children's literature and those who joined Rüttgers' call to follow the "God-given leadership of the *Führer*."[25]

Still, it was not clear to many educators among the latter group of enthusiasts that Hitler actually was out to reverse the Romantic concept of the *Volk* (folk). To the Nazis, it embodied what one ideologist called "the essential reality of race, tradition, mythos, and fate"[26] and what another one appraised as "the very spirit of homogeneity, solidarity, and organization"[27]—an idea that soon was to be echoed on thousands of Nazi posters bearing the slogan: "*Ein Volk! Ein Reich! Ein Führer!*" (One Folk! One Reich! One Leader!). In contrast to the Romantic concept, the Nazis' concept no longer stood for diversity within unity, but it implied a uniformity that made no allowance for individual differences. By abolishing the opposition and by levelling the "subjective element," the Nazis hoped to form a society that was totally committed to the *Führer* and the National Socialist ideology.

According to Meinecke, Hitler seized upon the idea of the "folk community" for two particular reasons: to get rid of the class-egotistical nationalism promoted by the heavy industry patrons of the bourgeoisie and to overtrump the Marxism of the Russian Bolshevists. While trying to preserve the natural groupings of society, he felt that they must be steered around and educated to serve a community including all of them. From the "Aryan racial point of view" it was a convenient means to transcend all social differences while boosting the average man's self image. The economic recovery, the reduction of unemployment, and large-scale recreation and travel programs for workers further strengthened the popular appeal of this concept.[28]

The Romantic concept of the "folk" was closely linked with that of the "community," but in their interpretation of these concepts the Romantic writers had granted the individual the freedom to select his own associations and to formulate his unique aesthetic, intellectual or political ideas. Both cultural and political Romanticism had thus been characterized by "diversity in unity" as far as their "Volkish" aspirations had been concerned. The Nazis consciously employed an ambiguous language to simulate this tradition. When Rosenberg, as the Nazis' chief ideologist, announced that the National Socialist Cultural Community (*Nationalsozialistische Kulturgemeinde*) had set as its ultimate goal the revival of German folk culture, this appeal sounded like an echo of Romantic thought and found a sympathetic reception by the German population who welcomed the idea of a cultural renewal on the basis of native folklore and the Nordic Germanic folk heritage.[29]

Rosenberg defined the Nazi ideology ambiguously as "an attitude rather than a dogma"[30] while referring to its objectives of forming the German people's attitudes toward the "fighting spirit" of the German nation. He began his career as Chief of the *Kampfbund für deutsche Kultur* (Fighter League for German Culture) in 1927, with the goal to counteract the "rootless" and "decadent" life of the cities by a return to the "healthy sources" of German nationhood still to be found among the peasants in the countryside. Later, this League was merged with the *Kulturamt* or *Kulturgemeinde* (Culture Office or Cultural Community) in the Third Reich that came entirely under Rosenberg's sphere of influence.[31]

From the beginning, Rosenberg's interest in the German cultural community was colored by his fascination with the Nordic Germanic folk heritage. He worked closely with the *Nordische Gesellschaft* (Nordic Society) and even sponsored its major journal *Der Norden* (*The North*).[32] Over several years, he tried to promote cultural exchange programs among German and Scandinavian writers and artists and also cooperated with the *Reichsbund für deutsche Vorgeschichte* (Reich Office for German Prehistory) on behalf of drawing up plans for a national institute dedicated to Nordic Germanic history and folklore. Throughout his career, he maintained intimate contacts with the *Institut für deutsche Volkskunde* (Institute for German Folklore), and even sponsored the publication of folklore journals by his Office.[33] These ties are important to remember if we consider the Nordic Germanic orientation of the National Socialist ideology and the significant role which German and Nordic Germanic folklore came to play in the Nazis' cultural politics.

Even the concept of folklore had changed its meaning since Romantic times, for the Nazis remained ambiguous about the distinction between the traditional folk heritage on the one hand and the new values of the folk state on the other. This was one of the major reasons why the status of folklore, as a science, was called into question after the war.[34] The National Socialists further confused the terms "Nordic," "Germanic," "Nordic Germanic," and "German," so as to create the impression that the present regime was merely a natural extension of the traditional past. To the Nazis, ambiguity itself served as an ideological tool.[35] Even Rosenberg's Cultural Community assumed the appearance of a "continuity" of thought in regard to what the art critic Strzgowski called "Germany's return to the Indo-Germanic North of Europe." While it paid homage to Nordic Germanic traditions and "Volkish thought" it also pretended to continue the Nordic Faith movement led by Bergmann and Günther in the twenties.[36] Only to some more critical minds it was evident that the Nazis had changed the original "faith community" into a "fate community" determined by the fighting spirit of National Socialism and its goal of political action.

As children were to become the most prominent members of such a future "fate community," and as all of children's literature during the Third Reich was subordinated to the Nazis' Volkish ideology, we may do well to take a closer look at its meaning. The Nazis' definition of ideological goals echoed the Romantic quest for an "organic" unity and a metaphysical "totality,"[37] although the new context changed its meaning to a "total sacrifice" of the individual to the state and a denial of existence of the individual outside of the folk community. According to Dr. Gross, Director of the Racial-Political Office, the system

Plate 7
Dr. Johann von Leers, *History on Racial Foundations*

of liberalism had created an "individualistic society" that was basically "unfree" in spirit. In order to regain his true freedom, he said, every individual should sacrifice his desires and goals entirely to the State. Only in this sense could he become a true "folk personality" that had the right to a so-called "higher existence." Like most of the Nazi ideologists, Gross appealed to the spirit of altruism and idealism when he spoke about the individual's contributions to the folk community:

> The human being no longer is a separate entity all by himself. . . .
> Born into the community of his people, he will feel the bond of the blood, and he will consider it the ultimate goal of his life to contribute his very best to the prosperity and preservation of this larger unit . . . Thus, it should come quite naturally to him that the meaning of his life no longer is bound up with his own small ego but with the community of his folk to whom he owes his life. His fate is inseparably linked with the destiny of his people.[38]

The Nazis identified the concept of the individual as "the essence of selfishness" under the influence of liberalism that National Socialism had to overcome. Instead, they hailed the "folk personality." Far from being a "personality" as Goethe had understood it in regard to a liberally educated person striving all of his life toward creative selffulfillment, the new "folk personality" was supposed to "fit into the whole of the community by submitting himself to all of its subsequent rights and duties."[39] In essence, it was the prototype of the "New Man" of the future, as the Nazis envisioned him. While contemplating the Nazi slogan "*Gemeinnutz geht über Eigennutz!*" (The Welfare of the Community has Priority over the Welfare of the Individual!), the literary critic Langenbucher explained that life in the folk community was the *only* life style that would guarantee to a person a "higher existence."[40]

In children's literature publications of the Nazi period such imperative statements were a common occurrence, as they formed an integral part of "folk education" to which literature was subordinated. Children's book authors usually would talk about the "noble goals" and "honorable obligations" of every individual to submit himself to the interests of the folk community. In one case, an author described this attitude as one requiring "an ethical sincerity, a deep inwardness, and a complete dedication to a given work or task,"[41] while another one warmly reminded his readers: "You are a part of the great German folk. This folk is a community which can exist only if all of its members are part and parcel of socialism. This means: think of the welfare of the whole, but remember, too, that in relation to the whole you are only a part."[42]

Germandom as a "spiritual task" lay at the very core of "folk education" which Rosenberg pursued in general terms with his Cultural Community, and which Reich Education Minister Bernhard Rust followed up through school and library reforms. In broad terms, "folk education" meant "community education" in the spirit of the National Socialist ideology. Ernst Krieck, who is generally considered the chief theorist of Nazi education, emphasized in this process the significance of Nordic Germanic folklore. Folklore itself would have to be transformed into a "total and politically oriented science," he said, "taking its orientation directly from the folk, in order to meet present-day standards."[43] This meant, of course, that folklore would have to blend old folk traditions with National Socialist values, so as to be of help in forming the "young team" of the future. Krieck was against a materialistic interpretation of race, and in fact, saw in such a view the direct reversal of its "real meaning." To him, as much as to Rosenberg, race and blood in and by themselves did not have meaning but took on significance only if they were matched by a "racial attitude" that he identified alternately as "Nordic," "Faustic," or as "the will toward fate." In modelling the "attitude toward fate" on the attitude of the Nordic Germanic peasant warriors and the saga heroes of the Nordic Germanic past, Krieck hoped to instill in young people a sense of determination to fight for the preservation of Germandom at all cost.[44]

In National Socialist "folk education" Professor Krieck and others pursued the idea that the "concrete" concept of the German folk community had replaced the "abstract" concept of humanity at large,[45] and that it was the first obligation of all writers and educators to instill in young people a genuine feeling for the "need" to sacrifice the personal will to the "will of the state." Reich Education Minister Bernhard Rust commented on behalf of the new National Socialist goals of education: "German youth now has shaken off the fetters of foreign cultures and accepted a life of masculine discipline including a willingness to sacrifice individual desires to the needs of the community. Thus, they have gained a new conception of community that, over a span of thousands of years, connects them with the heroic youth of Sparta."[46] Far from advocating a Greek model for German children and youth, however, Rust presented them with ideals of their Nordic Germanic "forefathers" who, as peasants and warriors, had tilled the soil and defended their tribes. He felt that especially after the internal divisions of Germany following World War I, it was of primary significance for National Socialism to provide youth with a new purpose in life and a deep faith in their folk heritage, their identity, and their destiny.[47]

To Krieck, as well as to Rust, Rosenberg and others, the Nazi ideology inevitably resulted in a peasant and ancestor cult that were both endowed with National Socialist meanings and objectives. In this context German and Nordic Germanic folklore assumed a new role in cultural politics, and also in children's literature, as they were meant to serve as a "political science." Folklorist Schmidt commented early in the thirties: "Although folklore is never rigid or absolutely at rest, it does represent a steady and permanent force. As the product of the native soil, it is an expression of the cultural community spirit, and as such, it reflects the folk soul but also the ideology of our culture."[48] He perceived in the new dual role of folklore a "catalytic force" capable of counteracting the instability, mobility, and diversity of city life and also, of bringing about a new unity of the German folk under the leadership of the National

Socialist Party. It was because of its assumed "rootedness" in Nordic Germanic peasant traditions that Krieck considered the Nazi ideology neither an "invention" of National Socialism nor a temporary means to support arbitrary politics but a "permanent force" of German culture. And yet, he did not regard it as a mere "inheritance" either but rather as an "obligation" to the future. The Nordic Germanic leaders and their followers had presented the Germans with heroic models that should provide old and young with a "stimulus to action," he wrote. In that sense, the legacy of the past implied a "task" for the future, a "will to become;" and folk education, consequently, was not to be understood as a finished product but as a process, also in the days to come.[49]

Since Romantic times, the German peasantry had always been considered as a class in which traditional folklore had been preserved much longer and more accurately than in the cities. Ever since the Brothers Grimm had begun to collect folktales from the German peasants, folklorists, and philologists had followed their example in collecting from the rural population the heritage of the past. Since those days, the image of the peasant, too, had risen in popular esteem, partially due to the nationalistic movement that had brought with it a greater respect for the common man and the vernacular. On the other hand, the beginning of the twentieth century had also introduced folklore studies pertaining to the cities—a trend which the Nazis largely ignored. To the Nazis, the peasant was not merely a member of a given class and a "preserver" of folk tradition, but a symbol of the Nordic Germanic ancestor representing the "blood-and-soil" idea of racial strength as much as the spiritual determination of a Nordic warrior. Consequently, they did not portray the peasant in idyllic and peaceful terms but more as the "heroic" warrior fighting for the preservation of his family and heritage.[50]

In 1935, Professor Hildebert Boehm was called to a chair in "Folk Theory" in Berlin, the first of its kind in Europe. It was meant to explore not only folklore as a political tool at home, in terms of its potential contributions to the Nazi ideology, but mainly folklore abroad. Folklore, race theory, and geopolitics combined were to serve the Nazis in strengthening Germandom abroad, both in the newly won "living space" areas in Eastern Europe and in the borderlands "endangered" by foreign cultures. Boehm called the folklore and peasant policy of the Third Reich not merely a temporary solution but a permanent policy aiming at the fight for Germandom and its preservation.[51] It is this goal that Hitler had in mind, too, when he said in 1933: "The question concerning the preservation of our ethnic identity can be answered only if we have found a solution pertaining to the preservation of our peasantry."[52]

At the beginning of the thirties, some practical considerations may have played a role in promoting the peasant cult, especially the peasant migrations to the cities. The rural population had declined from about 60% of the total population to 30%, and Hitler introduced various land reforms, the hereditary farm laws, and the new post of the Reich Peasant Leader, to which he appointed Walter Darré. Darré himself was thinking in biological terms when considering

Plate 8
"Mother and Child": Symbols of the Healthy Peasant Life

the peasant to be the perpetuator of the "Nordic race."[53] Statistics of 1937 indicated, however, that none of the practical measures taken had caused a substantial change in the percentage of the rural population. Still, the Nazi ideologists continued to promote the folklore and peasant policy as an "on-going" process in the manner as Krieck had advocated it, to build the "spiritual attitude" needed to consolidate the folk community of the Third Reich. Especially in children's literature and folklore publications of the Nazi period, the "Volkish" direction of the Nazis' cultural policy turned out to be a stable factor throughout the twelve-year existence of the Nazi Regime.

This "Volkish" ideology of National Socialism shaped the cultural policy of the Third Reich which essentially determined the direction of the Nazis' censorship and their promotion of children's literature and folklore. Since the Nazis considered children's literature and folklore important aspects of German "folk education," they selected, wrote, and re-interpreted them according to its guidelines.

The strong emotional and idealistic appeal of the Nazi ideology contributed to the relatively smooth transition of cultural trends from the Weimar Republic to the Nazi Regime. Whereas the Nazis used power and terror to reinforce their one-party system, they employed a "positive" cultural policy in order to establish long-range goals and to stabilize their system of controls. Totalitarian governments are seldom content with mere subjugation of the population but rather aim at a voluntary subordination of their subjects and a worship of the leader.[54] The Nazi ideology was intended to form a faithful and religiously devoted followership that had internalized not only the values of the Nordic Germanic past but also the values of National Socialism. Thus, the cultural policy of the Third Reich was not a temporary measure but one that was intended as a continuous process, just as Krieck had defined folk education. It was meant to last as long as the Nazi Regime itself. Due to the Nazis' clever manipulation of values pertaining to Romantic and Volkish thought of pre-Nazi times, the cultural policy took on an "evolutionary" rather than a revolutionary character, while promising a remedy to German cultural despair. Some writers came to the conclusion after the war that the mythos of Nazism was such a pervasive force, that, without its aid, the Nazi Regime could certainly never have established its reign as it did.[55]

If a number of scholars and educators, and a substantial portion of the German public became extremely gullible to the Nazi ideology, Hitler's "hypnotic power" undoubtedly had less to do with it than the Nazis' abuses of the German nostalgia for a national unity and a genuine folk community, and of the Romantic yearning for political order promising respect for the common man and social dignity for all. Only to the more discriminating minds it was evident from the very start that the Nazis' concepts of folk, community and personality actually stood in direct opposition to the Western humanitarian and democratic traditions; that unity for the Nazis meant uniformity, and that freedom implied slavery within a totalitarian system of controls.

Children's literature, possibly more than any other aspect of German culture during the Nazi period, was strongly affected by the Nazis' "positive" Volkish approach, for the ideologists knew well that especially young people are more susceptible to an idealistic appeal than to hate propaganda. As children's literature and folklore were the very media through which the Nazis hoped to shape the "attitudes" of the youngest members of the German folk community toward the Third Reich, these subjects offer a unique testing ground for their methods of indoctrination and their subsequent perversion of traditional humanitarian values.

Plate 9
The Führer Cult

NOTES

1. "Wider den undeutschen Geist" *Deutsche Kultur-Wacht* 9 (1933), 5.
2. "Bücherautodafé" *Frankfurter Zeitung* (May 7, 1933).
3. "Die Rufer" *Neuköllner Tageblatt* (May 12, 1933). See also: Joseph Wulf,

ed., *Literatur und Dichtung im Dritten Reich: Eine Dokumentation* (Gütersloh, Sigbert Mohn Verlag, 1963), pp. 42-45.

4. Josef Goebbels, "Undeutsches Schrifttum" *Deutsche Kultur-Wacht* 5 (1933), 13.

5. "Wider den undeutschen Geist" *General-Anzeiger für Bonner Umgebung* (May 11, 1933). See also Walter A. Behrendsohn, *Die humanistische Front. Eine Einführung in die deutsche Emigranten-Literatur*, Vol. I (1933-1935) (Zürich, Europa Verlag, 1946), p. 19.

6. Behrendsohn, pp. 20-21.

7. Axel Eggebrecht, "Bücherverbrennung war der Anfang" *Die Zeit* (May 20, 1977), 9-10. The article is based on interviews.

8. *Ibid.*

9. Thomas Mann went into exile. Dietrich Strothmann, *Nationalsozialistische Literaturpolitik. Ein Beitraq zur Publizistik im Dritten Reich* (Bonn, Bouvier, 1965), pp. 27-33, and "An Exchange of Letters by Thomas Mann" *Friends of Europe Publications* No. 52 (London, Friends of Europe, 1937), with a foreword by J.B. Priestley.

10. Ricarda Huch's letter was signed on April 9, 1933. Cited in Wulf, p. 27.

11. Harry Graf Kessler, *Aus den Tagebüchern 1918-1937* (Munich, Deutscher Taschenbuch-Verlag, G.m.b.H., 1965), p. 355.

12. Roger Manvill, *SS Gestapo: Rule by Terror* (New York, Ballantine, 1970), p. 355.

13. Walter Adolph, *Hirtenamt und Hitler-Diktatur* 2nd ed. (Berlin, Morus Verlag, 1965), p. 39.

14. Kessler, pp. 252-253 and p. 361.

15. Edward Y. Hartshorne, *The German Universities* (Cambridge, Mass., Oxford University Press, 1949). Cited in Karl Dietrich Bracher, Wolfgang Sauer and Gerhard Schulz, *Die nationalsozialistische Machtergreifung. Studien zur Errichtung des totalitären Herrschaftssystems in Deutschland* (Cologne, Opladen, Westdeutscher Verlag, 1962), p. 321.

16. Behrendsohn, pp. 17-24.

17. William Sheridan Allan, *The Nazi Seizure of Power: The Experiences of a Small German Town 1930-1935* (Chicago, Quadrangle, 1968), p. 224. Allan reports that in the small town of Thalburg about one fourth of all library books was destroyed.

18. See the Chapter XIV, footnote 2.

19. Hans Kohn, *The Mind of Germany: The Education of a Nation* (New York, Scribners's 1960), p. 53. Also: Christa Kamenetsky, "Political Distortion of Philosophical Concepts: A Case History—Nazism and the Romantic Movement" *Metaphilosophy* 3, 3 (July, 1972), pp. 198-218.

20. Ernst Nolte, *Three Faces of Fascism: Action Française, Italian Fascism, National Socialism* (Munich, Piper Verlag, 1965), pp. 343-345.

21. Cited by Walter Hofer, ed., *Der Nationalsozialismus: Dokumente 1933-1945* (Frankfurt, Fischer Bücherei, 1951), p. 120.

22. *Ibid.*, p. 121.

23. "Aus der Marburger Rede von Papens" (June 17, 1934), *Ibid.*, pp. 66-67.

24. Hans Schemm, cited by Nationalsozialistischer Lehrerbund, (National Socialist Teachers Association) eds., *Jahrbuch 1935* (Munich, Fichte Verlag, 1935), p. 263. See also p. 286.

25. Aley reports that immediately following the service in the Magdeburg Cathedral, the Nazi flags were sanctioned in front of the Church. See Peter Aley, *Jugendliteratur im Dritten Reich. Dokumente und Kommentare* (Hamburg, Verlag für Buchmarktforschung, 1969), pp. 13-19. The documents cited also include letters by Fronemann and Rüttgers, as well as Rüttgers' article on the Magdeburg Conference in the *Rheinische Lehrerzeitung.*

26. Hans Steinacher, "Vom deutschen Volkstum, von der deutschen Volksgenossenschaft und vom volksgebundenen Staat" in Paul Gauss, ed., *Das Buch vom deutschen Volkstum: Wesen, Lebensraum, Schicksal* (Leipzig, Klinckhardt, 1935), pp. 414-417. Heinz Kindermann went so far as to consider Herder's concept of the folk to be a concept characterized by "a biological attitude toward race." See Heinz Kindermann, *Die Sturm-und Drangbewegung im Kampf um die deutsche Lebensform* (Special Issue of the journal *Von deutscher Art in Sprache und Dichtung*, 1941/42), p. 33.

27. *Ibid.*

28. Friedrich Meinecke, *The German Catastrophe: Reflections and Recollections* (Cambridge, Mass., Oxford University Press, 1950), p. 215.

29. Alfred Rosenberg, *Das politische Tagebuch, 1934-35 und 1939-40.* ed. by Hans Günther Seraphim (Nördlingen, Deutscher Taschenbuch-Verlag, 1964), p. 243.

30. *Ibid.*, p. 24. Rosenberg also referred to the *Weltanschauung* as "an attitude toward the fate awaiting us outside" while hinting at the "fighting spirit" of the Germanic North.

31. Reinhard Bollmus, *Das Amt Rosenberg und seine Gegner. Zum Machtkampf im nationalsozialistischen Herrschaftssystem* (Stuttgart, Deutsche Verlagsanstalt, 1970), pp. 27-39. The imposing title which Hitler bestowed upon Rosenberg was "*Beauftragter des Führers für die Überwachung der gesamten geistigen und weltanschaulichen Führung der N.S.D.A.P.*" (Deputy of the *Führer* for the Control of the Total Spiritual and Ideological Leadership of the National Socialist Party).

32. Franz Theodor Hart, *Alfred Rosenberg, der Mann und sein Werk* (Munich, Lehmanns Verlag, 1939), pp. 94-100.

33. Bollmus, p. 340. For details of Rosenberg's plan see "Der Plan für ein Reichsinstitut für deutsche Vorgeschichte bis zur Entscheidung," *Ibid.*, pp. 162-173. Rosenberg was also in charge of the office for *Volkskunde und Feiergestaltung* (Folklore and Festivals). His pseudo-scientific approach to folklore and history were popular with the Party, but brought him criticisms, too, mainly from some scholars. See: "Rezensionen über Rosenbergs Mythus des zwanzigsten Jahrhunderts" in Josef Ackermann, *Himmler als Ideologe; Nach Tage-*

büchern, stenographischen Notizen, Briefen und Reden. (Göttingen, Musterschmidt, 1970), pp. 339-360 and pp. 82-89. Like Rosenberg, Himmler also drew up plans in connection with German cultural politics, particularly on behalf of "The Exploration of the Germanic Heritage," in connection with which he hoped to issue fifty volumes of German folklore and history dedicated to the Germanic North. Together with Wirth, he founded the society *Deutsches Ahnenerbe* (The German Forefathers' Heritage), whose journal, by the same name, was published by Rosenberg's office. See Ackermann, pp. 42-77. All of these activities point to the Nordic Germanic tendencies of the Nazi ideology.

34. Hermann Bausinger, "Volksideologie und Volksforschung" in Andreas Flitner, ed., *Deutsches Geistesleben und Nationalsozialismus* (Tübingen, Rainer Wunderlich Verlag, 1965), pp. 140-141. Also: Christa Kamenetsky, "Folklore as a Political Tool in Nazi Germany" *Journal of American Folklore* 35, 337 (July/Sept., 1972), 221-235.

35. Martin Broszat, *Der Nationalsozialismus: Weltanschauung, Programm und Wirklichkeit* (Schriftenreihe der Niedersächsischen Landeszentrale für Politische Bildung. Zeitgeschichte Heft Nr. 8) (Stuttgart, Deutsche Verlagsanstalt, 1960). See also: Ernst Aurich, *Drei Stücke über nationalsozialistische Weltanschauung* (Stuttgart, Kohlhammer, 1932), p. 14, and Jürgen Lützhoff, *Der nordische Gedanke in Deutschland* (Stuttgart, Ernst Klett Verlag, 1971). Lützhoff pointed out that the Nazis used the terms *nordeuropäisch* and *nordisch* (Northern European and Nordic) as racial concepts, while they employed the term *nordländisch* (northlandic) in reference to geographical locations. Broszat in particular emphasized that the Nazis used ambiguous language in the attempt to hide their true intentions behind such a "conglomerate" term as "Volkish," for example.

36. Alfred Rosenberg, "Nordische Wiedergeburt," in Dr. Walther Zimmermann, ed., *Nordische Wiedergeburt* (Berlin, Junker und Dünnhaupt, 1935), pp. 9-14. See also Ernst Bergmann, "Von der Hoheit des nordischen Menschen" *Germanien* 3 (March, 1933), 55-66 and F.K. Günther, "Der nordische Gedanke unter den Deutschen" in Zimmermann, ed. For further information on the concept of the "New Humanism" during the Nazi period consult Gerhard Salomon, *Humanismuswende: Humanistische Bildung im Nationalsozialistischen Staat* (Leipzig, Teubner, 1933) and Ernst Bergmann, *Deutschland, das Bildungsland der Menschheit* (Breslau, Hirt Verlag, 1933).

37. Kohn, p. 50. See also: Oscar Walzel, *German Romanticism* (New York, Putnam's Sons, 1967), pp. 21-33. The Romantic quest for "totality" had philosophical implications in regard to the search for unity of the arts and the sciences, of emotion and reason. To the Nazis, "totality" implied "total control" over all aspects of cultural and political life, and had little or nothing to do with the "Faustian" search for meaning in life.

38. Dr. Walter Gross, *Hauptdienstleiter*, (Director of the Racial-Political Office of the Party), "Rassenpolitische Aufgaben der Gegenwart" *Grundschul-*

lagen für die Reichsthemen der N.S.D.A.P. für das Jahr 1941/42., ed. by: Der Beauftragte des Führers für die gesamte geistige und weltanschauliche Schulung und Erziehung der N.S.D.A.P. (Rosenberg) (Berlin, Verlag der N.S.D.A.P., 1942) pp. 81-83.

39. Dr. O. Dietrich, *Reichspressechef*, (Director of the Reich Press Office), "Revolution des Denkens" *Freude und Arbeit* VI (June, 1936), 16.

40. Hellmuth Langenbucher, *Die deutsche Gegenwartsdichtung. Eine Einführung in das volkhafte Schrifttum unserer Zeit* (Berlin, Junker, und Dünnhaupt, 1940), pp. 10-11.

41. Oscar Lukas, "Das Wesentliche unseres Volkstums" *Das deutsche Mädel* (Leipzig, Adam Kraft Verlag, 1936), pp. 69-71.

42. "Der Türmer" in *Reichsjugendführung*, (Reich Youth Leadership Organization) ed., *Sommerlager und Heimatabendmaterial für die Schulungs- und Kulturarbeit der H. J.* (Schulungsplan für Juni, Juli und August) (Berlin, Zentralverlag der N.S.D.A.P., 1941), pp. 33-36. Among other things, we read here: "You are nothing, but your folk is everything, and this shall be the guiding principle of your life." See p. 20.

43. Ernst Krieck, "Reform der Lehrerbildung im Dritten Reich" in N.S. Lehrerbund, eds., *Jahrbuch 1935*, pp. 309-315. For a general evaluation of Krieck's theory of education consult Rolf Eilers, *Die nationalsozialistische Schulpolitik; Eine Studie zur Funktion der Erziehung im nationalsozialistischen Staat* (Cologne, Westdeutscher Verlag, 1963), pp. 5-35. See also Alfred Beck, *Erziehung im Grossdeutschen Reich* (Dortmund, W. Crowell Verlag, 1936), p. 123.

44. Ernst Krieck, "Die Objektivität der Wissenschaft als Problem" in *Schriften des Reichsinstituts für Geschichte des neuen Deutschland* (Heidelberger Reden von Reichsminister Rust und Professor Ernst Krieck) (Hamburg, Hanseatische Verlagsanstalt, 1936), pp. 27-30. Krieck emphasized here that the concept of "humanity" was much too broad and too abstract to make sense. Instead, Germans should look for "humanity" among their own members of the folk community, for the folk community was the only reality that truly existed. For the Nordic Germanic emphasis consult also: Ernst Krieck, *Dichtung und Erziehung* (Leipzig, Artamanen Verlag, 1933).

45. *Ibid.* p. 17.

46. *Ibid.*

47. *Ibid.*

48. Otto Schmidt, *Volkstumsarbeit als politische Aufgabe* (Berlin, Industrieverlag, 1937), p. 94.

49. Hans Schemm, "Der Totalitätsbegriff in der Erziehung des politischen Menschen mit dem Ziel Volk und Gott" *N.S. Lehrerbund,* (National Socialist Teachers Association), eds. *Jahrbuch, 1935,* pp. 286-288, and Krieck, "Reform . . . " p. 309.

50. Bausinger, See p. 125.

51. Max Hildebert Boehm, *Volkskunde* (Berlin, Weidmannsche Verlagsanstalt, 1936). p. 8. See also: Max Hildebert Boehm, *Volkstheorie und Volkstumspolitik der Gegenwart* (Berlin, Junker und Dünnahupt, 1935) and Wilhelm Stapel, "Entschiedene Kulturpolitik" *Deutsches Volkstum* (April, 1933), 313-319.

52. Adolf Hitler, cited in "Das Dorf wächst ins Reich" in *Volk im Werden* 4 (April, 1933), 11-12. On another occasion, Hitler said: "The Third Reich will be a peasant Reich or it won't be at all!" Cited in Dr. Karl Sachse, "Das Bauerntum in der deutschen Geschichte" in K.A. Walter, ed., *Neues Volk auf alter Erde: Ein Bauernlesebuch* (Berlin, Junker and Dünnhaupt, 1935), pp. 115-116.

53. Walter Darré, *Das Bauerntum als Lebensquelle der nordischen Rasse* (Berlin, Verlag der N.S.D.A.P., Franz Eher, Nachf., 1940/41). First published in 1934. Also: *Blut und Boden* (Berlin, Industrieverlag, Spaethe and Linde, 1936).

54. David Schönbaum, *Hitler's Social Revolution: Class and Status in Nazi Germany 1933-1939* (New York, Doubleday, 1966), pp. 159-186.

55. Bracher, Sauer, and Schulz, Introduction. This is an excellent definition of totalitarianism and the Nazis' idealistic appeal for the "folk community." For a distinction between authoritarianism and totalitarianism consult also: Michael Levin, "How to Tell Bad from Worse" *Newsweek* (July 20, 1981), p. 7.

3

The Nazis' Theory
of Volkish Literature

Like all aspects of German culture during the Nazi period, literature was transformed into an instrument of Volkish propaganda. Goebbels called it an expression of the "cultural will of the people,"[1] and the critic Heinz Kindermann, who originally introduced the concept of *volkhafte Dichtung* (Volkish literature) defined it in terms of its relationship to the mythos of the German blood, race, spirit, ancestors, landscape, and destiny.[2] Norbert Langer, whose definition of the concept was equally vague and ambiguous, referred to its special mission of preserving the German tradition at home and abroad, "wherever there are Germans."[3] In his view, Volkish literature was shared by all who were of German blood and who spoke the German language. Such definitions characterized the political and ideological role of literature in the Third Reich that had little to do with the self expression of individual authors.

The Nazi slogan:"*Das Buch—Unsere Waffe*" (The Book—Our Weapon) further indicated that literature played a vital role in the fight for German national unity under the rulership of the Nazi Regime. Books were to be written and to be used to "guide" all generations of readers in the ideology of National Socialism. Books were not only the most significant media of instruction but also of indoctrination. By means of the "right" type of literature the Nazis hoped to promote especially in young people the "right" attitude toward Party and State. During a meeting of the Reich Culture Chamber in November, 1934, State Secretary Funk defined art and literature as indispensable tools within the politics of the State, expressing his hope that they would serve to influence the German people by filling them with the spirit of the National Socialist idea.[4]

The Nazis saw children's literature as an integral part of Volkish literature, because they believed that it had to live up to the same "task" as all literature. Through it they hoped to achieve a control over their children's attitude toward the German folk community and the goals of National Socialism. Basically, they distinguished between three different categories of Volkish literature. The first one was folklore proper, from which they singled out all those German and

51

Nordic Germanic traditions that appeared to be well suited for the purpose of folk education, such as German folktales, Norse mythology, and the Nordic sagas, as well as German and Danish ballads and legends. The second category consisted of older German literature, including short stories, regional novels, historical novels, and certain excerpts from books that lent themselves well to a "Volkish" interpretation in the National Socialist sense. The third category was the new literature that was relatively slow in coming and that corresponded to the Nazis' requirements of "Volkish literature" without being dependent on the "right" interpretation. To be sure that the first two categories, which made up the bulk of children's literature during the first half of the Nazi Regime, would be interpreted in the proper manner, the Party and State censorship authorities would issue detailed "guidelines" for teachers, librarians and youth leaders. In addition, all editors of folklore journals and literature journals were placed under pressure to follow the National Socialist ideology in the interpretation and criticism of every article or book review published. Those who did not follow this demand were denied paper for printing or were ordered to cease publishing altogether.[5]

What we today plainly call "censorship," the Nazis expressed as "cultural guidance." In this activity they distinguished between two directions, one of which would move toward destroying all those elements in literature that did not fit their ideology, and the other one which would help them in their efforts to build the folk state of the future. The first one may be associated with the book purges, but it should be associated also with the willful distortion of folklore and portions of the older literature that were re-interpreted in a "National Socialist" manner. The Nazis never admitted that they were in any way doing something to art and literature that overstepped their boundaries. Hans Friedrich Blunck, President of the Reich Literature Chamber, used the gentle simile of a gardener's job to explain the task that Goebbels had assigned to him. He said that the State authorities would have to "pull out all of the weeds" from the "healthy bed of flowers," very much like a gardener who truly cared about his plants. If left untended, the weeds would choke the young plants and stifle their growth and development. "Thus," he concluded, "the State has the right to choose and select from among the literary creations and the authors according to its own will and desire. It has the right to do so—and it has always made use of this right—in order to counteract those movements that have a tendency to lead to the disintegration of German culture."[6]

As the removal of "un-Volkish" literature was an on-going process during the Nazi period and not confined to its early stages, the criteria used in this process are just as important as those connected with the promotion of "desirable" Volkish literature. At first, teachers and librarians followed in their selection procedures the general guidelines of the Nazi ideology and some more specific principles set forth in Goebbels' "black lists"—a periodic index of "un-Volkish" works that also included children's books. Later, Reich Education

Minister Rust urged all teachers and librarians again to screen the contents of their library holdings in view of the National Socialist "Volkish" requirements and to remove all of the remaining items that unnecessarily "cluttered" the book-shelves.[7] During the national conference in 1937, the National Socialist Teachers Association finally agreed to set up definite guidelines for the removal of "un-Volkish" literature and to implement these without delay. The ten points listed covered most aspects of the Nazis' censorship theory.[8] Significantly, the first one referred to the need of removing books that supposedly contradicted the "Nordic Germanic attitude." According to the attached explanation, this applied to works portraying unheroic characters, pacifistic themes, or certain "weaknesses" in German history. Implied in this statement was a simultaneous promotion of books dwelling on heroic themes and a "positive" world view. The second point concerned unwanted literature as far as the "wrong attitude to-ward Jews" and the racial question were concerned. It referred quite explicitly to books which portrayed Jews as "noble protagonists" but Germans as "treach-erous villains." Such themes were not to be tolerated, it said, nor others that presented a cooperation among different races or interracial marriages in a favorable light. The next following point, too, spoke against books depicting ideals of the brotherhood of man across racial lines. Specifically, it addressed the need of abolishing books that accepted the "imperialism of the Pope" while placing the value of the individual "monastic" life over the value of a life dedi-cated to the service of the German folk community.

The most drastic National Socialist censorship principles were those which were directed against works written by Jews or by persons who, for one reason or another, had expressed a dissenting view in regard to the Nazi Regime. Among the seventy Jewish writers whose works were to be withheld from chil-dren and youth were the names of Heinrich Heine, Else Ury, Jakob Wasser-mann, Franz Werfel, Ludwig Fulda, Alfred Döblin, Emil Ludwig, Arthur Schnitzler, Georg Simmel, and Stefan Zweig. Among the forty "dissidents" were those of Erich Kästner, Jack London, and Lisa Tetzner. In both cases, the Association's judgment was unrelated to literary criteria altogether, as it fo-cused primarily on biological-racial determinism on the one hand and on the authors' political and ideological attitudes on the other. It is evident that from the very beginning that such an application of Volkish book selection criteria ruled out altogether an evaluation of certain works of literature, simply, because some authors were singled out as "aliens" and "enemies" of the German folk community.

Some of the other criteria which the Association listed, at first sight ap-peared to be noncontroversial or even acceptable. Thus, some librarians initially may have sympathized with the request of removing books from the library shelves for so-called "reasons of national self-preservation and national secur-ity." Yet, who was to define what was dangerous to the nation's security? Given the tight security measures within the totalitarian state, as well as the Party's dogmatic opposition to free speech and the individual's right to an appeal, it turned out that such a vague guideline lent itself to arbitrary censorship actions. The same was true for the apparently universal selection criteria referring to the removal of books that were "out-dated" in their contents and "worn and unsightly" in their physical appearance, for even today librarians everywhere use common sense judgement in "weeding out" books that they consider to belong under these categories. Within the context of the Nazis' Volkish censorship, however, the Party leadership reserved the right for itself to determine what books were to be earmarked as "out-dated," and these criteria, too, easily gave the authorities an excuse to remove unwanted books from the library shelves. Many valuable works of German and world literature were now labelled this way, merely because they no longer served a particular purpose within the Nazis' folk education program.[9]

Some of the guidelines referred to the removal of books representing "sentimental clichés and moralistic tales." Such criteria appeared to resemble those used by Wolgast and the members of the former Children's Literature Association around 1900,[10] and for this reason were received sympathetically by educators. The difference was, however, that unlike the former critics, the Nazis really cared very little about aesthetic principles and quality control in children's literature, but mainly opposed books of this type because they had nothing to offer in terms of promoting the new didacticism of the National Socialist ideology. From their point of view, neither old fashioned moralistic tales nor sentimental and religious tales had a bearing upon promoting the heroic ethics needed for the "young team" of the future.

The new concept of Volkish literature as a "positive" instrument in promoting German folk education was as complex and ambiguous as the National Socialist ideology from which it derived its direction. Since the new concept of *volkhafte Literatur* (Volkish literature) sounded very much like *volkstümliche Literatur* (regional literature and folk literature, including folklore), and since, in addition, the Nazis often used them interchangeably, without necessarily referring to the more politically flavored concept of *völkische Literatur*, it came to be associated in many circles with the revival of idyllic literature dating back to the turn of the century.[11] Such an ambiguity not only led to confusions regarding the true meaning of the concept, but initially also contributed, at least partially, to the wholehearted support which some educators and former members of pre-Nazi Volkish groups gave to the National Socialist cultural policy. In many respects, the Nazis' emphasis on *volkhafte Literatur* for young children reminded them of what Severin Rüttgers and various Volkish groups in the Weimar Republic had tried to accomplish by strengthening the role of native folklore and German folk literature in the reading curriculum. It took them some time before they realized that the Nazis' ideological goals were aimed far beyond a mere "revival" of former Volkish trends.

The question then arises as to what exactly children's books were expected to accomplish within the new context of German folk education. During the early

Plate 10
"The Ancestor"

stages of the Nazi Regime, it was Hans Maurer, editor of one of the first bibliographical guides to Volkish literature for children and youth, who also gave one of the first definitions of its tasks. On behalf of the Hitler Youth Organization and the Reich Youth Library in Berlin, he defined the new goals of Volkish literature as follows:

We Expect of Good Books That They Will:
   1. Arouse among children an enthusiasm for the heroes of sagas, legends and history, for the soldiers of the great wars, the *Führer* and the

New Germany, so as to strengthen their love of the fatherland and give them new ideals to live by.

2. Show the beauty of the German landscape.

3. Focus on the fate of children of German ethnic groups living abroad and emphasize their yearning for the Reich.

4. Deal with the love of nature and promote nature crafts.

5. Relate old German myths, folktales and legends, in a language reflecting the original folk tradition as closely as possible.

6. Give practical advice and help to the Hitler Youth, both in relation to recreational programs and camp activities.[12]

Maurer's concern with the themes of nature and the German landscape, with German and Nordic Germanic folklore, and patriotic elements shows a clear correspondence with the themes emphasized in pre-Nazi times by the German Youth movement and in children's literature by Severin Rüttgers. Even the emphasis on the *Führer*, the "New Reich," Germandom abroad, and the Hitler Youth in part could still have been understood as a continuation of Volkish-political thought that prevailed during the twenties. In particular Maurer's attempt to revive the old folk traditions presented a skillful link between older popular trends and new directions in children's literature. Whereas the book selections in Maurer's *Guides* readily betrayed the exclusive concern with German themes, past and present, and a strong racial bias, the criteria as listed did not yet sufficiently alert those who had begun to look suspiciously upon the Nazis' literary policies.

When a few years later the National Socialist Teachers Association stated the criteria and requirements of Volkish literature as pertaining to children and youth, the guidelines clearly revealed not only a racial bias but also the crucial role to be played by children's literature in National Socialist folk education. It was now evident that the values derived from a new interpretation of the Nordic Germanic past were to be utilized for the purpose of an ideological indoctrination. Whereas Maurer had referred to folktales, myths, and sagas only in relation to traditional language patterns, the National Socialist Teachers Association emphasized the Nordic hero's "attitude toward fate" and his "inner victory in spite of a possible defeat," by associating both with the developing war ethics of the German folk community of the present time. All children's books would have to do justice to the German people, they wrote, namely by promoting a spirit of service and sacrifice for the German folk community, as well as by expressing confidence in the nation's victory. They should also convey to the young reader the need to accept one's fate with an attitude of confidence, an "inner victory," regardless of the outcome of a given battle. In this spirit writers should convincingly portray tragic and heroic characters, so as to appeal to young people. They concluded that such an attitude could be portrayed only by writers of German blood "and of racially related origin."[13]

GREAT HEROES OF GERMAN HISTORY
(From a Hitler Youth Yearbook)

KOENIG HEINRICH I·

Plate 11
King Henry "believed in the eastward expansion of the German Reich . . . "

Ulrich von Hutten

Plate 12
Ulrich von Hutten "fought for the people's rights."

The major emphasis in this definition of the role of children's literature lies in its needed support of the German "fighting spirit." In that sense, children's books, like all literature, represented an ideological "weapon" for the Nazis to establish the principle that the present was a direct continuation of the past, and that National Socialism demanded the same type of heroism as the Nordic Germanic "ancestors" had required. In the spirit of Norse mythology and the sagas, this implied a defiant attitude toward fate and a spirit of "action" rather than of resignation. Throughout the Nazi period, the Nordic heroes were put up as ideal models for children and youth. The newer writers, too, were expected to extoll their virtues through fiction. The critic Hellmuth Langenbucher demanded that writers should present their characters mainly in relation to the past, especially in regard to the nation's "storm and stress," so as to illustrate their heroic attitude toward the fate of the German people throughout history. A literary portrayal of such an heroic struggle, regardless of when it had occurred, would be most relevant to the present time. "Today it is expected of poetry, literature, drama, and film," he concluded, "that they show the heroic type of man . . . "[14]

The term "heroic literature" was but another word that the Nazis used for Volkish literature. Patterned upon the Nordic hero's attitude toward fate, it was meant to project the "New Man's" attitude toward the Third Reich. The Nazis also referred to the new literature as a literature characterized by *Wirklichkeitsnähe* (proximity to real life) while they claimed that it represented "National Socialist Realism."[15] At the same time, however, they considered it also as a "symbolic literature." Rosenberg defined the role of art and literature in terms of their capacity to exceed the immediacy of experience while employing symbols to express "the mythos of life."[16] Hitler, too, called attention to the "symbolic" function of art and literature in terms of their obligation to maintain the morale of the nation state and to develop "positive" ideals:

> They should arouse our national self-consciousness and stimulate the individual to greater achievements. In order to fulfill this task, they will have to become prophetic of all that is dignified and beautiful in life and of all that is natural and healthy. If indeed they do live up to this task, then no sacrifice is too great to promote their cause. If, however, they fall short of it, then we should not waste a penny on them, for if art and literature are not healthy and do not assure us of progress and longevity, they are nothing but symbols of degeneration and decay . . . [17]

The "symbols" of Volkish literature, as the Nazis understood them, were not the personal inventions of individual authors but the "overpersonal" creations of Volkish ideology employed in the service of the folk state. As such, they were linked with propaganda, although their apparent relationship to Norse mythology and religion, to Romantic Volkish and irrational thought endowed

Plate 13
"Storytelling" (From Hobrecker's Anthology): The Revival of German
and Germanic Folk Traditions

them with the glamour of a "mythos" of "deeper significance." These "symbols" were expected to be "positive" as much as advertisement and propaganda are expected to be "positive" if it is their aim to sell a given product. The Nazis did not really wish to sell a finished product but hoped to stimulate by "symbolic literature" the continuous process of folk education that would turn German children and youth into a homogeneous community of "true believers." Writers who dwelt upon the theme of human suffering, or on deplorable social conditions and suppressive circumstances were condemned as "degenerates." Thus, Volkish literature not only ignored the real present conditions of the people but also the "reality" of history and mythology while focusing exclusively on the "healthy" and successful image of German life in the past and in the present, for it was its ultimate goal to raise the "New Man" of the future. "There are symbols everywhere," said Rosenberg, "even in the so-called Nordic race."[18] Such a definition of symbols had very little to do with what modern critics call "symbolic expression" of art, or "symbolic action."[19] To Rosenberg and other Nazi ideologists symbols were predetermined images representing a conscious combination of National Socialist ideas and mythical images of the Nordic Germanic past. They shared with modern symbols a certain ambiguity, especially in regard to Volkish concepts of various kinds, yet even this ambiguity was a part of the Nazis' rational scheming to simulate prevailing Volkish trends in pre-Nazi days. The symbols of Nazism were essentially ready-made formulae meant solely to enhance the mythos of the Third Reich. What they lacked was an unrehearsed ambiguity rich enough to serve creative writers and artists as a basis for their own creative thoughts. As they carried a prescribed ideological message, they represented severe limitations to writers and artists.

In children's literature, as much as in all other spheres of German culture during the Third Reich, the new "symbolism" imposed on writers a conglomerate of clichés related to concepts of blood, soil, mythos, race, and the never-ending fight of the German nation. When writers attempted to remodel the reality of historical characters and events in historical fiction and biography, for example, the threadbare fabric of their models and the didactic intent of their symbols became all too evident and certainly did not convince. In one story, for example, the author portrayed William the Conqueror as the ancestor of Adolf Hitler, while glorifying both as determined fighters of the Nordic race.[20] Within the Nazis' context of symbolic thinking such a distortion of history was necessary and applaudable and the Party reserved for itself the right to reinterpret history and folklore as it saw fit, while ordering writers to follow the blueprints faithfully.[21]

The official Nazi definition of Volkish literature, particularly as it was promoted by Goebbels and the Reich Youth Leadership Organization, did not make a basic distinction between children's literature and literature intended for adult readers. The National Socialist Teachers Association was a little more moderate in this connection, but even they tended to ignore age group criteria on various occasions. Reich Youth Leader Baldur von Schirach explained this attitude in 1934 by referring to the changed emphasis of the literature available to youth: "Every true work of art addresses the whole nation, and as such, it also addresses youth."[22] Maurer supported this view by arguing that the most important task of Volkish literature was not to please or entertain children, but to promote the spirit of Germandom. He expressed his confidence in the fact that, at the present time, German children were mature enough to grasp the significance of this objective. "What they really want is literature that tells them more about the *Führer*, the nation, and the German people."[23] Even Lichtenberger, who in pre-Nazi days had so vigorously defended the need of preserving in children's books the "childlike appeal," now reasoned that even Theodor Storm in the nineteenth century had said: "If you wish to write for youth, don't write for youth!"[24] Fritz Helke, Director of the Reich Youth Literature Division in

Foto: Heinr. Hoffmann, Berlin

Plate 14
The Sentimental "Volkish Appeal": "We Love Our *Führer*, Our Home, and
Our Fatherland!"

Berlin, was a little more conscious of a certain methodological breach with the past, and thus felt obliged to add the following explanation:

> It is very evident that this list (of children's literature) does contain a great amount of literature for adults. Although to some persons this may appear a strange and unfamiliar practice, it does reflect one of the most important deviations in our attitude toward children's books in comparison with that which has prevailed in the past. Further, it does distinguish our policy from the policy pursued by former organizations.[25]

The former organizations were the Children's Literature Association and the Art Education movement of pre-Nazi days. Helke did not bother to explain why the attitude toward children's books had changed, nor what exactly the differences were, but merely announced the new policy as a dogma.

The National Socialist Teachers Association at least tried to explain to its members why Volkish literature for children now included so many works that originally had been written for adults. Their first reason was that the new writers simply had not come up with enough good books yet to satisfy the ideological demands and artistic standards of the authorities, and the second reason was that the selected works for older readers were so superb in expressing the new symbolism of the Third Reich, that educators simply could not do their job without them:

> If we wish to raise heroes, then we will have to expose our children early enough to the concepts of war and heroism. Yet, if the works of the newer writers do fall short of invoking the symbols of the great warriors who have fallen in battle, and if they fail to provide our youth with heroic examples, then they have done their writing in vain. In the poetry of Heinrich Anacker, Eberhard Wolfgang Müller, and Gerhard Schumann our young people will recognize their better selves. Also, if we want to develop in our youth the inborn German character, then we cannot do without the works of Kolbenheyer, Wilhelm Schäfer, and Emil Strauss.[26]

It is difficult to establish concisely what individual educators were really thinking about such a policy at the time, for they risked their personal safety by publishing a dissenting view; and if indeed they had dared to do so, nevertheless, the censors would probably not have permitted their articles to appear in print exactly as they had written them. The dissenting views that were published were usually confined to matters of pedagogical or methodological concerns but did not touch upon the vital issue of censorship itself. Thus, F. Jürgens, for example, complained in the *Jugendschriften-Warte* in 1934 that the leaders of the Hitler Youth Organization had displayed "sheer ignorance" in defining the concept of Volkish literature without an appropriate knowledge of psychology and childhood education.[27] Ludwig Göhring even made the point in 1938 that forty years of professional know-how could not simply be "wiped away" by those who were now in power, and that pedagogical and psychological considerations still played a role in evaluating children's books.[28] Neither one of them, however, addressed the more serious issue of the intrusion of ideological values into children's literature but seemed to take them for granted.

Some well known members of the former Children's Literature Association were equally ambiguous when stating their views on the status of children's literature after 1933. Franz Lichtenberger, for example, who at the beginning of the twentieth century had still defended children's literature against the intrusion of political and social objectives when demanding, that children's books first be evaluated for their portrayal of the "childlike" perspective, as well as for their literary and artistic qualities, now subordinated those criteria to ideological perspectives of Nazism. In 1940 he requested that children's books be judged according to the following criteria:

1. The National Socialist point of view.
2. An artistic and literary point of view (and, in the case of nonfiction, a scientific point of view).
3. A pedagogical point of view.[29]

In the article following this listing, he elaborated why the points mentioned would have to be considered in the order as stated. Such an "adjustment" to the Party's demands indeed appeared like a sad surrender of all the principles of liberalism that had still characterized much of the activity of the former Children's Literature Association he wrote, but by its very nature, the National Socialist point of view overruled all other considerations. Lichtenberger, however, even went on to condemn international and pacifistic trends in children's literature of pre-Nazi times. The only theories of value to come from that period were those of Severin Rüttgers, he wrote, as they provided a solid basis for the present revival of Volkish and nationalistic values in children's literature. He reminded teachers that, at the present time, children's literature primarily served the "trinity of race, folk, and God," which was the body, soul, and spirit of the German nation.

Another example of how prominent scholars of children's literature gradually yielded to the Nazis' pressure of *Gleichschaltung* was the case of Wilhelm Fronemann, a leading representative of the former Children's Literature Association. While in 1933, shortly after the Nazis' seizure of power, he had written a letter of protest to the Reich Minister of Education in Berlin, pledging for professional and supposedly more independent criteria in the evaluation of children's books,[30] his values gradually evolved in the direction of the new establishment. In 1934, he complained in an article published in the *Jugendschriften-Warte* that the newer children's literature publications still lacked the desired good quality, but somehow he seemed to have overlooked the more urgent issue pertaining to the political manipulation of children's books.[31] In 1939, he ap-

Plate 15
Hitler Youth Drummers:
Belief in Fate and Confidence in the Future

praised Severin Rüttgers' Volkish contributions to children's literature, while simultaneously expressing his admiration for Karl von Spiess' racial folktale interpretation, thus implying support for the pre-Nazi as well as the Nazi definition of Volkish literature.[32] Even more conspicuous was his recommendation that publishers should pay more attention to the promotion of children's books that dealt with geopolitics (*Raumplanung*), hereditary science, genealogy, and racial science, among others, as these served the present educational needs. "It is the highest goal of political education," he added, "to develop in the individual the feeling that he is an integral part of the racial folk community, and that he lives his life accordingly . . . "[33]

The ambiguous definition of the term "Volkish literature" had its source in the ambivalent attitudes of those who used it. First, there were those educators who rather naïvely believed that the Nazis' Volkish attitude indeed was nothing but an innocent concern with a German and Germanic folklore revival based on Romantic and patriotic sentiments. Secondly, there were those who since 1933 had openly embraced a radical change in attitude along racial and geopolitical lines. To these belonged the ideologists themselves and the members of the Hitler Youth Organization. Thirdly, there was a heterogeneous group of persons, among them many members of the National Socialist Teachers Association, who shifted from one point of view to another, while partially hiding behind Rüttgers' and Krieck's Volkish theories, yet neither clearly approving nor disapproving of the Nazi ideology. The ambivalent attitudes of these persons belonging to the third group especially helped the Nazis to assert their own policy of Volkish literature, as they accommodated the new "symbolic" interpretation, and, ultimately, their goal of ideological indoctrination.

On a broader scale, the political and ideological demands of the Party tended to prevail in regard to children's literature. Reich Education Minister Rust made some minor concessions to age group criteria and reading levels through his curricular reforms and "Basic Lists" for the school libraries, yet the goals of German folk education remained unchanged. Also, regardless of the concessions involved, the formal definition of Volkish literature always gave first consideration to the National Socialist point of view, even in regard to books intended for the youngest children.

NOTES

1. Rolf Geissler, *Dekadenz und Heroismus. Zeitroman und völkish-nationalsozialistische Literaturkritik* (Stuttgart, Deutsche Verlagsanstalt, 1964), p. 30. See also: Wilhelm Westecker, "Methode und Form der Buchbesprechung" *Bücherkunde* (March/April, 1937), 167-180.

2. Heinz Kindermann, *Dichtung und Volkheit: Grundzüge einer neuen Literaturwissenschaft* (Berlin, Volksverlag, 1937).

3. Norbert Langer, *Die deutsche Dichtung seit dem Weltkrieg: von Paul Ernst bis Hans Baumann* (Leipzig, Adam Kraft Verlag, 1941), p. 7.

4. Staatssekretär Funk, November, 1934. Cited by Walter A. Behrendsohn, *Die humanistische Front: Eine Einführung in die deutsche Emigranten Literatur, Vol. I (1933-1939)* (Zürich, Europa Verlag, 1946, p. 25.

5. To deprive publishing houses of paper supplies was just one of the less severe punishments by Party and State authorities in case of rule violations. Serious offenses usually resulted in more drastic measures. See Chapter 14 on "The System of Censorship." Also: Hermann Bausinger, "Volksideologie und Volksforschung" in Andreas Flitner, ed., *Deutsches Geistesleben und National-sozialismus* (Tübingen, Wunderlich Verlag, 1965), pp. 140-149.

6. Hans Friedrich Blunck, "Deutsche Kulturpolitik" *Das Innere Reich*, Vol. 1 (Munich, Eher Verlag, 1940), 63-65.

7. "Rust-Verordnung" cited in *Die Reichsverwaltung des N.S.L.B.*, (Reich Office of the National Socialist Teachers Association) eds., *Die Schülerbücherei* (Leipzig, Volksverlag, n.d.), p. 22.

8. *Ibid.*, pp. 23-25.

9. For a general description of Goebbels' attitude toward literature and literary criticism consult Westecker. Also: Bernhard Payr, *Das Amt Schrifttumspflege Berlin* (Berlin, Verlag der N.S.D.A.P., 1941). Two relevant articles about the new literary criticism in relation to children's books are: Heinrich Scharrelmann, "Über die Beurteilung und Stoff von Jugendschriften" *Jugendschriften-Warte* 42/1 (January, 1936), 23-25 and Udo Dickel, "Positive Buchbesprechung" *Jugendschriften-Warte* 44, 9-10 (Sept./Oct/, 1939), 139.

10. Irene Dyrenfurth-Graebsch, *Geschichte der deutschen Jugendbuchforschung* (Hamburg, Stichrate, 1951), p. 197. Also, see the related discussion of this issue in Chapter 1.

11. Peter Aley, *Jugendliteratur im Dritten Reich: Dokumente und Kommentare* (Hamburg, Verlag für Buchmarktforschung, 1969), pp. 3-30. See especially his analysis of the Magdeburg Conference. For a general discussion of the impact of the Nazis' "positive" folk culture and Volkish ideology consult Georg L. Mosse, *The Crisis of German Ideology: Intellectual Origins of the Third Reich* (New York, Grosset and Dunlap, 1964) and Hans Kohn, *The Mind of Germany: The Education of a Nation* (New York, Scribner's 1960) and Peter Viereck, *Metapolitics: The Roots of the Nazi Mind* (New York, Capricorn, 1964), pp. 67-74.

12. Hans Maurer, *Jugend und Buch im Neuen Reich* (Leipzig, Lehmanns Verlag, 1934), pp. 32-33.

13. *Reichsverwaltung des N.S.L.B.*, eds., *Die Schülerbücherei*, p. 60. See also: Marianne Günzel and Harriet Schneider, *Buch und Erziehung. Jugendschrifttumskunde* (Leipzig, Klinkhardt, 1943), pp. 157-158.

14. Helmuth Langenbucher, *Die Deutsche Gegenwartsdichtung. Eine Einführung in das volkhafte Schrifttum unserer Zeit* (Berlin, 1940), p. 37.

15. H. Boeschenstein, *The German Novel* (Toronto, Toronto University Press, 1949), p. 3. Boeschenstein said that the Nazis neglected universal human elements in favor of formalistic elements in their pursuit of a "realism" that was far removed from the reality of the conditions prevailing in the Third Reich. This notion can be confirmed by a stylistic analysis of children's books.

16. Alfred Rosenberg, *Der Mythus des zwanzigsten Jahrhunderts:* 2nd ed. (Munich, Eher Verlag, 1931), p. 251.

17. Adolf Hitler, "Volk und Kunst" in *Hirts Deutsches Lesebuch 8B* (Breslau, Hirt Verlag, 1940) p. 119.

18. Alfred Rosenberg, "Symbol und Rasse" *IBid.*, p. 49.

19. See, for example, R.R. Blackmur *Form and Value in Modern Poetry* (New York, Random House, 1957), p. 367. Blackmur considers art and literature as living, searching, forever changing processes—a definition that is quite contrary to the Nazis' didactic conception of "symbols."

20. Marion Marshak, "German Fiction Today" *The American Journal of Sociology* (January, 1944), 356.

21. Wilhelm Rödiger, *The Teaching of History: Its Purpose, Material and Method* (London, Friends of Europe Publications #57, 1938), pp. 3-10.

22. Baldur von Schirach, cited by Maurer, p. 45. Grunberger commented that the Reich Youth Leadership Organization officially defined the child below the age of ten as "the non-uniformed creature who has never participated in a group meeting or a route march." Richard Grunberger, *The Twelve-Year Reich; A Social History of Nazi Germany, 1933-1945* (New York, Holt, Rinehart and Winston, 1971), p. 277.

23. Maurer, pp. 13-14.

24. Franz Lichtenberger, "Die geschichtliche Entwicklung der Idee der Kindertümlichkeit" *Jugendschriften-Warte* 45, 9-10 (September/October, 1940), 75-80.

25. Fritz Helke, "H.J.-Arbeit am Schrifttum" *Der deutsche Schriftsteller* I, 1 (1936), 9.

26. *Die Schülerbücherei*, p. 88.

27. Fr. Jürgens, "Jugend und Buch im Neuen Reich; Eine Buchbesprechung" *Jugendschriften-Warte* 39, 12 (December, 1934), 85-87.

28. Ludwig Göhring, "Vom Wesen der Jugendschrift. Die Meinung eines alten Erziehers" *Jugendschriften-Warte* 33, 10 (October, 1938), 58-60.

29. Franz Lichtenberger, "Grundsätzliches zur Jugendschriftenfrage" *Jugendschriften-Warte* 45, 1-2 (January/February, 1940), 85-87.

30. Wilhelm Fronemann's letter to the Reich Minister of Education in Berlin was dated August 5, 1933. It is cited in full by Aley, pp. 15-16. For Barfaut's less favorable view of Fronemann see p. 215.

31. Wilhelm Fronemann, "Idee und Aufbau der deutschen Jugendliteratur

und die Frage der Jugendschriftenverzeichnisse" *Jugendschriften-Warte* 39, 1 (January, 1934), 1-2.

32. Wilhelm Fronemann, "Zur heutigen Lage der Jugendlesekunde" *Jugendschriften-Warte* 39, 2 (February, 1934), 25-28.

33. *Ibid.*, 28 and 26. Much more radical (and less ambiguous) in regard to racial issues were the definitions of the new tasks of children's literature as stated by Max Fehring, who in 1933 was placed in charge of all children's literature affairs in Hamburg. See Max Fehring, "Die geistigen Grundlagen der Arbeit am Jugendschrifttum" *Jugendschriften-Warte* 38, 7 (July, 1933), 49-52. Fehring clearly demanded a new direction in children's literature that would take its inspiration from the Volkish values of the past (including the heritage of Germanic folklore), but which would essentially integrate these with the Volkish ideals of the Nazi ideology and its racial objectives. In particular, see the definition of "*völkische Jugendschrift*" on p. 52.

PART II

The Interpretation of Children's Literature

4

Folktale, Germandom, and Race

The German folktale gained significantly in status and popularity during the National Socialist Regime, as the Party promoted it actively within the context of German folk education. A Party official put it quite plainly in 1935: "The German folktale shall become a most valuable means for us in the racial and political education of the young."[1] To the already fairly large German folktale collections in the libraries the Nazis added a great number of new publications early in the thirties, and the markets were flooded with series of paperbacks promoting the German folk heritage. The schools, too, officially supported this trend by paying close attention to the German folktale at all levels of education.[2]

On the surface, the folktale revival during the Nazi period resembled a similar one during the German Romantic movement. The Party emphasized this similarity while giving the impression that they were merely continuing a well established conservative trend based on a "neo-Romantic" faith in the German peasant. The wave of enthusiasm about the folktale revival could be felt particularly strongly among educators, writers, and philologists who had set their minds and hearts on Rüttgers' ideas pertaining to a renewal of German national identity through German folklore and "roots" research. During the German National Book Congress in Berlin in 1933, the main speaker focused on a recollection of nostalgic sentiments that the German folktale had provoked among writers of German literature. Among others, he referred to a writers' meeting not long before, when the host had taken from his book shelf a small, brown, leather bound volume of the *Kinder- und Hausmärchen* by the Brothers Grimm, while reflecting how much the simple yet vivid folk language of this work had inspired his grandfather. The speaker remembered that from there the conversation had turned to patriotic ideas and the present state of the nation. All of them had agreed whole-heartedly that it was their love of the German folktale and their love of their ancestors that had united them in spite of many individual differences. If ever again something new and creative would arise in German literature, he concluded, then it would have to reach the level of the simple German folktale, for in its sincerity and honesty it reflected the true spirit of Germandom.[3]

Patriotic sentiments of such a nature dominated the attitude of folklorists, educators, philologists, and writers during the early years of the Nazi Regime. An obvious racial bias was already evident in some of them, although in many cases there was more of an ethnocentric attitude toward the German folk tradition. In general, comparative and international folklore studies were on a decline, while there was a pronounced interest in the inherited folk tradition of the German peasant. Folklore of the city, too, became less popular as the cult of the German peasantry reached its peak. The German peasant evolved as a symbol of German "rootedness" in the Nordic Germanic past, and his village community out of which the German folktale originally had been born, now emerged as a symbol of the German folk community as a whole. In children's literature circles, and elsewhere, the German folktale was no longer considered a mere reflection of folklore or literature but "realistic evidence" of a community life founded in the Nordic Germanic past that had a special relevance to the present time. When during the Heidelberg Folklore Congress in 1935 the main speaker called the German folktale a "community forming agent" that had a bearing upon the community life of the German nation,[4] the ideological implications of such a statement could not be ignored, as it corresponded with the Nazis' own ambiguous Volkish terminology. At that time, all former theories pertaining to the German peasant community (like those developed by Tönnies, Sombard, Jahn, and Riehl, for example), had been officially assimilated by the National Socialist ideology that overshadowed all other interpretations, and it had become increasingly difficult for folklorists to pursue professional methodologies outside of its domain. Such innocent terms as *Volk* (folk), community, and national unity were endowed with a political meaning that was well understood by the majority of the population—particularly when they were used in a public address subject to Party surveillance.[5]

The exclusive Nordic Germanic interpretation of the German folktale became particularly evident in an article by Lorenzen, published in the same year in the *Jugendschriften-Warte*. Lorenzen demanded that teachers focus on a unified world view that reflected the old Germanic peasant culture, in order to guarantee that the discussion would have relevance to the folk Reich of the present.[6] All other approaches should be discarded, regardless of whether they applied to the theories of the Brothers Grimm, Benfey, Bédier, von Sydow, or renowned anthropologists and psychologists, as they had nothing to offer to enhance the current community spirit under National Socialism. Rothemund, Director of the Bayreuth Office for Youth Literature, officially sanctioned such a one-sided approach to the German folktale when he wrote: "Next to Norse mythology, the German legends, and the Nordic hero tales, it is the *German folktale* that helps most decidedly to develop a new racial consciousness and a positive attitude toward life under National Socialism."[7] Friedrich Panzer, too, saw in German folktales no longer simply an aspect of folklore or literature, but a reflection of the "true character" of the German nation. In his essay on "The Significance of Saga and Folktale for the Life of the Nation" he wrote in 1938 that teachers in particular should pay close attention to the Nordic Germanic origins of the German folktale, because folktales were older than myths and truly revealed the sources of Germandom.[8] He did not bother to supply the reader with evidence for such a theory. Like Karl von Spiess, in an essay on "The Folktale" that was published a few years later,[9] he assumed the position that the present time demanded an emphasis on those elements that made the German folktale "unique" in the world, while simultaneously, it required a rejection of all previously accepted approaches. In the preface to the work *Deutsche Märchen—Deutsche Welt* (*German Folktales—German World*), von Spiess further elaborated that many "foreign influences" had infiltrated the German folktale, and that now it was the task of folklorists, philologists, and educators to "purify" it to such an extent that its original Nordic Germanic roots would become evident to the reader. If thoroughly cleansed from all "un-Germanic" elements, the folktale would once more emerge as the "true mirror of the German folk soul."[10] At the present time it was of greater necessity than ever to restore the German folktale to its original meaning. He left no doubt that this "original meaning" could be viewed only in relation to selected themes and characters in Norse mythology which, in their turn, had a special significance within the context of the Nazi ideology.

The idea of "cleansing" the German folktale from "alien influences" represented yet another step in the direction of censorship. The Brothers Grimm, too, had drawn upon parallels between the German folktales and certain themes in Norse mythology, yet they had not gone so far as to exclude some tales, or portions of tales, from their collection, merely because they did not fit their theory. Neither had they done so in the interest of promoting "race consciousness" in a narrow and exclusive sense, for at all times they had kept alive their genuine interest in the folktales and myths of other nations.[11]

Such narrowing perspectives on folktale analysis had a definite impact on the selection and publishing trends of folktale collections for children. Whereas the censors generally left the older German volumes untouched, they altered newer editions by emphasizing the "German" and "Nordic Germanic" orientation and by using in their table of contents such sub-titles as "Of German Courage," "The Quest for Honor," and "The Stronger One Always Wins," or such book titles as *Deutsche Heldenmärchen* (*German Heroic Folktales*), *Germanische Märchen* (*Germanic Folktales*), *Nordische Märchen* (*Nordic Folktales*), and *Märchen des Nordens* (*Folktales of the North*). In the case of the last mentioned volume, they even mixed the genres of the German folktale and of Norse mythology, so as to underline more strongly the spiritual relationship between the two.[12] While there was no shortage of older and newer works pertaining to the German and Nordic Germanic folk traditions, children were more and more

Plate 16
Archetypes and Nazi "Symbols":
Grimms' Folktales as a "Mirror" of Female Virtues

deprived of folktales lying outside of this cultural area—with the exception of the *Arabian Nights* which the Nazis tolerated throughout the duration of the Third Reich. The German folktales themselves were "cleansed" from Christian tales and "foreign" elements, although such a process took time, and it was not consistently carried out in all new publications. The bulk of the German folktales were still re-told in the simple folktale style, and teachers and librarians generally were conscious of loyalty to the oral tradition in a given work, at least as far as its stylistic qualities were concerned.[13] From that point of view, German children in Hitler's Germany still benefited from the legacy of the Brothers Grimm, even though to a very limited degree.

One of the most pronouncedly racial folktale interpretations was Maria Führer's *Nordgermanische Götterüberlieferung und deutsches Volksmärchen* (*North Germanic Myths and the German Folktale*), which was published in 1939. Führer analyzed in this work ninety folktales of the Brothers Grimm from a new "symbolic" perspective that endowed the age-old Nordic Germanic mythical traditions with ideological meanings promoted by the National Socialist Party. "In the folktale we grasp the German character at its very roots," she wrote in the preface of her work, " . . . for we all feel instinctively and unconsciously that both the Nordic myths and our folktales have sprung from the same source."[14] What she really wished to imply in this statement was that the Nazi ideology, too, had sprung from these roots, and that folktales should be used effectively to enhance it.

Führer proceeded in such a way as to first link carefully selected folktale motifs with corresponding motifs in Norse mythology to "prove" their inner relationship—even in cases where there was no logical connection. In a rather forced attempt, she even went so far as to relate the white turtle doves in "*Aschenputtel*" (the German "Cinderella" story) to the black ravens of the Norse god Odin, while interpreting them both as "symbols of fate." In simple folktale riddles that came in patterns of three, she recognized the three mysterious deities questioned by King Gylfi (*Prose Edda*),[15] and in the folktale motif of the "water of life" she discovered the Norse well of Mimir from which Odin had gained his drink of wisdom. She would even draw on folk legends and bits of folk superstitions to prove her point that the symbols of life had been predominant in German folk wisdom. Thus, she referred to Frau Holle's Well (Mother Hulda's Well) in a Thuringian folk belief, for example, to show that wells were associated with "newborn babies." Frau Holle was the one who supposedly had brought the babies to German mothers, and she argued that therefore, all wells stood for "life and fertility."[16] Conveniently, she ignored the context of Norse mythology, according to which Odin received through his drink from Mimir's Well a terrible foreknowledge of doomsday and death.[17]

Following a similar bias in his methodology, Joseph Prestel alluded to the regional superstition of the *Hollezopf* (Holle pigtail) in Thuringia, which generally referred to an expression used to describe tangled women's hair, by pointing out that it was the mythical Frau Holle who had caused the entanglement.

Plate 17
Folktales of the North
Stories Retold from Norse Mythology

From here he then moved on to a discussion of the legendary *Holleborn* (well of Frau Holle), from which, according to German folk belief, the newborn babies were brought to earth. This proved, he concluded, that the motif of wells in German folktales symbolized life and fertility.[18]

The use of such symbols was no coincidence, for the Nazis created an institution called *Lebensborn* (well of life) in which selected "Aryan" women and unwed mothers were meant to serve the "racial up-grading" of the German folk Reich by producing children with men selected from the ranks of Aryan "supermen." The "symbols of life" in all spheres of German culture were intended to support the Nazis' "positive" population policy.[19]

As a result of focusing primarily on the "life giving" symbols in folktales, a number of philologists and educators produced some rather odd interpretations that bore indeed a greater resemblance to the Nazi ideology than to Norse mythology. Haacke, for example, selected from Grimms' folktales only the symbols of water, trees, swans, frogs, the moon, the spindle, and the sun, while viewing all of them in relation to the "positive forces of life" and the German wisdom gained "by instinct or blood knowledge." It was the responsibility of every educator, he wrote, to recognize in German folktales "the Nordic Germanic world view in symbols of nature."[20]

It became all too evident from a great number of related publications on the German folktale at that time what such a recognition of the "Nordic Germanic world view" did imply. It was no longer thought to be sufficient if educators merely expressed an appreciation of values linked with the past, as they were expected to link them with those of the present. Kurt Boehme commented in 1940 that the most characteristic motifs of the German folktale gave evidence of certain "masculine" qualities that expressed the Germanic drive for action. Such qualities were of vital significance for young people if they were to become true members of the German folk community:

> An emphasis upon the most characteristic motifs of our German folk-tales will give us sufficient insight into the nationality traits and attitudes of our people. These are: loyalty, courage, honesty, endurance under trying circumstances, a readiness to fight against enemy forces, and a manly mastery of difficult situations, due to an inborn drive for achievement. Victory is awarded only to the best, the most efficient, the most courageous, the most honest of men . . . [21]

In Boehme's view the German *Volksseele* (national soul) was also reflected in such traits as parental love and motherly love, and in combination with the masculine heroic values these corresponded to a high degree with the values reflected in the historical development of the German people as a whole.

Similar "desirable" character traits in the German folktale were singled out in the work by Dobers and Higelke, entitled: *Rassenpolitische Unterrichts-praxis* (*Racial-Political Practice of Teaching*). The authors proceeded very selectively in analyzing certain tales from Grimms' *Household Stories* that would be suitable for an interpretation along racial lines. After first discussing the need for the "Germanic masculine virtues" of courage, strength, loyalty, leadership, and service, they would then search out examples from Grimms' collection to illustrate their points. Through the following tales grouped under the heading of "Courage," Dobers and Higelke tried to prove that for many centuries the German and Nordic Germanic traditions had supported the same ideals as those which the Nazi Regime emphasized in German folk education at the present time. In their interpretation, courage was not merely "a virtue" but a specific "Nordic Germanic attitude" that also characterized German man. In the tale of "The Youth Who Could Not Shudder," they pointed out that the fellow who was apparently "stupid," in reality had more common sense than the so-called "clever" young man, who happened to be his brother. This implied, they explained, that the German folktale was essentially unconcerned about a person's degree of intelligence. What mattered, however, was the attitude of fearlessness, which showed the apparently "stupid" fellow to be a character of racial superiority. In the tale entitled "The Prince Who Feared Nothing," it was the Prince who was distinguished by fearlessness and self-discipline, both of which were Nordic and German qualities to be admired. In "The Drummer," too, these qualities marked the person who was racially superior to the rest of the characters. In this case, he was not only without fear, but he also could not be harmed by fire. This meant, explained Dobers and Higelke, that he shared the racial characteristics of the legendary hero Siegfried who, without fear, rode through a ring of fire. In the tale of "Iron Hans," the hero's courage was matched by strength, both of which were desirable racial qualities.[22]

In order to underline the "inborn Nordic traits" of the German folktale heroes, Dobers and Higelke proceeded in a similar fashion with other German folktales. Consistently they pointed out to educators that the hesitant and cowardly man had as little to do with the genuine German folktale tradition as the clever schemer who had in mind only his personal advantage. Of course, they could not deny the fact that there were quite a number of German folktales around, even among those collected by the Brothers Grimm, that simply did not fit such an interpretation but even contradicted it. Such an inconsistency in the folk tradition did not lead Dobers and Higelke to admit, however, that there were exceptions to the rule. On the contrary, they insisted that only the folktales which they selected and recommended for discussion were the genuine *German* folktales, whereas all those that portrayed "un-Germanic" character traits were quite simply "un-German" folktales that had been infested by foreign influences. Thus, tales portraying the German peasant as a ridiculous character or a pitiable fellow, tales that showed the defeat of an honest heroic man, or tales that characterized the main protagonist as a dishonorable or disloyal person were to be omitted from discussions with children, and editors should ensure that they were taken out of the folktale anthologies. The tales of "Clever Hans," "The Good Trade," and "The Clever Folk," for example, gave an undesirable, biased portrayal of the German peasant, showing him as a character of "bottomless stupidity." As such, these had as little to contribute to German folk education as the tale of "Clever Grethel," which they considered "a silly story about a greedy cook." They thought that a tale such as "The Child Mary," too, should be omitted, as it reflected some "race-alien" Christian motifs that were unsuitable for raising German children. "What distinguishes the *racial man* (it.) from the *race-alien man* (it.)," they concluded, "is his faith in the victory of the strong, the courageous, the beautiful, and the good human being over the greedy, cruel, ugly, and treacherous one."[23]

The German folktale also served the Nazis for teaching girls to become the "ideal Germanic women" for Hitler's Germany. According to Matthes Ziegler's *Die Frau im Märchen* (*The Woman in the Folktale*), the German folktale heroine represented the archetypal image of the Germanic woman. As such, she had no erotic characteristics but the same "healthy peasant spirit of those who originally told the tale."[24] These were, in Ziegler's view, the women among the

Plate 18
The Enchantment of the Fairy Tale

Nordic Germanic ancestors. "The folktale is a mirror of history—a mirror of the ideal image of the German and Nordic woman, and it represents a type of woman which today more than ever carries for us the eternal characteristics of the Nordic humanity."[25]

Ziegler saw in the German folktale heroine the archetype of a pure virgin who became the well deserved prize for the courageous hero who had overcome the dragon or the enemy by a vigorous and determined fight. She was his reward, but more than that: she was the needed complementary force for the fighting man, destined to perpetuate life and to give life. If at the end of most folktales the hero married the princess whom he had won by his actions, their marriage symbolized the life cycle and timelessness of the German nation. SS Leader Heinrich Himmler captured the very spirit of Ziegler's work when he wrote in its preface: "A people lives only as long and as happily in the present and future as it remembers its heritage and the great spirit of its ancestors."[26]

Joseph Prestel considered the primary virtues of the German folktale heroine to be those of innocence, patience, loyalty, diligence, and faithfulness. He, too, believed that she was "Germanic throughout," and in addition to appraising her virtues as a marriage partner, he set her up as a model for German girls and women at the present time, as she had such a positive attitude "toward the tribal home life close to the hearth."[27] Prestel considered the character of Aschenputtel as the archetype of the Nordic woman, for in it he saw reflected the ideal qualities of the Nordic Gudrun. Both women had been heroic examples of devoting their lives to others and showing a readiness to sacrifice themselves.[28] Above all things, it was their altruism that imparted to their names the spirit of eternity. Prestel further explained that finally, the folktale hero and the folktale heroine had given evidence of their "sound racial instincts" by selecting each other as marriage partners. "Whom does the princess choose? . . . She selects the courageous young man, the good natured, loyal man, regardless of whether he is a hunter or a shepherd." Together, the hero and the heroine of the German folktale had become "symbols of racial up-grading, the ideals of high racial quality and longevity."[29]

Whereas the Nazis promoted the German folktale with the main purpose of teaching children the "positive spirit of life" through selected symbols that suited their ideological objectives, they did not promote with an equal fervor the German literary fairy tale. Since both the folktale and the literary fairy tale had emerged side by side during the age of German Romanticism, each contributing equally to the development of children's literature, it may appear arbitrary at first sight that the Nazis should not have favored both. The reason for such a discriminatory treatment of the two genres lies in the fact that the Nazis simply found the German folktale more "useful" than the literary fairy tale in regard to German folk education. They did not reject the literary fairy tale altogether, yet they did not think that it had the same advantages as the folktale when it came to a search for symbols of life and eternity. Also, since it had neither Nordic origins nor "peasant roots," but more often than not reflected an individual author's personal philosophy of life, they thought that it lacked Volkish values.

Among the literary fairy tales, however, the Nazis saw some exceptions. Prestel, for example, singled out the tales of Brentano and Hans Friedrich Blunck. He favored these over others because they were "rooted" in some regional folk beliefs and thus came rather close to the spirit of the German folktale and the peasant heritage. On the other hand, he thought that many of the early Romantic fairy tales were nothing but "irrelevant playthings of the mind" and should be left aside.[30] These views found an echo among teachers, librarians, and censors at the time, and they were reflected also in Rust's *Basic Lists* for school libraries a few years later, in which literary fairy tales were represented only on a very limited scale. Krebs wrote in a *Denkschrift* early in the thirties that the early Romantic fairy tales represented a "tired pessimism" and a "sickly preoccupation" with elements of the grotesque and the bizarre that were absolutely unrelated to the "healthy German folktale spirit." Within such a scheme of values he wrote off the fairy tales of Tieck, Novalis, and E.T.A. Hoffmann as "morbid" and "out of touch with reality" while appraising the "life accepting" spirit of the German folktale above everything else.[31]

In the Nazis' evaluation of folktale and literary fairy tale we have a concise reflection of their larger debate pertaining to "healthy" and "decadent" literature and their standards for the evaluation of art and culture in general. Krebs even went so far as to apply the racial characteristics of a given author to his evaluation of his writings. In the case of Clemens Brentano, whose tales he generally approved, he faced a certain dilemma on account of his mixed German and Italian parentage. Finally, he decided that Brentano had inherited "the soft moods and the lighthearted spirit of life" from his Italian mother, yet the more valuable qualities of Germandom, namely "the spirit of toughness, pride, determination, and will power" from his father, which, fortunately, had had the greater influence on his writings.[32]

The application of such Volkish and racial criteria to the selection of children's literature severely limited the range of books which German children had available to them toward the end of the thirties. To reject the early Romantic fairy tale along with others that served no tangible ideological purpose meant to reject an essential part of the German literary tradition. According to Marianne Thalmann, a modern literary historian, the Romantic fairy tale not only belonged to one of the most imaginative and original literary creations, but it also bore the "seeds of surrealism" that marked the beginnings of modern literature.[33]

Some readers may wonder today how the Nazis' "symbolic" view of the German folktale compared with such symbolic folktale interpretations as those of Bruno Bettelheim or Max Lüthi, for example. Possibly the greatest difference between them is that the Nazis in their didactic over-concern with racial and Volkish values lost sight of international and universal perspectives on the folktale at large. By contrast, Bettelheim (as a student of Jung) consistently used folktales of various cultural traditions in searching out universal values of man. Like Jung, he had a deep faith in the dynamic life of an "inner world" shared by all peoples around the globe.[34] This "inner world" again was not merely one of "positive" values but it involved both the forces of "darkness" and the forces of "light." Max Lüthi, too, perceived in folktales the whole range of universal values reflecting the basic components of human existence: life and death, good and evil, as well as innocence and wickedness. In such contrasts he recognized complementary forces that characterized humanity at large. In his view, the folktale and its symbols represented "the quintessence of all poetry" that was one of the primary sources of all creative writing.[35]

Even though the Nazis promoted German folktale collections on an unprecedented scale, their brand of "symbolic" interpretation reduced their value to an instrument of National Socialist propaganda. Through the folktale's emotional appeal they hoped to foster in children not only a love of home and heritage, but also a love of heroic virtues that would serve as a basis for indoctrinating them in the values of the Third Reich. Whereas educators and folklorists today tend to perceive in folktales a potential bridge for international understanding, the Nazis saw in them a means to foster ethnic pride and a spirit of racial discrimination. In the final analysis, they cared less about preserving the German folktale itself than about developing a "tough minded" master race that would conquer and rule all of Europe.

NOTES

1. Alfred Eyd, cited in Kurt Boehme, *Die deutsche Volksseele in den Kinderdichtungen* (issued by the Reich Organization of the National Socialist Party) (Berlin, Verlag der N.S.D.A.P., 1939), p. 9. The book was issued within a series of ideological works for kindergarten teachers and youth leaders, in order to update their present teaching of children's literature.

2. For a more extensive discussion of such trends consult the chapters on the school libraries, the curricular reforms, and publishing trends. Also: Christa Kamenetsky, "Folktale and Ideology in the Third Reich" *Journal of American Folklore* 90, 356 (April/June, 1977), 169-178, and Christa Kamenetsky, "Folklore as a Political Tool" *Journal of American Folklore* 85, 337 (July/September, 1972), 221-236.

3. Paul Alverdes, "Das deutsche Buch" (A speech delivered during the German National Book Week in 1935). *Hirts Deutsches Lesebuch* (Breslau, Ferdinand Hirt Verlag, 1940), pp. 80-82.

4. Julius Schwietering, "Volksmärchen und Volksglaube" (A speech delivered during the German Folklore Congress at Heidelberg, Sept., 1934), *Dichtung und Volkstum* 36, 1 (1936), 68-78.

5. Boehm considered Schwietering as a proponent of "new ideas" that he associated with his own brand of *Volkssoziologie* (Volkish sociology). Max Hildebert Boehm, *Volkskunde* (Berlin, 1937), p. 3. Modern folklorists recognize his creative professional contributions to folklore, yet, simultaneously, they point to his ambiguous use of Volkish language and an exclusive concern with the German peasantry. Bausinger identified both these as characteristic of National Socialist inclinations, especially if they were combined with the concept of an "organic" folk community. Hermann Bausinger, "Volksideologie und Volksforschung," in Andreas Flitner, ed., *Deutsches Geistesleben und Nationalsozialismus* (Tübingen, Rainer Wunderlich Verlag, 1965), p. 134. Broszat claimed that *Völkisch* (Volkish) and Nazi ideology were identical, "if one understands by ideology a composite of intellectual attitudes." He considered them not merely within a strictly racial context but within a general "conglomerate" of ideas that had developed since the second half of the nineteenth century. Martin Broszat, *German National Socialism 1919-1945* (Santa Barbara, Clio Press, 1966), pp. 31-37. See also: Ralf Dahrendorf, "Soziologie und Nationalsozialismus," Flitner, ed., p. 117, and Ingeborg Weber-Kellermann, *Deutsche Volkskunde zwischen Germanistik und Staatswissenschaft* (Stuttgart, Metzlersche Verlagsbuchhandlung, 1969), p. 64.

6. Ernst Lorenzen, "Märchenursprung—Märchenforschung" *Jugendschriften-Warte* 43, 1 (January, 1938), 1-6.

7. Eduard Rothemund, "Das Jugendbuch in der deutschen Schule" in Hans Maurer, *Jugend und Buch im Neuen Reich* (Leipzig, Seemanns Verlag, 1934).

8. Friedrich Panzer, "Sage und Märchen in ihrer Bedeutung für das Leben der Nation" *Dichtung und Volkstum* 2 (1935), 203-245 and Gustav F. Meyer, "National-politische Auswertung der Volkssagen" *Jugendschriften-Warte* 42, 2 (June, 1937), 13-19.

9. Karl von Spiess, "Was ist ein Volksmärchen?" *Jugendschriften-Warte* 43, 7 (June, 1938), 143-150.

10. Karl von Spiess and Edmund Mudrak, *Deutsche Märchen—Deutsche Welt* (Berlin, Stubenrauch, 1939), 2nd. ed., Introduction. See also: Karl von Spiess, *Deutsche Volkskunde als Erschliesserin deutscher Kultur* (Berlin, Stubenrauch, 1934).

11. The following work presents ample evidence of Wilhelm and Jacob Grimm's great interest in folktales of other cultures and races: Wilhelm v. Steinitz Fraenzer, *Jacob Grimm zur 100. Wiederkehr seines Todestages.* (*Festschrift*). (Berlin, Akademischer Verlag, 1963.) Consult also Ludwig Denecke, *Jacob Grimm und sein Bruder Wilhelm* (Stuttgart, Metzler, 1971).

12. Nordische Gesellschaft, eds., *Märchen des Nordens* (Potsdam, Voggenreiter, 1940).

13. Edmund Mudrak, "Richtlinien für Märchenausgaben" *Jugendschrif-ten-Warte* 48, 12 (December, 1943). Book Review section. Such topics as loyalty to the original folk language continued to be discussed seriously among scholars, just as if Nazism had never entered the scene. As the Nazis did not consider such discussions as contradictions of their own demands, they tolerated them at length in educational and scholarly journals. In practice, they agreed with this concept only to the degree that it remained confined to the German and Nordic Germanic folk traditions—after they had excised the "folk-alien elements."

14. Maria Führer, *Nordgermanische Götterüberlieferung und deutsches Volksmärchen: 80 Märchen der Brüder Grimm vom Mythus her beleuchtet* Vol. III (Beiträge zur Volkstumsforschung) (Munich, Filser Verlag, 1939), p. 3. Issued by the Bavarian State Office for Folklore. Also: Maria Führer, "Nordgermanische Götterüberlieferung und deutsche Volksmärchen" *Jugendschriften-Warte* 44, 7 (July, 1939), 99.

15. For a comparison with the original source consult Snorri Sturluson, *The Prose Edda: Tales from Norse Mythology*, ed. by Jean I. Young (Berkeley, University of California Press, 1966), pp. 30-57.

16. Joseph Prestel, "Volksmärchen als Lebensdichtung" *Jugendschriften-Warte* 44, 7 (July, 1939), 99. See also Joseph Prestel, *Volkhafte Dichtung* (Leipzig, Klinkhardt, 1935), p. 43.

17. *The Prose Edda.* Although the *Edda* makes reference to the rise of Balder after Doomsday, the gloomy vision of the Sibyl dominates the Nordic world view. See also: Ellis Davidson, *Gods and Myths of Northern Europe* (Baltimore, Penguin, 1966), pp. 35-39.

18. Prestel, "Volksmärchen . . ." 99.

19. The Nazis' practical application of the concept of "racial upgrading" was the *Lebensborn* Association. Within the nine years of its existence, 11,000 children were born here by arranged "racially superior matings." 60% of the children were illegitimate—a term that Himmler wanted to abolish, for he hoped to promote temporary marriages in an all out effort to increase the "Aryan" population of Germany. Josef Ackermann, *Himmler als Ideologe: nach Tagebüchern, stenographischen Notizen, Briefen und Reden* (Göttingen, Musterschmidt, 1970), pp. 126-133. The trade mark of the *Lebensborn* was the Runic symbol of life, accompanied by a branch with oak leaves. See also Marc Hillel, *Lebensborn e.V.: Im Namen der Rasse* (Hamburg, Paul Zsolsnay Verlag, 1975).

20. Ulrich Haacke, "Germanisch-deutsche Weltanschauung in Märchen und Mythen im Deutschunterricht" *Zeitschrift für deutsche Bildung* XII, 12 (December, 1939), 603-616. Also: Hans Mohr, "Vom Ursprung und Wesen des Volksmärchens" *Jugendschriften-Warte* 38, 12 (December, 1933), 89-92.

21. Boehme, pp. 14-16. Also: Dietrich Klagges, "Die Märchenstunde als Vorstufe des Geschichtsunterrichts" *Jugendschriften-Warte* 45, 7 (July, 1940), 49-54. Both defended the view of the folktale as history and "folk reality."

22. Ernst Dobers and Kurt Higelke, *Rassenpolitische Unterrichtspraxis:*

Der Rassengedanke in der Unterrichtsgestaltung der Volksschulfächer (Leipzig, Klinkhardt, 1940), pp. 43-44. The strong racial bias of the authors is evident throughout the work.

23. *Ibid.*

24. Matthes Ziegler, *Die Frau im Märchen* (Kiel, Deutsches Ahnenerbe, e.V., 1935), with an introduction by Heinrich Himmler, *Reichsführer, S.S.*

25. *Ibid.*, Preface.

26. *Ibid.*, Introduction by Himmler.

27. Prestel, "Volksmärchen . . .," 99. Prestel recommended Brentano because of his "realism," and Blunck because of his rootedness in North German regional folk traditions. Among many other works, Blunck published *Von Geistern unter und über der Erde: Märchen und Lügengeschichten* (Jena, Diederichs, 1937), that represented a skillful blend of folk tradition and fantasy.

28. *Ibid.*

29. *Ibid.*

30. For some all too evident racial perspectives on folktales consult Reinhold Frank, "Das Märchen vom Däumling in deutscher und französischer Sprache" *Jugendschriften-Warte* 43, 11 and Ernst Tunman, "Ludwig Bechsteins Abstammung" *Jugendschriften-Warte* 43, 11 (November, 1938), 75. For a further documentation of similar grotesque racial views consult Peter Aley, *Jugendliteratur im Dritten Reich: Dokumente und Kommentare* (Hamburg, Verlag für Buchmarktforschung, 1969), pp. 106-107.

31. Dr. Albert Krebs, "Das Märchen der Romantik" (*Denkschrift*) *Document: MA-144/2. B&S Schnellhefter. Akt II. S.417ff.* The article is accompanied by Krebs' letter to the Headquarters of the National Socialist Party (typescript), which indicates that the Party was interested in the subject—at least in accordance with Krebs' view. Krebs' works were frequently recommended in educational journals. See "Bücherbrief" *Die Volksschule* 2 (April, 1939), 29-36.

32. *Ibid.*

33. Marianne Thalmann, *The Romantic Fairy Tale: The Seeds of Surrealism* (Ann Arbor, University of Michigan Press, 1970).

34. Bruno Bettelheim, *The Uses of Enchantment: The Meaning and Importance of Fairy Tales* (New York, Vintage Books, 1977), p. 309. Consult also Stith Thompson, *The Folktale* (Berkeley, University of California Press, 1977), which recognizes cultural differences within the context of comparative studies while pointing to various shared motifs as well. Also: Stith Thompson, "Myth or Folktale?" in Thomas Sebeok, ed., *Myth: A Symposium* (Bloomington, Indiana University Press, 1965).

35. Max Lüthi, *Once Upon a Time: On the Nature of Fairy Tales* (Bloomington, Indiana University Press, 1970) and Max Lüthi, *Das Märchen* (Sammlung Metzger, 2nd ed.) (Stuttgart, Metzlersche Verlagsbuchhandlung, 1964).

5

Norse Mythology and the Nazi Mythos

In Norse mythology the Nazis perceived the religion and spirit of their Nordic Germanic "ancestors." At the same time, however, they realized that it had excellent potential to be transformed into a symbolic view of life that might help to strengthen the ties of the German folk community with the Führer. When they began to popularize Norse mythology, they tried simultaneously to make it an instrument of their Volkish ideology. The strange fusion and confusion of concepts that resulted from such an interpretation led to a distortion of values in Norse mythology that was especially evident within the context of children's literature, for most of the books that dealt with this topic were intended for children and youth. Among them were individual tales retold for children's literature anthologies, as well as collections of myths interspersed with newer poems and stories based on traditional tales. In addition, the Party issued a great number of handbooks and guidelines for teachers and youth leaders to channel their interpretations of Norse mythology into the "right" direction. We will view this literature against the background of some unbiased older sources on the topic, but also in the light of ideological speeches and official statements that sought to enhance the "Nordic" world by making an active use of the new interpretation of myth.

The very concept of Asgard, the abode of the Nordic gods, appealed to the Nazis as a "heaven" for warriors. There were twelve halls in Asgard, of which Valhalla was the brightest one. Here lived the gods, together with the warriors who had fallen in battle, and whose golden shields now decked Valhalla's roof. After every battle on earth, Odin, the chief god, would descend to Midgard to select the bravest among the fallen warriors, and twelve maidens in armor, the Valkyries, would carry them across the rainbow bridge to Valhalla, to restore them to life. With renewed vigor, the warriors would join the ranks of Odin's selected army in Valhalla, and under his leadership they would engage in daily war games to stay fit for the final battle still to come. This final battle on doomsday, to which the Germans referred as the *Götterdämmerung*, was prophesied to bring defeat to all of the gods by the frost giants. In this myth the Nazis saw an inspiring symbol of the "eternal war." In his diary notes, Rosenberg recalled

Hitler's words at the Tannenberg monument in honor of the deceased Hinden-burg: "Dead warrior!" he had said, "Now enter Valhalla!" Rosenberg com-mented that these words had been understood by everyone around, even by the representatives of the Church.[1]

The Norse god Odin (who was also called Wodan or Wotan) appealed to the Nazis primarily because he reflected the somber and defiant image of what they considered their "ancestors," the peasant-warriors of the Nordic Germanic past. To them he was the archetype of an authoritarian leader who had accepted the destiny of war as a final challenge to his pride and honor. The Nazis conven-iently ignored the fact that, according to the *Edda*, the original source of Norse mythology, Odin had not just been a god of war but also a god of the "hanged," a god of justice, and above all, a god of poetry.[2] They insisted that Odin was a "Nordic god," and that all other interpretations were to be laid aside, particu-larly if they related some speculations pertaining to the non-Aryan origins of Odin.[3] Thus, folklorists and children's book writers were no longer at liberty to view Odin as a god of many roles. As an archetype of "Nordic man," Odin was supposed to emerge as "the eternal mirror of the Nordic soul and of primeval strength," as Rosenberg himself put it. He thought that at the present time, Odin was as much alive as he was five thousand years ago.[4]

Such an interpretation may be better understood within the Nazis' concept of war as a symbolic expression of the National Socialist "Nordic" world view, which was, at the time, understood as an heroic world view. In 1942, when Himmler addressed the SS-Division "Viking," he referred to war as a "law of life" affecting the world of animals as much as the world of man. "Beware of the people who are not willing to sacrifice their lives!"[5] he warned the men. The SS symbol of the Viking Division, he explained, represented the runic symbol of the sun wheel, the swastika, which meant that all of life was war, and that the world had survived only because of it.

The Nazis evidently found it more effective to reinforce their world view by a selective approach to Norse mythology than merely by references to Darwin's theories, especially when it came to educating children in the spirit of the Na-tional Socialist *Weltanschauung*. Reich Education Minister Rust complained that the schools had failed in strengthening children's consciousness of their own folk heritage. Children knew more about Olympus than about Asgard and Valhalla, and they were better acquainted with the Greek gods and heroes than with Odin, Thor, and Balder, or with the heroes of the Nordic sagas.[6]

In an attempt to present Norse mythology in this new light, early in the thirties Karl Dilg issued a voluminous interpretation guide for elementary school teachers that was strongly recommended by the National Socialist Teachers Association. In this work he transformed Odin into "the mighty friend of the warriors" who helped to restore the "holy order" of the land:

> Midgard means war in defense of the peasant's soil . . . Work and
> war for the sake of Midgard have the blessings of the gods . . . Life in

Midgard is life in the peace of the gods, for *Bifröst*, the friendly bridge, connects the order of Midgard with the order of Asgard. If this order, the holy Odal, is threatened, then the peasants become warriors, and Odin, the mighty friend of the warriors, will assist and protect them in battle.[7]

Dilg saw in the "holy Odal" no longer just a symbol of the past but also of the present order under the new regime in which war was justified in the name of defense, and in which the peasant had emerged as a symbol of the German nation. Obviously, he implied that the "New Order" of National Socialism, too, had the blessings of the gods.

In another guidebook to Norse mythology, Ledermann and Prestel urged teachers to make children aware of the fact that the word "*odal*" had originated from the word "*odil*," which meant "*edel*" (noble) in German. Consequently, the sacred meaning of the peasant's estate, the *Odal*, implied the "holy and *noble* obligation" of all Germans to defend the German folk community against the enemy forces, and in Norse mythology it should be interpreted as the German man's "fight for German nationhood."[8] Ledermann and Prestel made no distinction between the tribal community of the past and the German *Volksgemeinschaft* (folk community) of the present, but referred to both as if no time had elapsed since the Middle Ages, and as if the past were identical with the present. That this confusion was not accidental but was integral to the very essence of the Nazis' new interpretation of Norse mythology, is evident also in the same writers' discussion of Odin as the leader of warriors. They wrote that in Valhalla the dead warriors would form "a new community under the leadership of the *Führer*," thus hinting at the identity of Odin or Wotan and the *Führer* of the Third Reich, Adolf Hitler. They likened the dead warriors in their eternal "fight for order and survival" to the German people under Hitler's rule who were also destined to fight "until the end of all times." In summing up their discussion of the Nordic concept of war, they stated: "An ethical task of the highest order has been preserved for us in our time that is meant to be the guide for all of those (men) here on earth who are sacrificing their lives on the battlefields in loyalty to the *Führer*."[9] In this way, they, too, raised the "order" of Valhalla to a kind of heavenly command that was sanctioned by the gods themselves.

The concept of Odin as an archetype of the *Führer* was not limited to works related to myth interpretation for children. Naumann called the world view of Norse mythology "a mythos and a lesson" while pointing out its relevance to the present time.[10] In leaning upon Heidegger's concept of *Führer* and *Gefolgschaft* (leader and followers, in the Nordic sense of *comitatus* or retinue), he implied the concepts of loyalty and dedication to service as they had been understood in the saga literature. In this sense, he also discussed "the *Führer's* will toward tragedy" as a spiritual power that set him above fate.[11] In confronting fate, Odin had become the leader of all gods, wrote Naumann, and he had emerged not only as an ideal for all Nordic Germanic heroes but for all Germans at the time.[12] More explicitly, Heidegger referred to a comparison of Odin and Hitler in his regrettable inaugural address in 1933 as president of Freiburg University, in which he told his audience, among other things, that an absolutist regime demanded an authoritarian *Führer* in the Nordic spirit, so as to create and maintain the desirable unity of a nation. "The ideal leader is the founder and preserver of the entire nation's goal," he said, "and the realization of his goal determines the historical existence of the *Volk*."[13] Not all of Heidegger's philosophy was built on such thoughts, and he later realized that he had unwittingly supported a regime with which he did not really identify. His ideas, however, found support among the Party leadership and in educational circles, where they were echoed in numerous interpretation guides to Norse mythology issued to teachers. Some philologists admitted that Odin, like Goethe's Dr. Faustus, had been a thinker and a quester, too, but in most cases they agreed that his ultimate wisdom had been his spirit of *action*. Unlike the philosophical and hesitant Hamlet, Odin had not lost a moment in preparing actively for the final battle to meet his ultimate fate.[14]

The Norse god Thor emerged as the second most significant god within the context of the Nazis' myth interpretations. In the *Edda* he was known as the mighty god of thunder. Equipped with his hammer, *Mjöllnir*, and his belt of strength, he would ride across the stormy northern skies in his wagon drawn by goats. He was pictured as a red-bearded fellow with a stature like that of a tall hero, who was eager at all times to reach for his weapons in settling an argument or defending Asgard. There is certainly much humor in the portrayal of Thor's various adventures which children enjoy even today, but he is not an image of nobility or civility, and his rough dealings have to be viewed within the context of tribal life and thought.[15]

The Nazis, however, were out to make Thor into a god of noble character and strength, whose actions, however barbaric they appeared to be, were justified in the name of "defense." Guidebooks warned teachers not to equate Thor's actions with "brutal force," as he had never attacked anyone except for the sake of peace. Thus, the Nazis interpreted the use of force as a legitimate means to an end, particularly if the safety of the "peasant community" was at stake. Dilg presented Thor as a god of the peasants, as well as a god of the settlers. He called him "a builder" in the sense that his defense of the peasant estates could be interpreted also as a defense of the German settlers who tilled the soil in the newly acquired "living space" areas of Eastern Europe. With that interpretation, he raised him to a god of the German peasants both at home and abroad:

> Thor is the mighty friend of the peasants, the protector of Nordic men who fight in defense of their soil . . . It is our political goal to follow Adolf Hitler's command: "Either we will be a peasant folk or we won't be at all!" This should serve us as a guideline. Therefore, it is our political task to create in our children's minds the image of the peasant with all of his spiritual and racial power. The peasant is the pillar of the state.[16]

Thor fährt über Mitgard   Wilhelm Petersen

Plate 19
"Thor Rides Across Midgard"

A number of other critics, and philologists, too, portrayed Thor as a pleasant and vivacious god who with his strength, reliability, and stability represented "the peasant soul" of the German people—a god on whom one could depend in regard to building and expanding the German lands. As he was "rooted in the soil"[17] and preserved German community order by his protective actions, he came to be declared the guardian of the "blood-and-soil" program, particularly in regard to the Nazis' settlement plans in Eastern Europe.[18] Children were told that Thor, as a god of the settlers, helped Germans in the border areas and in the newly settled lands to preserve their cultural identity and unity within an ethnically "alien" and potentially hostile environment. Thor's sympathy, they were taught, was always with the Germans, never with those who had been driven from their land.

Some educators suggested that Odin and Thor should be viewed as complementary forces, as together they symbolized the tragic fate of the German nations from which arose their defiant attitude toward life. Odin was the wanderer and the warrior, and Thor was the fighting peasant defending German settlements at home and abroad. Together, they might be viewed symbolically as the very image of the swastika, the Nordic rune of the moving sun wheel, as they represented the moving power of Germandom itself.[19] All of the Nordic gods combined, as Leopold Weber suggested in a popular work for young people, represented essentially the spirit of victory. "The exterior form of this ancient faith has long crumbled away," he wrote in *Die Götter der Edda* (*The Gods of the Edda*), "yet we hope that the spirit that once created it will find enough strength to rise again to a new life, and that it will be victorious over everything that is alien to our race."[20]

Balder, the Nordic god of the sun, took up a very special place in German children's literature of the Nazi period, and also in the relevant interpretation guides for teachers. In the *Edda* he is known as the son of Odin, the god of light, but also the god of spring time and hope. His birthday was on December 21st, the date of the ancient solstice celebration, after which the days would grow longer again.

The Nazis saw in Balder a symbol of Germany's reawakening to power, and in his rise to glory they perceived a god-given promise of better days to come for the German nation. In a handbook for elementary school teachers, Lohrmann reminded teachers that Balder's victory over darkness and his symbol of light should not be interpreted in seasonal terms but within the ideological context of National Socialism:

> Yet, one day, the sun god will arouse to a new life all those who have fallen into a deep sleep . . . Adolf Hitler, who has made us a gift of the new flag of light (with the symbol of the swastika), is our Führer, to whom we have sworn *loyalty* and *service* (as the retinue) at this hour. He has given us light in the hour of darkness: *Heil Sieg!* (Hail Victory!)[21]

In ancient Germanic times the people had hailed their gods, but now the *Heil Sieg!* evolved into the new *Sieg Heil!*, the "battle cry" employed at National Socialist rallies.

RUNIC SYMBOLS FOR GERMAN YOUTH:
"The Wisdom of the Nordic Forefathers"

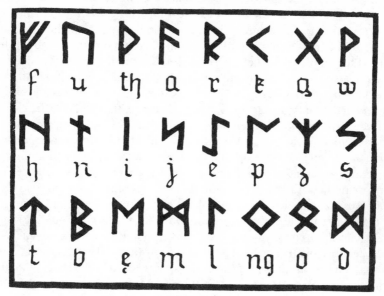

Plate 20
The Runic Alphabet

Plate 21
Stone with Runic Carvings

In a number of German Christmas books published after 1939, the symbol of light emerged in a new context enhanced the Nordic Germanic myths and customs rather than the spirit of Christ. Since the churches were not outlawed, many traditional Christmas legends and Bible stories were still available to children through their church libraries or the books in their home libraries dating back to pre-Nazi times, although they became rare items in bookstores and on the school library shelves. To all appearances, the contents of children's books related to this season had not changed much, as there were still many references to Santa Claus, the Christmas tree, lighted candles, gingerbread, reindeer in the wintry forests, as well as to toys and gifts behind frosted panes or in the department stores. There was the same spirit of joy, it seemed, that usually accompanied the holy advent season, and yet, one thing was missing: the Christ child in the cradle. Although there were photographs and paintings in abundance representing the serene oneness of mother and child, they referred to German mothers, the New Year, and the coming of the Thousand Year Reich. In some cases, the sun god Balder took the place of Baby Jesus, and *Frau Holle*, the old woman in one of Grimm's *Household Tales*, who was popularly known to German children for causing snow to fall from the sky whenever she would shake her heavy feather beds, played a substitute for Mother Mary. An example of this trend is an anthology of Christmas stories issued by the Party in 1940 and dedicated by Heinrich Himmler "To Women, Mothers, Men of the *SS* and the Police."[22]

One story in this volume is entitled "The Search for Balder." Two children took a walk through the deep, dark forest in mid-winter in search of the sun. The little birds hopped from the snowy branches to join them, and even the rabbits and the foxes left their holes to accompany the children in their quest. Finally, they came to a mountain and entered a long passage way leading to a cave. For a long time they crept along in utter darkness, until suddenly they were blinded by a bright light shining at them from a glittering crystal hall. When they had become accustomed to the light, they discerned in one corner a mysterious glow that shone like a halo above the head of a woman and a child who were seated on a throne. Struck by a sense of wonder, the children fell upon their knees, but the woman beckoned them to come closer: "Don't be afraid, my dear children," she said, "for I am Frau Holle, and this babe here is Balder, my newborn son, who was given to me this night."[23] Then she gave each one of the children an apple and gently told them: "Now rise, and go out into the world to tell all men that Balder is risen, that Balder is born again!" The children rose happily and with joy in their hearts followed Frau Holle's advice. Upon reaching the outside of the cave, they saw that the sun was shining again, more brightly than ever before. Balder has risen indeed, they thought, and now a new life could begin!

In this case, the author took the liberty of giving Balder a new mother, for Frau Holle belongs to a familiar folktale by the Brothers Grimm.[24] It is not too

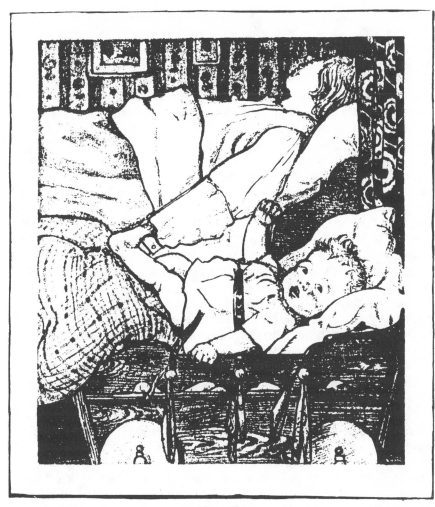

Plate 22
The Mythos of the Child:
Enhanced by the Republication of Older Children's Books

difficult to guess that the two children were meant to represent the nation's search for a leader, and that the reborn Balder came to symbolize the "good news" that Adolf Hitler, the "redeemer," finally had been sent by God to save Germany from utter darkness and destruction. On the other hand, the Nazis obviously borrowed a good portion of this story from the Christmas story. The "strange glow" surrounding mother and child is reminiscent of the scene in the manger, and the words spoken by Frau Holle: "Now rise, and go out into the world . . ." sound like the message of the Angels to the shepherds in the field.

It did not seem to perplex the Nazi writers in the least if they retained in their "Nordic" Christmas stories some allusions to the customary Christian celebration, as long as these were restricted to a general emotional appeal of the season. In general, however, the newer writers searched for these seasonal references among the Norse myths themselves, and also in old German folk legends. They would utilize older German literature as an inspiration, or, on a selective basis, even some of Hans Christian Andersen's tales.[25] They would also refer to such folk beliefs as the return of the deceased family members on Christmas Eve, and Odin's "wild ride" on horseback on the twelve nights after Christmas. In all of the old stories, however, they tried to establish a connection with the new symbols of the Third Reich. Thus, the *Weihnachtsmann* (Santa Claus) emerged in one such story as a descendant of Odin, and Odin as the symbol of the *Führer*.[26] In another story, the memory of the dead was related to the German nation's memory of the fallen German soldiers and the future battles still to come.[27] One author asked: "What is Christmas?" and then gave the answer himself: "It is the joy in the German love of life, in growing and becoming, in mothers and newborn babies. In the true Germanic spirit, these babies are not merely born to live but to fight: to fight for the preservation of German blood and soil . . ."[28]

The Norse myth of doomsday underwent a very peculiar transformation in the Third Reich. According to the *Edda*, it represents the end of all times. The sun will swallow the moon, there will be long winters of darkness, and finally, the frost giants will destroy the rainbow bridge connecting Midgard with Asgard. The gods will all fall in battle, there will be floods, and a great fire will consume everything, even Yggdrasill, the gigantic World Esh rooted in the soil whose top branches support the dome of Asgard.[29]

In the following poem on Yggdrasill, written for children, it is evident that the Nazis preferred to view the World Esh as an "eternal tree" as if doomsday would never come. The poem itself comes to represent the Nazis' political view of Norse mythology and their frantic search for "symbols of life"—even where they do not exist in the genuine folk tradition. It is no accident that the poet focused on Yggdrasill "at the beginning of time" rather than "at the end of all days," as he tried to create a new *mythos* from the old myth that would project the eternity of the German nation:

Yggdrasill

There grows a tree
At the beginning of time,
Clasping together heaven and earth . . .
Always in sap,
Covered forever
With fruit and blossoms,
This mighty giant
Eternally rules
The vastness of space.

Germanic Customs during the "Light Celebration"

Plate 23
The Sun Wheel

Plate 24
The Light Pyramid

Plate 25
Traditional Lanterns
With "the Tree of Life"

High in its branches,
Touching the clouds,
Breathe our forefathers,
Happy, at ease;
Deep down below,
Ceaselessly striving,
Building and toiling
Are we, the descendants.[30]

The *Edda* makes no mention of the ancestors residing up high in Yggdrasill's branches; nor does it refer to the descendants "building and toiling" deep down below the tree. Instead, it mentions a mean eagle at the top and Nidhoggr, a vicious dragon, below, both of whom are constantly fighting. In addition, it tells that Nidhoggr is constantly gnawing at the roots of the tree, thus causing its gradual decay.[31] A poet is, of course, at liberty to use myths in his own way and to create symbols and fantasies that are a part of his personal view of life. Essentially, this is what Tolkien did with Celtic and Norse mythology, or what inspired C. S. Lewis and Lloyd Alexander in their work. No serious critic would think of accusing Richard Wagner of combining various sources of Norse mythology and deviating from all of them to a certain degree when he composed his *Ring der Nibelungen (Ring of the Nibelungs)*. Yet, there is a great difference between a *voluntary* deviation from a mythological source for the purpose of expressing one's own creative thoughts and a deviation that is prescribed by the censors. In regard to the poem on "Yggdrasill," the interpretation of the world tree follows all too obviously the prescribed guidelines for Volkish literature for it to be mistaken for an original interpretation. Had the poet dared to present Yggdrasill as a tree doomed to fall and crumble, most likely, his poem would not have seen print, and certainly it would not have been included in a children's literature anthology approved for use in the public schools.

When Nazi writers did refer to the idea of doomsday, they used it as a background or foil against which they would offset the heroic attitude of the Nordic gods as a bright contrast. They explained that by defying fate, the gods demonstrated that they had overcome it spiritually; or else, they used the doomsday mood in Germany after World War I as a foil to Hitler's rise to power, while comparing his ascent to that of Balder after the darkest night.[32] In both cases, it was hope, not despair, that characterized their interpretation of the *Götterdämmerung*.

There is a brief passage in the *Edda* that hints at the possibility of a resurrection of the gods after doomsday has passed. Balder and the gods are assembled peacefully, it says, and the "golden chessmen" are lying next to them in the grass.[33] Scholars have commonly interpreted this reference as an influence of Christianity upon the *Edda*,[34] but the Nazis saw in it only a promise of the rise of Hitler and the Third Reich toward a glorious future. Thus, Seidenfaden wrote in his preface to a children's literature anthology including selections of folklore and literature from ancient Germanic times to the present: "Faith recreates. It brightens the darkest day, while illuminating it with eternal light. It symbolizes the future of order and discipline, both of which carry their own reward, and it stands for the nationhood created by God, which means that after death and destruction we see the coming of the New Reich."[35]

It was this hope for life and resurrection that characterized the selection of Volkish literature from past to present, and it was faith in the reassertion of the Germanic-Nordic heroic spirit that permeated all ideological thinking. To express this faith more effectively, the Nazis engaged not only poets and painters in the task of creating a new mythos from the myth of the past, but also craftsmen, architects, and business firms. Runic symbols, especially those symbolizing life, victory, and the sun appeared in children's book illustrations, on entrance doors, barns and theaters, on wooden plates, cradles, ash trays, and even on Christmas cookies. All of these were supposed to express not only Germany's "rootedness" in the Nordic Germanic past but also her invincible strength and will power in overcoming all obstacles in her path toward a glorious future.[36]

In the history of myth interpretation we find such distinguished nineteenth century scholars as Max Müller and M. Cox whose solar interpretations of mythology appear to have been somewhat similar to the Nazis' interpretation.[37] In the first place, however, these scholars concerned themselves with an analysis of mythology itself, not with its uses and interpretations in regard to political ideology. Secondly, as one-sided as they may have been in their exclusive views pertaining to the origin of myths, they considered at least the full course of the sun and, unlike the Nazis, did not ignore its "setting." Thirdly, their basic approach was a comparative one involving cross-cultural studies of myths from many nations. The Nazis, however, remained ethnocentric in their concern with the folk tradition and did not wish to consider myths outside of the sphere of their Nordic Germanic "ancestors."

We may perceive another surface similarity between the Nazis' conception of myth as an "active force" in establishing the "order" of a folk community, and Malinowski's theory pertaining to the function of myth within a tribal community.[38] Malinowski observed that in primitive communities priests and tribal leaders promoted myths and rituals in an effort to reinforce an established folk tradition, thus leading also to a greater stability of the tribe. By contrast, however, the Nazis were less interested in perpetuating the folk tradition in its inherited form than in superimposing upon it their own political ideology. Whereas the Nazis constantly paid lip-service to the value of Norse mythology, they did not so much pursue it out of respect for their ancestors' heritage but in order to strengthen the mythos of the Third Reich. Essentially, the mythos of Nazism was not a myth of the people but only an ideology that simulated an organic connection with the genuine folk tradition.[39] Also, if the Nazis referred

Plate 26
The Revival of Germanic Symbols
in Traditional Christmas Pastries

Plate 27

to "community order," they did not have in mind a traditional order that evolved from an organic community life, based on inherited customs and general consent, but an order of the "rank-and-file," founded on the principles of a totalitarian state.

Viewed from this perspective, the Nazis' interpretation of the Norse mythology is not so much a reflection of a sustained "theory" but of a totalitarian ideology placed at the service of German folk education. The dogmatic interpretation which the Nazis attached to the myths created the paradox that German children at that time became acquainted with their own folk tradition only to a very limited degree, even though they read more myths than ever before.

NOTES

1. Hans Günther Seraphim, ed., *Alfred Rosenberg: Das Politische Tagebuch, 1934-35 und 1939-40* (Munich, Deutscher Volksverlag, 1964), p. 55. Regarding other Nazi references to Norse mythology that were commonly understood at that time, such as the *"Unternehmen Valkyre"* (Mission Valkyrie), see Albert Speer, *Erinnerungen* (Berlin, Propyläen Verlag, 1970), pp. 387-404.

2. The many names and roles of Odin are enumerated in the *Prose Edda*. Snorri Sturluson, *The Prose Edda: Tales from Norse Mythology*, ed. by Jean Young (Berkeley, University of California Press, 1966), pp. 48-49. Comparative perspectives on Odin were explored by Jacob Grimm, *Deutsche Mythologie* (Göttingen, 1835), reprinted in Jacob Grimm, *Teutonic Mythology*, Vol. I (New York, Dover, 1972), pp. 95-96. Decidedly one-sided interpretations of the Nazi brand appeared in Hermann Schneider, *Die Götter der Germanen* (Tübingen, J. B. Mohr, 1938), p. 219 and Ulrich Haacke, "Germanisch-deutsche Weltanschauung in Märchen and Mythen im Deutschunterricht" *Zeitschrift für deutsche Bildung* 12, 12 (December, 1933), 6-9.

3. See, for example, Wilhelm Ledermann and Joseph Prestel, *Die deutsche Sage im Unterricht* (Munich, Verlag Oldenbourg, 1927), p. 227. The authors called Odin a god of the peasant nobility and also a god of the "master race." See also Haacke, p. 11 and Julius Petersen, "Die Sehnsucht nach dem Dritten Reich in deutscher Sage und Dichtung" I *Dichtung und Volkstum* 35, 1 (January, 1939), 27. Alfred Rosenberg saw in Odin a god worthy of comparison with King Frederick the Great, Germany's "soldier king." See Seraphim, ed., p. 163. A general analysis of prevailing trends in folklore research and publications during the Nazi period appeared in Hermann Bausinger, "Volksideologie und Volksforschung," in Andreas Flitner, ed., *Deutsches Geistesleben und Nationalsozialismus* (Tübingen, Wunderlich Verlag, 1965), pp. 140-147.

4. *Nationalsozialistischer Lehrerbund* (National Socialist Teachers Association), "Aufruf des N. S. L. B. zur Pflege germanisch-deutschen Schrifttums" *Deutsches Bildungswesen* 10 (October, 1933), 317-322. Rust's demand for an emphasis on Germanic folklore studies is restated within the context of a general appeal to German educators on this behalf by the National Socialist Teachers Association.

5. Heinrich Himmler. "Rede des Reichsführers der SS vor den niederländischen SS-Führern der Waffen-SS, Anlässlich der erstmaligen Verleihung der Leistungsrune" (October 3, 1944). Munich, Institut für Zeitgeschichte, Document No. *MA 316-4827-29.*

6. "Aufruf." The same "appeal" was reprinted in "Aufruf des N.S.L.B." *Hamburger Lehrerzeitung* (October 30, 1933), 456.

7. Seraphim, ed., p. 163

8. Karl Dilg, "Von der Bauernsage zur modernen Bauernnovelle" *Die Volksschule* 35, 5 (June, 1939), 109-112.

9. Ledermann and Prestel, p. 225.

10. Hans Naumann, *Germanischer Schicksalsglaube* (Jena, Diederichs, 1934), pp. 68-69.

11. Martin Ninck, *Wodan und der germanische Schicksalsglaube* (Jena, Diederichs, 1935).

12. Naumann, pp. 68-77. See also: Hans Naumann, "Altgermanische Philosophie" in *Zweites Nordisches Thing in der Böttcherstrasse zu Bremen* (Bremen, Veröffentlichungen der Väterkunde, 1934). This work, issued in the form of proceedings related to the above mentioned Nordic Conference in Bremen, brought out systematically some of the new ideological views on Norse mythology.

13. Alexander Schwan, *Politische Philosophie im Denken Heideggers.* (Series: *Neue Freiburger Beiträge zur Politikwissenschaft*). (Cologne, Westdeutscher Verlag, 1965), pp. 92-93. Schwan commented also on Heidegger's speeches in November and December, 1933. Consult also the critical views of C. W. Lewalter with respect to Heidegger's "Nordic" world view in "Wie liest man Sätze von 1935? Zu einem politischen Streit um Heideggers Metaphysik" *Die Zeit* (Hamburg, August 13, 1953) and Christa Kamenetsky, "Nordic Existentialism: Myth and Philosophy in the Literary Politics of Nazi Germany" *Revue des langues vivantes* XLII, 4 (April, 1976), 339-357.

14. Haacke, 10-12.

15. Such renowned German writers of earlier days as Johann Gottfried Herder, who was largely responsible for the pre-Romantic revival of Norse mythology, had been far more sceptical in regard to certain rough and wild aspects of Thor's character and actions: " . . . *jene Wildheit bleibe älteren Zeiten!*" (Such a wild spirit should remain a part of older times!) he wrote in his essay "Zutritt der nordischen Mythologie zur neueren Dichtkunst." See Bernhard Suphan, ed., *Herders Sämmtliche Werke* (Berlin, 1894), Vol. XXIII, p.

314. For a scholarly and unbiased discussion of the character of Thor see also: H. R. Ellis Davidson, *Scandinavian Mythology* (Toronto, Hamlyn Publishers, 1970), p. 47.

16. Dilg, pp. 109-110.

17. Haacke, 6-9.

18. Fritz Lübbe and Heinrich F. Lohrmann, *Deutsche Dichtung in Vergangenheit und Gegenwart: Ein Führer durch die deutsche Literatur* (Hannover, Karl Meyer Verlag, 1943), p. 86.

19. Haacke, 16.

20. Leopold Weber, *Die Götter der Edda* (Munich, Verlag Oldenbourg, 1934), pp. 13 and 18. See also Ledermann and Prestel, p. 225. Most of Weber's books were published prior to the Nazis' seizure of power, yet his brand of Volkish thoughts, even though in many respects not identical with those of the Nazi ideologists, pleased the authorities enough to include his works in the basic recommended library lists and most of the other recommended book lists for children. The Hans Schemm Prize for German Youth Books was awarded to him in 1936/37 for his contributions to the popularization of Norse mythology. Special mention was made of his works *Asgard* (1920), *Midgard* (1924) and *Grettir, the Icelandic Hero*. See "Leopold Weber" *Jugendschriften-Warte* 42, 11 (November, 1937), 72-75.

21. Hubert Breuer, *Die völkische Schulfeier*, 3rd ed. (Bochum, Verlags- und Lehrmittelanstalt, 1940), pp. 221-226.

22. Heinrich Himmler, ed., *Weihnachtsbuch: Buch der Heimat* (Berlin, Verlag der N.S.D.A.P., 1944/45), Introduction.

23. *Ibid.* The story's title was "*Balder's Wiedergeburt*," pp. 35-39.

24. Frau Holle appears in one of Grimm's folktales as an old woman—without a child. According to the sources on Norse mythology. Balder's mother was Frigg, Odin's wife. For an unbiased view consult O.E.G. Turville-Petr, *Myth and Religion of Ancient Scandinavia* (New York, Holt, Rinehart and Winston, 1964), pp. 110-124. See also Sir James Frazer, *The New Golden Bough*, ed. Theodor H. Gaster (New York, The New American Library, 1959), p. 667.

25. *Nationalsozialistische Deutsche Arbeiter Partei* (Nationalist Socialist Party), eds., *Deutsche Kriegsweihnacht 1941* (Berlin, Verlag der N.S.D.A.P., 1941), pp. 45-49.

26. *Ibid.* The editors selected their material from a great range of folk customs related to older centuries, as well as from familiar stories, including Hans Christian Andersen's "The Fir Tree." Obviously, they tried to preserve the sentimental appeal of such tales while relating them to ideological themes unrelated to the Christian festival.

27. Frazer, pp. 608; 721-725. Frazer gives only the original folk customs. To these the Nazis added their own meanings.

28. Klaus Dörner, ed., *Das deutsche Jahr. Feiern der jungen Nation.*

102   *Interpretation of Children's Literature*

(Munich, Zentralverlag der N.S.D.A.P., Franz Eher, Nachf., 1939), p. 179. See also: Hellmuth Lehmann-Haupt, "What the Nazis did to Children's Books" *The Horn Book Magazine* (May, 1949), 220-230. While the author was correct in observing the missing image of the Christ child in children's books at that time, he ignored the abundance of references to mothers and newborn babies that took their place. Also, he did not mention the substitution theme contained in references to "Baby Balder."

29. Sturluson, pp. 88-89.

30. Johannes Linke, "Yggdrasil" *Hirts Deutsches Lesebuch* (Breslau, Hirt Verlag, 1933), pp. 199-200. See also Seidenfaden's work cited below, and W. von Bülow, "Die Heiligkeit und Ewigkeit des lichttragenden Lebensbaums" Hagal 14, 2 (1937), 1. Von Bülow compared the runic symbol of Yggdrasill with other pagan symbols of light and life, including what he called the "original" Christmas tree.

31. Sturluson, pp. 54-56.

32. Petersen, Part II, 146-182. In his conclusion of the two-part article, Petersen drew a straight line from the prophecies of the Edda to the coming of the "savior," Adolf Hitler, pp. 181-182.

33. Sturluson, pp. 31-32.

34. Turville-Petr, pp. 110-124.

35. Theodor Seidenfaden, *Das deutsche Schicksalsbuch* (Freiburg i. Breisgau, Herder Verlag, 1936), Preface.

36. Consult Rust's Basic Lists in the chapter on School Libraries. Also: Bausinger, p. 141, and Georg Mosse, *Nazi Culture* (New York, Grosset and Dunlap, 1966), p. 288. The Nazis' "bible" of runic lore was Hermann Wirth's *Aufgane der Menschheit* (Jena, Diederichs, 1928), along with his two-volume work *Die heilige Urschrift der Menschheit* (Leipzig, Klinkhardt, 1936). Rosenberg mentioned both works several times in his *Mythus*, and they continued to be included among the recommended works in school libraries.

37. For a comprehensive discussion of the solar myth theories defended by Müller and Cox in the previous century, consult Richard Dorson, "The Eclipse of Solar Mythology" in Thomas A. Sebeok, ed., *Myth: A Symposium* (Bloomington, Indiana University Press, 1955), pp. 25-63.

38. B. Malinowski, "Myth in Primitive Psychology" in Malinowski, *Magic, Science and Religion* (Garden City, N. Y., Doubleday, 1954).

39. For a discussion of the mythos in relation to a totalitarian state consult Ernst Cassirer, *Vom Mythos des Staates* (Munich, Europa Verlag, 1949). Some relevant observations on the artificiality of such a mythos, appear also in Henry Hatfield, "The Myth of Nazism" in Henry A. Murray, ed., *Myth and Mythmaking* (Boston, Beacon Press, 1968), pp. 209-211.

6
Saga Ethics
and Character Training

The heroic sagas of Iceland and Norway held a special fascination for the Nazis. According to Professor Krieck, the leading educational theorist of the Third Reich, German folk education would be seriously incomplete without a study of the sagas.[1] What particular values did the Nazis perceive in these tales, and how did they manage to adjust them to fit their ideology and German folk education?

Our discussion will focus on three major aspects that motivated the Nazis to interpret the sagas to their ideological and political advantage. The first one of these we will call the purpose of identification. This aspect was very similar to that which had motivated them to turn to Norse mythology. As in the myths they hoped to find in the sagas evidence of an historical past, the spirit of which could be presented as if it were still alive at the present time. In assigning children to read the sagas, the Nazis hoped to lead them not only to a greater interest in the life and thought of the heroic past, but to an identification with their "ancestors." Systematically, they tried to get across to them the idea that the past and the present were one and the same.

Secondly, the Nazis perceived in the sagas an excellent means of teaching children the "right" attitude toward the folk community and such values as honor, fate, loyalty, and blood revenge. This aspect we will call the purpose of idealization, for in praising the virtues of the saga heroes, the Nazis gave the impression that these were the very models upon which children and youth should pattern their lives. "The ethics of the sagas create for us *a mirror of our folk*!" wrote Professor Vogt in 1933. Even though he conceded certain limitations, he concluded: "These ethics are of immeasurable value for us today."[2]

The third aspect which will concern us here is the purpose of justification. The Nazis perceived in the judicial system as it was reflected in the sagas, a system governed by organic and flexible laws that came in very handy to explain to young and old why it was necessary and justified to expand German boundaries beyond the given borders into Eastern European territories. What Christian ethics and Roman laws would have condemned, the Nordic Germanic laws seemed to support and even to sanction.

103

Essentially, the sagas provided the Nazis with a new basis for a system of ethics that Rosenberg called "eternal" and "German throughout." He compared the sagas to the compositions of Bach, the sermons of Meister Ekkehart, and the monologues of Goethe's Faust. "All of these are but different facets and expressions of the very same soul." he said in his *Mythos*, "of the very same soul, the very same creation of the human will, and of the same eternal powers that first took form in the god Odin or Wotan."[3] What he had in mind was not a cult of the past but the formation of the "New Man" of the future.

The sagas were reprinted for children and youth in numerous editions, and the texts were left relatively unchanged. New were the interpretation guides for teachers that accompanied them. One of the leading saga guides was Lohrmann's work, entitled *Die altnordische Bauernsage in der deutschen Erziehung (The Old Nordic Peasant Saga in German Education)* which the Party officially recommended for the use of teachers in the public school. In his preface, Lohrmann defined the purpose of saga studies as follows:

> If we talk about Germanic traits in our time, we will have to remember our ancestors who were peasants and knew how to defend themselves. . . . Our life in Germany today is based on a deep faith in the values of the National Socialist ideology, namely those of blood and soil, honor and loyalty. These values are responsible for our nation's progress and significance in the world. We should reach the point when nobody will dare to talk about these Germanic values without having consulted the Icelandic sagas.[4]

Lohrmann strictly followed the historical interpretation of the sagas within the context of the new ideological guidelines. He reasoned that if young Germans were to identify with the characteristic attitudes of their "ancestors," it was mandatory that the sagas be viewed as an "historical reality" rather than as fiction, for the past and present were essentially characterized by the same spirit. "Let us awaken their pride and arouse their enthusiasm for the Germanic past, their own past," he wrote, and he advised teachers to make their discussions of the sagas as relevant to the present situation as possible. "Could Blundketil live among us today? Let us try to place him right into our present-day village community. If students become aware through such a discussion that he is a Germanic man, then we have reached our goal."[5]

How could the saga hero Blundketil possibly have fitted into the German village community? What values would he have presented, and how could such values serve as an example to modern-day youth?

The saga interpretation guides would usually point out first of all that men like Blundketil had been totally committed to the cause of community life. In times of peace, they had been peasants, rooted in customs, folk traditions, and tribal laws. They had plowed the soil owned by the community, without thinking of their personal "profits." Their tribe had been their extended family—just as the German *Volk* was the extended family of the village community at the present time—and to this family they were wholly bound by honor and loyalty. If honor demanded it, they would exchange the plow for the sword and fight with vigor and determination until death.

Hitler himself characterized the Nordic fighting spirit as the "all-or-nothing" attitude,[6] while setting it up as an exemplary virtue for the followers of the Nazi Regime. In explaining such an attitude to elementary school children, suggested Lohrmann, teachers should draw upon parallels between the heroes of the sagas and the brave soldiers of World War I. He referred to a letter that had been written in this spirit by a volunteer of the German Army in 1917: "To live loyally, to fight defiantly, and to die laughingly . . . Do you know this Germanic wisdom? This is the formula to which I cling!"[7] This was not the peasant ancestor speaking, said Lohrmann, but his transformed double, the Nordic warrior who had followed the call of his destiny.

Educators would explain to children that from the basis of Nordic man's total dedication to his tribe arose his sense of honor and his loyalty to the leader. Such a loyalty, commented one writer at that time, could have arisen only from a *voluntary* retinue in battle, and thus it resembled in every respect the German people's retinue in regard to Adolf Hitler. "Fighting for the sake of the community and a readiness to sacrifice one's life: these are the highest ethics arising from the sagas!"[8] Baetke claimed that fate and honor were not merely "principles" or "concepts" but the very "reality of the *Volk*," for both were essentially determined by the warrior's acceptance of his fate. Somehow it escaped Baetke and others that the *Führer* of the present regime enforced the "voluntary" service; that he himself rose to determine the fate of the German nation by dictating its course; and that, unlike the tribal leader of long ago, the German Army did not leave it up to the free decision of the soldier if he wished to fight or not.

It appears ironic to us today that the Nazis should have identified the voluntary service of the Nordic Germanic peasant warrior with the compulsory duty of German men to fight for the *Führer*. Yet, the Nazis needed ideals rooted in the heritage of the past that would inspire German youth more than mere propaganda. Thus, an educator commented in 1933: "The sagas will give our children a true and unfalsified picture of Germandom . . . They will convey to them an ideal image of purity and virtue, along with those reflecting spiritual toughness, determination, and strength. From the sagas they will inherit a positive attitude toward life."[9] Such character ideals as obedience, "toughness," self-discipline, and pride were, according to Dobers and Higelke, the very qualities of the superior race that German youth had inherited from their "ancestors," and these needed cultivation beyond measure.[10]

To a much greater extent than most of their colleagues, Dobers and Higelke subscribed to an overt racial interpretation of the sagas. In their work *Rassenpolitische Unterrichtspraxis (Racial-Political Practice of Teaching)*[11] they followed Bartels' theory from around the turn of the century that identified the literature of a given area with the "racial soul" of a given people. Even more so, they hoped to strengthen the racial soul by a pronounced emphasis on the sagas. All too obviously, however, they distorted the sagas' values of loyalty, service, and discipline into the totalitarian principles of the Hitler Regime. By speaking about "total discipline" and "absolute obedience" to the leader, they not only omitted to mention the saga heroes' choice in selecting and following their leaders, but also their personal conviction of what was honorable and what was not—matters that were not even a subject of discussion for members of a totalitarian state.

The ethics which Dobers and Higelke underlined in the sagas, in many respects reflected those demanded by the Hitler Youth Organization and its leaders. The "Twelve Commandments of the Hitler Youth," which every boy was forced to memorize and accept upon his honor during the initiation ceremony, stated, among other things, that "loyalty and unselfishness" were the first considerations. Further, they spelled out that the members were expected to serve the Organization and the National Socialist Party with pride, to be self-disciplined, to prove their courage, to be active rather than to be idle or talkative, and to be ready to fight for the Party's cause. Such demands as: "A true National Socialist must be a real comrade," and "Treat your comrade as you would like him to treat you" were supposed to instill in young people respect for their peers and to develop their "team spirit" and love of the "folk community." In many respects, such demands were reminiscent of the Germanic leaders' expectations regarding the honor and loyalty of their followers. There was one major exception, however, which made all of the difference: the followers of the Hitler Youth, unlike the saga men, were not allowed to use their own critical or moral judgements. Significantly, two of the Hitler Youth Commandments addressed this point by stating: "The leader is always right!" and "Whatever serves the interest of the (National Socialist) movement, and through it serves the German nation, is always right."[12] It was an established fact, that only the leaders of the Hitler Youth Organization had the right to make important decisions. It was also understood, that whatever they considered to be good for National Socialism was considered to be good for the nation as a whole, and that in the interest of such an objective all means were justified and sanctioned.

The most extreme racial interpretation of the sagas was offered by Reich Leader of the S.S., Heinrich Himmler. Early in the forties he himself saw to it that thousands of paperbacks pertaining to the saga literature were distributed among the soldiers fighting at the front lines. On one such an occasion he addressed a divison of Mountain Volunteers as follows:

> Many essays in these pamphlets are concerned with the heroic history of the German people, exactly as they are reflected in the sagas of the Norsemen. By using the term *"saga,"* people sometimes give the impres-

sion as if they were talking about stories that were not true. We, however, consider the sagas as history. They are based upon history, and in ancient times they were indeed regarded as history by the Norwegians and the Danish, and our own forefathers.[13]

Being concerned with providing the necessity of following the virtues of the "forefathers," Himmler did not even consider the question when and why the sagas had been considered literature and mythology as well. Also, it lay in his interest to merge the terms German and Nordic Germanic, so that he might more emphatically call for a renewed emphasis on such saga ethics as to *"fight loyally*, practice *absolute obedience*, and work toward a *genuine community spirit.*" He concluded his speech by pronouncing: "But the main virtue is obedience. Also for this Division the law applies that says: S.S. Men! Your honor means *loyalty!*"[14] To Himmler, the sagas were historical "proof" of a racial attitude that made soldiers out of ordinary men. Regardless of the literary distortions involved, he twisted their meaning to serve his goal of building up a fighting unit whose members were determined to shed their last drop of blood for the *Führer*.

Most educators at the time did not even go as far as Dobers and Higelke by adopting the code of ethics of the Hitler Youth and its overt racial bias. Instead, they preferred to present the leadership-followership concept of the sagas more in terms of Professor Krieck, while appealing to young people's sense of idealism. Philologist Meyer, for example, argued that in discussing the sagas and German legends with children in the elementary school classroom the following values should receive major attention:

1. Service to the community
2. Sacrifice for the community
3. Courage and unselfishness
4. Respect for the person
5. A sense of responsibility
6. National pride
7. Faith and loyalty (The Germanic concept of *Gefolgschaft*)
8. Heroism
9. Honor
10. Self-discipline[15]

By referring directly to Krieck's writings on the topic, he wrote: "All of the saga hero's power, all of his possessions, all of his loyalty, and all of his actions are linked to his sense of honor, if the situation demands it. If necessary, he will sacrifice even his own life."[16] Not once did he mention "absolute obedience," nor did he overdo it by talking about "total subordination to the *Führer*" or blind obedience. This does not mean that such values were not implied, but it is very characteristic of many educators' writings at the time that they pursued the method of "positive propaganda" by attempting to build up enthusiasm for the nation and the *Führer*, rather than to incite young people openly to a hatred of "alien races."

Instead of presenting the saga ethics of loyalty as an absolute demand, for example, educators were more inclined to prove it a vital necessity, not only for the sake of protecting the nation and the *Führer*, but also, for protecting the lives of the individuals fighting for him. In that sense, one educator wrote:

> The idea of *loyalty* meant something very important to the Germanic people, and it does mean something very important to us today. Every single member of the large group of followers should show as much honor and readiness for sacrifice and loyalty as those living closest to the *Führer*. If they were to leave the *Führer*, they would be helpless. A *Führer* always must be at the top. This is the reason why we find at his side the most efficient members among the retinue.[17]

In this way, they were able to present the *Führer* as a caring father who gave his followers security in return for their loyalty and sacrifice. Also, they built up children's pride in belonging to the selected group of followers that served the *Führer*. Obedience and sacrifice thus did not emerge as categorical imperatives or threats but as pledges of honor sanctioned by the "cause." Such euphemism was wide-spread at the time. Gustav Neckel, a renowned philologist and folk-lorist,[18] referred to the loyalty of the saga heroes as "a principle of metaphysical importance to the whole nation"[19] that was of particular relevance to the present, and Naumann, too, presented this aspect in idealistic terms that simultaneously made it an appraisal of the desired attitude toward the *Führer*.[20]

Since the Nazis placed so much emphasis on idealism in regard to loyalty, service, and sacrifice, it is small wonder that some members of the Hitler Youth Organization during the final stage of World War II fought fanatically to the bitter end, still believing faithfully that they had lived up to the legacy of their ancestors in standing loyally by their leader, be it in victory or defeat. After returning from his long-term sentence in the Spandau prison, Hitler's architect, Albert Speer, once commented in an interview that a confusion of such ideals had led him to become a victim of an unquestioning faith and an unconditional loyalty to the *Führer*. Only too late had he realized that a loyalty of this type was based on a blindness in regard to ethical principles, and that, in essence, it could never be reconciled with responsible action.[21]

Interpretation guides for teachers also distorted the traditional concept of loyalty in relation to such German legendary heroes as Siegfried, Dietrich von Bern, Wieland the Smith, and Lohengrin.[22] In an article printed in the *Jugend-schriften-Warte* in 1939, for example, one author argued that Hagen, the killer of Siegfried, had only revenged his new Queen Brunhilde, and thus, was more loyal to his homeland, Burgundy, than to his blood brother Siegfried. This meant that he deserved a higher respect than it was generally granted him, for he had placed his loyalty to the fatherland above his loyalty to a personal friend.[23] Obviously, it disturbed the writer of the article very little that he swept aside centuries of scholarship on the *Nibelungenlied*, merely in the interest of fostering a new idealism based on a perverted principle of loyalty to the nation.

The perversion of literary values was even more evident in regard to interpretation guides affecting the principle of loyalty in books edited for girls. A book entitled *Des deutschen Mädels Sagenbuch (The German Girl's Book of Legends)*[24] portrayed such German heroines as Kriemhild, Thusnelda, Elsa von Brabant, and Mechthild not in their well known traditional contexts but in situations in which the author obviously tried to underline their roles as loyal women and mothers, just as the Nazis admired them. In the following scene, for example, we find a stereotyped situation of domestic peace that is actually very alien to the spirit of the *Nibelungenlied*. Siegfried himself does not appear as a knight on horseback but as a happy father, and Kriemhild demurely sits by the window engaged in embroidery work:

The happiness of the young couple was complete only when a son was born to them whom they named Gunther. Gunther grew up to be a de-

Plate 28
The Nibelungenlied

Plate 29
Siegfried Fighting the Dragon

Plate 30
Hagen von Tronje: Old and New Concepts of Loyalty and Revenge

lightful child, and when the grandfather would rock his grandchild on his knees, while the child's mother would sit by the sunny window with her embroidery, Siegfried would take leave from his duties of ruling the country and join the group instead, thinking all the while that he was the happiest man on earth.[25]

The author did not even name Kriemhild, but referred to her only as "the child's mother." Such a reference obviously was meant to call to the reader's attention the ideal of motherhood which the Nazis so consciously promoted. Also, the author did not name the grandfather but referred to him only generically in the stereotyped situation showing him rocking the child on his knees. Such an image was meant to idealize the "link" between the generations, the line of "continuity" from past to present, and the concept of Germany's promise in the future that was derived from her "roots" in the past. Ironically, however, the scene as a whole came much closer to the sentimental clichés of the old-fashioned girls' books than to National Socialists "realism" which the Nazis tried to superimpose even upon the old legends.

On the other hand, girls were also encouraged to read the sagas in the very same editions that were on hand for boys. Many educators felt that such characters as Bergthora (Njal's wife), and Aud (Gisli's wife) had shown such a deep loyalty and respect for their husbands that it would not harm girls at all to read the relevant sagas in their entirety. While boys might learn from the sagas how to become tough and loyal men, girls might learn from them how to become devoted, proud, and loyal women. According to a librarian's view early in the forties, the sagas were to be considered a "much healthier diet than the sweet girls' books."[26] Obviously, it had not occurred to her that some of the saga books written for girls contained the same "sweet" sentimental clichés as the older girls' books.

Mainly, however, the sagas were considered a healthy diet for German boys, and an inevitable tool for making them spiritually "tough," and revengeful, just as the "hardy generation" of the Third Reich required. There was no question about the Nordic hero's determination to fight defiantly until the bitter end. He would rather prefer to plunge himself into his enemy's sword laughingly, spitting into his face, than retreating from the battlefield or shamefully dying of old age or of illness in the comforts of his home. Revenge and honor moved him to action, and defiantly, he would overcome the idea of inner defeat. He might be physically crushed, but his spirit would remain unbroken. It was this spirit of defiance which the Nazis called the "masculine spirit" of the sagas. While applauding and idealizing it, they would frequently contrast it with the "soft and feminine spirit" of Christianity and humanism, both of which they called "passive," "cowardly," and "folk-alien."[27]

Even young boys of kindergarten age were supposed to be introduced to the

Plate 31
Ancestor Worship:
"Germanic Dress, 2,000 Years Ago"

concept of "spiritual toughness" through stories adapted from the sagas. Benzing, for example, included in his guidebook for kindergarten teachers some tales that were intended to bring out in boys the warrior spirit of their "ancestors."[28] One of these referred to little Thorgild, a five year old boy who had to prove to his brothers and friends that he was ready, after all, to participate as an equal in their tough war games. What did he do? At night, when everyone was fast asleep, he quietly climbed out of bed, took his father's big spear that was leaning against a wall, and tiptoed out of the house. Once outside, he approached his father's favorite horse, and with one big blow he killed it on the spot. Thereupon he swiftly returned to his room and went back to sleep. Benzing commented as follows on the meaning of the story: "Thorgild has shown that he possessed the correct attitude of a warrior—a blood heritage of his father. And now he was permitted to participate in the games of his brothers."[29]

Without saying more, Benzing implied the lesson that Thorgild had done the right thing in killing the horse, for it was toughness that counted the most. He had proven to his friends and brothers that he had the "right" racial instincts of a warrior to be taken seriously. Benzing still underlined this theme by telling another story about the changeling, Leif, who was ruthlessly attacked by the twins who proved to be the rightful heirs to a king's throne. How did they prove it? One day the king observed that the twins attacked little Leif who was sitting upon the throne, playing with a golden bracelet. They merely pushed him aside and wrested the bracelet away from him, whereupon Leif began to wail loudly. Benzing commented that it was then that the king suddenly knew that Leif was not his rightful son but a changeling of low birth, and that he ordered the queen to give Leif away to the servant and to raise the twins instead.[30] He further explained that this story could well be used to show young children that the saga heroes were a "race of warriors" to whom toughness mattered more than anything else.

Dobers and Higelke in their guide for elementary school teachers included a related story about little Grimwald, who after a bloody battle had been carried off on horseback by his captor. Realizing his very last chance, Grimwald had suddenly drawn his little toy sword and hit his captor with it over the head. The man was so surprised that he fell off the horse—and was killed on the spot. In a similar vein to Benzing, Dobers and Higelke independently concurred that little Grimwald thus had proven himself to be the true son of a heroic warrior, "for he was willing to risk all, and thus earned the greatest reward!"[31]

One of the most significant values which the Nazis emphasized in their interpretation of the saga literature was the "ideal" of blood revenge. A number of educators argued that revenge actions grew out of the Nordic spirit of determination and defiance, and that they were direly needed in Germany at the present time, in order to assure law and order.[32] Others would relate it to the spirit of "masculine toughness" that was needed to save the German nation.[33] In that sense, they reasoned, revenge was not only a virtue but a necessity, a challenge for German men, and an inevitable fate. In a reading textbook for eighth graders, Martini called revenge "a higher life experience, an action unparalleled, in which man can find happiness and pride . . . It is a most noble and honorable attitude—an attitude that at the same time is characteristic of the Nordic Germanic race."[34] In discussing the saga heroes' motivation for action, Martini used the present tense throughout, thus leaving it unclear if he referred to the past or to the present.

We may wonder why the Nazis were so insistent on sanctioning the spirit of revenge within the context of their saga discussions and the German folk education program. Such an emphasis might be understandable perhaps in times of war when all thoughts are geared toward armament and the draft, but significantly, many of the discussion guides pertaining to the sagas were issued during the early thirties. Thus, we must look for some ideological reasons in this connection, some of which were related to pre-Nazi Volkish-political thought pertaining to Germany's fight for nationhood and the reassertion of her "well deserved" safe position in Europe. After 1933, the Nazis frequently still referred in school textbooks and anthologies to the "treacherous" Peace Treaty of Versailles, in which Germany, like the legendary hero Siegfried, had received a murderous "stab-in-the-back." They presented the case in such a way that it appeared as if the Hitler Regime had come to power only because it fulfilled the long awaited prophecy of setting right all wrongs, inside of Germany as well as in the former German culture areas abroad. The revenge ethics of the sagas thus came in handy to explain to children why Germany should not forgive her former enemies but try to regain what formerly had belonged to her. They implied that revenge, like honor, loyalty, and spiritual "toughness," was an inherited trait that was as justified at the present time as it had been in the past.

Ultimately, the Nazis employed the sagas to justify their aggressive actions against the Eastern European nations, while they presented their own territorial expansions into those areas as something like an historical custom that had been initiated by their Nordic Germanic "ancestors." Lohrmann, for example, referred to the saga of Ulf in order to demonstrate that the Nordic Germanic tribes had acquired new "living space" whenever they had felt an organic need to do so. Such an assertion of territorial "rights," he argued, was nothing but a response to a "natural law" that could be understood within the context of "organic justice."[35] Meyer defended the case of the Viking conquests along similar lines by warning his readers not to label them as "exploits" nor as "aggressive actions," because the territorial conquests of these heroes had been "noble manifestations of the Nordic spirit—a fulfillment of the principles of good followership . . . and a true assertion of the genuine nobility of the master race of Europe."[36] No footnote was needed to teach the young reader that Hitler's expansions eastward, too, were to be considered nothing less than noble manifestations of the Nordic spirit and "the genuine nobility of the master race of Europe."

Both Lohrmann's and Meyer's saga interpretations corresponded to the geopolitical views expressed at that time by Karl Haushofer.[37] Haushofer, too, had defended Germany's drive to the east as a "natural right" based on Germany's need for "living space." The same pattern of argument was echoed in many of the speeches by Rosenberg, Goebbels, Himmler, and Hitler, in all of which we rediscover the idea of justifying present actions in the name of so-called age-old traditions and inherited "rights." Walter Gross, Leader of the Racial-Political Office of the National Socialist Party, put it this way in 1935: "The Germanic nation is a mobile and elastic nation, and as a fish needs water, so Germanic man needs space."[38] Whereas in relation to adult audiences the Nazis would not hesitate to make frequent references also to Darwin and his concept of the survival of the species, they much preferred in the educational context that teachers would relate such views to the life and thought of the Germanic "ancestors." As history and folklore were sanctioned by tradition, the Nazis felt that their values had a chance of being received enthusiastically by children and youth if presented through the sagas rather than alone through the subjects of biology, racial science, and geopolitics.

By attaching to the saga interpretations the purposes of an identification with the present, an idealization of heroic virtues, and a justification of aggressive expansionist policies, the Nazis turned the Germanic folk literature into a useful instrument of Volkish propaganda. Their references to the traditional past added authority and weight to their statements, and, most significantly, they helped them to add the desired emotional appeal. Ironically, the Nazis cared very little about the fact that in this process they distorted the very heritage which supposedly they respected like a "sacred fountain" of German nationhood.

NOTES

1. Ernst Krieck, *Dichtung und Erziehung* (Leipzig, Armanen Verlag, 1933). Also: Ernst Krieck, "Reform der Lehrerbildung in Schule und Erziehung im Dritten Reich" *Nationalsozialistischer Lehrerbund* (National Socialist Teachers Association), eds., *Jahrbuch 1935* (Berlin, Verlag der N.S.D.A.P., 1935), 286-288. The very fact that the National Socialist Teachers Association printed Krieck's essay in its *Yearbook* implied that his theories were officially sanctioned by the Association.

2. Walther Heinrich Vogt, "Das altgermanische Schrifttum in unserer höheren Schule" *Deutsches Bildungswesen* 12 (December, 1933), 343-349.

3. Alfred Rosenberg, *Der Mythus des 20. Jahrhunderts* (Berlin, Verlag der N.S.D.A.P., 1935), p. 289. See also: Ferdinand Clauss, *Die nordische Seele: Eine Einführung in die Seelenrassenkunde* (Munich, J. F. Lehmanns Verlag, 1940), pp. 49-50.

4. Heinrich Lohrmann, *Die altnordische Bauernsage in der deutschen*

Erziehung (Series: *Volkhafte Schularbeit*) (Erfurt, Kurt Stenger Verlag, 1938), p. 135.

5. *Ibid.*

6. Hitler frequently used the expression "*Alles oder nichts!*" (All or nothing!) in relation to his concept of a "total war."

7. Lohrmann, pp. 173-181.

8. Gerhard Salomon, *Humanismuswende: Humanistische Bildung im nationalsozialistischen Staate* (Leipzig, Teubner, 1933), pp. 12-13. Salomon and others referred to the Nazi ethics as principles based on the so-called "Third Humanism" that was essentially pagan and unrelated to Classical Humanism or Christianity. See also Walter Baetke, *Vom Geist und Erbe Thules* (Göttingen, Van Hoechst and Ruprecht, 1944), p. 56.

9. Rudolf Limmer, "Geschichte, Sagen- und Märchenunterricht" *Deutsches Bildungswesen* (July, 1933), 105.

10. Ernst Dobers and Kurt Higelke, *Rassenpolitische Unterrichtspraxis: Der Rassengedanke in der Unterrichtsgestaltung der Volksschulfächer* (Leipzig, Klinkhardt, 1940), p. 19.

11. *Ibid.*

12. Harwood L. Childs, tr., *The Nazi Primer: Official Handbook for the Schooling of Hitler Youth* (New York, Harper and Brothers, 1938), pp. 1-10. See also: H. W. Koch, *The Hitler Youth: Origins and Development, 1922-1945* (London, McDonald and Jane's, 1975), pp. 116-117. According to Koch, about 7 million boys and girls took the "loyalty oath" as members of the Hitler Youth Organization (and the League of German Girls). See also: Baldur von Schirach, *Idee und Gestalt der Hitler-Jugend* (Leipzig, Klinkhardt, 1934).

13. Heinrich Himmler, "Heldische Forderungen" (Document). *Himmler vor den Führern der 12. SS Freiwilligen der Gebirgsdivision.* January 11, 1942. Institut für Zeitgeschichte, Munich, Document No. *MA 316-4842-62.* See pp. 9-10.

14. *Ibid.*, pp. 11-12.

15. Gustav F. Meyer, "Nationalpolitische Auswertung der Volkssagen" *Jugendschriften-Warte* 40, 2 (February, 1935), 13 and Gustav Meyer, "Erziehliche Wirkungen der Volkssage" *Jugendschriften-Warte* 38, 7 (July, 1933), 52-54.

16. *Ibid.*, 17. The citation refers to Krieck's work *Menschenformung*, p. 154.

17. Karl Dilg, *Die deutsche Bauernsage in der Schule* (Leipzig, Otto Harrassowitz, 1935), p. 106.

18. Most of Neckel's works were published in the pre-Nazi period, and they are generally regarded as works of solid scholarship. The peculiarly slanted passages may be ascribed to later editions. Among other works on Nordic hero tales strongly recommended by the censorship authorities were Leopold Weber's *Asgard*, Gustav Schalk's *Meisterbuch deutscher Götter- und Heldensagen*, and Severin Rüttgers' *Nordische Heldensagen*.

19. Gustav Neckel, *Die Welt der Götter* (Leipzig, Otto Harrassowitz, 1933), p. 101. Neckel wrote: "And when in our time the *Führer* of the German Reich pronounces at an official state burial ceremony the words: 'Dead Warrior! Enter Valhalla!,' then he reasserts an aspect of the ancient faith, as has been said, while pointing to the very essence of the Germanic world view." For a number of similar attempts to equate the heroic world view of the past with that of the present, see also: Hermann Lorch, *Germanische Heldendichtung* (Leipzig, Friedrich Brandstätter, 1934), particularly pp. iii and iv, and Peter Aley, *Jugendliteratur im Dritten Reich: Dokumente und Kommentare* (Hamburg, Verlag für Buchmarktforschung, 1969), pp. 107-120. Neckel's concept of loyalty in "metaphysical" terms relates to his work *Vom Germanentum*, (Leipzig, Otto Harrassowitz, 1944) (edited by Heydenreich and H. M. Neckel) pp. 85-91.

20. Hans Naumann, *Germanischer Schicksalsglaube* (Jena, Diederichs Verlag, 1934), p. 68.

21. Phil Donahue, "Interview with Albert Speer," PBS Television, November, 1977. A related observation was made by Reich Youth Leader Baldur von Schirach in his memoirs entitled *Ich glaubte an Hitler* (Hamburg, Mosaik Verlag, 1967), pp. 132-133.

22. An abundance of works were made available to children on German hero tales. (See the chapter on publication trends). Curriculum surveys of the Nazi period show that these works usually preceded the sagas within the context of classroom discussions, although the sequence of presentation was not fixed. See Meyer, "Nationalpolitische Auswertung der Volkssagen . . . " 13-17.

23. Dr. Franke, "Hagen und Siegfried" *Jugendschriften-Warte* 44, 5 (May, 1939) 81-91.

24. Erna Seemann-Segenitz, *Des deutschen Mädels Sagenbuch: Germanische Frauengestalten* (Berlin, Heinius und Co., Verlagsgesellschaft, 1934). In her introduction, the author addressed the German girl, to whom she dedicated the book: " . . . I hope you will like what this book will tell you about heroic women of long ago. What you will find high spirited and honorable in these pages, be sure to practice yourself at all times!"

25. Eugenie Erlewein, "Nordische Sagenwelt und Schule" *Deutsches Bildungswesen* (November, 1933), 327-328.

26. Ella Manz, "Gedanken zum Lesegut heranwachsender Mädchen" *Jugendschriften-Warte*, 47, 7/8 (July/Aug., 1942), 51-52.

27. Rosenberg, *Der Mythus*, pp. 49-50. See also: Joseph Prestel, "Der Wandel des Heldenbildes" *Jugendschriften-Warte* 40, 7 (July, 1935) 45-47, and Ludwig Wolff, *Rittertum und Germanentum im Mannestum und Heldenideal* (Marburg, Wegener, 1942), pp. 58-78.

28. Richard Benzing, *Grundlagen der körperlichen und geistigen Erziehung des Kleinkindes im nationalsozialistischen Kindergarten* (Berlin, Zentralverlag der N.S.D.A.P., Franz Eher Nachf., 1941), p. 9. Selected stories from the sagas

for younger children were also cited in Marianne Günzel and Harriet Schneider, *Buch und Erziehung; Jugendschrifttumskunde* (Leipzig, Klinkhardt, 1943), pp. 135-140, and in Walter Baetke, *Kinderleben und Kindererziehung im alten Norden; nach den Isländersagas* (Göttingen, Von Hoechst und Ruprecht, 1943).

29. *Ibid.*, p. 11.

30. *Ibid.*, p. 14.

31. Dobers and Higelke, p. 21.

32. Alois Bauer, "Isländische Altzeitgeschichten in der deutschen Schule" *Deutsches Bildungswesen* (December, 1933), 322.

33. Erlewein, p. 327.

34. Fritz Martini, "Der Geist der germanischen Heldendichtung" *Deutsches Lesebuch für höhere Lehranstalten* (Teubners deutsches Unterrichtswerk, 6. Teil für Klasse 6) (Berlin, Teubner, 1940), 119-120.

35. Lohrmann, pp. 173-181.

36. Herbert Meyer, *Rasse und Recht bei den Germanen und Indogermanen* (Weimar, 1942), pp. 64-68. See also Bernhardt Kummer, *Midgards Untergang. Germanischer Kult und Glaube in den letzten heidnischen Jahrhunderten* (Leipzig, Adolf Klein Verlag, 1937), p. 68.

37. Karl Haushofer, "Deutscher Osten" *Lesebuch zur deutschen Geistesgeschichte* (Berlin, Junker und Dünnhaupt, 1935), pp. 4-25.

38. Walter Gross, *Leiter des Rassenpolitischen Amtes der N.S.D.A.P.* (Director of the Racial-Political Office of the National Socialist Party), "Nordische Rasse und nordische Weltanschauung in den Kämpfen unserer Zeit" in Karl Zimmermann, *Die geistigen Grundlagen des Nationalsozialismus* (Leipzig, Adolf Klein Verlag, 1933), pp. 33-38. For a related discussion of the Nordic Germanic concept of "natural and organic law" justifying territorial conquests, consult Dr. jur. Roland Freisler, *Präsident des Volksgerichtshofes* (President of the Volkish Court of Justice), *Das Reichsdenken des jungen Europas* (Berlin, Verlag der N.S.D.A.P., 1943), p. 60.

7
Fiction:
From Myth to Mythmaking

The National Socialists expected that fiction for children and youth follow the same ideological path as folklore and nonfiction. "Only during the time of liberalism did people use to think that fiction had no purpose beyond itself,"[1] commented one critic in the *Jugendschriften-Warte* in 1934, while reminding teachers that now it was their primary task to keep in mind the political objectives of the State when selecting and discussing children's literature.

At the beginning of the Nazi Regime not enough of the newer fiction was as yet available to make the transition an easy one, and the Nazis realized that much of their initial success in introducing folk education through literature would depend on their careful selection of older works of literature as well as a suitable ideological interpretation. Among the older works, two genres in particular received much attention in this connection: the peasant novel and the historical novel.[2] Neither one of these had been specifically written for children or youth in pre-Nazi days, yet the Nazis recognized in them some valid "Volkish" themes that might lend themselves well to a re-interpretation in the light of National Socialist values.

From the peasant novels of pre-Nazi times they selected primarily those of Löns, Rosegger, Stifter, Storm, and von Droste-Hülshoff, partially because they reflected a love of home and country, and partially, because they contained symbols of "mythical strength" that showed the peasant as a peaceful man rooted "eternally" in the customs and traditions of his forefathers, be it in regard to his community life, his work behind the plow, or his "fighting attitude" when it came to the defense of his kin in times of war. Löns' *Mümmelmann*, for example, was a selection favored for younger children, in an attempt to convey to them the love of nature and the North German landscape, whereas they would use his *Wehrwolf* for older children in order to illustrate the concept of the Germanic spirit of defiance and defense.[3]

Among the older historical novels, the works of Friedrich Griese, Will Vesper, Hans Friedrich Blunck, and Hans Grimm received primary attention,[4] next to those of Felix Dahn and Gustav Freytag. Langenmeier wrote in 1935 about Griese's *Das letzte Gesicht* (*The Last Face*) that it portrayed in an exemplary way the mythos of the "eternally young primeval strength of the German peasantry."[5] Like no other author before him, Griese had known about the mystical correspondence between man and nature, and the very soul that spoke to Germans from their native landscape. As a member of the Reich Literature Chamber, Griese himself had become well aware of this "desirable" element in his novel that made it so acceptable to the Nazis. Thus, he wrote in the new preface to the reprint of his work in 1935: "At no other time was the landscape so much loved and conjured up as in our time. The only and single answer to this phenomenon is that we are ready to recognize in the landscape a significant share of the eternal, vital, and active forces that have shaped the present and that will shape the future of our entire nation."[6] This wording prefigured the Nazis' "blood-and-soil" theory, although originally Griese had not perceived it so explicitly.

It is interesting to observe that Vesper, Blunck, and Grimm were also members of the Reich Literature Chamber, and that each one of them consciously promoted his own novels by catering to the National Socialist ideology in new prefaces and introductions to reprints of their older works. Will Vesper's novel *Das harte Geschlecht* (*The Hardy Generation*) had its setting in Iceland around 1,000 A.D. Vesper himself explained its relevance to modern times when he addressed his young readers in the preface:

> The stories which I will tell you here did happen a thousand years ago. You may object to such a remote setting by thinking: "What do we care about such old tales?" But you should realize that we can justify before God that one thousand years are only as much as one day, and that in those times people weren't really so very different from us today. After all, it is our blood that pulsed through the hearts of those men.[7]

Moreover, it was not only the blood that Germans today shared with their "ancestors," he pointed out, but such concepts as honor, loyalty, and destiny. Above all, these men had been defiant, and they had known how to fight and how to accept defeat—just as the Germans of today. According to Vesper's own words, the characters of his novels were like "resurrected saga heroes" and at the same time, like "Germans of the present time."[8]

As President of the Reich Literature Chamber, Hans Friedrich Blunck was in a position to promote his own novels as much as he wished. In his case, however, they expressed so vividly the spirit and attitude of the Germanic "forefathers" that they might have been promoted by the censors even if he had not held this post. Moreover, they were among those works that were rather popular among younger readers—in fact, had been popular since pre-Nazi days. Blunck distinguished himself by two genres: literary fairy tales based on re-

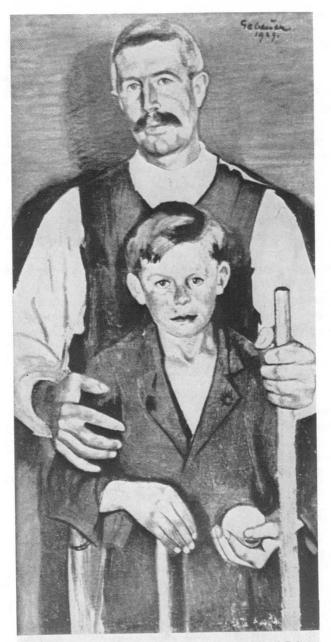

Vater und Sohn   Paul Gebauer

Plate 32
"Father and Son" as Earthbound Peasants:
The Peasant Novels Outnumbered All Others

gional folk legends and superstitions of North Germany, and historical novels rooted in the Nordic Germanic past. The censors usually recommended the "fairy tales" for younger readers, especially his *Märchen von der Niederelbe* (*Fairy Tales of the Lower Elbony River*), while they reserved his trilogies *Werdendes Volk* (*Developing People*) and *Urvätersaga* (*Forefathers' Saga*) for older children and youth. In *Werdendes Volk* the heroes were unmistakenly based on images of the "forefathers." Rotlusohn was a hero of the Saxon wars; Hoyer was a major of the closing Middle Ages; Berend Fock appeared as a sailor of the Germanic past. All three of them, and others, emerged as peasants and warriors of Nordic Germanic times, driven by a certain spirit of restlessness, creative energy, and a strong determination to find an answer in their search for God.[9] They were pagan characters in the strictest sense of the word, yet (just as the Nazis preferred them in their time), they were neither barbaric nor primitive in their attitudes but noble, spirited, and heroic. The same could be said about the characters of Blunck's *Urvätersaga*, in whom the Nazis perceived an ideal reflection of the "noble ancestors."

The works of Hans Grimm, too, had taken their inspiration from the saga literature, even in pre-Nazi times, and the Nazis now found them very suitable literature for children and youth. Paul Fechter commented on their characteristics in 1954: "Like in the Saga of Ref, the Clever One, in the Saga of Nornagest, or in the Saga of Grettir the Strong, there is in Grimm's novels the very style of the Icelandic peasant stories told in the thirteenth century. It was not so much the old Germanic peasant that fascinated Grimm, nor the warrior doomed to his final battle, but the Nordic Germanic man as a colonist who fought for his "living space."[10] The theme of the Germanic man's "fight for living space" made Grimm's novels especially valuable to the Nazis, as they hoped to promote through it the idea of the German fight for ethnic identity abroad, along with a justification for the German "need for living space." It is for this reason that Stutzki wrote in 1936 that students should be made aware of the relevance of Grimm's novels to modern political goals.[11]

Grimm's novel *Volk ohne Raum* (*People without Space*) became a plea for German living space, for the North German colonists in South-West Africa. Paul Fechter called the book the greatest political novel since Grimmelshausen's *Simplicius Simplicissimus*, and during the Chicago World Fair in the thirties, it was displayed among "the Seven German World Wonders."[12] The Nazis referred to Grimm as "the pathfinder of Nordic thought" and with great ease interpreted the major theme of the novel as the present German need for "living space" in Eastern Europe, while searching in it for a moral justification for their ruthless expansionist theories and practices.[13] As they portrayed the peasant not as a peaceful settler but as a fighting colonist determined to sacrifice his life for the preservation of his blood and soil, teachers found in the work much "useful material" for relevant classroom discussions touching upon the political situation of the Third Reich.

Plate 33
Blunck's Regional Tales of North Germany:
A Promotional Success like his Nordic *Trilogy*.

The theme of the preservation of Germandom abroad was also treated in a great number of newer works appealing to a younger age group than did the works of Grimm. In a review of about 200 children's books pertaining to this topic (both fiction and nonfiction), Karl Götz listed and discussed such titles as J.M. Velter's *Jürgen in Australien* (*Jürgen in Australia*), Götz' *Kolonistenkinder fahren nach Deutschland* (*Colonial Children Travel to Germany*), Quindt's *Peters Djungelferien* (*Peter's Vacation in the Jungle*), or *Im Eselwagen durch die U.S.A.* (*In a Donkey Cart Through the U.S.*). Regardless of whether the setting of such novels was Australia, South America, Africa, or the U.S., the major themes were usually related to the plight of Germans fighting for their ethnic identity and survival amidst foreign surroundings. Here and there, they involved a bit of adventure and excitement in the plot, yet primarily, they would try to emphasize the strength of Germandom abroad. In his introductory note to these children's book reviews, Götz stated:

Of the approximately 35 million people of German blood living beyond the German borders, about 34 million are citizens of foreign states. The new name which we have given them is *Volksdeutsche* (Folk Germans). About one million people are *Reichsdeutsche* (Reich Germans) . . . As a rule, today we consider all persons of German blood who live in foreign states as *Auslandsdeutsche* (Germans Abroad), regardless if they have become citizens of those states or if they have retained their German citizenship.[14]

Within this context, the Nazis claimed the entire 35 million Germans living abroad as their own, for according to the law of "blood-and-soil," they belonged to the German race, to German culture and history. In case of Eastern Europe, they also claimed the areas that in the past or in the present had been settled by persons of German origin. Taking on this ideological demand, children's books were meant to teach children that Germans had certain "inalienable" rights on the basis of their culture and origin. A particular genre developed in children's literature that dealt with the subject of Germandom abroad. It was its specific task to convince children of these "natural" rights, and to strengthen their bond of kindship with Germans living in other parts of the world. Götz, who was one of the more successful writers of these books felt it was the writer's task first to transmit to children through fiction a knowledge of German life abroad, and secondly, to do so "with the necessary warm *feeling* for their compatriots in foreign lands," so that in case should the need arise, they would be motivated enough to fight for their brothers beyond the German borders.[15]

The characteristic style of these novels is unlike the sagas and consists in the main of sentimental clichés. It is studded with expressions of joy and tears (reunion scenes) or delights and ecstasies (coming "home" to the German Reich). Not even Müller-Hennig's *Wolgakinder* (*The Volga Children*) was free of this disease. After a long journey from Russia, two children finally arrive in what they call "the holy land": "Imagine! every single child here is *German*, speaks, reads and writes *German*—but naturally, it's because *it is Germany!*"[16]

The political novel for children and youth emerged at the beginning of the thirties, but not in sufficient quantity to satisfy the Party's demands for this type of literature. Its major themes revolved around the leaders of the National Socialist movement, their victories and their sacrifices for the "cause." Among these were books celebrating the life and death of Herbert Norkus, Horst Wessel, and Schlageter. Alois Schenzinger's *Der Hitlerjunge Quex* (*The Hitler Youth Named Quex*) was by far the most popular work of this genre, and according to Nazi critics most satisfactorily lived up to the National Socialist standards of fiction for youth.[17] It had an active plot, a convincing central character, and above all, a theme that demonstrated the "need" for the Hitler Youth Organization and the National Socialist ideology in a credible way. The story was told in the first person narrative by Heini Völker, the son of a worker in Berlin. Heini's father appeared as a crude character with "underground" connections and a general lack of sensitivity, who tried to impress Heini with his Communist affiliations that supposedly defended the "welfare of the Proletariat." Heini, however, felt repelled by his father's bad habits (drinking) as much as by his "cause," and in his view, the Communists were no more than groups of

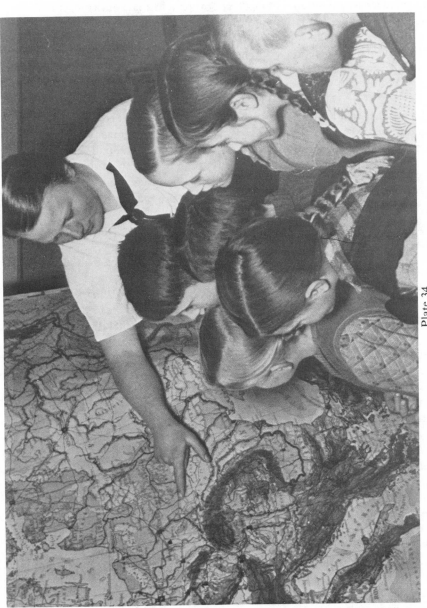

Plate 34

GREATER GERMANY:

"In these areas beyond our eastern borders live 35 million Germans of German blood. According to the law of 'blood-and-soil,' they belong to us."

"loafers" standing around at street corners and labelling people as "dictators" or "capitalists," while lacking order, discipline and a genuine faith in ideals. As Heini made the acquaintance of an older boy in the Hitler Youth movement, he developed a strong sympathy not only for him but also for the Hitler Youth Organization. Through him he gained respect for the Nazi ideology which seemed to satisfy the people's longing for community and meaning in life. "I want to feel my blood and that of others who have the same blood as I," an older Hitler Youth told him once. "We have to become a natural community again. . . "[18] Heini joined the Organization where he found a real purpose in life, a purpose that his home life had denied him. Later, he became a martyr of the movement. The *Jugendschriften-Warte* praised Schenzinger's work in 1934 as "an outstanding work of fiction" deserving the attention of all German children and youth. "This is an honest and a strong book. It portrays life true to reality, while it fascinates the reader. It is effective because it convinces you. . . The idea which Heini Völker embodies is not a dead concept but one that comes alive through the thoughts and actions of those who believe in it. The comradeship, the "New Order," loyalty to the *Führer* and readiness for sacrifice are described in a truly credible way. . . "[19]

Some books about the Hitler Youth, however, were treated in more critical terms. Mohr, for example gave a relatively negative evaluation of Viera's *Utz kämpft für Hitler* (*Utz Fights for Hitler*) and Joest's *Ulla, ein Hitlermädel* (*Ulla, a Girl of the Hitler Youth*). Viera's book he condemned on the basis that it was flavored by a spirit of scepticism rather than heroism, and that it simply did not and could not arouse young readers to enthusiasm for the National Socialist Party. To the second work, too, Mohr did not apply literary criteria but evaluated it by ideological standards. Ulla was portrayed in the manner of a character in one of those old fashioned girls' books, he wrote, as her attention throughout the work focused on bourgeois trivialities. Neither one of these works presented the "Nordic ideals" in a simple and straight forward manner.[20]

One of the genres that became available to German children in great quantity toward the end of the thirties concerned fiction dealing with war. Prior to World War II, myths and sagas of the Germanic North, along with the historical novels of Dahn, Freytag, Blunck, and Jünger had satisfied the Nazis' ideological demands pertaining to the didactic message that war should be recognized as a "principle of life." These works were still considered mandatory reading, but critics pointed out that more books were needed to portray a heroism of the Nordic Germanic type within a modern setting, books that actually convinced young readers of the reincarnation of the Nordic Germanic fighting spirit characterized by loyalty and determination. Prestel indicated that this type of heroism could be found in older works, provided teachers would see and discuss them in the right light:

In the broadest sense, the word "hero" implies a close kinship with the words "followership" and "defense." Regardless of whether it is the heroism of Arminius, Topler of Rothenburg, Henry of Plauen, Harm Wulf of the peasants' defense community (H. Löns), the Baker of Limberg (W. Schäfer), Pioneer Peters or Major Erckert in the Kalahari (H. Grimm), or of an army volunteer, Stewart of the Group Bosmüller (Beumelberg): at all times, the true heroism is demonstrated by a character who has strong will power and an unfaltering determination to dedicate his life to a greater cause. He is a great example of integrity and an ideal of Volkish virtues. . . . [21]

Pacifistic works like Remarque's *Im Westen nichts Neues (All's Quiet on the Western Front)* had made it to the incinerator and to Goebbels' "black lists" by 1933,[22] since they were deemed to be contrary to the "fighting spirit" of the National Socialist attitude. Still, there were a number of books on children's book shelves even after the purge, that, for the Nazis' taste, dwelt too much upon the absurdities of war, including the idea of senselessness of human suffering. The authorities insisted that such portrayals were to be avoided under all circumstances. New war books should vigorously emphasize the Nordic Germanic heroic virtues with reference to the present and future German folk community. In this connection, symbols should be effectively used to enhance the meaning of the National Socialist "reality."[23]

During the first years of the Third Reich teachers and youth leaders had a difficult time to find suitable literature of this kind in the bookstores. By 1939, the choice seemed to broaden, as a great number of inexpensive paperbacks became available that dealt with the topic of war. It was all too evident to educated persons, however, that most of these had been composed for financial gain and quick consumption. Although they were popular with young readers, these war books (for which educators coined the word *Kriegsschundschrifttum* or war kitsch) offended not only by their cheap looking appearance but also by their clichés of patriotism, their focus on the thrills of war adventures, and their shallow sense of humor.[24]

Taking into consideration the lack of better war books that were specifically written for children, as well as increasing Party pressures to treat this topic, teachers turned to works of a higher quality that could not be considered children's literature in any sense of the word. Thus, they gave much attention to the war novels by Beumelberg, Zöberlin, Timmermann, Wittek, and Jünger, even though they made up difficult reading materials. For older children they recommended most highly Jünger's *Unter Stahlgewittern* (*Under Thunder Storms of Steel*), on the basis that it had been inspired by a genuine respect for Nordic Germanic heroism characterized by such attitudes as strong determination, defiance of the enemy, acceptance of fate, and an unquestioning loyalty to the German folk community.[25] Undoubtedly, the Nazis' Volkish interpretation was needed to emphasize such values, for they were not necessarily evident in some of Jünger's works that had been composed in pre-Nazi days. Even in the work mentioned it could hardly be said that Jünger's heroes shared the Nazis' attitude

Die letzte Handgranate   Elk Eber

Plate 35
"The Last Hand Grenade"——
The Rise of Heroic Themes after 1939

toward the German folk community. Interpretations of this kind, however, were an integral part of the Nazis' folk education program that fulfilled the Party's demand for showing a continuous line from the Nordic Germanic past to the National Socialist present.

After the beginning of World War II, the National Socialist Teachers Association issued several series of paperbacks of their own to remedy, among other things, the lack of suitable war literature for children. Some of these were anthologies containing excerpts of war novels by the writers mentioned above, while others represented new writings. Yet, these new war books, of all genres, were characterized by the Nazis' ideological didacticism. In an effort to anticipate the Party's demands, the writers of these works all too consciously composed their stories in accordance with certain formulae. Consequently, their characters were lifeless, the dialogues represented clichés, and the plots remained unconvincing. In the manner of didactic Sunday School writers, the authors would sometimes end a book by addressing the reader directly, just to be sure that he had brought across the message clearly enough. Thus, Menningen, for example, would remind his readers in *Der Kanal brennt* (*The Canal is Burning*): "German Youth! You, too, will march across the grave, and across many other ones, so as to cut out a path for the freedom of our people, and a lasting peace of honor!"[26] In his work *Stützpunkt Z wird genommen!* (*Stronghold Z Will be Taken!*) Diekmann followed up his war story with the comment: "He was ready to sacrifice the very best that a soldier has to give: his own life;"[27] and then told his younger readers that they should not feel sorrow for the fate of this hero, as he had been loyal, brave, and dedicated to the fatherland. The consolation for death lay in the loyalty of a soldier to the nation, as it showed that he had given his life to the "New Order," thus demonstrating by his actions the ideal attitude of the "follower" to the nation.

Less preachy and very popular with young readers was Wittek's *Durchbruch anno achtzehn* (*Breakthrough in the Year 1918*). Critics praised Wittek's books above many others, as they managed to bring home the message of heroism through the action itself rather than through sermonizing. According to Prestel, Wittek had the skills of "a superior writer" by making his characters come alive in their fulfillment of heroic duty to the community.[28] Even so, given this "message," Wittek's work was not less didactic than the rest.

It was the same Erhard Wittek who, under the pseudonym of Fritz Steuben, became the most popular writer of fiction dealing with the American Indians (next to Karl May, of course).[29] In 1931 he published *Der Rote Sturm* (*The Red Storm*), which was followed by *Schneller Fuss und Pfeilmädchen* (*Fast Foot and Arrow Girl*) as well as several volumes of books concerned with the great Chief Tecumseh. For *Tecumseh* he received the German youth book prize for fiction in 1938/39, the *Hans-Schemm Preis*,[30] awarded by the Dietrich Eckart Library under the auspices of the National Socialist Teachers Association. It may come as a surprise that at a time when racial prejudice dominated much of the selection process for books in general, the Association should have given its recognition to a work dealing with the "Redskins," as the Indians were popularly called in Germany.[31] The answer lies not only in the preceding success of Karl May who through his *Winnetou* books (extending over one hundred volumes) had sparked German enthusiasm for books about American Indians in general, but in fact that Wittek portrayed his Indians as if they were Nordic Germanic warriors. The very language in which he depicted Tecumseh's concern with tribal honor and tribal unity seemed to reflect the language of the sagas. Even though his plots were nonpolitical in nature, reflecting a setting related to the Indian wars around 1800, the "fighting attitude" of the American Indians in his novel corresponded to the Nazis' expectations of heroism in children's books. Wittek-Steuben wrote in a letter to Rothemund, then Director of the Reich Division of Youth Literature in Bayreuth, the main censorship office of the National Socialist Teachers Association:

> What motivated me to concern myself with this theme was the desperate struggle of a noble people for their home and soil; their heroic resistance in face of the incessant flood of the white man, and the hopelessness of their struggle. In Tecumseh I have characterized a man who had to experience defeat in spite of his defiance, and in spite of what we may call his genius.[32]

As the author was as well versed in Norse mythology and the Nordic sagas as in the Nazi ideology, and in addition, was a skillful writer, he did not face the problems as did many of his colleagues who regressed into an old-fashioned type of didacticism. In Tecumseh he created the mythical image of Odin himself—well confined, of course, to the heroic warrior interpretation of the Nazis. He emerged here as the greatest of all warriors who, with a foreknowledge of doomsday and final defeat, would fight with determination to the very end, thus accepting his fate heroically. Tecumseh, like Odin and the saga heroes, never retreated from the battle field, but he knew how to deal with destiny.

Many of the newer writers tried to adjust to the Party's demand for books portraying Nordic Germanic heroism, by simply placing the setting of their fiction several centuries back, or even in prehistoric times. Thus, some wrote adventure stories based on historical events or such personalities as Arminius and Widukind. These stories did not live up to the standards set by Freytag, Dahn, or Blunck, but at least they fulfilled enough criteria to get into print and to be sold. Above all, they helped to save the integrity of those who composed them, for it wasn't to every writer's taste to glorify the exploits of war. Sonnleitner's *Höhlenkinder* (*The Cave Children*) was one such work. It seems ironic that it should have passed the censorship tests,[33] as cavemen are indeed a bit remote as a theme for literature expected to deal with "Socialist Realism." The very fact that it focused on Nordic Germanic cavemen, however, made it acceptable, even though the author created another "Robinson Crusoe" book rather than one paying homage to the heroic virtues of the "forefathers."

Two works by Annemarie von Auerswald focused on the Germanic woman, namely *Sonnwill* (*Will-of-the-Sun*) and *Radkreuz* (*The Wheel Cross*), both of which bore the subtitle: *Eine Erzählung aus der Germanenzeit* (*A Tale of Germanic Times*). The titles betrayed not only a Nordic Germanic but also a National Socialist interpretation, for both the sun and the wheel cross, as runic symbols, appeared in various adaptations in Nazi symbols, including the swastika.[34] Of interest for our analysis is that these works attempted to portray the virtues of Germanic women in association with the new role of women in the National Socialist Regime. When a reviewer noted in 1936 that *Sonnwill* portrayed better than any other book "the character and fate of Germanic women," he left no doubt that he had in mind her biological-racial strength and her gift to give life and health to children. His citation from the author's work shows that she shared his view:

> With the newborn child in his arms, the peasant now stepped forward to the bed of his peasant wife. She brushed her heavy blond hair from her forehead and looked at him with a smile. Then she raised her arms to accept what was her own, and he gave her the child. A holy event had embraced them all: a new link had been added to the long, eternal chain of generations!"[35]

It is apparent that the reviewer cared more about the "chain of generations" concept in regard to the Nazis' positive population policy than he did for literary quality, for he added without further comments about the work's intrinsic merits: "This book is a definite gain for every folk library and school library!"[36]

The censorship authorities did not automatically take out of circulation all books that did not promote an aspect of the Nazi ideology, whether in regard to the present Regime or the Nordic Germanic heritage or both, but would often just give them bad reviews. It appears, however, that the reviewers were more strict with boys' books than with girls' books. Since boys were considered the ones who would have to "carry the flag" of the Third Reich in the future, the Nazis were much more demanding with regard to ideological education. A case in point was the popular adventure story, either in form of detective fiction, mystery novel, or crime novel. In 1940, there were still enough of these books around to cause an outcry by educators and censorship authorities. The first group was upset about the large quantity of *Schundliteratur* (kitsch) that supposedly corrupted young people, whereas the latter was more concerned with the "waste of time" that the reading of these novels represented, as they taught nothing that was "useful" to the folk community. Obenauer wrote accordingly: "If a man or a boy sails a ship across the ocean, for the sole purpose of writing a book about his experiences, he doesn't prove that he is courageous or productive. This type of "heroism" is *unrelated to community interests.*"[37] According to these criteria, *Robinson Crusoe* might also not have made it onto the Nazis' approved reading list, for Robinson was a "loner" for more than twenty years, with only the limited company of Friday and the goat. Ironically, however, this became a strongly recommended book throughout the Nazi period—partially because it was deemed to be of *practical* help for the growing Hitler Youth. On the whole, however, the censorship authorities remained consistent in giving negative reviews to works that did not serve the ideology.

The old fashioned girls' book, which remained one of the most popular and absolutely "un-Volkish" and "unpolitical" genres, represents an example of where the authorities would seem to have been rather lenient. Considering the smug bourgeois milieu of these works and their preconcern with the social norms of the upper middle class, we may wonder why the Nazis did not condemn them as "outdated," particularly as they frequently portrayed the female characters as the spoiled and dependent daughters of distinguished lawyers, doctors, professors, or high government officials, roles that had no bearing upon the eductional ideals of the Nazi Regime. The girls shown in these novels were usually raised in luxurious homes away from the "low village community," and the spacious park gardens surrounding the private villas of their parents were usually walled off from "common intruders," with dogs guarding their privacy. The families generally employed a large staff of servants, sent their girls to expensive boarding schools, and the girls themselves never worked nor "served" anyone except their own god of leisure. Still, the censors did not officially prohibit such books.

On the other hand, educators very much deplored their incredible plots and sentimental clichés. Rothemund commented that it was a pity that there were no better books available to girls, although he was confident that the day would come when writers would produce novels for them with characters that were decent, clean, and true to life. In the meanwhile, an attitude of tolerance might be in order, as far as these books were concerned, for even though they were trite, sentimental, and highly predictable, they satisfied the emotional needs of girls.[38] Nevertheless, such an attitude of tolerance, expressed by the highest authority (Rothemund was Director of the Youth Literature Office in Bayreuth), showed a definite decline in standards since Wolgast's times. Around the turn of the century, educators had proceeded much more radically against sentimental and pretentious books than was the case during the Nazi Regime.

The most popular girls' books of the nineteenth century writers were those written by Emmy von Rhoden, Ottilie Wildermuth, Johanna Spyri, and Agnes Sapper. Among the early twentieth century girls' book writers they preferred Else Ury, Emma Gundel, Magda Trott, Margaret Haller and Enid Blyton. Essentially, Rhoden's *Trotzkopf* (*Obstinate Child*) did not differ much from Ury's *Nesthäkchen* (*Little Nest Hook*) or Trott's *Goldköpfchen* (*Little Golden Head*). Each of these works was issued in a series of as many as twelve books, and in every case the little girl was introduced with the first volume as a charming three to five year old who still used "baby talk." As the series progressed, the little girl grew up to be a bigger girl, a school girl, a teenager, a young lady, a young lady with a fiancé, a bride, a mother, and finally a grandmother.[39] In some respects these works continued the tradition of the eighteenth century educational novel, the *Bildungsroman*, as it is called in Germany, although the very concept of "education" was translated here into social patterns of expectations that aimed at social "adjustment" rather than at personality development.[40] It was easy to predict from the start that misbehavior would be corrected, that quarrels and hatred would turn into tolerance and love, and that the little "tomboy" who sometimes overstepped the boundaries by teasing her friends or playing tricks on her teachers, at the end of the fifth or sixth volume would turn into a charming young lady endowed with all the social graces under the sun.

Other, more modern girls' books were slow in coming, but at last they did arrive. Their covers were bright and cheerful, showing girls in uniform, girls on the farm, girls in the household, girls engaged in sports activities like rowing, swimming, and running. On the surface, these books appeared to be relevant to the present life of the Nazi Regime while capturing the modern image of the girl in action. There was no time for embroideries, garden parties, and gondola rides, they seemed to say, for now there was the call for duty. Such titles as *Pack zu, Gisela!* (*Pitch In, Gisela!*), Blitzmädel Ulla (*Ulla, the Air Force Auxiliary*), *Kamerad Schwester* (*Nurse, Our Comrade*), and *Juttas Pflichtjahr* (*Jutta's Year of Duty*) suggested active involvement, liberation, and exciting experiences away from home. In their imagination girls left their sheltered homes and private lives to join the ranks of those who had tasted the freedom of action. The illustrations, too, gave every indication that life under the new Regime meant duty, but also fun. These books seemed to be more thrilling than mystery novels, for they promised to reveal what girls actually experienced as war nurses, communications aides, or helpers on the farms, in the factories, or behind the front lines.

Soon, however, many girls began to lose their initial interest in this genre, for they discovered on their own that mainly the setting was different from the other works of fiction they knew, but that thematically there was not much of a change. The librarian Ella Manz complained early in the forties, that with their many clichés and sentimental scenes the new girls' books all too strongly resembled their old-fashioned counterparts from around the turn of the century.[41] Unfortunately, the girls were still shown in the typical "wait-and-see" attitude, passive rather than active. Why did so many of the books end on the note that a charming young officer or a broad shouldered lieutenant embraced the young lady to carry her off to the altar?[42]

The most characteristic feature of the new girls' books was that they retained their attitudes toward the traditional virtues of motherhood, social adjustment, and family involvement. Even if the new authors introduced their female characters to roles outside of the home, they did so primarily by placing them in auxiliary positions. Girls "helped," "volunteered," "assisted," and "pitched in," but they did not study to enter a profession, or to supervise, manage or control their jobs independently. From that point of view, it did not matter if they were shown in the domestic environment or behind the front lines, for their attitude was marked by the spirit of dependency. In addition, these books emphasized the great need for girls to set examples in their service to the folk community. This made them especially didactic, for even if they dealt with leaders of the *B.D.M. (Bund Deutscher Mädchen,* or League of German Girls), they were portrayed as persons characterized by loyalty and dedication to the "cause," sometimes in aggressive roles or as fanatics, but never as sceptical or independent individuals. In any given role the first duty of girls remained "service and sacrifice."

The portrayal of girls and women as characters in fiction for young people reflected the Nazis' attitude toward women in general. First, women were meant to carry out biological functions and domestic duties, in order to strengthen the growth and wellbeing of the family which Hitler considered the "core cell" of the German folk community. Beyond this duty, they were expected to help in various community organizations to aid the *Reich* and the *Führer.* Women were not encouraged to pursue a higher education, they were not allowed to join the Party, and they were strongly discouraged from "competing" with men in the job market.[43] The heroism of the woman, as the Nazis perceived it, lay in her physical stamina needed to breed and raise children and in her quiet strength in regard to solving daily problems and smoothing human relations. This is why they considered her the "guardian of life" for the generations to come.

Many works of fiction for children and youth that were written during the Nazi period were simply too tendentious to outlast the Third Reich. The modern setting alone was not enough to give them a lasting appeal, as often they lacked convincing characters and "preached" all too obviously the new didacticism of the National Socialist ideology. The patterned plots and stereotyped characters both in the novels for boys and the novels for girls fulfilled their ideological functions, yet they lacked some unique human qualitives that might have given children a more permanent basis for an identification with their feelings and actions. Thus, it was partially due to the failure of the newer children's literature authors that at least during the thirties the older publications, including folklore, the peasant novel, and the historical novel did prevail in the publishing trends.

On the other hand, there are many indications that along with German and Nordic Germanic folklore the peasant and historical novels were bound to stay on the recommended book lists for children and youth, because the Nazis perceived in them an ideal expression of their ideological values. In 1942, Wilhelm

Westecker, a renowned literary critic of the Nazi period, commented that they were far more than passing "fads" in German cultural life. The peasant novel and the historical novel forcefully counterbalanced the "decadent" literature concerned with urban life, while they helped to stabilize the growth and development of the German nation. "Under no circumstances should the peasant theme vanish from our sphere of interest," he wrote, "nor from the creative concern of our writers!"[44] In children's literature the same concern was voiced throughout the Nazi period.

The peasant novel and historical novel survived the year 1945 when "Doomsday" finally arrived to end the totalitarian regime of the Third Reich and with it the Nazis' censorship system. In various new editions, and with changed prefaces and introductions, they made their reappearance in the postwar years and many of them are still in print today.[45] Along with them have survived a number of works simulating a prehistorical setting, such as *Höhlenkinder* (*Cave Children*), mainly because they appeal to children's sense of adventure within a Germanic "Robinson Crusoe" type of setting, while they avoid a portrayal of racial stereotypes. Very much alive today are also the old-fashioned girls' books from earlier days. They take up only a relatively small portion in comparison with the modern girls' books, but obviously they still hold their sentimental appeal for by-gone days.[46]

Gone, however, is political fiction for youth, along with all political fiction aimed at an overt racial and ideological instruction. *Der Hitlerjunge Quex Quex* and *Blitzmädel Ulla* were prohibited after the end of World War II within the framework of the Denazification policy,[47] and thus it is difficult to estimate if these two works would still find a limited popular audience today. Along with the rest of the bloodless and didactic novels for children and youth they were shipped to archives in the United States and experienced the same fate as other captured war materials. Only here and there a copy of them escaped the "clean-up" procedure after World War II as a quaint reminder of a twentieth century "didactic age." It is questionable if their threadbare plots and their political ideology would still capture a young reading audience in our time. After Nazism itself became irrelevant, the "message," too, was lost, and there was little else that might still appeal to children on a personal basis in human terms.

NOTES

1. Hans Mohr, "Zur Frage der politischen Jugendschrift" *Jugendschriften-Warte* 39/6 (June, 1934) 41-44. See also Wilhelm Fronemann, "Zur heutigen Lage der Jugendlesekunde" *Jugendschriften-Warte* 44/2 (February, 1939) 24.

2. Horst Geissler, *Dekadenz und Heroismus. Zeitroman und völkisch na-tionalsozialistische Literaturkritik* (Stuttgart, Deutsche Verlagsanstalt, 1964), pp. 11-13, and H. Boeschenstein, *The German Novel 1939-1945* (Toronto, Toronto University Press, 1949), p. 15. According to both authors, peasant novels during the Nazi period outnumbered all others.

3. Georg Clasen, "Hermann Löns in der Volksschule" *Jugendschriften-Warte* 39/10 (October, 1934) 1-6. For a discussion of Löns' novels in regard to ideology, consult Georg L. Mosse, *The Crisis of German Ideology* (New York, Grosset and Dunlap, 1964), pp. 67-88.

4. *Reichsstelle zur Förderung des deutschen Schrifttums* (Reich Office for the Promotion of German Literature), ed., *Die hundert ersten Bücher für na-tionalsozialistische Büchereien* (München, Zentralverlag der N.S.D.A.P., Franz Eher, Nachf., 1934). Among others, the list includes the works of Löns, Miegel, Blunck, Vesper, Griese, and Hans Grimm. See also Rust's school library recommendations (See chapter on school libraries). It should be noted that Blunck, Grimm, Griese, and Vesper were among the newly appointed members of the Reich Literature Chamber in 1933. Joseph Wulf, *Literatur und Dichtung im Dritten Reich: Eine Dokumentation* (Gütersloh, Sigbert Mohn Verlag, 1963), pp. 234-235.

5. See Theodor Langenmaier, *Deutsches Schrifttum unserer Zeit* (Bamberg, Büchners Verlag, 1940), p. 78.

6. Norbert Langer, *Die deutsche Dichtung seit dem Weltkrieg, von Paul Ernst bis Hans Baumann* (Leipzig, Adam Kraft Verlag, 1941), p. 97.

7. Will Vesper, *Das harte Geschlecht.* Cited in Franz Schonauer, *Deutsche Literatur im Dritten Reich* (Freiburg, B. Walter Verlag, 1961), pp. 78-79.

8. *Ibid.*

9. Langenmaier, p. 78.

10. Paul Fechter, *Geschichte der deutschen Literatur* (Gütersloh, Bertelsmann, 1954), p. 598. See also Wolfgang Stammler, "Das dichterische Schaffen in Norddeutschland" in H.F. Blunck, ed., *Die nordische Welt* (Berlin, Propyläen Verlag, 1937), pp. 548-564.

11. Erich Stutzki, "Hans Grimms 'Die Olewagen Saga' im Deutschunterricht" *Zeitschrift für deutsche Bildung* 12, 9 (September, 1936) 445.

12. Wulf, pp. 294-295.

13. Peter Zimmermann, "Kampf um den Lebensraum. Ein Mythos der Kolonial-und der Blut- und Boden-Literatur" In Horst Denkler and Karl Prümm, eds., *Die deutsche Literatur im Dritten Reich: Themen. Traditionen Wirkungen* (Stuttgart, Reclam, 1976), pp. 165-183.

14. Karl Götz, "Auslandsdeutsches Schicksal in der Jugendschrift" *Jugendschriften-Warte* 41, 6 (June, 1936), 43-46. The programmatic character of this literature is particularly evident in the parallel bibliographical listing of children's fiction and non-fiction on this topic, as well as of numerous geopolitical, geographical, and historical background reading material for teachers.

15. The Nazi slogan "*Heim ins Reich!*" (Home to the Reich) frequently was used even in essay contests for children and was meant to present a forced annexation of territories (Austria, the Sudetenland, etc.) as a celebrated "homecoming event." In this context it refers to the "homecoming" of German children from German areas and settlements abroad.

16. Erika Müller-Hennig, *Wolgakinder; Die Geschichte einer Flucht* (Berlin, Steglitz, Junge Generation Verlag, 1940), p. 51.

17. Renate Jaroslawski and Rüdiger Steinlein, "Die politische Jugendschrift; Zu Theorie und Praxis faschistischer deutscher Jugendliteratur" in Denkler and Prümm, pp. 305-330.

18. *Ibid.*, pp. 312-314. Karl Aloys Schenzinger, *Der Hitlerjunge Quex* (Berlin, Propyläen Verlag, 1932), p. 62.

19. Mohr, 42.

20. *Ibid.*, 43.

21. Joseph Prestel, *Volkhafte Dichtung. Besinnungen und Durchblicke* (Series: *Völkisches Lehrgut. Schriftenreihe zur Neugestaltung des Volksschulunterrichts*), p. 19. See also Peter Aley, *Jugendliteratur im Dritten Reich; Dokumente und Kommentare* (Hamburg, Verlag für Buchmarktforschung, 1969), pp. 131-142.

22. M. Sturm, "Die Kriegsbücherei der deutschen Jugend" *Jugendschriften-Warte* 48, 11/12 (Nov./Dec., 1942) 91. The novel was banned not only because of its pacifistic attitude but also because of its "technical style" that did not enhance the Nazi ideology. See Ronald Gray, *The German Tradition in Literature: 1871-1945* (Cambridge, Harvard University Press, 1965), pp. 60-61.

23. Herbert Cysarz, "Zur Geistesgeschichte des Weltkrieges; Die dichterische Wandlung des Kriegsbildes" in Walther Linden, "Volkhafte Dichtung vom Weltkrieg und Nachkriegszeit" *Zeitschrift für Deutschkunde* 48, 1 (Ja., 1934), 1.

24. The Party's fight against "*Schmutz und Schund*" was directed primarily against trite entertainment literature, including pornographic material. See "Verschärfter Kampf gegen Schund und Schmutz," *Jugendschriften-Warte* 38, 5 (May, 1933), 38. The Nazis continued to enforce some laws on this behalf which had been initiated by the Art Education movement and were first put into effect in 1926.

25. Wilhelm Westecker, *Volksschicksal bestimmt den Wandel der Dichtung* (Berlin, Zentralverlag der N.S.D.A.P., Franz Eher, Nachf., 1942), p. 67. See also Karl Riha, "Massenliteratur im Dritten Reich," Denkler and Prümm, pp. 281-305 and Karl Prümm, "Die antidemokratischen Kriegsromane" Denkler and Prümm, pp. 144-154.

26. Walter Menningen, *Der Kanal brennt! (Series: Kriegsbücherei der deutschen Jugend*, Vol. 111) p. 32. Cited by Riha, p. 285.

27. Ernst Günter Diekmann, *Stützpunkt X wird genommen* (Kriegsbücherei der deutschen Jugend, Vol. 113), p. 32. Cited by Riha, p. 285.

28. Prestel, p. 19.

29. Irene Dyrenfurth-Graebsch, *Geschichte der deutschen Jugendbuchfor-schung* (Hamburg, Stubenrauch, 1951), pp. 206-207.

30. Jaroslawski, p. 320. See also Aley, pp. 174-175.

31. *Ibid.*, p. 322.

32. "Aus einem Briefe Witteks" *Jugendschriften-Warte* 45/1 (1940) 19. Steuben (a pseudonym for Wittek) felt that Indian books were much more than simple adventure stories. He maintained that Tecumseh eventually had to fail because his people were not united as a *Volk*.

33. Consult the chapter on school libraries.

34. Consult the book review section in *Bremer Nachrichten und Weser-Zeitung*, October 6, 1938.

35. Annemarie v. Auerswald, *Sonnwill. Eine Erzählung aus der Germanen-zeit* (Dresden, Meinhold u. Söhne, G.m.b.H., 1938).

36. *Bremer Nachrichten und Weser-Zeitung.*

37. Franz Friedrich Obenauer, "Über das Abenteuerbuch für die Jugend" *Jugendschriften-Warte* 45, 1/2 (Ja., Feb., 1940) 11-12.

38. Eduard Rothemund, "Das Jugendbuch in der deutschen Schule" in Bernhard Payr and Hans Georg Otto, eds., *Das deutsche Jugendbuch* (Munich, Volksverlag, 1939), pp. 38-39.

39. Malte Dahrendorf, "Das Mädchenbuch" in Gerhard Haas, ed., *Kinder-und Jugendliteratur. Zur Typologie und Funktion einer literarischen Gattung* (Stuttgart, Reclam, 1976), pp. 263-288.

40. *Ibid.*

41. Ella Manz, "Gedanken zum Lesegut heranwachsender Mädchen" *Jugendschriften-Warte* 47, 7/8 (July/Aug., 1942) 49. See also: Eva Kaulfers, "Was wird am liebsten gelesen?" *Jugendschriften-Warte* 48, 10 (October, 1943) 61-62.

42. This applies to complaints by the critics Graebsch, Manz, Kaulfers and others mentioned previously.

43. Andreas Flitner, "Wissenschaft und Volksbildung" in Andreas Flitner, ed., *Deutsches Geistesleben und Nationalsozialismus* (Tübingen, Rainer Wunderlich Verlag, 1965), p. 252. See also: Richard Grunberger *A Social History of Nazi Germany, 1933-1945* (New York, Holt, Rinehart and Winston, 1971).

44. Westecker, p. 91.

45. Kurt Tauber, *Beyond Eagle and Swastika. German Nationalism Since 1945* (Middleton, Connecticut, Wesleyan University Press, 1965), Vol. I, pp. 640-642.

46. Dahrendorf, pp. 287-288.

47. Tauber, Vol. I, pp. 40-47. Consult also his chapter on the Denazification policy.

8

The Role of the Classics

The Nazis approached the classics of children's literature from racial as well as "Volkish-political" perspectives, so as to determine their ultimate "usefulness" for German folk education. In their screening process they would reject all works whose authors were of Jewish origin, but also works that even belonged to the genres of the adventure story or fantasy, unless they lent themselves to their own brand of a "Volkish" interpretation. Further, they would reject works whose human and universal values did not fit the values of their totalitarian regime or were even considered as contrary to the National Socialist ideology.

First of all, they would give consideration to works that were of German origin or generally belonged to what they considered the German culture area, which included not only Austria and Switzerland but also the Netherlands, Denmark, Norway, Sweden, and Iceland.[1] With works from these countries alone they found they had enough to establish in children a feeling of identity with their "roots." Among the favored works were the folktales of the Brothers Grimm, the German legends and epics, the German chapbooks of the Middle Ages, as well as works representing "folk humor," such as *Till Eulenspiegel (The Merry Pranks of Tyll)*, Hoffmann's *Struwwelpeter (Slovenly Peter)*, Wilhelm Busch's *Max und Moritz. (Max and Moritz)*, and Storm's *Der Kleine Häwwelmann (The Little Häwwelmann)*. Austria would give them the *Nibelungenlied (Song of the Nibelungs)*, Switzerland would surrender to them Spyri's *Heidi*, and Denmark would have to let go of Andersen's *Fairy Tales*. All three they considered to be as much steeped in German and Germanic thought as were Rembrandt's paintings or Mozart's music.[2] On the same basis they also made room for Selma Lagerlöf's *Nils Holgersson* from Sweden.[3]

Outside of the "German culture area," however, the Nazis showed a very limited interest in children's classics. Lewis Carroll was, for their taste, too nonsensical to be taken seriously. The works of Dickens and Mark Twain they simply ignored. Neither of these authors were prohibited (as was the case with the works of G.B. Shaw and Rudyard Kipling, for example),[4] but most likely the Nazis found it difficult to translate the social criticisms of Dickens and

139

Plate 36
Theodor Storm's *Der kleine Häwwelmann* Remained on the German Classics List

Twain into the "positive world view" of National Socialist Realism. If we recall Dickens' *David Copperfield*, or Mark Twain's *Tom Sawyer* and *Huckleberry Finn*, we realize that it might have presented the Nazis with a problem indeed to detect in them some traces of "social virtues" that might have served German children as a model to live by. In principle, Reich Education Minister Bernhard Rust did not care to promote books by "foreign authors" or of foreign cultures, since he considered it his primary task to make German children familiar with their own roots in the past and their "tasks of tomorrow."[5]

Hardly a recommended book list issued in the Third Reich omitted Johanna Spyri's *Heidi*. The critics praised the work as *German* in spirit, on account of its natural simplicity and spontaneity, and its closeness to nature. In her unspoiled character, Heidi might present a model to German children, they said, as she was joyous, humble, and truthful, unselfish, and "life accepting" in her ways. Also, she had a strong "social consciousness" as she aided poor Clara and cared for her grouchy old grandfather. Modern youth indeed might take such an attitude as an example. Judging by all the positive comments that the critics made about Heidi as a protagonist, we begin to realize that the Nazis ignored various aspects of her character that make her less perfect but more human. Like nineteenth century critics of the didactic school they made her appear as if she had been a good child only—like a real sister of Little Goody Two-Shoes, a girl without a fault—which was not exactly the character as Spyri had portrayed her.

On the other hand, the Nazi critics objected to some aspects of Spyri's original work that did not correspond to the National Socialist ideology. This referred in particular to her references made to the Bible, to sermons and pious conversations. Under the pretext that such references were "out-dated" and would only "bore" a modern child, one critic recommended that the following changes be made if *Heidi* were to be judged an "acceptable" book:

1. Omit archaic phrases and expressions that are a part of the original edition.
2. Omit long religious songs and didactic sermons.
3. Transform the "pious atmosphere" of the work into a modern middle class setting.[6]

In other words, new editions of *Heidi* were expected to reveal not Christian thoughts but common sense; not religion but "contemplation"—or better still: more action; not forgiveness and repentance but simply a love between grandfather (ancestor) and his grandchild.

In reflecting about our own present-day abridgements of Spyri's *Heidi*, we may come to the conclusion that unknowingly we have used the Nazis' criteria in many of our modern editions. Certainly, there is little religion left in them, and common sense talk has replaced the pious conversations. The difference is, of course, that we have had the child reader in mind in making such abridgements, and not the dictates of a totalitarian regime.[7] Also, we have still retained the option of using one edition or another, whereas the Nazis were striving for uniformity and limited choice. In totalitarian countries like Nazi Germany all abridgements were subject to censorship, just like the original editions of the works in question and their reviews. In some cases, the Nazis even took the original works out of circulation while permitting only some particular abridgements to remain in print and on the bookshelves.

How consistently the Nazis applied the criteria of Volkish literature to all literature, we may observe especially well in three well known children's classics that had been long-time favorites with German children: Defoe's *Robinson Crusoe*, Swift's *Gulliver's Travels* and Beecher Stowe's *Uncle Tom's Cabin*. All three of these works were still available to German children during the Nazi period, although none of them was recommended in the original editions based on their first translations into the German language. In each case, the authorities pressed for abridgements and modifications along ideological lines, without taking into consideration the authors' original intentions or the child's point of view. Although in each case the arguments guiding the discussion were somewhat different, they all reflected the Nazis' primary concern to make children's books an instrument of German folk education.

In 1937, the *Jugendschriften-Warte* carried a debate on the suitability of *Robinson Crusoe* to modern educational principles. The literary merits of the work were not in the focus of attention, but the questions if and how a German child might improve his citizenship by reading the work. In two instances, the critics underlined the so-called "Nordic virtues" of Robinson Crusoe as exemplary and worthy of consideration. Whereas Arbeiter praised Robinson's Nordic spirit of "defiance,"[8] Holler applauded his Nordic attitude toward fate, his bravery, self-reliance, and his "Germanic resourcefulness" in managing to survive on the desert island. Such virtues as diligence, inventiveness, and bravery were the marks of a Nordic "outdoor type of man" who loved action, not the traits of a "bookish man." Children continued to respect Robinson for his actions, his general attitude toward work, said Holler, and eventually, they might transfer this respect to the German peasant and the German worker in the German society. It was the essential lesson of the book that "God helps those who help themselves."[9] Beyond this lesson, however, something else could be learned from Robinson as a character: his ideal attitude toward the community:

> We owe all of our material and spiritual accomplishments to the community, and only that person who has lived in isolation as long as Robinson will truly be able to estimate the spiritual and material values of human life. Whoever acts according to the principle: "*One for all and all for one!*" will be a socialist. Welfare can grow and develop only in cooperation with others. Therefore, we all will have to subordinate our desires to the welfare of the community![10]

Aside from the fact that it is certainly a most far-fetched example to refer to Robinson Crusoe (of all characters!) as a "community man," the interpretation cited above clearly reveals the didactic intent of the Nazis' approaches to literary criticism. Evidently, the ideological message was more important to Holler than the book itself. Just as didactic critics of the nineteenth century and earlier would take children's book reviews as an excuse to preach the gospel of virtue, so did the Nazi critics grasp every opportunity to preach the "gospel" of the folk community.

Nevertheless, Holler insisted that the following revisions be made of Defoe's work if the book were to be considered acceptable for German children at the time:

1. Robinson and Friday must not appear as equals, regardless of their relationship with each other. The concept of "humanity" as Defoe had emphasized it, unfortunately had given the impression, that a certain degree of equality indeed existed between these two characters—an impression that should be avoided under all circumstances.

2. The scene referring to the marriage of the Spaniards to some native women should be omitted, as it offended the German concept of racial purity.

3. Friday should not be shown as accompanying Robinson on his further travels but as staying behind in his native land.

4. Robinson should be presented as a contemporary *German hero*, for in that way German children would be better able to identify with him as a character. Campe's edition of *Robinson* should serve as a guideline in this connection.[11]

Holler's essay reflects his primary concern with the Nazis' racial biological values, according to which "humans" and "subhumans" were not allowed to "mingle." It is of particular interest to see how the new concept of "humanity" is applied here to literary criticism. Holler's suggestion to change the ending of the book in such a way as to leave Friday behind on the island,[12] essentially reaffirms the Nazis' belief in the basic "inequality" of the races.

We cannot ignore, of course, that long before the Nazis came to power there had been a number of "Robinsonnaides"—variants on the theme of Defoe's books—many of which had taken great liberties in the re-interpretation of the Robinson Crusoe theme. Among the better ones was Campe's *Robinson der Jüngere (Robinson the Younger)*, which appeared as early as 1779, sixty years after Defoe's book was first published. Campe stranded his Robinson on a desert island without the resources and tools that Defoe had granted him from the shipwreck, thus enabling him to re-establish civilization.[13] The ending of the work is different from Defoe's version, too, in that Robinson the Younger returned to his old father to live the life of a useful citizen, whereas Friday is shot by the followers of his own tribe. This version pleased Holler more from the National Socialist point of view, although he insisted that it should be "updated" to make Robinson into a more contemporary hero. In conclusion, he suggested that children might to a greater advantage read other books than the Robinson Crusoe books currently available to them, particularly those which reflected more keenly the spirit of their Nordic Germanic "ancestors." He recommended to them, among other works, Blunck's *Urvätersage (Forefathers' Saga)* and Sonnleitner's *Die Höhlenkinder (The Cave Children).*[14]

Some critics not only objected to certain portions of Defoe's *Robinson Crusoe*, as did Holler, but to the work as a whole. Beitlein, for example, felt that it did not express at all the spirit of the present, and that no editing job could hide the fact that it had been written several centuries ago. He especially disliked Defoe's "overemphasis on reason" and his "optimistic utilitarianism," along with his "humanism." None of these could be reconciled with the National Socialist ideology. Children were far better off if they read Blunck's works instead. *Robinson Crusoe* simply wasn't a "folk book" at all, since it lacked the legendary background of a *Dr. Faustus.*[15]

The debate in the *Jugendschriften-Warte* remained open-ended, although it ended on a critical note, as far as Defoe was concerned. The editors, however, still felt it worthwhile to list various modern adaptations of *Robinson Crusoe* available in the bookstores, among which Campe's edition was mentioned first.[16]

Gulliver's Travels, too, stirred up some different opinions. Swift was not outlawed in Germany at that time, and his works were still available to German children. Like in the case of *Robinson Crusoe*, abridged editions of *Gulliver's Travels* had been in circulation in pre-Nazi times, but now the question was opened as to whether the work as such should be given into the hands of children or not. In the first case, argued some fanatic critics, the book was a fantasy and therefore not very useful for German folk education. There was really little or nothing in it that would serve to prepare German children for life in the German folk community. One critic wrote that the book as a whole stood in direct contrast to the concept of German folk education, as it presented such a bleak view of society. In particular, he objected to the fourth part of the work, in which Gulliver returned to the paradise of the horses (the Houyhnhnms), while leaving no doubt in the reader's mind that he preferred the company of the horses to that of men. He felt that since Swift's attitude to society reflected nothing but bitterness and contempt, his writing would have an adverse effect upon children's attitudes toward society in general. Swift really belonged to the eighteenth century, he concluded. In the twentieth century, however, he had lost the target of his satire, for his social criticism had become "irrelevant." It could not be denied that the work had won its place in world literature, but it was unsuitable reading material for German children.[17]

Yet another book from the children's classics list became a subject of controversial opinions during the early thirties: Harriet Beecher Stowe's *Uncle Tom's Cabin.* In 1935, Schneider attacked some critics in the *Jugendschriften-Warte* who had advocated the view that the book should be recommended to children, on the basis that it was suspenseful and close to the "real life experience" within a significant historical and ethnic setting.[18] Schneider found such an evaluation of the work unexcusable. He wrote that Beecher Stowe had given a "false" portrayal of the Negro character. This meant, that Blacks should not have been shown so sympathetically. It was simply "wrong" if slaves emerged as more talented, more diligent, and more loyal than the members of the white race. How could Beecher Stowe have dared to portray the white man as wicked, mean, and heartless, while depicting Uncle Tom as an "honorable slave"? Such a character portrayal was a contradiction in terms, as it distorted the factual truth and only confused the young reader. Germany owed it to her great colonial pioneers that books would present the racial question *"realistically."* Further, he commented: "In a state which by means of a gigantic struggle is determined to upgrade its race within the context of the Volkish rebirth of the nation, books of this kind cannot be tolerated."[19] In the *Jugendschriften-Warte*, where this article was printed, Schneider obviously had the final word on this topic, as no reply appeared in the following issues. This situation reflected the dominant trend at the time. Even though *Uncle Tom's Cabin* did not appear on Goebbels' "black lists," it also was not recommended by Reich Education Minister Rust for the school libraries in 1937, nor at a later date.

Schneider's review provides another insight into Volkish literature, as the Nazis perceived it. His demand for "realism" and the "truth" not only denied historical truth but also earlier perceptions of a common humanity of man. For the sake of promoting the "Volkish rebirth," the Nazis would go so far as to remold history itself.

Another testing ground for Schneider's conformity to National Socialist Realism is his demand that the concept of loyalty in *Uncle Tom's Cabin* should not be presented as the equivalent of slavish subordination. Loyalty was a proud Germanic concept, he said, derived from the Nordic Germanic leadership-followership principle, and it was "unrealistic" to present it in a "false" way.[21] How realistic would it have been indeed, if Harriet Beecher Stowe had shown Uncle Tom as a hard, determined but loyal Nordic Germanic saga hero? It appears that Schneider would have preferred the book to be rewritten in reversed roles, attaching all the moral deformities to the Negroes, and creating a lily-white Uncle Tom equipped with all the "exemplary" virtues of the Nordic Germanic peasant-warrior.

Finally, let us consider the fate of Karl May's *Winnetou* and the other novels by May about the American Indians that had been on the children's classics list since the late nineties. *Winnetou* belonged to the type of book (like *Uncle Tom's Cabin*) that was extremely popular without being of more than average literary value.[22] Karl May was a native of Saxony, and like Beecher Stowe, had created in his protagonist a noble person whose fate was of deep concern to children as well as adult readers of all ages. In three volumes, *Winnetou* revolved around the great chief of the Apaches, showing him as a man of great dignity, fearless-

100 Jahre Karl May

1842 / 25. Februar / 1942

Es ist ganz klar, daß die erste hundertjährige Zeit-
epoche, die nun ihrem Abschluß entgegeneilt und er-
füllt ist von einem arbeitsreichen, fruchtbaren 70jäh-
rigen Leben Karl Mays, eine Unmenge von Stellung-
nahmen, authentischen Äußerungen, Zeitungsartikeln,
Broschüren und sonstigem Schrifttum, das mit ihm in
Zusammenhang steht, hervorgebracht hat. Diese hundert Jahre Karl May waren voller Unruhe, Ärger und
Trübsal für den schwer ringenden Schriftsteller selbst,
und der Rest brachte Verwirrung in sehr viele Köpfe
oder gar Abneigung gegen seine Person und Ver-
werfung seiner Werke. Das ist der bekannte Weg
eines für seine Ideale kämpfenden Mannes aus dem
Volk! Karl May hat ihn beschritten, aber erfolgreich
beendet. Zu seinem 100. Geburtstag wollen wir ihm
von Herzen gratulieren, denn die Wogen um ihn
haben sich geglättet, und er mag sanft ruhen im
Wigwam der Ewigkeit, getragen von der Liebe seines Volkes. Es ist mit Bestimmtheit zu erwarten, daß
sich im Februar 1942 die gesamte deutsche literarische
Welt ebenso vor dem Hundertjährigen verneigt wie
unsre Zukunft, unsre Jungen und Mädel, es tun werden. Auf siegreichem Vormarsch in ein freies Groß-
deutschland wird uns auch Karl May begleiten!

Erich Venn.

Aus dem ‚Betriebswart‘, Werkzeitschrift der Betriebs-
gemeinschaft Preußische Elektrizitäts-Aktiengesellschaft
und angeschlossener Unternehmungen. Nov./Dez.-
Heft 1941.

Karl-May-Verlag / Radebeul bei Dresden

Plate 37a
"100 Years of Karl May" (Advertisement of 1942)

Afrika, den 27. April 1941

Sie werden erstaunt sein, einen Kriegsberichtergruß aus der Wüste Lybiens zu erhalten. Aber ich darf Ihnen verraten, daß wir hier sehr fleißig Karl May lesen und uns genau wieder so daran ergötzen wie damals, als wir Jungen waren und uns nach fernen Lancer sehnten.

Jetzt sind wir Männer. Stuka-Männer sogar! Im fernen Lande sind wir nun, und zwischen Kämpfen und Schreiben bleibt sogar noch Zeit, ein flottes, leichtes Buch zu lesen.

Meine Pimpfe, deren Führer ich bis zu Ausbruch des Krieges war, hatten nun die prachtvolle Idee, mit der Reihe nach alle drei Ihrer heißgeliebten Winnetou-Bände zu schicken, und siehe da — sie werden von uns nahezu verschlungen ...

Im übrigen hoffe ich, mich als 'Old Shatterhand', der ja auch kämpfen und schreiben mußte, bestens zu bewähren. Es kann eigentlich für einen Jugendführer kein besseres Ziel geben, als das, auch einmal von der Jugend so gehört zu werden, wie dieser Karl May.

Kriegsberichter Horst Kanitz

Karl-May-Verlag / Radebeul bei Dresden

Plate 37b
Karl May's Stories about the American Indians:
In Support of the Heroic Spirit
(Advertisement of 1941)

ness, strength and gentle nobility, a man whom all admired. Essentially, the glorification of the "Red Man" was a European Romantic theme, but May wove it into the context of an action filled adventure story. In all, he published sixty-five volumes about the American Indians that sold more than two million copies in Germany alone. His success was almost instant, and in the early days of the Nazi period his books were widely read, especially by boys. In their envy, his friends nicknamed him for one of his characters: "Old Shatterhand."[23]

The Nazi authorities reacted somewhat ambiguously to Karl May's novels, and until 1937 it was not at all clear whether they supported or condemned them. The reason for this ambiguity was two-fold. In the early thirties not enough books were available that presented German children and youth with the ideals of the Germanic warrior as the Nazis would have liked to have seen them portrayed. Consequently, they thought that the books by Karl May presented a kind of substitute. Even though they dealt with the "Red Man," that is with a "non-Aryan" race, they represented certain attitudes toward war and community life that might be reinterpreted positively within the context of German folk education. Besides, and this was by far the more weighty reason, many of the Nazi authorities themselves had been (and still were) fans of Karl May and did not wish to part with their boyhood memories. This may appear to be an odd and incredible situation within the context of the Nazis' rationally calculated cultural politics, yet it explains the inconsistency with which the works were treated. It is well known that Reich Propaganda Minister Josef Goebbels and Reich Air Minister Hermann Göring were very fond of *Winnetou* and his "Red Brothers." In 1934, even Reich Culture Minister Hans Schemm still spoke about the "Karl May spirit" in positive terms, while alluding to the bravery, initiative, and endurance of his great heroes.[24] At that time the Karl May festivals were initiated in Saxony, under the sponsorship of the Party.[25]

The situation changed when Reich Education Minister Bernhard Rust officially took control over school libraries and curricular matters in 1937. Even though he did not "ban" the works of Karl May, he publically referred to "the Karl May nonsense" and urged teachers and librarians to channel children's interests into different yet related directions, be it toward Cooper's *Leatherstocking Tales* or Fritz Steuben's books about the American Indians, as both Cooper and Steuben had more to offer than Karl May in terms of presenting credible heroic characters.[26] Critical reviews of May's novels frequently would camouflage their ideological and didactic intentions by merely referring to them as "unrealistic," "outdated," or "unbelievable." Usadel, for example, employed all three of these euphemisms, and in addition, wrote that the Karl May books presented the danger of inciting young people to "run away from home." His main point, however, was that May gave children and youth a "false idea" about the nature of mankind,[27] which meant, in the Nazi terminology, that he did not project into his characters strongly enough some Nordic Germanic heroic ideals with which they might identify.

After the beginning of World War II, when more of the newer works of fiction and also more of the war books were available to young people, the Nazi ideologists strongly aimed at increasing their popularity as they embarked on a battle against the still more popular classics and older works which, in their view, had nothing to offer to modern youth. Thus, Gert Bennewitz wrote in 1940:

> Before the time when our great German past had begun to speak to us, Winnetou and Old Shatterhand were still the heroes of our youth, and the courage and bravery of a foreign people had to serve as a basis of our ideals. But what are all those Indian stage props, the peace pipes, and the feather adornments to us, in comparison with the replica of a Germanic sword or the jewelry, and the tools of our Germanic ancestors, such as we present them to our youth today? The courage of Siegfried, the loyalty of Hagen, and the love of Kriemhild mean more to us today than the most beautiful tales of other countries, for we can perceive in them the very voice of our own racial soul.[28]

If Bennewitz had had his way, most likely he would have outlawed not only Karl May's tales along with those of Cooper and Steuben, but also the still popular German children's game of "Redskins and Palefaces," while replacing the whole genre of American Indian adventure stories with sagas of the Norse and with German legends.

Essentially, the Nazis' approach to children's classics was based on ethnocentric and racial criteria that served the primary goal of fostering didactically among children the values of the National Socialist ideology. As such, the Nazis' attitude toward children's literature emerged as the very opposite of that which the German Children's Literature Association around 1900 had defended under the leadership of Heinrich Wolgast. Whereas Wolgast had considered children's literature as an integral part of world literature that should be free from a didactic bias, regardless if it was religious, educational, social, or political in nature, the Nazis aimed primarily at promoting a bias through children's books. In their limited perception of literature, they consciously ignored the very qualities that had won the classics world recognition in the first place, namely their timeless and universal human appeal that for so many years had touched the hearts of children. As they had no respect for the integrity of the classics and their original meaning, they also had no scruples to "adjust" them to the needs of the National Socialist state, either by slanted abridgements or reinterpretations, or by banishing some of them altogether from the children's bookshelves. Like all aspects of culture, the classics came to serve the Nazis only as a means to another end.

NOTES

1. See, for example: *Reischsjugendführung, Presse-und Propagandadienst* (Reich Youth Office; Press-and Propaganda Division), eds., *Jahrbuch der Hitlerjugend (1935-1941)* 6 vols. (Berlin, Verlag der N.S.D.A.P., 1935-1941). Practically every given volume referred to the concept of "Greater Germany" in these terms. Consult also: Fritz Brennecke, ed. *Vom Deutschen Volk und seinem Lebensraum; Handbuch der Hitlerjugend* (Munich, Eher Verlag, 1937), pp. 93-109, and Harwood Childs, ed., *The Nazi Primer: Official Handbook for the Schooling of Hitler Youth* (New York, Harper and Brothers, 1938), pp. 105-112. Here we read, among other things, that the German culture area extended even beyond the area where the German population lived outside the German Reich, whether in Eastern Europe or elsewhere, particularly in the lands of non-German peoples who had received their historical consciousness and their national character from Germans.

2. See chapter 1. We may remember here that Langbehn referred to Rem-

brandt as a "German." Children in Nazi Germany were brought up with the idea that Mozart and Salzburg were as much a part of Germany as was all of Austrian literature.

3. See chapter on school libraries. All of these works were recommended by Reich Education Minister Bernhard Rust for use in the public schools and libraries.

4. Dietrich Strothmann commented at some length about the fate of foreign books in German translation. See Dietrich Strothmann, *Nationalsozialistische Literaturpolitik. Ein Beitrag zur Publizistik im Dritten Reich* (Bonn, Bouvier, 1965), pp. 332 and 265.

5. Bernhard Rust, *Das nationalsozialistische Deutschland und die Wissenschaft (Heidelberger Reden von Reichsminister Rust und Professor Ernst Krieck)* (Hamburg, Hanseatische Verlagsanstalt, 1936), Minister Rust emphasized here that only if German youth were willing to tear themselves loose from foreign influences of every kind, might there be hope to realize the future "folk Reich" soon. He spoke here at length about the dangers of the *Überfremdung der Kultur* (foreign influences on culture), among which he also counted the concept of "humanity" (*Humanitätsidee*). Such influences and ideas that involved all of humanity were not only too vague and too abstract, he said, but contrary to the Nazis' desire to develop pride in the German national character. See in particular pp. 16-18.

6. Hildegard Stausch, "Kleine Beiträge: Die Werke der Johanna Spyri in neuer Bearbeitung" *Die Bücherei* (October, 1942), 30-35.

7. This is not meant as an excuse for poor abridgements of the classics in our time, of which we have an abundance. At its best, an abridgement aids the younger reader without destroying the integrity of the work as a whole, and without changing the characterization or the theme of the book.

8. Bruno Arbeiter, "Ein neuer Robinson" *Jugendschriften-Warte* 44, 9-10 (Sept./Oct., 1939), 134-135.

9. Ernst Holler, "Robinson: Ein Jugend-und Volksbuch" *Jugendschriften-Warte* 44, 9-10 (Sept./Oct., 1939), 136.

10. *Ibid.*, 138.

11. *Ibid.*, 137.

12. *Ibid.*, 139.

13. For a general discussion of the various *Robinson Crusoe* editions and adaptations consult Bettina Hürlimann, *Three Centuries of Children's Books in Europe* (Cleveland, World Publishing Company, 1939), pp. 103-105.

14. These works had their setting in ancient Nordic Germanic times and reflected in their own ways man's struggle for survival. Otherwise, they had little to do with the theme of Robinson's island existence.

15. Hermann Beitlein, "Ist Robinson wirklich ein Volksbuch? Zur Aussprache über das Robinsonproblem" *Jugendschriften-Warte* 44, 11-12 (Nov./Dec., 1939), 154-155.

16. Strothmann, pp. 300-353.

17. Hermann Beitlein, "Robinson und Gulliver und die deutsche Jugend" *Jugendschriften-Warte* 44, 9 (October, 1939), 129. Defoe's original work, along with Swift's, was still listed alongside a number of recommended adaptations of more recent times in Beitlein's article. This means that even though some critics were sceptical of the "usefulness" of the original editions of the work, they did not take them out of circulation. Beyond doubt, however, Campe's abridgement received a more favorable review than did Defoe's, and in the case of *Gulliver,* seven modern abridgements were listed, of which five focused on the first two parts in the work only. In and by itself this is not unusual in children's book editions; but in this case, the listing followed a rather critical view of the other two parts, and therefore may have encouraged educators to buy the abridged versions rather than the original translation.

18. This view was cited and attacked by Rudolf Schneider, "Kann *Onkel Toms Hütte* noch als deutsche Jugendschrift angesprochen werden?" *Jugendschriften-Warte* 45, 1-2 (Ja., Feb., 1940), 6. Schneider agreed that the work was still very popular with children at the present time, yet he questioned its "educational value."

19. *Ibid.,* 7.

20. *Ibid.,* 8.

21. *Ibid.,* 7-8.

22. Strothmann, p. 239. See also: J. Foerster, "Ein Trick des Karl May Verlags" *Jugendschriften-Warte* 38, 3 (March, 1933) 22.

23. Peter Aley, *Jugendliteratur im Dritten Reich: Dokumente und Kommentare* (Hamburg, Verlag für Buchmarktforschung, 1969), pp. 175-179.

24. *Ibid.* See also: Georg Usadel, "Nationalsozialistische Forderungen des Jugendschrifttums" *Jugendschriften-Warte* 41, 1 (January, 1936), 36.

25. See chapter on puppet plays etc.

26. Aley, 175-177.

27. Usadel, 37.

28. Gert Bennewitz, *Die geistige Wehrerziehung der deutschen Jugend* (Series: *Schriftenreihe für Politik und Auslandskunde*) (Berlin, Junker und Dünnhaupt, 1940), pp. 16-17.

9

Picture Books
between Continuity and Change

Two years after the Nazis' seizure of power, Hugo Wippler, an active member of the National Socialist Teachers Association, published a series of articles in the *Jugendschriften-Warte* on the role and significance of the picture book in German folk education. His views were taken seriously by the Association which then put him in charge of a national workshop on this topic and later reprinted excerpts from his writings in an official handbook on children's literature.[1]

In line with the ideological requirements of Volkish literature, Wippler first of all listed the "undesirable" qualities of picture books available to German children that no longer had a justification for existence. Among these, he singled out religious themes and sentiments, themes of tolerance toward other races, an over-emphasis on urban life, an interest in fantasy and the "miraculous" element, and a preconcern with deplorable, problematic or morbid situations. None of these elements were suitable for picture books, he said, whose first task it was to raise children in a healthy Volkish atmosphere. Further, he condemned picture books that characterized children as spoiled and over-protected creatures who had not learned to share their lives and goods in a community. He also rejected picture books portraying lonely, dreamy, moody or unstable children, as such portrayals were not conducive to raising the new generation. He claimed that all of these characteristics belonged to the age of liberalism—an age of permissiveness that had bred an unhealthy climate for raising families within the German folk community.

What the new age demanded, said Wippler, were ideals of self-discipline, cleanliness, orderliness, and courage. Picture books, perhaps more than other works of literature, could do much to develop these ideals in very young children. The following themes would be acceptable for the picture book in the Third Reich:

1. Folk rhymes and folktales.
2. Customs, traditions, festivals of Nordic Germanic origin; symbols of the Germanic past.

3. Modern German achievements: highways, bridges, transportation.
4. Home and country; the German landscape.
5. Protection of the German forest.
6. Protection of mother and child.[2]

Although none of these criteria mentioned race propaganda, they were all rooted in the general orientation of the National Socialist ideology. Emphasis was given to pride in national and ethnic origin (to the degree that it was rooted in the Nordic Germanic tradition), a love of home and country, and respect for the symbols of life and nature in general. Pride in technological achievements was viewed here side by side with pride in the folk heritage of the nation. Wippler still warned authors and illustrators to abstain from all artificial things that evoked the image of an "estranged city life," and they should always prefer a portrayal of farm life and farm animals to a superficial world of entertainment characterized by "silly talking beasts."[3] Picture books were seen to have a deep responsibility to help develop in children a "healthy" appreciation for nature and the German folk community, while creating such "timeless symbols" as windmills, peaceful harvest scenes, etc. He concluded: "Picture books shall *conserve* the timeless values of our folk ethics, they shall *guard* the traditional heritage of our forefathers, and they shall *fight* for the organic world view of the Führer."[4]

In a Party sponsored publication of 1935, Boehme called for a "blood-and-soil" orientation of picture books that would not only reflect the German peasantry and its "rootedness" in Nordic Germanic traditions, but also the "battle for German nationhood" as Hitler had demanded it. "To our savior, Adolf Hitler, we should be grateful for his initiative at having plucked the evil by its roots,"[5] he said, while pointing to the "decadent life style" of the cities, and the "disintegrating" influences of Bolshevism, liberalism, and internationalism. The only cure for Germany as a nation he saw in an educational emphasis on folklore and Volkish values, beginning at the kindergarten level.

The discussion of "Volkish" values also affected educators' concern with the style of the picture book. In 1933, the National Socialist Teachers Association passed a resolution to fight all *Kitsch* and commercialism in children's book illustrations, and to promote the value of traditional folk art.[6] During a conference on the picture book sponsored by the Reich Ministry of Propaganda at about the same time, the main speaker demanded that the picture book should unmistakenly reflect the "German style," which meant, he said, that it should deal with German characters, German folk and community life, and the German folk heritage. As such it should evolve into a true "folk book" for every member of the German family, and at the same time into "a true medium for our work in National Socialist education."[7]

The Nazis' frequent references to such terms as "folk art," "German style," and "folk book" seemed to suggest that the Volkish values of the past were identical with Volkish values of the present. What added to the confusion of such conglomerate terms was that some well established writers and critics of the former Children's Literature Association assured German educators that indeed, nothing had really changed. Thus, Rüttgers wrote in 1936 that the German picture book used to be and still was "a book of the people and by the people,"[8] just as if Nazism didn't exist.

Critical reviews of picture books, too, were characterized by such ambiguities.[9] Kressner, for example, pretended to fight commercialism, yet he showed a much greater concern about the "non-Nordic" portrayal of Santa Claus who in one case had been portrayed as a pipe smoking grandfather in a rocking chair—not at all like the Norse god Odin riding on horseback.[10] Illustrators might do well, he suggested, to return to native folklore and show it in the "new light."[11] The new folklore interpretation, of course, had as little to do with genuine folk art as had Santa Claus with Odin, which serves to show that Kressner cared less about folk traditions than ideology.

In yet another review, the issue was brought up again, this time in reference to a supposed lack of taste in the illustrations. The reviewer commented that in many picture book illustrations the "more serious Nordic Germanic spirit," as it had still emanated from the illustrations of such great German masters as Albrecht Dürer and Ludwig Richter, had been replaced by "cheap Hollywood clichés." This was especially evident in picture books on the Easter theme, he wrote, in which there were simply too many *Kitsch* illustrations that had nothing to do with genuine folk art. There were books showing Easter bunnies who tied ribbons into their tails, who brushed their mustaches like gentlemen, who travelled by boat, train, and motor cars, smoked cigars, and amused themselves like city folk in dancing halls. "The world of the Easter bunny has gone berserk," he complained, "and the masquerades become wilder and sillier with every book. . . "[12] While we can still sympathize with the reviewer in regard to the last mentioned point, his true concern really had little to do with art itself. This is very evident from his objection to the portrayal of bunnies that pushed baby carriages in the public parks, as such images made a "mockery" out of German women and mothers, and thereby offended the concept of "sacred German motherhood." The reviewer's Volkish didacticism became especially obvious in his derogatory comments about Koch-Gotha's classic picture book, *Die Häschenschule (The Bunny School)*,[13] for it completely ignored the work's artistic qualities, its warm sense of humor, and its subtle and childlike appeal to younger readers, simply because it showed rabbits in the habitat of human beings. Would a modern reviewer ever think of judging Beatrix Potter's *Peter Rabbit* on such a basis?

On the surface, the Nazis' selection criteria for picture books were conservative in nature. For young children they searched out the illustrated folktale and legend, as well as picture books on nursery rhymes, riddles, and German folk songs. Folklore was so much in evidence and in such an abundance that it looked indeed as if not much had changed since pre-Nazi days. Even the picture posters by nineteenth century illustrators were still in circulation. The conserva-

SOME CRITICAL VIEWS OF NEWER GERMAN
PICTURE BOOK ILLUSTRATIONS (1938)

Plates 38a (top) and 38b (bottom)
"The rabbits are too 'human': they dance, they skip rope, they swim . . . they push
baby carriages in the parks, and they even smoke cigars!"

Plate 39a
"Some illustrations are too cluttered and too abstract to appeal to the child."

Plate 39b
"German children should not be exposed to 'Hollywood parades' in their picture books."

Plate 39c
"Here the illustrator tries too hard to be 'cute' and childlike in his appeal!"

Plate 40
Koch-Gotha's *Bunny School*:
A Work Popular with Children, Yet Less Desirable from the Official Nazi Point of View

tive trend was also reflected in books pertaining to the German rural setting, including farm animals and the world of nature. Picture book fantasies, too, were among the books actively promoted, but only those that corresponded in their major themes to the folktale theme and still preserved what the Nazis called "the healthy view of life."

The expressed intent behind new folktale editions for younger children often pointed to the "link" between the generations and the continuation of the folk spirit from the past to the present. Paul Alverdes' words: "The human being cannot be understood without the ancestors who have lived before his time"[14] sounded as Romantic and unpolitical as those of Hobrecker in his introduction to the illustrated anthology of old German songs for children, *Lieder und Bilder für Kinder* (*Songs and Pictures for Children*), in which he reminded children that the old songs "from another time" were still as much alive at the present time as they had been a thousand years ago.[15] The nineteenth century engravings by Richter, von Schwindt, and other German masters evoked the spirit of days gone by, and do not at all appear to be relevant to the new demand for National Socialist "Realism," unless we grasp their Volkish-didactic meaning within the context of German folk education.

A number of older folktale books for younger children were brought out with new illustrations during the Nazi period; but many of them were also reprinted in the very same way in which they had been originally published, often without an additional preface or introductory comment pointing to the new Volkish policy of Hitler's Germany. Reprints without changes were made of Fritz Kredel's works, for example, and those of Else Wenz-Viëtor. Both illustrators had contributed much to the art of picture book illustrations since the first decade of the twentieth century, and their works were entirely nonpolitical in nature, if we take them literally. Why, then, would the Nazis care to reprint their works? Between 1933 and 1942 Wenz Viëtor added to her long list of publications 41 additional picture books, including illustrated editions of the fairy tales of Bechstein, Andersen, and the Brothers Grimm.[16]

The answer may lie in the nature of Wenz-Viëtor's illustrations that enhanced simultaneously the world of plants and animals and the world of the German folktale. The National Socialists used her illustrations in different ways without tampering in any way with her style. Thus, they adopted her fairy tale illustrations for youth hostel calendars, and even issued a miniature book of her illustrated *Däumeling* (*Tom Thumb*) that was given away in return for donations collected by the members of the League of German Girls on behalf of the *Winterhilfswerk* (Winter Air Program). Tom Thumb, for that matter, was not turned into a cocky Hitler Youth, but in Wenz-Viëtor illustrations he remained the same jolly folktale character as the Grimms had described him in their *Kinder-und Hausmärchen* more than one hundred years earlier. When in 1941 Thienemann published her illustrated book of Andersen's *Däumelinchen* (*Thumbelina*),[17] the work itself did not betray any National Socialist inclinations. The Nazis merely welcomed and promoted it because, in their view, Andersen's stories came very close to the Danish and Nordic Germanic folktale world and like the German folktale, his tales reflected what they considered an "organic view of nature."[18] Else Wenz-Viëtor remained one of the most favored illustrators of German picture books throughout the Nazi Regime, mainly because her work consistently reflected a poetic view of the natural environment, just as it had first appeared in her earlier work *Blumenhimmel* (*Flower Heaven*). In commemmoration of her sixtieth birthday, the editors of the

Judgendschriften-Warte paid a special tribute to her work and deeply expressed their appreciation for her Romantic contributions to the world of the German picture book—a view that still had "relevance" at the present time. The very wording of such a tribute appears odd if we consider the fact that it was published in 1942 when Germany was already at war with many other nations, yet it does show that the Romantic view of nature still held its place in German children's book illustrations at that time:

> She embodies the spirit of Romanticism which we Germans will never lose. With her warm sympathy for animals, be it in regard to the biggest bear or the tiniest insect, both of whom she has created with human sympathy, she keeps us in close touch with nature and a sense of poetry.[19]

Even if occasionally the illustrator had "humanized" some of her creatures by giving them facial expressions, she was still honored because she had retained their natural characteristics as a species apart from man.

On the other hand, Else Wenz-Viëtor also illustrated some books that obviously bore some more pronounced ideological messages than the folktales. A case in point are her rather static and "naturalistic" illustrations of an animated nature book by Marga Müller, entitled *Die vom Wegrain* (*Those by the Wayside*). The book served two purposes: to instruct children in the names and characteristics of simple weeds and flowers growing by the wayside, and secondly, to instruct them in certain ideological values that were of relevance to the present. It was animated only to the extent that the flowers talked with the bees, and the birds, and the butterflies, without, however, ever entering the world of true enchantment. From a modern point of view, this book indeed did make a "mockery" out of humanity by politicizing even the "world view" of the dandelion, and by forcing the National Socialist perspective even onto the wind itself. Yet, no reviewer at that time would have dared to denounce it on that basis, as its values corresponded to those of German folk education. Following is a conversation between Mrs. Dandelion, who is about to "wilt away" of old age, and the jolly wind, called Mr. Lustikus:

Mrs. Dandelion: Yes, and I am Mrs. Dandelion. The difference between us is that I did not idle away my time by the wayside like you. Instead, I have had to work hard all of my life.

Mr. Lustikus: Such a brave one you are! Indeed, it is true that you have had a difficult life. However, if you wish to achieve great things, you must fight against odds in life. You do deserve to live on!

And quite gently, Mr. Lustikus embraced Mrs. Dandelion and carried off her children, the seeds.

Plate 41
A Child's Botany and the Concept of National Survival:
"Thus Mrs. Dandelion did not live in vain, for her life will continue in the lives of her children . . . "

Mr. Lustikus: She has produced the pollen for the bees. She has given her leaves to the people for their salads; to those who knew her secret, she has given medicine as well. Thus, the old Mrs. Dandelion did not live in vain; her life will continue in the lives of her children.[20]

This dialogue can be understood on several levels. First of all, it gives evidence that the book belongs to nonfiction rather than to fantasy. It is true that nature is animated here, that the wind is like a father, that the dandelion is like a mother with her children, and that both of them talk. Yet, the purpose of the talk all too clearly betrays a lesson in botany and biology. The conversation is not tied to a plot in the conventional sense, but serves primarily the function of conveying to children more dramatically the idea that dandelions produce pollens which are good food for the bees; that their leaves make good salad for humans, and also medicine; and that they multiply by seeds which the wind carries in many directions. Beyond this information, it provides no stimulus to the imagination.

The wind, however, still gives children the "realistic" message that Mrs. Dandelion had a purpose in life beyond her own existence: to live on in the lives of her children. Today, we may be tempted to interpret such a message merely as a theme related to the cycle of nature. Within the context of the Nazi ideology, however, the dialogue implied and emphasized something more, namely that industry, productivity, and sacrifice were the "unselfish virtues" sanctioned by the National Socialist folk Reich of the *Führer*. As such, it echoed the Nazi slogan: "You are nothing, your *Volk* is everything!" which conveyed to young and old alike that the individual should be ready to sacrifice everything for the community of the German folk, since the folk was eternal, whereas the individual was only a replaceable cog. Thus, didactically, the book introduced children not only to various wild flowers and their characteristics; but also to the Social Darwinist message that, as Hitler once put it, "life is a cruel struggle and has no other object but the preservation of species. The individual can disappear, provided there are others to replace him."[21]

Fairy tales with a "purpose" were not as easily produced as illustrated folktale editions for children, as they had to be composed with the Nazi ideology in mind. Judging by the Nazis' requirements for the picture book, they were also not as urgently "needed" as the folktale picture book or the illustrated nonfiction picture book. Occasionally, however, the censors permitted the publication of a fantasy, provided it resembled the folktale, or at least bore a "realistic" message at the end of the story. The Nazis preferred "healthy" conclusions that clearly distinguished dream from reality while pointing to the virtues of life in the German folk community. In the picture book fantasy *Was Ursel Träumte* (*What Ursel Dreamt*), for example, the author and illustrator relate the adventures of little Ursel and her Teddybear on a flying rocking horse at midnight. On top of the clouds they watch the angels bowling and frolicking, until St. Peter discovers their hiding place and sends them straight down to earth again. He appears like a strict policeman taking care of "law and order." Upon waking up in bed at home, Ursel muses: "Oh my! Naturally, stuffed toys can't really talk! My rocking horse doesn't have wings after all, and none of us is really in heaven!"[22] The young reader is no longer kept in doubt about what is a dream and what is reality, and with St. Peter he is meant to conclude that dreams are "nothing but nonsense!"

In Rendel's *Märchenflug ins Bienenland (Fairy Tale Flight into the Land of the Bees)* there was even a fantasy with a touch of social realism. In this case, an elf accompanies Hans and Trude to the land of some giant bees, only to give them a long lecture on the virtues of the bee society. Hans would have liked to stay a little longer, but the elf reminds them that, after all, "The Earth is a nice place, too. . . ."[23]

It was fortunate for German children that the Nazis in their demand for the "Volkish" book selected a relatively large number of works from pre-Nazi days that still qualified for German folk education. Not only did this apply to folklore material and works related to the peasant and nature theme, but also to some of the German "classics." Theodor Storm's *Der kleine Häwwelmann (The Little Häwwelmann)* was available to German children throughout the Nazi period, and so were Wilhelm Busch's *Max und Moritz (Max and Moritz)* and *Hans Huckebein (Hans Huckebein)*, as well as Dr. Hoffmann's *Der Struwwelpeter (Slovenly Peter)*.[24] Partially, these works were categorized as "regional literature," and partially as representative examples of "folk humor." It is also possible that the small town and rural milieu of these picture books helped to keep them alive during the Nazi period.

Besides, there were still a good number of illustrated works on the children's bookshelves that were better known by the illustrators than by the titles. Among them were the already mentioned works of Else Wenz-Viëtor, but also the picture books of Gertrud Caspari, Ernst Kreidolf, Fritz Kredel, Elsa Eisgruber, Otto Ubbelohde and Ruth Koser-Michaëls, all of whom had achieved fame in pre-Nazi times under the sponsorship of the German Children's Literature Association. The Nazis not only "tolerated" them but praised them highly for their genuine "commitment" to the German folk spirit. It is true that each one of these illustrators had in various and unique ways enhanced the spirit of nature, of elves, dwarfs, and "root children," although none of them exactly represented what the Nazis required of the "German folk style" in ideological terms. What made them so very acceptable to the Nazis was that even their fantasies were closely related to the spirit of the German folktale.

In glancing at the Nazis' selected reading lists for younger children, one might easily gain the impression that not much had changed in comparison with pre-Nazi selections, as so many titles look very familiar and unrelated to politics and ideology. Such an impression is misleading for two reasons. First, it does not take into consideration what books are missing from the list that used to belong to the standard works for German pre-schoolers, and secondly, it ignores the books outside of the schools and school libraries that were available to children in the bookstores and in the bookstalls. A representative example of a selective conservative listing of recommended books for pre-schoolers was published by Dr. Marianne Günzel in 1943. Let us examine this list first of all in

Plate 42
Nineteenth Century Didacticism: *Slovenly Peter* Survived the Purge.

view of what books are listed before we try to detect what categories are missing.

First, we find here, as usual, evidence of the Nazis' preconcern with the Volkish theme in terms of an emphasis on folktales and traditional nursery rhymes, followed by an interest in folk humor and the theme of nature (animals, birds, the seasons) and in the rural environment (picking blueberries, growing corn, making bread). Among the best known older illustrators we recognize Caspari, Hoffmann, Wenz-Viëtor, Kreidolf, and Kressner, and besides, those of the traditional "picture posters." A few new books have been added to the list to represent more contemporary topics pertaining to transportation (airplanes, trains) and to war (the German Army), but the conventional topics far outnumber these. The sub-headings of the list also use conventional titles and do not betray an ideological orientation at all, for with the exception of category 5 that corresponds to a traditional German genre not well known in the United States, the rest looks very familiar.

RECOMMENDED PICTURE BOOKS
(Age Group 2 - 6)

1. *Picture Books for the Very Young Child*
   Caspari, *For Our Youngest Ones.*
   Gorn, *My First Book.*
   Hoffmann, *Slovenly Peter.*
   Wenz-Viëtor, *Bakersman, Bakersman.*

2. *Folktale Picture Books*
   Brakow, *Little Hans in the Blueberry Forest.*
   Kreidolf, *The Meadow Dwarfs.*
   Kressner, *The Dwarf Book.*
   Olfers, *Something About the Root Children.*
   Watzlick and Rossner, *Where is Hans Everywhere?*

3. *Humorous Picture Books*
   Brochmann and Kressner, *The Little Deer.*
   Bohatta-Morpurgo, *Heinzel Wanders Through the Year.*
   Caspari, *From the Animal Nursery.*
   Klenkens, *The Bird ABC.*
   Mosig, *Little Long Ear.*
   Osswald and Kranz, *The Dear Animals.*

4. *Informational Books*
   Benary and Skarbinea, *Picture Book about the German Army.*
   Bergmann, *The Song about Bread.*
   Kiepenheimer and Scheel, *The Seasons.*
   Kranz, *Who Will Ride With Us?*
   Lindeberg, *We are Riding on the Railroad.*

5. *Picture Posters* (*Bilderbogen*)
   Lübeck Picture Poster No. 1, "The Conquest of the Air."
   Lübeck Picture Poster No. 2, "The History of Trains."
   Munich Picture Posters.
   Staffer Picture Poster, "The Nurse's Clock."[25]

What, then, is missing here? We observe that first of all there are no books pertaining to prayers or religious themes.

Absent from the list are also books on nonsense verse (unrelated to traditional verse)—simply because they didn't have a definite function to fulfill within the Nazis' folk education program. The same reason applied to the omission of fantasies based on an author's free imagination. To the Nazis, such books were not only "un-Volkish" but even "alien" or "sickly" in spirit—and often suspect of hidden anti-Nazi propaganda. Missing from the list are also picture books representing life in the urban community—not to mention those representing the bleak view of city life. Critical portrayals of German life were not wanted, regardless to what themes they applied. Most of all, on this list we miss picture books representing the peaceful coexistence of ethnic groups, or works showing different cultures in a friendly way. There were no books listed at all that portrayed children's friendship across racial lines or within the context of international relations.

Such omissions reveal that in spite of all their talk about "continuity," the Nazis changed young children's reading experiences substantially by focusing on an exclusively German and racial perspective. Even within the range of the conventional literature left on the library shelves after the purge, German children's exposure to liberal and humanitarian values across racial lines was severely restricted. To those educators who had whole-heartedly supported Wolgast's plea for quality control and an unbiased, world-open picture book for the youngest readers, it must have been a painful experience to realize how the Nazis gradually destroyed all professional standards and humanitarian values that they had developed in a painstaking effort over a period of forty years. There was not much they could do to reverse this policy, as it was enforced by totalitarian controls, yet in the final analysis, much was still left to their own conscience, as far as the full implementation of the ideological guidelines was concerned. The two-way T.V. screen in the corner of the classroom from which "Big Brother" was watching every word that the teacher spoke to the children was still a matter of the planned future.

The changing trends in pre-school education of the Nazi period were even more obvious in some popular picture book biographies glorifying Hitler, heroes of German history, and leaders of the National Socialist Party. It has been suggested that the books about "little Adolf" were the only real fantasies written during the Nazi period.[26] Authors and illustrators tended to portray him as the German "superman" who defied wind and weather, overpowered all enemies and obstacles, and always came out "on top." Even the little Austrian village boys seemed to sense that he was the "destined leader" of the German nation. Tall tales such as these resembled to some degree some of our own nineteenth century biographies about our national leaders that appeared there as "too-good-to-be-true" characters without fault. In both cases, we encounter a combination of an idealized heroic image supported by the author's strong didacticism. The difference however, lay in the fact that Hitler was a less worthy subject than Lincoln or Washington, and that, consequently, the sweet tales about him had little or no foundation whatsoever in the historical reality.

After 1939, many picture books about war were sold in the bookstores, among them some very simplistic and sensational tales often no longer than twelve pages. Like their counterparts in fiction, they were intended to appeal to all age groups and to stimulate their enthusiasm about the German war effort. Many teachers and librarians consciously abstained from discussing them, as their literary and artistic qualities were very poor,[27] and even the censorship authorities only selected a very few among them for their recommended book lists, as, in their view, they did not portray the "fight for German ethnic identity" convincingly enough. On the other hand, the Hitler Youth Organization and the League of German Girls frequently were less discriminatory in their tastes and found them suitable enough as propaganda material.

There was still another type of picture books available to young children that found support mainly from fanatic groups and individuals who purchased them in the book stores or in bookstalls. This concerned the category of anti-semitic books preaching hatred and contempt for the Jews. While we do not find such works included on the official book acquisition lists for school libraries or in plans for the reading curricula in the public schools, they were an integral part of the Hitler Youth indoctrination program. As a theme, the "fight against the Jew" even cropped up in school readers, in children's literature anthologies, and in children's journals, and it also formed an integral part of the Hitler Youth recreation program.

One of the most prejudiced picture books of this kind was produced by Elvira Bauer in 1936 under the title: *Trau keinem Jud' auf grüner Heid. . .Ein Bilderbuch für Gross und Klein* (*Don't Trust a Jew on the Green Heath. . . A Picture Book for Big Folks and Little Folks*).[28] Significantly, it was published by the Stürmer Verlag, known for its anti-semitic publications. It contained a story that was no story in the traditional sense, as it lacked an active plot. Its theme, presented in some crude rhymes, pertained merely to the contrast between the Jew and the German, their history of enmity, and the lesson that was to be derived from it. It began:

> The Devil is the father of the Jew.
> When God created the world,
> He invented the races:
> The Indians, the Negroes, the Chinese
> And also the wicked creature called the Jew. . .

Further, the "story" tells how God created also the "proud and beautiful German" and gave him a piece of land that he tilled with diligence and success. Meanwhile, the Jew stood by idly, shying all responsibilities, yet waiting only to snatch away the harvest that the Germans had produced. As a "parasite" and "son of the Devil" he is portrayed not only as physically repulsive, equipped with every attribute of the stereotype, but also as morally corrupt. Whereas he is shown to lie, cheat, and steal, the German is portrayed as honest, upright, and noble:

> The German is a proud man
> Who can work and who can fight.
> Because he is so beautiful and courageous,
> He has always hated the Jew.
> Here is a Jew, as all can see,
> The vilest man that'll ever be.
> He thinks he is a handsome lad,
> Although he is the ugliest brat.

And the moral of the story is:

> Remember, my child, what Mother has told you:
> Don't buy anything from a Jew.[29]

The illustrations accompanying the text show the Jew as a repelling and mean looking creature, while they idealize the noble features of the German. In one case, they depict how German children drive away some Jewish children from their school building and playground while making faces at them. In the illustrations the Jewish children look lowly and ugly, as if they deserved their fate, whereas the German children look cheerful, healthy, and active. The pictures clearly were meant not to tell a "story" at all but to dramatize merely the "needed" German fight against alien invaders.

On the whole, picture books available to German children through the kindergartens and the public schools promoted the Volkish theme in various forms: through German folktales and the Nordic Germanic folk heritage; through a glorification of nature and the German landscape, the German peasantry, and German achievements of the past and of the present. Lacking, however, were fantasies unrelated to folk traditions, along with realistic works touching upon real problems in urban life. Lacking were also works that merely served the purpose of enjoyment, or that fostered a human understanding across racial and ethnic lines.

The didacticism of the new picture book lay in its Volkish theme and was to be implemented fully through an interpretation along ideological lines. Within the context of literature interpretation guides and critical book reviews the implications of the new Volkish approach emerged as one that sacrificed literary and artistic standards to ideological goals. While some critics still pretended to fight *Kitsch* and to stand up for quality control, it became their primary concern to judge the picture book solely by its capacity to serve as an efficient means to another end, namely to form in young children the "right" attitude toward the fatherland and the *Führer*.

NOTES

1. Hugo Wippler, "Die volkserzieherische Bedeutung des deutschen Bilderbuches" *Jugendschriften-Warte* 44/8 (Aug., 1935), 115. The article was extensively quoted in the authoritative work issued by the Reich Youth Literature Office in Bayreuth: Bernhard Payr and Hans Georg Otto, eds., *Das deutsche Jugendbuch* (Munich, Deutscher Volksverlag, 1942), pp. 49-50.

2. *Ibid.* See also Hugo Wippler, "Kleinkind und Bilderbuch" *Jugendschriften-Warte* 41/5 (March, 1936), 33-34.

3. *Ibid.*

4. Kurt Boehme, *Die deutsche Volksseele in den Kinderdichtungen* (Berlin, Verlag Zentrale der deutschen Arbeitsfront, 1935), pp. 1-26.

5. *Ibid.*, see also Kurt Boehme, "Die deutschen Kinderdichtungen als Spiegel der Kinder- und Volksseele" *Jugendschriften-Warte* 45, 9-10 (Sept./Oct., 1940), 70-73.

6. Wippler, "Die volkserzieherische Bedeutung. . . ", 116.

7. "Über das Bilder- und Kinderbuch; Arbeitstagung der Verleger, Autoren und Zeichner im Reichsministerium für Volksaufklärung und Propaganda" *Jugendschriften-Warte* 46, 9-10 (Sept./Oct., 1941), 72-73.

8. Severin Rüttgers, "Gedanken zur Bilderbuchfrage" *Jugendschriften-Warte* 46, 9-10 (Sept./Oct., 1941), 34-35.

9. Franz Lichtenberger, "Die geschichtliche Entwicklung der Idee der Kindertümlichkeit" *Jugendschriften-Warte* 45, 9/10 (Sept./Oct., 1940), 65-70. For a historical perspective on the topic consult Irene Graebsch, *Geschichte des deutschen Jugendbuches* (Leipzig, Otto Harrassowitz, 1942), pp. 193-222.

10. Children's literature critics in general have confirmed the conservative trend. Irene Dyrenfurth-Graebsch, *Geschichte des deutschen Jugendbuches* (Hamburg, Stubenrauch Verlag, 1951), Chapter 8, and Peter Aley, footnote 26b. The idea pertaining to the confusion of "Volkish" values, however, may be best perceived in the study by Bausinger, although it does not make specific references to children's books but only to folklore interpretations. Hermann Bausinger, "Volksideologie und Volksforschung" in Andreas Flitner, ed., *Deutsches Geistesleben und Nationalsozialismus* (Tübingen, Rainer Wunder-

lich Verlag, 1965), p. 117. Bausinger analyzes here the "conglomerate" of terms used in connection with the "Volkish" National Socialist ideology. It is evident from this analysis that it was not merely understood in racial terms.

11. Rudolf Kressner, "Weihnachtsbilderbücher" *Jugendschriften-Warte* 42, 12 (December, 1937), 8-13.

12. Rudolf Kressner, "Der Osterhase im Bilderbuch" *Jugendschriften-Warte* 43, 2 (February, 1936), 11-16. This view corresponds largely with Wippler's demands in his essay "Über das Bilder- und Kinderbuch. . . ", 73. See also: Ivor Sörensen, "Bilderbuch, illustriertes Jugendbuch und seine Beurteilung" *Jugendschriften-Warte* 41/12 (December, 1936), 93-99 and Ilse Berg, *Die Entwicklung der deutschen Märchenillustration* (Munich, Bruckmann, 1944).

13. Fritz Koch-Gotha, *Die Häschenschule. Ein lustiges Bilderbuch* (Hamburg, Alfred Beck Verlag, 1934), 2nd ed.

14. Paul Alverdes, ed., *Deutsche Märchen* (Hamburg, Zigaretten-Bilderdienst, 1939), Introduction. Loose illustrations were supplied for this book by a cigarette factory in Hamburg, free of charge, for each purchase of a package of cigarettes.

15. Karl Hobrecker, ed., *Lieder und Bilder für Kinder. Volksmund und Volkstum aus der Zeit Ludwig Richters* (Leipzig, Velhagen and Klasen, 1944). Hobrecker was also responsible for many fine folktale editions published during the Third Reich. Besides, illustrated folktales were published by the well known illustrator Fritz Kredel, who singled out two tales by Grimm, "*Die sieben Geisslein*" (The Seven Little Goats) and "*Das tapfere Schneiderlein*," (The Brave Little Tailor) and the tale by Hauff, "*Zwerg Nase*" (The Long Nosed Dwarf) for new picture books. Ruth Koser Michaëls brought out richly illustrated folktale anthologies based on selections from Grimm, Bechstein, and Hauff, Gertrud Eisner's richly illustrated *Märchenbuch* (*Book of Folktales*) appeared in 1940, and Timmermann's picture books of Philipp Otto Runge's tales were published in 1943. Consult also: Peter Aley, "Das Bilderbuch im Dritten Reich" in Klaus Doderer and Helmut Müller, ed., *Das Bilderbuch in Deutschland von den Anfängen bis zur Gegenwart* (Weinheim, Beltz Verlag, 1975), p. 341.

16. Dyrenfurth-Graebsch, pp. 361-385.

17. *Ibid.*

18. The inclusion of Danish, Norwegian, and Swedish children's books (in translation) emerges as a trend also in the so-called "Basic Lists" for school libraries issued by Reich Education Minister Bernhard Rust in 1937 and 1939 respectively. (Consult the chapter on school libraries.)

19. "Die Malerin Else Wenz-Viëtor: 60 Jahre alt" (Editorial) *Jugendschriften-Warte* 47, 3-4 (March/April, 1942), 243.

20. Marga Müller, *Die vom Wegrain*, ill. by Else Wenz-Viëtor (Munich, Verlag Josef Müller, 1940), p. 30.

21. H.R. Trevor-Roper; *Hitler's Secret Conversations 1941-1944* (New York, Stradford Press, Inc., 1953), p. 37. The slogan cited earlier appeared on hundreds of Nazi posters and also in children's textbooks.

22. Elisabeth Bantzer, *Was Ursel träumte*, ill. by Hildegard Bantzer (Leipzig, Rudolf Schneider Verlag, 1936).

23. Georg Rendel, *Märchenflug ins Bienenland; Eine Erzählung für Kinder* (Stuttgart, Frank'sche Verlagsanstalt, 1936), p. 145. One of the most popular "bee" stories that was heading the bestseller list in the Third Reich was Waldemar Bonsels' *Die Biene Maja.* (Stuttgart, Deutsche Verlagsanstalt, 1942). Originally published in pre-Nazi times, this work was much more imaginative than Rendel's work, although even here we detect much talk about the virtues of community life (albeit within the context of the bee society). On the whole, however, it was less didactic, and today it is still widely read by German children as a fantasy. (Consult also the chapter on publishing trends.)

24. For a general discussion of the mentioned children's classics consult Bettina Hürlimann, *Three Centuries of Children's Books in Europe* (Cleveland, World Publishing Company, 1954). Official guidelines recommended by the Party confirm that some of the old classics among the German picture books were still highly recommended as "folk books" of the German people. See Marianne Günzel and Harriet Schneider, *Buch und Erziehung: Jugendschrifttumskunde* (Leipzig, Klinkhardt, 1943), pp. 42-43. Also: Josef K. Scholz, "Vom deuschen Bilderbuchverlag" *Jugendschriften-Warte* 31, 1 (January, 1937) 3-5 and Harriet Schneider, "Das Buch im Kindergarten, Hort und Erholungsheim" *Jugendschriften-Warte* 45, 11-12 (December, 1940), 83-84.

25. Günzel and Schneider, pp. 42-43. The *Bilderbogen* (picture posters) were over-sized illustrated sheets of paper issued in large portfolios. Some librarians also framed them. With or without an accompanying text, they contained picture stories, some of which had been designed by famous nineteenth century illustrators (among them Wilhelm Busch). During the Nazi period, a great variety of new *Bilderbogen* were printed, the bulk of which contained woodcuts and engravings of earlier decades. See also: Erich Parnitzke, "Alte und neue Bilderbogen" *Jugendschriften-Warte* 41, 5 (May, 1936), 35-36.

26. See, for example, Karl Springerschmidt, *Eine wahre Geschichte* (Stuttgart, 1936). Ironically, this "True Story" contained very little of the truth. A bibliographical discussion of picture books and other works about Adolf Hitler appeared in W. Krohn, "Der Führer in der Jugendschrift" *Jugendschriften-Warte* 39, 5 (May, 1966) 33-36. For a more elaborate critical discussion of this topic consult Aley, p. 341.

27. Graebsch (1942 edition). This edition contains a chapter that was drastically abbreviated in the later edition which the author published under the name Dyrenfurth-Graebsch. The review of picture books glorifying Hitler states that the Hitler biographies were intended to acquaint children with the fighters of National Socialism and their goals, while reminding them of the

"spirit of history" and the "need to sacrifice". Graebsch did admit that many of the war books for children did not meet literary and artistic standards, yet she felt that young people were in a "need" of this type of reading material at the present time. As a whole, the chapter is uncritical of the ideological influences on children's books—an attitude that was revised in the post-war edition of the work.

28. Elvira Bauer, *Trau keinem Jud' auf grüner Heid'* . . . *Ein Bilderbuch für Gross und Klein* (Munich, Stürmer Verlag, 1936). For a corresponding prejudiced view of the Jew see also the following essay printed in a children's journal issued by the National Socialist Teachers Association: "Der ewige Jude" *Hilf-Mit* (Supplement to the journal *Die Volksschule*) (July/August, 1939), 7-8. For additional comments on Bauer's text consult Bettina Hürlimann, pp. 174-175 and Peter Aley, *Jugendliteratur im Dritten Reich: Dokumente und Kommentare* (Hamburg, Verlag für Buchmarktforschung, 1969), pp. 183-184. Aley quotes the full German text.

29. *Ibid.*

PART III

The Uses and Adaptations of Children's Literature

10

Primers:
The ABC's of 'Folk Education'

The Nazis realized that for many children the primers were the first picture books they would be allowed to take home, where their parents, too, would have an opportunity to read them. Since approximately 300,000 first graders annually studied the primer, Party and State authorities decided that it would be of great significance to start children early in learning about some elementary aspects of German 'folk education': faith in the *Führer*, Adolf Hitler, a love of the country, and service and sacrifice for the German folk community.[1]

Early in the thirties many primers still represented an odd mixture of old and new values, in which the first generally retained the upper hand.[2] Publishers frequently reprinted pre-Nazi primers with only minor changes, such as the insertion of some sayings by Hitler, Party slogans, or stories about the swastika flag. In regard to illustrations, too, they would rely on reprints of traditional etchings or woodcut engravings, while only here and there adding a few drawings of the Hitler Youth or men in uniform. It was only later in the decade when newer writings and illustrations became available in greater quantity and when the pressure of censorship increased, that the primers began to reflect the National Socialist ideology in more obvious ways.

The fusion of old and new values sometimes produced some strange hybrid creations. In a primer dating back to 1936, for example, the nineteenth century illustrations of ladybugs and cuckoos contrast oddly with the pictures of soldiers. They appear even more odd if they are misplaced to illustrate Hitler's maxims: "Learn to make sacrifices for your fatherland!" "All of us will have to die but Germany will live!" or "In your folk community lies your strength!"[3] We may wonder what ideas may have crossed a child's mind when associating the pictures of two swallows nesting under a house gable, or bluebells and daisies in the field, with Hitler's reminders to be loyal, courageous, honest, brave, comradely, and dedicated to the "great cause."

In the same primer there is an old engraving of a child with folded hands, kneeling in front of an open window overlooking a summer meadow bathed in the bright morning sun. The poem accompanying the illustration is entitled *"Gebet"* (Prayer). Contrary to expectation, however, it does not invoke God's blessings of the child himself but of the *Führer* and the fatherland.

> Prayer
> Protect, God, with your hand
> Our dear fatherland.
> Give strength and power to our *Führer*,
> And help him in his difficult task.
> Turn away our nation's sorrow
> Give all of us work and bread this morrow.[4]

The poem was meant to build up confidence in the *Führer*'s cause. If God Himself was asked to help him, could there be anything wrong with his plans? Like the image of a good father, the Führer emerged as the person who cared for all and who tried his best to bring work, bread, and security. In this task, of course, he needed strength and power, and if God was to give to him both, who was to deny God's blessings in whatever he would undertake? Thus, a simple poem like this was meant to develop the child's loyalty to the leaders of the Third Reich.

The primers of the Third Reich did not only contain poems about the *Führer*, but also stories and anecdotes. Usually, they were short and limited to brief episodes, but with great intensity they tried to convey the image of a fatherly man who cared for all, was generous and friendly, and above all, loved children and animals. In the story entitled "A Happy Day," the major theme concerns the excitement experienced by school children as they anticipate the *Führer's* visit to their village. The following scene is preceded by the announcement of the postmaster's wife that the *Führer* had just entered mainstreet with his motorcade:

> Now everyone is getting excited. We all want to run to the door, but the teacher says: "Wait! Stay in here! Heini and Franz, you two will hoist the flag at the window, be quick about it! Lenchen and Hanne, you two will run into the garden and get some flowers! The rest of you, line up along the sidewalk! As soon as the *Führer* will have arrived here, we will sing a song for him.
> "There is the *Führer*! *Sieg Heil!*" (Hail Victory!)[5]

The teacher maintains "order and discipline," while keeping the children back from running to the door. Then he divides the tasks evenly among two boys and two girls and gives instructions for their behavior in the street. Finally, however, he lets go his restraints, as all of them cheer their *Sieg Heil!* No more words are needed to convey the catharsis involved.

Gebet.

Schütze, Gott, mit deiner Hand
unser liebes Vaterland!
Gib zu seinem schweren Werke
unserm Führer Kraft und Stärke!
Wende unsres Volkes Not:
Arbeit gib und jedem Brot!   H. Sommer.

Der Kuckuck als Wahrsager.

Kuckucksknecht,
sag mir recht,
sag mir klar
auf ein Haar,
wieviel Jahr
ich leben möcht'!
Belüg mich nicht,
betrüg mich nicht,
sonst bist du der rechte Kuckuck nicht!

Volksgut.

Kuckuck.

Der Kuckuck auf dem Zaune saß;
es regnet' sehr, und er ward naß.

Plate 43
A Prayer for the *Führer*:
Adoption of Folk Rhymes for Developing Children's Allegiance to the Fatherland

A second story strewn amidst folk songs and old riddles concerns little Reinhold who manages to stand right in the front row where the music is playing in honor of Adolf Hitler who has come to town in his private plane.

> Suddenly Reinhold shouts: "He is coming! He is coming!" All turn their heads and look up. The boy is right! Quickly, the plane approaches and then lands, quite close to where Reinhold is waiting. The *Führer* gets out of his plane. "*Hail! Hail to Hitler!*" the people shout. Adolf Hitler greets back with a smile. At this point, Reinhold no longer can restrain himself. In the twinkling of an eye he rushes past the S.A. men, runs across the free place toward the *Führer* and stretches out his hands to him. The *Führer* laughs at Reinhold, and hand in hand he walks with him to the car. Reinhold will never forget this moment.[6]

Little Reinhold's joy of anticipation is described here in a manner of an almost religious love and devotion. Hitler is the smiling Savior passing his hands over the blond heads of the boys and girls who greet him with flowers. He seems to say: "Let the Little Ones come to me . . . " When little Fritz, in another primer story, personally hands him a fresh bouquet of garden flowers, he is invited by that "great man" to ride along for a little while on the steps of his open car. Fritz describes the event as if a miracle had happened to him![7]

The portrayal of Hitler in the primers does not substantially change in the later years of the Third Reich. He continues to emerge as the kind and benevolent leader of the German people who "knows what is best for all" and who acts only out of the generosity of his heart.

After 1939, primers began to reflect a stronger preconcern with topics related to everyday experiences of the new "folk community" of the Third Reich. Although even at that time we still find in them numerous folktales, folk songs, riddles, and other traditional primer material, the text as well as the illustrations focus to a greater degree upon images of National Socialism represented by marching soldiers, banner-waving Hitler Youth, May Day parades, solstice celebrations, and other Party-sponsored activities. In combination with the pictures, the simple primer language conveyed the message of National Socialism as effectively as poster propaganda. Whereas in former times, the most important goal of the primers had been to teach children reading along with some traditional ethics, now it became their first concern to convey the message of the Third Reich and to form the young characters in the spirit of German folk education. In this process, methodological concerns were sometimes subordinated to ideological goals. In the Primer *Von Drinnen und Draussen (From Inside and Outside)*, for example, various letters of the alphabet are introduced in association with some aspects of the National Socialist movement. The letter "h" is related to the shouts of a Hitler Youth marching song: "*Ho hei ho*" which

Der Führer kommt!

Der Führer spricht:

Lerne Opfer bringen für dein Vaterland!

*

Wir sind vergänglich, aber Deutschland muß leben!

*

In deinem Volke liegt deine Kraft.

*

Ihr müßt treu sein, ihr müßt mutig sein, ihr müßt tapfer sein,
und ihr müßt untereinander eine einzige große,
herrliche Kameradschaft bilden!   Adolf Hitler.

Plate 44
Early Conditioning: "The *Führer* is Coming!"
Flowers for Hitler and Citations from his Speeches

then leads to the Nazi salute: *"heil heil" (hail, hail),* and finally to the simple
primary text relating further "h" combinations conveying the meaning that two
boys marched alongside the parade, enjoyed it, and ran home again.[8] From a

methodological point of view, children had been exposed to a total of eleven words containing the letter "h," yet, it was obviously of greater significance from the Party's point of view that they were introduced to the Nazi salute, the image of the marching Hitler Youth, and the symbol of the swastika flag. The accompanying illustration shows in the foreground a little girl with her doll and a little boy with his hoola hoop, both of them watching the parade passing by. It seems to suggest: "Wouldn't it be nice, if you could march, too?"

In the case of the letter "F," represented by the words "*Fahne, Feier, Feiertag*" (flag, celebration, holiday), the ideological message appears to be more important than the alphabet lesson itself, for the words succeeding them are "*singen, grüssen—fröhlich*" (to sing, to salute—being joyous), of which only one applies to the letter involved. The text itself, too, illustrates the "joy" of National Socialism, yet hardly more than that:

> Music, music!
> There comes the parade!
> Listen, the boys are singing a song!
> In front march the musicians,
> Then come the banners.
> The Hitler Youth carry the pennants,
> The drums and fanfares.
> Listen to the sound of the drums!
> They all march in the same step,
> In rows of three.
> We salute the flag.
> *Sieg Heil* (Hail Victory) to the Führer![9]

The child reading this page of the primer has been invited to imagine the bright sights and exciting sounds of the marching Hitler Youth, including the flags and uniforms, the beat of the drums and the resounding steps on the pavement. The final exclamation: "*Sieg Heil* to the *Führer!*" is meant to recreate the enthusiasm at the Nazi rallies that were all too familiar to young and old in those days. In its abrupt style, the primer language as such shows a resemblance to the military command and the brief orders used by the Hitler Youth leaders, thus emphasizing action and obedience rather than passive contemplation.

Germans who were not "lucky" enough to fight for the *Führer* at the front line, had an opportunity at home to give their share of "sacrifice" by knitting socks for soldiers, by collecting scrap metal or old papers for recycling, or by sacrificing their Sunday dinner and eating instead what was called "*Eintopf*," a one-course dish consisting of a thick vegetable stew or soup with little or no meat. This custom was introduced by the Party in an attempt to induce Germans to donate their savings to the *Winterhilfswerk*, (Winter Aid Program), which partially subsidized the needy and partially equipped the front line sol-

Plate 45
"The *Pimpfe* March through Town"

diers.[10] How the spirit of "sacrifice" to folk and fatherland was conveyed through an alphabet lesson concerning the letter "E" may be conceived from the following example:

E Ei   E EI

> *A one-course dish—on Sundays.*
> *A bowl. A thick soup.*
> *give donate - rich poor*
> *Just a soup. Yes, but a thick soup.*
> *A bowl. One-pot. Mother, too, shall have Sunday.*
> *There are few dishes to wash.*
> *Emma and Ella rinse them.*
> *We sacrifice—Sacrifice Sunday.*[11]

In more direct terms, some primers referred to the Winter Aid Program itself, which during the early forties had the active support of all schools and youth organizations. Not only were children drafted to collect money from passersbys at street corners, but they were also engaged to go from house to house to solicit old rags, scrap metal, books, newspapers, and even old bones for recycling purposes, so as to counteract the increasing raw materials shortage during the war years. Public schools usually served as collection stations and awarded certificates and badges to the most successful collectors. The following excerpt from a primer shows how the National Socialists tried to convey to children a certain spirit of altruism in their efforts, and how they taught the very young what it meant to help the *Führer* if one was willing to sacrifice.

> Fight all waste!
> Mother doesn't let anything spoil.
> She uses up all of the left-overs.
> We children are not allowed to throw away the
>   crusts of bread.
> Recently, the teacher gave us a memo to take home.
> Now mother is saving all of the bones, big ones,
>   little ones, thin ones, thick ones.
> We take them to school with us.
> In this way, we are helping the *Führer*.
> Our *Führer* says:
> Nobody shall go hungry!
> Nobody shall freeze!
> *SA*-men collect money
> For the Winter Aid Program.
> Gerhard takes his toys.

E Ei – E Ei

Eintopf – Sonntag
Ein topf   Sonn tag

Eine Schüssel. Eine dicke Suppe.
Ei ne   Schüs sel.   Ei ne   di cke   Sup pe.

geben spenden – arm reich
ge ben   spen den   arm   reich

Ei ne Sup pe nur. Ja, a ber ei ne di cke Sup pe.
Ei ne Schüs sel. Ein topf. Mut ter soll auch Sonn tag ha ben.
Es ist we nig zu spü len. Em ma und El la spü len.
Wir op fern – Op fer sonn tag.

Plate 46
"A ONE-COURSE DISH—ON SUNDAYS"
A Primer's Call for Sacrifice

Helga takes her doll:
All sacrifice—all help.[12]

Both Gerhard and Helga are set up as examples in giving what was dear to them. The Primer suggests to the young reader that true sacrifice demands that one give in an unselfish way, and that it is not enough to collect bones and scrap metal without caring for the National Socialist cause. The words "*our Führer*" remind of the prayer "Our Father . . . "—a similarity which was calculated to add a feeling of sanctity to the person of Adolf Hitler, and to promote faith and trust in his actions.[13]

The portrait of Hitler that emerges from the primers and readers for younger children indeed is that of a loving father who cares for the German folk community as a good shepherd might care for his sheep. A case in point is the story of two little girls who from their own allowance money buy flowers for Hitler on his birthday, and a big sausage for his shepherd dog, Wolf, and deliver these to him personally. They are warmly received in his study and eagerly listen to his talk in which he tries to convey to them his great respect for women and girls and their new role in society.

> Then he came to speak about the great task which we girls and German women would have to fulfill within our nation. We noticed the great respect with which he spoke about German women and about the brave generation of our mothers who were so willing to bring sacrifices for the cause. In listening to him, we really took pride in the fact that we girls, too, had been given a significant task by the Party, and that the *Führer* did not only count on boys but on girls, too.[14]

The didacticism of this account is somewhat softened by a little scene toward the end of the story, when Hitler reportedly cut off a piece of sausage, placed it on Wolf's nose, and let him jump for it: "You may believe me, this impressed us very much, and you may guess why I said to the *Führer*: 'My goodness, Herr Hitler, you really do have an excellent way of training dogs!'"[15] Such a sentimental scene completes the image of Hitler as a kind man who cares not only for the nation as a whole but also for children, not only for boys but also for girls, and not only for people but also for dogs. It was intended to impress the young readers with the idea that Hitler was the right leader for the German people, as he was "down-to-earth," warmhearted, and above all, "human."

All nations glorify their leaders to some extent, and here and there legends develop around them that make them appear stronger, kinder, and perhaps wiser than in real life. Primers of pre-Nazi times, too, had emphasized charismatic leadership qualities while playing upon patriotic sentiments.[16] Was this case so very different?

To answer this question, we will have to realize that the scene portrayed above, with all of its sentimental and human appeal, represented a gross contrast to the true conditions in a totalitarian state in which the individual was considered a replaceable cog in a big machine. The folk community concept of Nazism left as little room for personal sentiments as did the racial theory based on pseudo-scientific principles. The irony was that while Hitler indeed may have been kind to his dog, he had no sympathy for millions of Jews and "subhumans" of other races, including their children. To the Nazis, Jews always remained Jews, regardless if they had assimilated the National Socialist ideology or not. Whether Hitler really cared for his own nation may also be challenged on many counts, and even more so, whether he was concerned about the welfare of German children. Even though hundreds of photographs showed him with a smiling face in the company of German children,[17] he was ready to "sacrifice" every one of them when it came to the final decisions in his Bunker in 1945. Within the broader context of the Nazis' scheme of efficiency there was no room for individual human sympathy if it lay outside of the immediate interests of the German folk state.

It is another irony that the Nazis' call for a conservation of energy and resources and their demand for "sacrifice" as far as the German population was concerned, coincided with their involvement in an aggressive war involving an extravagant waste of resources. Whereas in 1932 Germany had spent only one percent of its gross national product on defense, it spent 61 percent in 1943![18] Neither newspaper collections, old bone collections, nor scrap metal collections cards allowing for only a few grams of meat per person per week, the "one-course dish" on Sundays was no "sacrifice" in which people had a choice but an economic necessity. Why, nevertheless, would the primers so consistently emphasize the need for individual sacrifice?

The answer is not to be found in the *Realpolitik* of the Third Reich, nor in the economic conditions of the time but in the Nazi ideology itself. The National Socialist ideology demanded the individual's *total* dedication to the German folk community and its leaders, not merely occasional support when the proper situation would arise. This required an acknowledgement and faith in the infallability of the *Führer* and his Party, absolute loyalty, and a determination to fight for his cause, regardless at what price. In order to develop such an attitude in children, the Nazis appealed to their *feelings of love* for whatever values they considered important: the home, the German landscape, the German nation, the German ancestors, the folk community and the *Führer*. Through primers they hoped to develop in children—and also in their parents—a sense of unity and purpose within the present National Socialist Regime.

Primers gave children the impression that they themselves were important to the Third Reich, and that they could already carry out some responsibilities in regard to the German folk community. Hitler was not only kind to children, the primers seemed to say, but he also recognized their contributions and potentialities. Such trust on the part of the *Führer* invited the trust of children as much as their loyalty and respect. Little did they know at the time that ultimately, their faith in the Regime would imply a total abdication of democratic freedoms, and that they themselves, as individuals, were deemed important only to the degree that they contributed to the smooth and efficient operation of the totalitarian state.

NOTES

1. Eduard Rothemund, "Das Jugendbuch in der deutschen Schule" in Bernhard Payr and Hans Georg Otto, ed., *Das deutsche Jugendbuch, 4 Vorträge gehalten auf der Jugendbuchwoche in Bayreuth* (Munich, Deutscher Volksverein, 1942), pp. 68-70. For a discussion of the role and function of illustrations see: Robert Böttcher, "Die Fibel, das wichtigste Bilderbuch der deutschen Jugend" *Jugendschriften-Warte* 42, 9 (September, 1937) 61-64.

2. Peter Aley, *Jugendliteratur i Dritten Reich; Dokumente und Kommentare* (Hamburg, Verlag für Buchmarktforschung, 1969), pp. 218-219. Aley partially ascribes this trend to economic considerations.

3. "Der Führer spricht" *Deutsches Lesebuch für Volksschulen* II (Frankfurt/Main, Diesterweg, 1936), p. 11.

4. "Gebet" *Ibid.*, p. 11.

5. "Ein froher Tag" *Ibid.*, p. 9.

6. "Der Führer kommt" *Ibid.*

7. "Der Führer kommt" *Von Drinnen und Draussen: Heimatfibel für die deutsche Jugend* (Frankfurt/Main, Diesterweg, 1942).

8. *Von Drinnen und Draussen*, p. 17.

9. *Ibid.*, p. 51.

10. In regard to the Winter Aid Program, Hitler is cited in a reader for older children: "We will try our best to educate the German people in the spirit of sacrifice." See Adolf Hitler, "Zum deutschen Winterhilfswerk" *Von deutscher Art* V, pp. 145-148. For a general discussion of community work and donations see H.W. Koch, *The Hitler Youth: Origins and Development, 1922-1945* (London, McDonald and Jane's, 1975), pp. 116-136.

11. *Von Drinnen und Draussen*, p. 42.

12. *Mein erstes Buch* (Dortmund, 1937). See also: Peter Aley, "Das Bilderbuch im Dritten Reich" in Klaus Doderer und Helmut Müller, eds., *Das Bilderbuch; Geschichte und Entwicklung des Bilderbuches in Deutschland von den Anfängen bis zur Gegenwart* (Weinheim, Beltz, 1975), p. 353.

13. Much of the language in the Nazi Primers is characterized by sentimental clichés and expressions of bombast. For an analysis of style consult Peter

Hasubek, *Das deutsche Lesebuch in der Zeit des Nationalsozialismus: Ein Beitrag zur Literaturpädagogik zwischen 1933 und 1945* (Hannover, Hermann Schroedel Verlag, 1972), pp. 160-162.

14. *Von deutscher Art* I.

15. *Ibid.*

16. Hasubek, p. 35. Consult also: A. Pudelko, "Das erste Reichslesebuch und seine Gestaltung" *Deutsche Volkserziehung* 3 (March, 1936), and Rolf Eilers, *Die nationalsozialistische Schulpolitik* (Köln, Opladen, Staat und Politik, 1963).

17. Photographs and illustrations of Hitler in the primers and readers for younger children usually have a sentimental appeal also, while showing him surrounded by boys and girls. Often, he appeared with a smile, graciously accepting their well-wishes and flowers, while shaking their hands in return, patting their heads, or giving autographs. He was shown in a more "heroic" pose for the upper grades.

18. Henry M. Pachter, *Modern Germany: A Social, Cultural, and Political History* (Boulder, Colorado, Westview Press, 1978), p. 213. The state of the German economy during the war is described on pp. 216-217.

11

Readers:
Textbooks in Ideology

The German reading textbooks published during the National Socialist regime were expected to contribute an essential part to the Nazis' folk education program. Early in the thirties, however, there were still a great number of different texts in circulation,[1] which very much displeased Rosenberg. He consequently ordered Bouhler and the Party Censorship Office to examine all of the current textbooks in use, and to screen them carefully with a view to their ideological orientation. Bouhler carried out this survey systematically and came to the conclusion that more was needed than a mere "weeding" process, namely a uniform *Reichslesebuch (Reich Reader)* for the entire nation.[2]

It was Reich Education Minister Rust who began to implement this idea actively. First, he ordered that all of the old Readers be taken out of circulation, and that the new editions should then be used in their place. Before such new editions be distributed among the public schools, however, they would have to be checked carefully so they conformed to the following ideological principles:

1. Blood and Soil.
2. Leadership and Followership.
3. Honor and Loyalty.
4. Service and Sacrifice.
5. Struggle and Work.[3]

Under the title of *Deutsches Reichslesebuch (German Reich Reader)* Rust proceeded slowly but surely to issue the 5th and 6th grade volumes in 1935, the 3rd grade volume in 1936, and the 3rd and 4th grade volumes in 1937. The 7th and 8th grade volumes followed in 1939/40. Even at this late date, other Readers were still in general use, but since 1939 they followed at least in principle the five points that Rust had stated as mandatory ideological guidelines.

It was one of the peculiarities of the Reich Readers that they made some allowances for variations within the structural and ideological unity of the work. This was done mainly to make room for regional characteristics of the native folk heritage and landscape in the diverse German culture areas. Whereas the "core" of the Readers underlined in the same consistent way the five major principles listed above, the so-called "home parts," which in 1939 existed in twenty-two variations, focused on regional writers and poets, local legends, and experiences reflecting the past and the present in familiar surroundings. The idea behind such an orientation was that the German people would more easily be led to unite under the banner of the swastika flag if they were solidly "rooted" first of all in their feelings for home and family.[4]

The educational theory behind the Readers was based on the teachings of Professor Krieck.[5] Rothemund acknowledged his influence on this idea by calling attention to the link which Krieck had established between the concepts of family, race, and Germandom. He thought that, ideally, the Readers should become something like "family bibles" that would find their place in every German household.[6] The passage below illustrates how selectively the editors of the *Reichslesebuch* would pursue these objectives:

> Only those reading materials were selected for inclusion in the Readers that are rooted in our common folk heritage, that reflect our blood and soil, landscape and tribes, and that, in general, are of such a nature as to appeal to the child's innermost being, thus helping him in his development.
>
> In particular, materials were chosen that serve the purpose of cultivating our knowledge of Nordic literature, the sagas and folktales, and of prehistory and history. The meaning of blood and soil is conveyed poetically through themes related to folklore, Germandom abroad, and stories about the life experiences of families throughout the generations.[7]

Obviously, editors gave priority to the blood and soil concept over those concerning the child's "innermost being" in the traditional sense. Now the concept of child development itself had been linked with Krieck's concept of "Nordic virtues" that implied honor, loyalty, service, and devotion to the folk community;[8] Löffler considered the Reader a "folk forming agent,"[9] and in the words of Reich Minister Rust himself, it was to "serve the ideological education of young German people, so as to develop them into fit members of the folk community—members who are ready to serve and to sacrifice."[10]

In selecting stories and poems for the Readers, editors were, first and foremost, subject to the general rules of censorship that prohibited the publication of "un-Volkish" materials. On the one hand, this included literature written by Jewish writers or dealing with the Jews in a favorable way. These rules also excluded literature touching upon Christian themes or ideals projecting the unity of mankind regardless of race, creed or religion, and even some neutral informational or purely cultural items pertaining to other lands. On the other hand, censorship barred editors from including German literature dealing with some past or present national problems or failures, aspects of "decadence," or "unheroic" moments in German history. All controversial subjects or unresolved questions were simply omitted, along with anything that might throw an unfavorable light upon the present government.[11]

In compliance with such "taboos," and within the guidelines of Volkish literature in general and Rust's specific demands for the Readers, editors would first of all turn to the "home parts." In this section they would offer selected regional literature and local legends familiar to the people in a given area of Germany. Possibly it represented the most conservative and least political section of all, although it did fulfill the "Blood and Soil" requirement. From here editors would move on to selections from German and Nordic Germanic folklore, including some tales collected by the Brothers Grimm, stories from the *Edda* and the sagas, and selections from the *Nibelungenlied (Song of the Nibelungs)* and other German medieval epics and heroic tales. This section represented the "core" of the Readers, as it dealt with the "roots" of Germandom in which all Germans had a share, regardless of their regional characteristics. Such selections were particularly well suited to meet the Party's requirement for an emphasis on the concepts of leadership, service, honor, and loyalty.

In order to do justice to the above mentioned first three guidelines of Rust, editors had available to them, of course, the whole range of German literature, including poetry, fiction, and nonfiction, from the early Middle Ages to the twentieth century.[12] In making their selections, they put aside all considerations pertaining to the integrity of a given work, an author's point of view, or respect for the traditional heritage and its intrinsic merits. They followed only one overruling objective, namely to tailor the selections to the ideological views of National Socialism. As a result of such a ruthless approach to literature, history, and tradition, the selections listed in the Readers often appeared to be rather incongruous in relation to each other. At first glance we may be puzzled indeed by seeing the name of Baldur von Schirach right above that of Frederick the Great, or by reading a quote from Mussolini following a citation by Fichte:

> All great things in this world have come
> about because of loyalty!
>
> > (*Baldur von Schirach*)

> It is not necessary that I live,
> but it is necessary that I do my duty!
>
> > (*Frederick the Great*)

> Whoever fights has the right on his side,
> but whoever shuns fighting has forfeited
> his right.
>
> > (*Fichte*)

Whoever is not ready to die for his faith
is not worthy of possessing it.

(*Mussolini*)

To become German means to be
loyal, good, strong, and joyous.

(*Gorch Fock*)[13]

The riddle's answer lies in Rust's guidelines calling for an emphasis on "Honor and Loyalty," "Service and Sacrifice," and "Struggle and Work." Placed into a new context right between a saying by Hitler and some "wise words" by Himmler or Rosenberg, even a poem by the great eighteenth century writer Johann Wolfgang von Goethe seems to take on a new meaning:

Go, Obey My Beckoning

Go, obey my beckoning,
And use your young days well:
Learn early to be wise.
On the scales of fortune
The perfect balance is seldom attained.
You must either
Rise or fall,
Rule and win—
or serve and lose.
Choose your own lot:
Suffer or triumph,
Be an anvil or a hammer.

(*Johann Wolfgang von Goethe*)[14]

It is not difficult to imagine that teachers were expected to relate this poem within the new context to Hitler's concept of service, sacrifice, fight, and work. In this process it may be seen that Goethe's concept of self-discipline in the individual's task of shaping his own personality and fortune might easily have been perverted into the National Socialist maxim that "might is right." The difference in point of view was substantial: Goethe still saw the individual as a free personality who was both the anvil and the hammer as he chose his own lot; the Nazis saw in the hammer the symbol of the master race that chose war to subordinate other nations and races. Within a totalitarian system of government the individual had no choice but to serve, to work, to sacrifice, and to fight for the *Führer*, unless he preferred to be crushed by the "hammer" itself.

The table of contents of many of the Readers published during the Nazi regime reflect the same incongruous mixture of writers and literary selections.

To the uninformed, the listing of names from any one of such tables would not necessarily betray an ideological emphasis at all, for it might include not only selections from Goethe and Schiller, but also from Klopstock and earlier writers. Only a closer analysis would lead the critical observer to detect the Nazis' Volkish emphasis, also in some selection from the works of Brentano, Wackenroder, Grillparzer, Stifter, Storm, and Keller. The Nazis' ideological intent was, of course, more evident in their selections from works by Fichte, Arndt, Riehl, Nietzsche, de Lagarde, and von Moltke, even though in these cases, too, the quoted passages created the false impression that these writers in their time had prophesied the coming of Hitler and his "folk Reich." Generally, the newer writings of Carossa, Miegel, Brockmeier, Kolbenheyer, Anacker, and Menzel[15] held their place in the Readers, simply because they were approved by the Reich Literature Chamber. It appears that the editors' inclusion of Volkish literature followed various objectives, for they utilized everything "useful" from political Romanticism through the Germanic Faith movement. Another volume of the same Reader also included excerpts from the "Nordic" novels of Hans Friedrich Blunck, and selections from the works of Hans Grimm and Paul Ernst, all of which in one way or another focused on the struggle of the German or Nordic Germanic peasantry.

In an attempt to convey more emphatically the concepts of battle and sacrifice, editors were not beneath inventing poems by listing them anonymously under such titles as "A Runic Inscription." Whatever the ancient Germanic tribes used to carve in stones sometimes took on the power of magic or prophecy, and often represented the very "wisdom" of the ancestors which the editors now hoped to convey in a new light. The following "inscription" is in itself "unpolitical," yet the editor's interpretation accompanying it provide a clue to its ideological significance.

A Runic Inscription

The peasant Gulli had five sons.
Bravely, Asmund fell in battle at the Fysund River,
And Assur was killed in far away Rome.
Holm Halfdan was killed.
And Kari died at Dunder;
Bur is different.
Kari cut these runes.[16]

The editor commented:

This inscription on a Runic stone in Högby in East Gothland is a symbol of the Viking race. Four sons fell in battle: the firstborn fell in Sweden, where he defended his home and country; the second one died in the service of Rome; the third fell in battle against the Danes at Born-holm; the fourth one found his death on a Viking trip to Scotland. The youngest son, however, was only "different," which means that he was not less loyal by taking care of his father's peasant estate at home.[17]

It is common knowledge that Runic inscriptions did not carry footnotes. Neither did the saga literature make mention of Gulli and his five sons.[18] Thus, it is tempting to assume that the editor or one of his staff members made up the verse, including the interpretation, in order to create some vivid symbols of the Nazis' concept of the struggling Nordic Germanic peasants who gladly sacrificed their lives on the battlefields, be it at home or abroad. In this context he justified Bur's "difference" by referring to another Nordic virtue: work and service at home. He was the peasant tilling the soil, the necessary complement to the warrior brothers.

Under the topic of "Heroes of the Nordic Race" another Reader even went so far as to include Spartan proverbs and tales about such Greek heroes as Heracles, Daedalus and Icarus, Hector, Achilles, and Odysseus while appraising their "Nordic heroic" qualities.[19] Interspersed among such heroic tales were sayings by Nazi leaders whose words seemed to presuppose a continuity from the "Nordic Hellenes" to the National Socialist Regime. In one of the Readers, Hitler's own words underlined Germany's absolute need for peasants, at the present and also in the future: "That our folk can exist without cities, we know from German history, but it is impossible to imagine that Germany could exist without the peasant."[20] Often quoted in this context were also Sohnrey's poem, beginning with the lines: "Peasant fist and peasant wit,/ Although seldom praised,/ Are our country's source of strength,/ Our victory and power. . . ,[21] or the anonymous *Niedersachsenlied* (Song of Lower Saxony):

> From the Weser to the Elbe,
> From the Mountains to the Sea,
> We are the sturdy bulwarks:
> The sons of Saxony are we.
>
> Strong as our oak trees,
> Eternally we stand
> When the storms are sweeping
> Across the German land.[22]

In both cases, the "peasant poems" are more than samples of local color literature to be placed in the "home parts" of the Readers, as they symbolize the concept of the working and fighting German peasantry that constituted the very core of the Nazi ideology. The oak tree became symbolic of the peasantry, for the Nazis perceived in it the same "eternal" and stable element of Germandom.

Plate 47
"Peasant Strength: Free on German Soil"
(Illustration from a School Reader)

It was, as one Reader stated it, "the hand of the eternal peasant" that had become the symbol of Germany's hope for the future.[23]

Sometimes the German peasant was portrayed in contrast to the Jew. In the children's journal *Hilf-Mit*, for example, which was used as a supplementary reading text in the elementary schools, a number of stories depict the peasant as a blond Aryan superman characterized by honesty and diligence, while showing the Jew as a despicable "subhuman," a usurper and a thief.[24] In the *Reichslesebuch* such a portrayal of stereotypes was relatively rare, as Rust's guidelines aimed at developing in children pride in their folk heritage rather than racial hatred of "aliens" in an overt manner. On the other hand, editors would sometimes include selections of older German literature (taken out of context) that portrayed the Jew as a filthy solicitor craving for nothing but money. A case in point is a passage from Wilhelm Raabe's famous work *Der Hungerpastor* (*The Hunger Pastor*) which was cited in 1943 in the *Deutsches Lesebuch für Volksschulen* (*German Reader for Elementary Schools*), obviously not for literary but for purely ideological reasons.[25] In Readers for the secondary schools, too, there were occasional anti-semitic quotations by Hitler, Himmler, and other Nazi leaders, and even by Luther, Schiller, Arndt, de Lagarde, Treitschke, Moltke, Chamberlain, and Langbehn.[26] The Nazis calculated that if such biased views were subtly interspersed with folklore and literature that mainly appealed to a feeling of national pride, or that expressed the need for a folk community, they would be more effective in the long run than if they would make up the bulk of the Readers' contents.

Many more stories in the Readers, for example, portrayed the peasant as a colonist and settler in his plight to defend Germandom abroad. Stories of this kind seldom suggested that the Germans first drove away the native population before they called upon the German peasant to settle the newly won "living space" in Eastern Europe. Neither did they mention that German peasants were sometimes forced to leave their homeland to settle in the east. Instead the reading selections preferred to portray the settlers as American pioneers, the only difference being that the Germans moved eastwards instead of westwards. Moreover, the Nazis pretended that the farmland which the peasants now inhabited had been nothing but a wasteland prior to their arrival, thus giving them all of the credit for having produced the rich harvest which the land would miraculously yield after they had worked it with the spade.

In the following story, a group of German peasants finally arrive at their place of destination far in the east. To all appearances, however, the promised land looks like a great disappointment: there is nothing but barren grassland, all scorched and brown, and only in the far distance a little rivulet cuts its way through a canyon. "It's a lost Paradise," exclaims one of the peasants, while looking about very pessimistically. "When Adam and Eve were driven out of Paradise by an angel, they certainly couldn't have found more thistles and thorns than what we find here!" It is Bellmann, their leader, however, who straightens them out by calling upon their "peasant honor," their German pride in work, and their spirit of determination in spite of all adversities:

> Suddenly he threw himself upon the earth, clasped the soil with both of his hands and called out: "All, all of this shall be ours? Shall all of this belong to us? All of it—as far and wide as we can plow the soil? Men! Do you realize what that means? Weren't you all poor and without land at home? And weren't there fences all around and border markers at every corner? And wherever you walked, didn't the landowners whistle after you and chase you away? Free is God's earth, and the land belongs to all, if not inside of Germany then in Russia," he said, while jumping back on his feet.[27]

The story goes on to tell how the peasants are moved to tears by Bellmann's speech, and how suddenly they begin to see everything in a new light. Without hesitating much longer, they take up their spades with renewed vigor and start digging, so as to prepare the land for their new settlement. It appears that the sentimental appeal of the story was intended to build up a warm feeling for the "good earth" in general and especially for the German peasants in the east.

A number of nonfiction writings, too, were used in the Readers to explain to children the German need for "living space" in Eastern Europe. Sometimes, essays would point out that the Nordic Germanic "ancestors" with their self discipline and spirit of determination had given an example of how in times of trouble they had all united across the borders in order to fight together. Thus, the *Deutsches Lesebuch* (*German Reader*) of 1940 reminded students: "In the memory of our great forefathers, we, too, should take up the challenge and accomplish great deeds in the future,[28] which echoed Hitler's own words to German youth: "Don't ever forget that man's right to possess (and till) his own land is the holiest right on earth!"[29] The *Handbuch für die Hitler Jugend* (*Handbook for the Hitler Youth*) explained that territorial conquests in Eastern Europe were nothing but attempts to "repossess" the lands that formerly had belonged to the German culture areas. Culture areas it defined as areas in which there was still evidence of German or Germanic folklore, the German language, German customs, traditions, architecture, art, music, or "national character." Young people were told that it was not only morally justified to claim such areas, but that it was Germany's "holy duty" to do so at any price.[30] What Germany, as a unified nation under Hitler, now attempted to accomplish with pride was to unify also all of the scattered German settlements abroad while "Germanizing" the very soil on which they happened to be established. One Reader put this quest into a poetic form that resembled the Old German poem of Merseburg, generally referred to as the *Merseburger Zaubersprüche* (*Magic Formulae of Merseburg*). The very imitation of the rhythm of this well known verse emphatically underlined Hitler's "will" to fuse together the scattered German colonies:

Borderland Oath
Folk join folk,
Blood join blood,
Flame join flame:
Rise to the sky, holy embers,
Move on from tribe to tribe!

Folk join folk—
A stream of sacrifices
Shall unite all hearts!
High above the German dome
The sun of God shall rise.[31]

In the Old German poem, the God Wodan had tried to cure a broken leg of Balder's colt by chanting:

Leg join leg,
Blood join blood,
Limb join limb,
As if they were glued together![32]

No leg is to be healed in the Nazis' poem, but the scattered "tribes" are to be welded together: "Blood join blood. . . " The new references to the moving flame, the holy embers, and the rising sun hint at Balder as much as at Hitler prophesying a better life to come. In this context the "German dome" emerges as a symbol of Greater Germany itself.

The Nordic Germanic peasant very frequently appeared in the Readers as a warrior, be it as a knight of the Middle Ages, a soldier of the peasant wars, a hero of World War I, or a fighting youth in the dawn of the National Socialist movement. In the reading selection entitled "Langemarck 1914," there is an example of what the author himself called "an apocalyptic dream of Nordic Germanic dimensions." Amidst a surprise attack, just when thousands of hand grenades seemed to explode at once to set the sky on fire, a broad line of soldiers moved forward horizontally as if drawn by an invisible force. As they marched ahead, step by step, they sang the German national anthem, and in the darkness they appeared "as if they were creatures of the Nordic sagas, with glowing faces, burning eyes . . . " Gradually, their song faded away as one by one tumbled to the ground: "Voice upon voice became silent, as forehead after forehead sank forward and downward upon the wet earth."[33]

Another fighting hero who did not acknowledge defeat was Lieutenant Schlageter, who, as the Nazis put it, was treacherously killed by a "stab in the back"—like the legendary Siegfried: "All of us will die eventually in one way or another; but only one met his death like this: they bound him to a post and kicked him from behind. Later, an officer still placed the mouth of his pistol at

Plate 48
"BEFORE US LIES GERMANY"
(Flag Citations)

his temple, for the firing squad alone couldn't do the job . . . "[34] The author tells how Schlageter had been a peasant's son. Raised in the Black Forest, he had descended from the mountain on horseback; a blond and strong fellow, innocent at heart, pure and proud: the very image of his ancestors . . . It appears to have been no coincidence that the editor placed a poem entitled "Siegfried—Hagen" right after the Schlageter story, beginning with the lines:

> Hero with the golden hair
> And the heavy sword . . . [35]

In this way, he first of all raised the fate of Schlageter to mythical dimensions, for the whole nation had mourned for Siegfried and sworn revenge when he was treacherously killed in the forest. The political and ideological dimensions to both he provided by including in the volume references to the "stab in the back" that Germany had suffered by the Peace Treaty of Versailles—an unjust treatment that called for nothing but retribution. The logic behind such a grouping of stories, legends, and historical accounts was to justify Germany's overt acts of aggression, wherever they might occur, on the basis that war was needed to restore political justice to the German nation and to raise the German people's pride that assumedly had been trampled into the dust.

Death and injustice called for action in the name of revenge. This was also the message of a story recorded in the form of "diary entries" by Joseph Goebbels, Reich Minister of Propaganda. A Reader of 1939 cited these entries possibly in an attempt to bring home the message to German youth that their fate, too, was the fate of Norkus and the nation. The very style of the diary entries simulates the terse language of the sagas that tell of heroes who knew how to face death:

The Hitler Youth Norkus

January 24, 1932:

In Moabit, a little boy of the Hitler Youth was stabbed to death.

January 26.

I pass by the same place where he was slain, and I still recognize the imprint of a small bloody hand on the wall next to which he died.

January 29.

On an ice cold day, we carry the Hitler Youth Norkus to his grave. My heart overflows when I speak to the children and the men who have gathered around the small coffin. The father of the boy is brave beyond all measure. A simple worker, ash gray in his face, he raises his hand during the Horst Wessel song and sings with wrath and bitter pride: "*High Raise the Flag!*"[36]

As a narrator, Goebbels is sentimentally involved in the story ("My heart overflows . . . "), yet his economic description of Norkus' death and burial, and his reference to the "ash gray face" of the father singing defiantly the Horst Wessel song, clearly betray his attempt to sketch in Norkus' fate the fate of the

Plate 49
Siegfried in a School Reader:
A Symbol of Germandom, Fearlessness, and Strength

Nordic peasant warrior. Reich Youth Leader Baldur von Schirach once wrote: "When our German children say: 'Herbert Norkus,' then more is involved than a mere naming of a single human being whose fate has been told . . . This little comrade has become a *mythos* of *our young nation*, the symbol of a martyr for all of our youth who bear the name of the Hitler Youth."[37]

Just as Schlageter and Norkus emerged in the Readers as new archetypes of the German hero whose image was formed on the model of the saga hero, so Hitler himself appeared like the risen Siegfried, or like the still older image of the Nordic Germanic "ancestors." Will Vesper clearly referred to this ancient legacy when he wrote in his poem about the *Führer*:

> May it come alive again,
> This ancient custom of forefathers' days:
> There rises the *Führer*
> From the midst of the people . . . [38]

Vesper called him *Führer* and *Herzog* alternately. *Herzog*, (duke), in the Germanic sense, referred to the leader in battles who rode out ahead of the army. Thus, Vesper, like many other poets of the Nazi period, raised Hitler to an archetypal image of a warrior who had come to lead the German nation toward justice. Vesper closed the poem on the lines:

> He who led his followers in battle
> Was called the *Herzog* of the Reich.
> *Herzog* of the Reich you are,
> This is how we see it.
> For a long time already
> You have lived in the heart of the nation![39]

Words such as these invoked the image of Odin on horseback followed by his warriors in the great battles of Asgard. Viewed from this perspective, Hitler, the *Führer* and *Herzog*, only seemed to continue what Odin had begun long ago.

The National Socialist ideology clearly emerged in the German Readers of every brand, in spite of some variations that still persisted after Rust had introduced the *Reichslesebuch*. Above all, the theme of the heroic German and Germanic peasantry provided the link between past and present, and also between poetry, fiction, and nonfiction selections. The *mythos* of the peasant warrior helped editors and writers to fulfill Rust's requirements for the themes of blood and soil, honor and loyalty, service and sacrifice, and struggle and work. Above all, however, it provided the very source from which the Nazis gathered their ideals of the leadership and followership principle on which the very concept of folk education was built. The Readers projected these ideals in various forms, so as to lead children and youth toward the National Socialist folk community of the future.

Plate 50
"Marching Toward the Great Future"
(From a School Reader)

NOTES

1. Dietrich Strothmann, *Nationalsozialistische Literaturpolitik; Ein Beitraq zur Publizistik im Dritten Reich* (Bonn, Bouvier, 1968), pp. 58-62.

2. *Ibid.*

3. Erich Löffler, "Das deutsche Lesebuch und die Jugendschriftenarbeit" *Jugendschriften-Warte* 41, 1 (January, 1936) 18-21.

4. Peter Aley, *Jugendliteratur im Dritten Reich. Dokumente und Kommentare* (Hamburg, Verlag für Buchmarktforschung, 1969), pp. 90-92. See also Peter Hasubek, *Das deutsche Lesebuch in der Zeit des Nationalsozialismus: Ein Beitrag zur Literaturpädagogik zwischen 1933 und 1945* (Hannover, Hermann Schroedel Verlag, 1972), pp. 64-69. Some of the titles were: *Hirts Deutsches Lesebuch (Hirt's German Reader)*, published in Breslau; *Lesebuch für Hauptschulen (Readers for Main Schools)*, published by the Office of Education, and *Von Deutscher Art (Of German Kind)*, published at Frankfurt.

5. Eduard Rothemund, "Das Jugendbuch in der deutschen Schule" in Bernhard Payr and Hans Georg Otto, ed., *Das deutsche Jugendbuch: 4 Vorträge gehalten auf der Jugendbuchwoche in Bayreuth* (Munich, Deutscher Volksverlag, 1942), p. 68.

6. *Ibid.*, pp. 68-70

7. Löffler, 18-21.

8. Ernst Krieck, *Nationalsozialistische Erziehung* (Series: *Grundlage, Aufbau und Wirtschaftsordnung des nationalsozialistischen Staates*) (Berlin, Industrieverlag Spaethe und Linde, 1938).

9. Rothemund, p. 68.

10. *Ibid.*

11. *Ibid.*, Rothemund commented that the Reader was to be at the core of the school curriculum, thus forming the nucleus of all curricular activity. For this reason, he felt that it was "of fundamental importance for the study of literature in the public schools."

12. Part III of the Reader *Von Deutscher Art*, for example, involved the following topics: Jests and Adventures; The Struggle with Nature; Hunters, Shepherds, Fishermen and Peasants; Knights and Mercenaries; Heroes of the Germanic and German saga; Icelandic Men, Vikings, Hanseatic Brothers; Fight for the *Reich* and the Folk; German Outposts of Duty. Part V of the same Reader included the topics: German Living Space, Landscape and Tribes; Germans in the World; Of German Work; Contemplation; Leaders Fighting for Nation and Folk; Heroism of the People.

13. Corresponding citations can be found in most school Readers for practically all grade levels. See also N.S.D.A.P. (National Socialist German Workers' Party) eds., *Freude, Zucht und Glaube; Handbuch für die kulturelle Arbeit im Lager* (Potsdam, Voggenreiter, 1937), pp. 30-34.

14. Johann Wolfgang von Goethe, "Geh, gehorche meinem Winken" *Von deutscher Art; Ein Lesebuch für höhere Schulen*, Part I (Frankfurt/Main, Verlag Otto Salle, 1939). The reference to volume numbers rather than to specific grade levels allowed for a certain flexibility in the use of these school Readers.

15. *Das ewige Deutschland: Ein deutsches Lesebuch für die achte Klasse* (Frankfurt/Main, Diesterweg Verlag, 1941).

16. "Das Schicksal eines Vikingerstammes" *Von deutscher Art* III, p. 176.

17. *Ibid.*

18. There are sagas and myths about Gulli, Halfdan, Asmundar and Bur, for example, but they are unrelated. See Jan de Vries, *Altnordische Literaturgeschichte* I and II (Berlin, Walter de Gruyter and Company, 1964).

19. *Von deutscher Art*, Part II, pp. 140-155. Some writers at that time emphasized the contrast between "Homer's weeping heroes" and what they called "the masculine spirit of the Nordic heroes." See Hermann Harder, *Das germanische Erbe in der deutschen Dichtung: Ein Überblick* (Potsdam, Voggenreiter, 1939). On the other hand, Alfred Rosenberg, in *Der Mythus des zwanzigsten Jahrhunderts* (Berlin, Verlag der N.S.D.A.P., 1935), p. 289, developed the idea that Norse culture influenced Greek culture.

20. Adolf Hitler, cited in the chapter "Heimaterde" in *Von deutscher Art*, Part I, p. 161.

21. Heinrich Sohnrey, "Bauernfaust und Bauerngeist" *Von deutscher Art*, Part I, p. 162.

22. "Niedersachsenlied" *Von deutscher Art*, Part II, p. 59.

23. Karl Heinrich Waggerl "Bauernnot" *Von deutscher Art*, Part V, pp. 105-106.

24. The *Hilf-Mit* children's journal was published by the National Socialist Teachers Association, and it appeared as a regular supplement to the journal *Die Volksschule*. A highly prejudiced story about the German peasant and the Jew was published under the title "Der Bauernkönig von Hessen" *Hilf-Mit: Illustrierte deutsche Kinderzeitung* I (1937) 9. The author, Dr. von Leers, a famous agronomist at that time, presents his case as if the Jews were guilty of all the injustice experienced by the peasants. "Peasants, wake up!" the story opens, "The Jew holds you in his claws! Defend yourselves!" The story as a whole is representative of the Nazis' racial bias, as it caricatures the Jew not only as a usurper shunning work, but even as a "cursed bug." The school Readers treated the racial question frequently in terms of genealogical research, "family histories," and history studies. Consult also Hasubek, pp. 52-53.

25. Hasubek, p. 59.

26. *Ibid.*, pp. 58-59.

27. "Die Ankunft der deutschen Siedler an der Wolga" *Von deutscher Art* Part III, pp. 256-258.

28. Fritz Martini, "Der Geist der germanischen Heldendichtung" *Deutsches Lesebuch für höhere Lehranstalten*, Part VI. (Bochum, Verlag und Lehrmittel-Anstalt F. Kamp, 1940), pp. 113-114.

29. Adolf Hitler, "Das ganze Deutschland soll es sein!" (Preface cited from *Mein Kampf*) in *Der Lebensraum des deutschen Volkes* (Series: *Deutscher Wille; Schriften für die deutsche Jugend*), (Berlin Verlag der N.S.D.A.P., n.d.), p. 1.

30. Harwood L. Childs, ed., *The Nazi Primer: Official Handbook for the Schooling of the Hitler Youth* (New York, Harper & Brothers, 1938), pp. 4-6.

31. Heinrich Gutherlet, "Grenzlandschwur" *Von deutscher Art*, Part III, p. 159.

32. The "magic spell" is typical of the kind of poetry recited during National Socialist festivals and celebrations. It has also been referred to as the "blood and soil mysticism."

33. Hermann Timmermann, "Langemarck" *Von deutscher Art*, Part V, pp. 211-213.

34. Ulrich Sander, "Schlageter" *Ibid.*, pp. 242-245.

35. Josef Weinheber, "Siegfried—Hagen" *Ibid.*, p. 245.

36. Joseph Goebbels "Hitlerjunge Norkus" *Von deutscher Art*, Part III, p. 166.

37. Baldur von Schirach, "Vorwort" in Gerhardt Mond, *Herbert Norkus: Das Tagebuch der Kameradschaft* (Stuttgart, Beusselkietz, 1936), pp. i-ii.

38. Will Vesper, "Dem Führer" *Hirts deutsches Lesebuch für Jungen* Part I (Breslau, Ferdinand Hirt Verlag, 1939). The same poem is also included in *Von deutscher Art*, Part I, which indicates its popularity among the editors of school Readers.

39. *Ibid.*

12

Puppets, Plays, and Politics

The Nazis promoted children's plays on a much broader scale than had ever been tried before in Germany. Through dramatic activities of various kinds they hoped to foster in children an emotional involvement in the German folk community, its heritage, and its political goals. In a way, they seemed to implement the theories of Severin Rüttgers in the twenties that had called for stage adaptations of folklore for the sake of strengthening in young people a feeling of patriotism and a desire for national unity.[1] Of course, Rüttgers could not have foreseen the extremes of which the Nazis would be capable in their pursuit of ideological goals.

The beginnings of the revival of Volkish drama in the German public schools were still balanced by the fact that the National Socialist Teachers Association not only recommended the use of ideological-political plays but also those based on older literature and old German and Nordic Germanic folk traditions. About three-fourths of the plays recommended in the *Jugendschriften-Warte* between 1933 and 1934 were adaptations of folklore and selected older works of literature.[2] The Hitler Youth Organization, by contrast, pursued a more radical break with the past from the very outset by focusing attention on plays of the newer type.[3]

The ideological-political plays recommended by the National Socialist Teachers Association, as well as by the Hitler Youth Organization, were meant primarily to develop in children faith in the Third Reich. The themes were much more abstract, such as Germany's struggle toward nationhood, the preservation of Germandom abroad, the destiny of the German peasantry, or the heroes of German history and of the National Socialist movement. They frequently aimed at mass participation, while depending on large groups of choral speakers. The play *Deutschland steht auf (Germany Arises)*, for example, called for one hundred children for the choir, yet only four actors. The threadbare plot that held the play together still provided for a certain unity of action, but in many respects the play resembled a ritual, or a cult celebration rather than a play.[4]

Many of the plays included on the recommended lists after 1933 revolved around Norse mythology and medieval folk traditions, and thus might be grouped under the category of the folklore adaptations, although some of these had been transformed into symbolic expressions of National Socialism. In the play *Am Johannesfeuer (At the Fire of St. John's Day)* the traditional Nordic fire symbols evolved into symbols of life and the national strength of the Third Reich. This effect was also achieved by the play *Heiliges Licht (Holy Light)*, in which the Nordic rune of the sun, the wheel cross, came to symbolize the heroic deeds of Charlemagne and Wittekind, both of whom emerged not only as models of German but also of Nordic heroism. Characteristically, Charlemagne was presented not as a Frankish emperor but as the German *Kaiser*. The legend of Perceval found its adaptation in *Herzeleyde (Herzeleyde)*, a play named for Perceval's mother. She was not the same character as the medieval poet Wolfram von Eschenbach had portrayed her, however, but a Nordic model of female strength. The editors of the *Jugendschriften-Warte* saw in her "a symbol of all German mothers in their attitude toward fate."[5] In other words, the playwright remodelled Herzeleyde in accordance with the Nazis' concept of motherhood, thus transforming her from a convincing unique character into a bloodless National Socialist symbol.

On the whole, the leaders of the Hitler Youth Organization were less critical of the artistic qualities of a given play than were the leaders of the National Socialist Teachers Association. In addition, they were not only tolerant of themes underlining a racial bias, but they even promoted them as an integral part of their ideological indoctrination program.

The members of the National Socialist Teachers Association, many of whom had attained a higher education through colleges and universities, could not so easily overlook the fact that the newer plays often lacked art and a power of conviction the more they turned into mouthpieces of shallow propaganda. Even the more fanatic ideologists among them demanded a stronger emotional appeal founded not on rational calculation but on a thorough appreciation of Volkish literature. Thus, they appealed to the playwrights to produce plays which could be taken seriously as an art form, and to turn for their inspiration toward such writers as Wilhelm Raabe or Hanns Johst, for example, and also to German and Nordic Germanic folklore.[6]

As it took time to write such plays, the National Socialist Teachers Association in the meanwhile promoted many plays that had been composed in pre-Nazi days.[7] Among these were a great number that represented adaptations of German folktales (mostly by the Brothers Grimm), German legends, medieval chapbooks, and also old German Christmas pageants, and puppet plays. With the exception of the old German Christmas pageants, these plays were retained, with some ideological adjustments, throughout the Nazi period, as they made up an essential part of what the Nazis considered Volkish literature. It is for this reason that in 1934 the *Jugendschriften-Warte* still continued to include among

Plate 51
The Folktale Play Remains Popular at Christmas Time

the officially recommended plays twelve traditional old German Christmas pageants with clear references to Mary, Joseph, and the Christ Child in the manger.[8] Only gradually were such plays replaced by others that focused entirely on German and Nordic Germanic folk customs or on blueprints for solstice celebrations in the National Socialist interpretation.

At the beginning of the Nazi Regime, the old puppet plays were still re-printed and performed in the traditional manner. The main protagonist of the *Kasperletheater* (Kasper Theater) was Kasper, who with his long nose, his fool's cap and his quick wit had entertained German children since the Middle Ages. Kasper never vanished from the stage during the Nazi period, but the adjust-ments made to his characteristic attitudes and values were quite striking. It did not take the Nazis long to realize that the *Kasperletheater*, with its strong emo-tional appeal, especially for younger children, could be turned into an effective medium of ideological indoctrination. In 1935, Hugo Wippler published a study that was officially sponsored by the National Socialist Teachers Associa-tion. It concerned the use of the puppet show within the context of German folk education, and its recommendations were addressed to German teachers, pup-peteers, marionette players, and youth leaders. In summary, Wippler urged the following "adjustments" to the traditional puppet plays:

1. Strengthen race consciousness, and omit characters representing alien races.
2. Omit characters representing the guardian angel or the devil.
3. Emphasize the need for strong actions.
4. Emphasize folklore material, such as plots based on folktales, myths, legends, sagas, etc.
5. Promote the community spirit.
6. Abstain from ridiculing the working class, the policeman, the army, or life under the present regime.
7. Promote enthusiasm for some contemporary German achieve-ments, such as transportation, vehicles, machines, etc.[9]

The most obvious adjustments referred to an omission of characters that betrayed the Christian influence on the *Kasperletheater*, namely the guardian angel and the devil. Instead of dealing with them in the customary way, Kasper was expected to rely on his own resources. Of course, it was now legitimate to send the policeman and even the army to his aid, whenever he needed them—provided they were represented in as honorable a fashion as the guardian angel had been. The devil was easily replaced by the figure of a robber or a dragon, although puppeteers and marionette players now had to be cautious in their use of words. Undoubtedly, the prescribed task of promoting "enthusiasm for con-temporary achievements" and the German folk community, stifled their sense of humor, and their free use of irony and wit. Customarily, no character in the traditional puppet shows had been exempt from ridicule, for as in the compar-able English "Punch and Judy" shows, it was the everyday aspect of life in all its vitality that had served as the basis for exaggeration and humor. To elevate the ordinary to the level of the sublime and therefore beyond ridicule meant to deny children the very source of laughter to which they had been accustomed.[10]

Plate 52
Ideological Blueprints for Traditional Puppet Shows
(Nineteenth Century Illustration from Hobrecker's Anthology of 1944)

In 1936, the National Socialist Teachers Association also placed similar restrictions on actors and directors of children's theaters. It demanded that folktales, not fantasies, should serve as the basis of plays performed on stage, and that these folktales should be German in every respect. For this reason, they urged teachers and theater directors to avoid "Hollywood clichés" under all circumstances, to replace the French ballets by German folk dances, and to use as background scenery German landscapes (preferably the German fairy tale forest), or images related to Norse mythology. The Association stated these demands in the name of good taste, the unity of genuine folk art, and the seriousness of the German folktale.[11] All too obviously, however, the repeated request for Germanic characters and traditions betrayed the spirit of national exclusiveness which at that time also dominated their folktale interpretations. A number of additional rules restricting the use of literary fairy tales, as well as the actors' customary spontaneous interactions with the young audiences during the performances gave a clear indication of the Nazis' growing imposition of censorship on children's theater.[12]

Within the various restrictions as set out by the National Socialist Teachers Association, however, teachers were still relatively free to make use of traditional puppet shows and plays that previous generations of German children had enjoyed. At least, this held for those plays that the Nazis did not consider to be in direct conflict with their ideology. In a recommended list of puppet plays in 1934, the Association still included such titles as *Kasper und der Teufel (Kasper and the Devil)* and *Kasper und die Prinzessin (Kasper and the Princess)*, for example, and at Christmas time the German theaters, at least until the beginning of the war, sponsored performances based on Grimms' folktales, without changing the characters' speeches into political propaganda.[13]

Plays sponsored by the leaders of the Hitler Youth Organization were another matter entirely. Racial prejudice became a dominant theme in many of them, as these leaders were more fanatic in their application of ideological demands as stated in the Hitler Youth Commandments. At the same time, they showed less hesitation than did German teachers and philologists in distorting the national folk heritage solely for the sake of promoting National Socialist ideals. In a speech to the Hitler Youth assembled to celebrate National Theater Week in 1937, Reich Theater Director Rainer Schlösser stated their radical orientation quite bluntly when he said:

> We know today that art and life within a nation are closely interrelated. Political leadership, art, and defense, essentially move into the very same direction. Just as Germany, as a nation, has asserted herself as a big power . . . ,so the will to power has stirred in all of us. After having shaken off all alien influences, we will assert ourselves again as a spiritual force of great magnitude.[14]

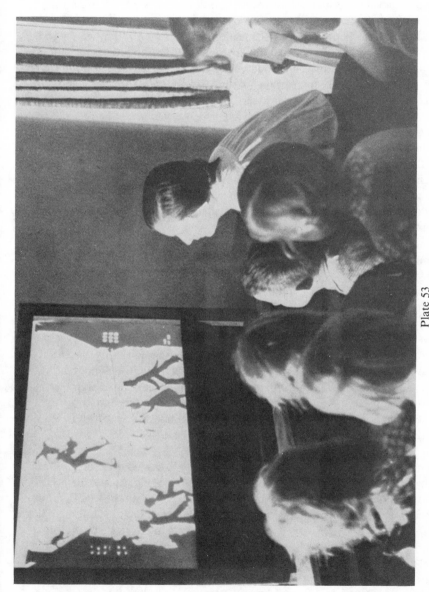

Plate 53
"The Pranks of Merry Tyll":
Medieval Folk Themes in Shadow Plays

By "alien influences" he meant Jews, Communists, and all those forces that had dragged Germany into a whirlpool of "decadence" for which the Nazis knew only one remedy: German folk art with a National Socialist interpretation.

Plays and the texts of puppet shows printed for use in the Hitler Youth recreation camps betray how far the leaders of this organization would go in applying racial values. In one play, Kasper is still the leading character, but his role has been changed to accommodate the Party's didacticism. The good characters are not only of German origin but they also represent the "blood and soil" image: the Peasant and his daughter, Grethel. The bad characters are the Dragon, who is portrayed as a Jew in disguise (by the name of Isidor) and the Red Commissioner, portrayed as a Communist who plays the feigned role of a helpful policeman. The Peasant is in despair, as Grethel has been abducted. The Red Commissioner proposes that the Peasant should give him a sackful of gold to deliver to the Dragon. With this gold he would convince the Dragon to return Grethel to him. The peasant agrees to the plan and gives him the gold willingly. Fortunately, Kasper finds out, just in time, that the Dragon is really Isidor with whom the Commissioner hopes to share the gold.

The following quote represents the editor's summary that even includes comments on the children's anticipated reactions to the show:

> And now, fate takes its course. Just when Isidor appears on the stage with the Red Commissioner, still continuing in his discussion with him on how they will share the gold and get Grethel out of the hiding place, Kasper emerges from behind a bush where he has secretly overheard their plotting. (The children in the audience quiver with joy!). And: "Whack!"—He hits Isidor over the head with his club. (The children in the audience holler with excitement.) Isidor now shakes and trembles. (What a great *national* hero he is!). Kasper, however, grabs him firmly by the collar and then gives him a big kick with his boot, so that Isidor flies high up into the air—high, high up, as far as Palestine! . . . [15]

The summary continues by stating that the Red Commissioner, disguised as a Dragon, returns Grethel to the Peasant along with the gold. Kasper then vigorously attacks the Dragon with his toothbrush and knocks out the Red Commissioner in the process. In conclusion, he carries the remains of the Dragon to the Museum of Natural History. The editor comments in reference to the actual performance of the play: "Kasper should not be portrayed merely as a jolly good fellow, but also as a character who knows how to deal with the problems of life in the right way."[16]

In pre-Nazi days, too, Kasper had made active use of his club, whenever the occasion arose to defeat a dragon, a robber or a wicked witch, but usually this had happened in the interest of morality, not in the name of racial prejudice and ideological warfare. This difference was not simply one of degree, but involved the very nature of ethics under the Nazi Regime.

The theaters of the future, as the Nazis envisioned them, were already implemented during the Third Reich, namely in the form of the so-called *Thing-theater* (*Thing* theaters, named after the old Germanic law courts). These were meant to appeal to all age groups, adults and children alike. As open-air theaters, they were inspired partially by the Greek amphitheaters and partially by Wagner's Nordic operas. By 1935, the Nazis had constructed twenty-five of these theaters in Bavaria alone, but they planned to build four hundred throughout Germany, so as to stage large-scale shows that would lead to well rehearsed audience involvement. Many of these plays were based on Norse mythology and German history, both of which emerged as symbols of National Socialism. As in the Nazi rituals, every move was to be carefully calculated and controlled, from the opening speeches to the concluding songs and the singing of the national anthem.[17]

As early as 1935, Professor Krieck, the Nazis' chief ideological theorist, considered the strong emotional impact of the *Thingtheater* as one of the most

Plate 54
Kasperle Prior to 1937: Still Fighting with the Devil

Plate 55a
Kasperle after 1937 (as Viewed by the Hitler Youth): Fighting the "Dragon"

Plate 55b
. . . and the Jew!

important factors in German folk education, primarily because it helped to get children actively involved in the German folk community.[18] Maria Glanz, author of *Das Puppenspiel und sein Publikum (The Puppet Play and Its Audience)* defined in similar terms the ideological significance of the puppet plays when she wrote in 1941:

> A new Germany has arisen, and with it, our faith in what is genuine, simple, and original—a Germany in which we have come to realize once more the true meaning of the folk community that is ready to experience the stage spectacle and to believe in it. In an environment of such a receptivity, the puppet plays have to fulfill a cultural-political task.[19]

Comments such as these affirmed a national policy in which plays for all ages were considered as educational tools in the service of the German folk community.

On the whole, the National Socialist Teachers Association pursued a more moderate course in carrying out the "cultural-political task" of the Third Reich. Throughout the Nazi period, recommended lists of plays issued by the Association included a number of older works based on the German folk tradition. This trend continued even during the war years when many more of the newer works were available. We may explain this relatively balanced approach by the Association's general conception of Volkish literature and its "positive approach" to censorship and propaganda, which resulted in a greater emphasis on themes based on folklore and national roots than on those promoting racial prejudice. On the other hand, the Hitler Youth Organization selected predominantly the newer plays and showed no hesitation in distorting traditional plays and characters in the interest of a crude racial propaganda.

The general direction of both organizations was to replace children's plays gradually by rituals and festivals for children and youth.[20] This meant that in the future the "New Order" of regimented mass performances might have replaced even the traditional forms of plays—not just their meanings. In such a context, art and tradition would have been subordinated entirely to the symbolic expression of National Socialism.

NOTES

1. Dr. Rudolph Murtfeld, "Severin Rüttgers als Erwecker des Sinnes für volkhafte Dichtung" *Jugendschriften-Warte* 44, 1 (January, 1939), 6-10. The

author makes special reference to Rüttgers' promotion of Volkish literature through plays and dramatic activities.

2. "Neue Spiele für die Schul-und Jugendbühne" *Jugendschriften-Warte* 39, 4 (April, 1934), 27-31. See also "Neue Bücher zum Schul- und Laienspiel" *Jugendschriften-Warte* 38, 7 (July, 1933), 56-57.

3. Plays for the members of the Hitler Youth Organization were published periodically in the journal *Die Spielschar*, and reference notes to plays were listed in *Wille und Macht.*

4. "Neue Spiele . . . ", 30.

5. *Ibid.*, 31.

6. See "Schul- und Jugendbühne: Neue Spiele aus der Zeit und für die Zeit" *Jugendschriften-Warte* 38, 11 (November, 1933), 85-86. The editor referred here to Joseph Goebbels' observation that it was not enough to promote German culture through marching bands.

7. Some of these appeared in reprints, yet others were also newly composed in the traditional manner.

8. "Neue Spiele . . . " The annotations make no reference whatever to National Socialism, but instead emphasize the traditional *German* character of the plays.

9. Hugo Wippler, quoted in Kurt Boehme, *Die deutsche Volksseele in den Kinderdichtungen* (issued by the Reich Organization of the National Socialist Party). (Berlin, Verlag der N.S.D.A.P., 1939), p. 39. One of the newer titles cited by Wippler was *Kasperspiele zur Gestaltung deutschen Gemeinschafts-lebens (Kasper Plays for Building the German Community Spirit).*

10. For a discussion of the traditional German puppet shows consult Inge-borg Haas, "Zur Geschichte des Kindertheaters" in Gerhard Haas, ed., *Kinder-und Jugendliteratur; Zur Typologie und* Funktion einer literarischen Gattung (Stuttgart, Reclam, 1976), pp. 435-465.

11. Fritz Bauer, "Das Stiefkind; Ein Gespräch zwischen dem Intendanten des Theaters Allstadt und Franz Bauer in Nürnberg" *Jugendschriften-Warte,* 41, 12 (December, 1936), 92. See in the same issue Friedrich Bonn, "Zur Kritik des Weihnachtsmärchens," 90-92. The interview by Bauer is so didactic that it appears to have been staged merely for the purpose of getting across to the readers the new cultural-political demands of the Party in regard to children's plays.

12. Compare the chapter on folktale interpretations. Aley observed that it was commonly used as a euphemism by the Nazis to exercise censorship under the pretext of fighting *Kitsch* in the interest of genuine German folk art. See Peter Aley, *Jugendliteratur im Dritten Reich: Dokumente und Kommentare* (Hamburg, Verlag für Buchmarktforschung, 1969), pp. 171-172.

13. "Neue Spiele . . . " 32.

14. "Der kulturelle Wille der Jugend" *Frankfurter Zeitung* (April 14, 1937). Consult also Dr. Rainer Schlösser, "Jugend und Dichtung" in *Der Autor* (Feb./

March, 1937), 5. Schlösser's official title was *Reichsdramaturg*. Since 1940 he also was in charge of the *Reichsstelle für Jugendliteratur*, the censorship office for youth literature that was attached to the Hitler Youth Organization. Consult the chapter on the system of censorship. The above mentioned Theater Week involved a total of 250,000 boys from the Hitler Youth throughout Germany.

15. Reichsjugendführung, ed., *Freude, Zucht, Glaube: Handbuch für die kulturelle Arbeit im Lager* (Potsdam, Voggenreiter, 1937), pp. 140-142.

16. *Ibid.*, p. 142.

17. In some of the *Thingtheater* runic stones were even erected next to the stage to emphasize the Nordic Germanic heritage of National Socialism. See Josef Wulf, ed., *Theater und Film im Dritten Reich* (Gütersloh, Sigbert Mohn Verlag, 1969), pp. 184-189. This documentation includes a number of bibliographical references to National Socialist publications pertaining to the *Thingtheater,*

18. Konrad Klug, "Erziehung zur Gemeinschaft im deutschen Thingspiel" in Ernst Krieck, ed., *Volk im Werden* 34, 3 (1935), Heft No. 8, 453-464.

19. Lucia Glanz, *Das Puppenspiel und sein Publikum* (Berlin, Stubenrauch, 1941), pp. 83-95.

20. The editorial statement in the *Jugendschriften-Warte* of 1933 already indicated this trend. See "Neue Spiele . . . " 30.

13
Volkish Rituals
for Children and Youth

In the rituals and celebrations which the Nazis sponsored for children of all ages, Norse mythology and all the old Germanic customs and traditions experienced a renaissance as never before. At the same time, they became festive occasions for the recital of the new poetry which reflected the past, and yet, prophetically also the future. The Nazis did not merely conceive of such events as staged "spectacles," but they hoped to promote through them a spirit of "total community involvement" based on deep faith in the *Führer*. In a handbook for elementary school teachers Dörner wrote in 1941 that the New Order of National Socialism had revived the original Germanic feeling for the rhythm and cycle of the sun year. Once again all Germans could rejoice in celebrating, as in by-gone days, the common heritage of customs binding together the folk community: "The living customs and traditions, together with our own experiences during times of struggle, are now the very sources of our rituals."[1]

The National Socialist calendar of events reflected two types of rituals celebrated annually. The first type indeed seemed to be founded in traditional folk customs, whereas the second one was more directly related to National Socialist heroes and events. The following outline, suggested by Dörner as a guide for teachers and Hitler Youth leaders, makes reference to both types of rituals, those rooted in the past, and those relevant to the present regime:

January 24:	Frederick the Great's Birthday
	Herbert Norkus was killed
	Flag Day
January 31:	Germany Arise!
	The March into the Reich
	Torchlight Processions
February and March:	Spring Festivals:
	Mardi Gras

First Day of Spring
Celebration of Light
Easter
Children's Festival

April 20:   *The Führer's Birthday*

May: May Tree
                 May 1: Youth Day (Assembly in the
                            Olympic Stadium, Berlin)
                 Folk Customs related to May
                     Labor Day

June 21:   Summer Solstice:
                     Fire and Fire Formulae
                     Solstice Customs
                     Solstice of the Young Team

September: Reich Party Day

October: Thanksgiving Day (Day of the Peasant)
                     Harvest Festivals
                     Harvest Customs

November: Memorial Month
                     November 9: Day of the Fallen Heroes
                     Celebration of Langemarck

December: Christmas Time
                     Poems by von Schirach
                     Christmas
                     Winter Solstice (poetry)
                     Celebration of the Solstice (outline)
                     Sayings
                     Peasant Customs at Christmas
                     The Art of Giving
                     Holy Night
                     Festival of the Family
                     "High Night Sky of the Clear Stars"[2] (song)

Judging by the literature which we analyzed in the chapter on school reading textbooks, Frederick the Great, as Prussia's disciplined "Soldier King," belonged as much to the Nazis' celebrated heroes as Herbert Norkus or the *Führer* himself. It is well known that both the workers' May Day parade and the National Socialist Youth Day in May had as little to do with Nordic Germanic folk customs as the celebration of Langemarck. All of these occasions would thus be part of the category of National Socialist celebrations in which references to the Third Reich would be expected.

On the other hand, the Nazis also transformed traditional folk festivals such as the light celebration in spring time, the summer solstice, the harvest festivals and the winter solstice into Nazi rituals. Thus, Dörner was only partially honest when he wrote that such occasions had become the very sources of the rituals celebrated in honor of the living customs and traditions. Essentially, the Nazis were not only very selective in their approach to tradition, but also utilitarian. Folklorist Strobel defined the National Socialist attitude toward the past more concisely by stating in a Party-sponsored guidebook for ideological training camps in 1941: "The age of a tradition is not enough. Important alone is its usefulness for the present and the future."[3] "Useful," in the Nazis' definition, meant that a custom might be used effectively on account of its emotional appeal to convey National Socialist symbols, so as to form young people's attitudes toward the "folk Reich" of the future. The traditional Christian festivals, such as Christmas, Easter, and Pentecost were considered useful only to the degree that they could be transformed into "German pagan customs" on the one hand and Nazi rituals on the other.

The perversion of values which arose from such a forced transformation was based on pseudo-scientific explanations by the Party leaders. The Nazis were too diplomatic merely to take away from the German people the traditional Christian holidays. While they tolerated existing traditions in the private sphere, they attached official statements to their blueprints for "Nordic Germanic folk celebrations" that were intended to help teachers explain to their students why the schools now celebrated the Solstice instead of Christmas. Rosenberg claimed that the Church had merely "adopted and integrated into her rites" what she had inherited from the myths and rituals of the Nordic Germanic ancestors. Therefore, it was only fair to restore the old customs that rightfully belonged to the people.[4] Other Party authorities commented that the very term *Weihnachten* (the German word for Christmas) had been derived from the words *geweihte Nächte* (blessed nights), which originally had designated the twelve nights before the Solstice (Balder's festival), when Odin and his army of warriors had come to earth, roaming on horseback through the countryside.[5] Some Church authorities were intelligent enough to recognize the true origin of their festivals, wrote Strobel in one of his handbooks on celebrations, and they were humble enough to give priority to the "light celebrations" of the ancestors over the Christian celebrations. He recalled that in a small German village at one time the pastor had lit the first candle for his Christmas tree in the church on the bonfire that had been lit in honor of Balder.[6]

A closer examination of the Nazis' blueprints, especially for the solstice celebrations, will show further that the celebrations were turned into solemn rituals with a very strong emotional appeal that were only partially geared toward a revival of old customs. By far the greater effort was spent on seeking a certain "relevance" of the old Nordic festivals to the present National Socialist Regime.

The summer solstice, according to a handbook for the public schools, was supposed to be celebrated with students in the outdoors, preferably in a valley or on a mountain top, outside of the city and under the open sky. The seriousness of the ritual was to be retained throughout, as it implied "a holy commitment to the spirit of life."[7] The following outline was suggested on behalf of the sequence of events:

The Summer Solstice

We are standing at right angles around a pile of logs.

Song for All:	"Let the Flag Fly in the Wind"
Speaker:	"Folk desires folk, Flame desires flame. Rise to the sky, holy flame, Move on from tribe to tribe.

Lighting of the Bonfire.

Speaker:	"Look, the Gate is Gleaming" (Poem by Baldur von Schirach)
Song for All:	"Rise, Flame, Rise"
A Comrade Speaks:	"The Meaning of the Solstice" (a short speech). Again, the fires shine brightly on the mountains. We have reached the summit of the year and glance backwards to past events and achievements. Many tasks have been completed, and many new ones have been given to us by the *Führer*. Let us move on to new goals . . . " Note: The speech should not deteriorate into a long lecture.

Drums	
Camp Leader:	"We remember those who have fallen in battle and in fighting for the National Socialist movement." One minute of silence. Three wreaths are thrown into the flames (made of oak leaves or branches of fir).
First Speaker:	"To those who have died in the great wars!"
Second Speaker:	"To those who have died in the German Revolution! To German youth, their initiative and dedication!"

Plate 56a

Plate 56b
THE SUMMER SOLSTICE:
Fire Leaps and Hymns to the *Führer*

Song for All:	"Here we stand loyally . . . "
Fire Leaps:	"We are the fire, we are the flame. We burn before Germany's altars. We carry the drums across the land: We are the fanfares of the battles." (After the fire has burned down, we step back from it and watch silently.)
Fire Watch (Vigil)	
	Quietly, boys and girls move back to camp.[8]

The nature of the speeches and the very selection of songs and poems for the occasion give little indication that Balder was the center of the ritual. To the contrary, all of them were geared toward certain aspects of National Socialism that were to be commemorated by this occasion. The poem "Folk desires folk" was meant to express the concept of national unity; von Schirach's poem employed the symbol of the "gleaming gate" in reference to Hitler's coming; the words spoken during the fire leaps (which used to be lovers' leaps) referred to the idea of sacrifice for the country ("We burn before Germany's altars"); the drums, the wreaths for the fallen soldiers, and the reminders of the "German Revolution" were intended primarily to lead the participating children toward a renewed oath of loyalty to the *Führer*. Thus, the song for all begins: "Here we stand loyally . . . " "We do not belong to ourselves," Himmler once addressed a group of the Hitler Youth celebrating the summer solstice, "but with our bodies, our souls, and our characters, we belong to the *Volk* alone. In order to place a seal on our commitment, we are gathered here today to take a vow of loyalty to that man who has restored to us freedom and honor. May our work be made holy through this flame."[9]

Practically all children's literature anthologies issued during the Third Reich included a large section on poetry to be used during the solstice celebrations.[10] In a strange way, most of them combined allusions to Norse mythology and the spirit of the "ancestors" with an appeal to fight for the idea of National Socialism. In a poem cited by Prestel, for example, the ancient "fire call" for the solstice is transformed into a battle cry of the Nordic warriors, and simultaneously, into a call for war in defense of the fatherland:

Fire Call

Glow, red fire!
Take your course
Through the land.
Burn in all German states.
Arouse all those

In need of courage.
Glow, red fire!

Burn, bright light!
Throw your flame
Into the darkness.
Light the path
For young and old.
Protect our victory.
Throw your flame, bright light!

Fly high, you sparks.
Fly high into time.
Announce battle and war
To all who quarrel,
To all who hesitate to act.
Fly high, you sparks!

Flame, warm our hearts!
Tell everyone early his duty.
Tell everyone early his task.
The blood is our duty,
The blood is our task:
Flame, warm our hearts![11]

In the next poem, the *Führer* becomes the rising Balder himself who promises light and liberty. It also implies, however, that only if the Germans would voluntarily surrender their own desires to the "will" of the *Führer* while accepting him as their divine leader, then liberty would follow for the nation as a whole.

Hymn to the Führer

From thousands of hearts we cry in despair:
Our Führer! Enslave us, Master! Make us free!
Millions are bending their heads in silent devotion:
Redeemed!
The pale morning sky bursts into flames:
The sun is rising!
And with the sun rises the Reich![12]

A spirit of prayer dominates this "hymn," which may remind us of some Christian prayers, were it not for images of the rising sun and the bursting flames that are more closely related to the Norse god Balder and the solstice than to Christ. On the other hand, the idea of redemption, used here for the sake of a stronger emotional appeal, was borrowed from the Church. Such borrow-ing practices were rather common in National Socialist celebrations of various kinds,[13] although they did stand in a direct contradiction to the Nazis' supposed ideal of "purifying" the rituals of their "ancestors" from Christian influences.

In general, however, references to Norse mythology suited the Nazis much better, as they permitted them to give vital expression to the idea of fight for the sake of revenge, or that of dying with honor on the battlefield. The following poem, for example, hinted at the Nordic warriors' ultimate obligation to join the ranks of Odin's *Einherjer* in the final battle against the frost giants. At the same time, of course, it was an invitation to die for the *Führer* and the fatherland:

High Raise the Flag

Under the flag with a mighty gust
We all march forward, as forward we must:
Under the flag we fly,
Under the flag we die.
Under the flag in the glimmering light
We enter the eternal fight:
High raise the flag![14]

Whereas the summer solstice celebration was meant to bring together the German "faith community" and the German "fighting community" both in the spirit of Norse mythology and National Socialism, the winter solstice celebra-tion, too, emphasized this goal, but more so the spirit of hope for better times to come. The indoor setting of the celebration, and the use of Christmas trees, candle lighting ceremonies, classical music, and selected (non-Christian) Christmas songs added a more serene and sentimental touch to the occasion. Essentially, the Nazis translated the Christian "advent" season into a season in celebration of the coming of the *Führer* and the rise of the Third Reich, both of which found their symbolic expression in the birth of Balder. The suggested outline for solstice celebrations in the public schools listed below combines traditional Christian and Nordic Germanic folk customs with the message that the seasonal renewal is a renewal of the German nation:

Christmas Celebration

Introductory Music   (violin orchestra)
First Speaker: "We light the wreath of light.
The year renews itself
And finds a new beginning.
The glow of candle light
Reminds us of the past . . . "

Song:	"We Light the Candles"
Reading: a.	"We Pass Through a Dark Room in Great Silence"
b.	"The Light has returned to Us after these Dark Days"
Orchestra:	(Violin and horn: Bach, Pesel, Telemann).
Reading:	"Today, Germany faces the sun again and looks into the future with hope. We will erase all lies for all times and will help the truth to come to light again. The brightness of the hills shall penetrate the darkness of the valley . . . "
Song:	"High Night Sky of the Clear Stars" (accompanied by violin and horn).
Words of the Führer:	"The *Führer* says: whoever has faith in his heart has the strongest power on earth."
Speech.	
Orchestra:	(Violin and piano: Gluck, Bach, Händel)
Candle Lighting Ceremony:	
	Two representatives of the German League of Girls light the four candles on the Christmas tree.

Plate 57
The National Socialist Winter Solstice Celebration

Hohe Nacht der klaren Sterne

Hohe Nacht der kla-ren Ster-ne, die wie

wei-te Brük-ken ſtehn über ei-ner

tie—fen Fer-ne, drüber unſ-re Her-zen gehn.

Hohe Nacht mit großen Feuern,
die auf allen Bergen ſind–
heut muß ſich die Erd' erneuern
wie ein junggeboren Kind.

Mütter, euch ſind alle Feuer,
alle Sterne aufgeſtellt;
Mütter, tief in euren Herzen
ſchlägt das Herz der weiten Welt.

Worte und Weiſe: Hans Baumann

Plate 58
"High Night of the Clear Stars":
. . . A Welcome Song for a Christmas Celebration without Christ

A boy of the Hitler Youth Organization speaks: "Now we have lighted the candles, and each single one lights up a thought within us. The lights shall burn:
— for the heroes who have died for Germany.
— for women and mothers, as they give eternity to our folk.
— for our fighting soldiers at the frontline.
— for all Germans abroad in foreign lands.
— for our fatherland, Germany, and for our victory.
And *all* of the lights burn for our *Führer*, Adolf Hitler. He created the new, the eternal German Reich, and he will lead us to victory.

Concluding Words: "The Master of Ceremonies extends our greetings to the *Führer*."

National Anthem: "Germany, Germany above everything, above everything in the world . . . "

Leader (addressing the audience):
"And now remember that everyone of you shall light a red candle tonight in the solstice fire, so as to place it on your Christmas trees at home."[15]

A Hitler Youth handbook, entitled *Deutsche Weihnachten, Brauchtum und Feiergestaltung* (*German Christmas, Customs, and Celebrations*), advised youth leaders to omit for stage decorations all references to Christianity, and to use instead such images as Odin's victory over the dragon, Little Red Riding-hood's resurrection from the womb of the Wolf, Snow White's reawakening, or Sleeping Beauty's redemption, as such references to Nordic Germanic and German folklore best expressed the spirit of contemporary life in Germany at Christmas time.[16] Such instructions were not given in an arbitrary manner, for they conformed to the general concern of the authorities to cultivate rituals that would combine traditional folklore and inherited customs with the ideological message of the Third Reich. Alfred Rosenberg himself was in charge of the Reich Office for Folk Festivals that coordinated celebrations and rituals in all German towns, and even in the villages.[17] Reich Propaganda Minister Goebbels further agreed with Heinrich Himmler, Reich Leader of the SS, that the solstice celebrations of all the folk festivals should be given especially close attention.

On December 12, 1938, Himmler held a conference on solstice celebrations in Bormann's office, in which he referred to Goebbels' strong support of the idea pertaining to a nation-wide revival of this custom in the "National Socialist style." Of particular interest in this connection was his observation that the winter solstice celebrations tended to be less popular than the summer solstice celebrations, as they were in conflict with the prevailing Christian traditions at Christmas time. In order to avoid such a conflict, the National Socialist authorities should make some concessions to the better known established customs. This meant, to include the popular Christmas songs, along with readings of stories from the older German regional writers describing the traditional German Christmas celebrations.[18]

How these instructions were actually put into practice we have already observed in the outline of the "Christmas Celebration" cited above. Following is an authentic diary entry of a boy from the Hitler Youth who, for the first time in his life, celebrated Christmas away from home in the "new style." If we are to believe Leni Rieffenstahl's propaganda films, it appears indeed that the boys of the Hitler Youth were full of awe as they listened to the voice of the *Führer*, and that their glowing faces reflected the spirit of "total dedication" to the cause of the Third Reich.[19] The diary, however, confirms what the Nazi authorities themselves knew all too well: that the rituals sponsored by the public schools and the Hitler Youth Organization at Christmas time in reality did present a strong conflict with prevailing customs, in spite of certain adjustments.[20] The Hitler Youth commented how in the serious part of the celebrations poems were read to them by Theodor Storm and C.F. Meyer, and how some girls from the "Working Team" had given a choir performance. Up to this point, the celebration had been bearable but then the "new style" had added to it an unpleasant taste of artificiality:

> Lieutenant B. read to us a long and extremely boring Christmas letter, which was probably printed by the Party, and thereafter came a lecture. Of course, it was one of those in the new spirit: the celebration of light was in the center of attention. I think that with such a symbol alone one can't really celebrate Christmas, for it's all not really related. For us, the true reason for celebrating Christmas is the birth of Christ. . . "[21]

The boy continued to describe how during the candle lighting rituals, a small incident had occurred as an unrehearsed surprise: suddenly a group of boys in the background began to sing on their own "Silent Night, Holy Night . . . ," and then the whole assembly joined in, even the leaders, as if touched by a miracle. Later, an old veteran spontaneously told them the story of how Ernst Moritz von Arndt had come to write the children's song: "And Now It's Really Christmas," and everyone felt at home again.

Significantly, the diary did not mention at all the "Nordic Germanic" spirit of the festival which the Party officials tried so hard to get across to children and youth, although it expressed the boy's feelings of disgust at having to listen to "unrelated" letters and lectures.

The irony of the Nazis' "folk festivals" was that the common folk had very

Plate 59
Youth Rally:
"One Folk—One Reich—One Leader"

little to do with them, as they were centrally planned by the authorities.[22] They were rituals of the "New Order" in the sense that it was their primary goal to instill in children and youth faith in the *Führer* and a loyal dedication to his cause. At the same time, as this chapter has shown, they were carefully planned in such a way as to give the effect the Nazis were merely continuing an age-old Nordic Germanic tradition. The references to Norse mythology, particularly in the poems and symbols used during the solstice celebrations, were not just meant to "replace" Christian references, but to strengthen actively the "Nordic virtues" of Hitler's "Young Team": loyalty, dedication to the *Führer*, the spirit of revenge, and faith in the Nazis' mission of an "eternal war."

If here and there the Nazis' rituals were characterized by some inconsistencies or were met with a spirit of scepticism, we must realize that they were intended as blueprints for the future. The Nazi authorities considered the rituals and festivals on the same level as all other aspects of Volkish literature, namely as a significant aid in the on-going process of German folk education. They hoped, however, that in the long run, the strong emotional impact of the rituals might bring better results than all of the literature combined that children read in books.

NOTES

1. Klaus Dörner, ed., *Das deutsche Jahr: Feiern der jungen Nation* (Munich, Eher Verlag, 1939), pp. 171-172.

2. *Ibid.*, pp. 3-7 and Introduction. For additional plans consult Reichsjugendführung, ed., *Freude, Zucht, Glaube. Handbuch für die kulturelle Arbeit im Lager* (Potsdam, Voggenreiter, 1937). Also: Hans Baumann, *Das Jahr überm Pflug* (Munich, Eher Verlag, 1935) and *Wir zünden das Feuer* (Jena Diederichs, 1938); Wolfram Bruckemann, ed., *Ewiges Volk* (Leipzig, Arwed Strauch Verlag); Hermann Roth, *Die Feier* (Leipzig, Arwed Strauch Verlag, 1941), and Erna von Vocano-Bohlmann, *Jugend im Jahresring* (Potsdam, Voggenreiter, 1937). Rosenberg's *Kulturgemeinde*, in addition, issued periodically complete plans for the celebration of National Socialist rituals.

3. Hans Strobel, ed., *Volkskundliche Grundlagen der Feiergestaltung* (Berlin, Verlag der N.S.D.A.P., 1941), p. 83.

4. H.G. Seraphim, ed., *Das politische Tagebuch Alfred Rosenbergs: 1934-35 und 1939-40* (Munich, Deutscher Taschenbuchverlag, 1964), pp. 243-244, and Alfred Rosenberg, *Der Mythus des Zwanzigsten Jahrhunderts* (Munich, Eher Verlag, 1933), p. 165.

5. "Lichtfeier" (advertisement of books and brochures pertaining to the National Socialist "Light Celebration") *Jugendschriften-Warte* 44/12 (December, 1939). See also Dörner, p. 171. For an equivalent type of program sponsored by the Party for soldiers during the war (including the almost identical songs and stories used for children), consult: Nationalsozialistische Deut-

sche Arbeiter Partei, eds., *Deutsche Kriegsweihnacht 1941* (Berlin, Verlag der N.S.D.A.P., 1941), pp. 45-49.

6. Dörner, pp. 115-116.

7. Dörner, pp. 115-116.

8. *Ibid.*, pp. 116-118.

9. Himmler, cited by Dörner, pp. 115-116. On behalf of Himmler's interest in reviving the solstice celebrations on a national scale, among the members of the German army, too, see Heinz Höhne, "Der Orden unter dem Totenkopf: Die Geschichte der S.S." Part IV, *Der Spiegel* 46 (November 7, 1966), 105-107.

10. Not only children's literature anthologies, but also handbooks on literature meant for teachers usually included a large section on the uses of literature and poetry in Nazi rituals and festivals.

11. "Feuerruf" *Von deutscher Art. Ein Lesebuch für höhere Schulen*, Part I. (Frankfurt, Verlag O. Salle, 1939), p. 176.

12. Cited in Hellmuth Langenbucher, *Die deutsche Gegenwartsdichtung. Eine Einführung in das volkhafte Schrifttum unserer Zeit* (Berlin, Junker und Dünnhaupt, 1940), p. 221.

13. Gamm pointed out a certain similarity between the "Credo" of the Church and the Nazi ritual. See Hans Jochen Gamm, *Der braune Kult; Das dritte Reich und seine Ersatzreligion. Ein Beitrag zur politischen Bildung* (Hamburg, Rütten und Loening Verlag, 1962). For additional examples consult also Georg Mosse, *Nazi Culture* (New York, Grosset and Dunlap, 1966), p. 288.

14. Joseph Prestel, *Volkhafte Dichtung* (Leipzig, Klinkhardt, 1935), pp. 81-83.

15. *Deutsche Kriegsweihnacht*, p. 58.

16. Günter Hartmut, *Deutsche Weihnachten, Brauchtum und Feiergestaltung* (Halle, Teut Verlag, 1937), pp. 28-30.

17. The so-called *Amt für Feiergestaltung* (Office for Festivals and Rituals) was under Rosenberg's jurisdiction within the *N.S. Kulturgemeinde* (National Socialist Cultural Community).

18. Friederichs, "Report über eine Konferenz mit dem Reichsführer der SS in Bormanns Hauptquartier." *Document*, marked: "*Vertraulich!*" (confidential!). Munich, December 16, 1938. (Present at the conference were Himmler, Bormann, and Friederichs. Friederichs wrote the report for the *Stabsleiter*.). *Document No. FA 131*, Munich, Institut für Zeitgeschichte.

19. See Francis Fergusson, *The Idea of a Theater* (Garden City, Doubleday & Co., 1953), p. 106. Also: Richard Moran Barsam, *Film Guide to 'Triumph of the Will'* (Bloomington, Indiana University Press, 1975).

20. Some other Nazi rituals, such as the "Initiation of Youth," also met with some public resistance, mainly because it conflicted with the prevailing practice of the Protestant Confirmation in Northern Germany. Gauleiter Schleswig

Holstein, Rundbrief." *Document No. 1121 / 21*, first folder. Institut für Zeitge-schichte. See also Höhne, pp. 105-107.

21. Klaus Granzow, *Tagebuch eines Hitlerjungen, 1943-1945* (Bremen, Karl Schünemann Verlag, 1965), pp. 144-145. The diary, according to the preface, is based on an authentic script.

22. See footnote 17.

PART IV

Methods and Limitations of Control

14

The System of Censorship

The control over children's literature in Nazi Germany was closely linked with the control over literature in general. In both cases, the authority was divided between Goebbels and Rosenberg representing the State and the Party respectively. The *Reichsschrifttumskammer* (Reich Literature Chamber) with its various subdivisions had the executive power to prohibit books and to punish authors, publishers or booksellers who did not abide by its rules. The various documents published by the Reich Literature Chamber became laws to the nation. According to a decree of November 1, 1933, everyone in Germany had to submit to its screening process all materials that were connected with "the creation, reproduction, recital, spiritual or technical interpretation, distribution, maintenance, trade or sale of cultural goods."[1] The following document, dating from 1935, may convey an idea of the all-embracing nature of censorship as Goebbels had designed it:

> The Reich Literature Chamber issues a list of harmful and undesirable literature containing all works of literature opposed to the cultural and political goals of the National Socialist State. It is prohibited by law to publish, sell, lend, borrow, issue, advertise, sell, or store these books. This prohibition applies to works of authors of Jewish or semi-Jewish origin, even if their works are not included in the above mentioned list, and it is also applicable to the literature in the newly acquired territories in the east.[2]

Goebbels issued such a list periodically, which was consulted by Rosenberg's various censorship offices. On occasion, it referred to books for young people under the age of eighteen, although it made no special provisions for children's literature.

The Reich Literature Chamber assigned the task of censorship to various sub-branches, including, among others, the Reich Office for Folk Libraries, headed by Reich Education Minister Bernhard Rust. Besides, there were addi-

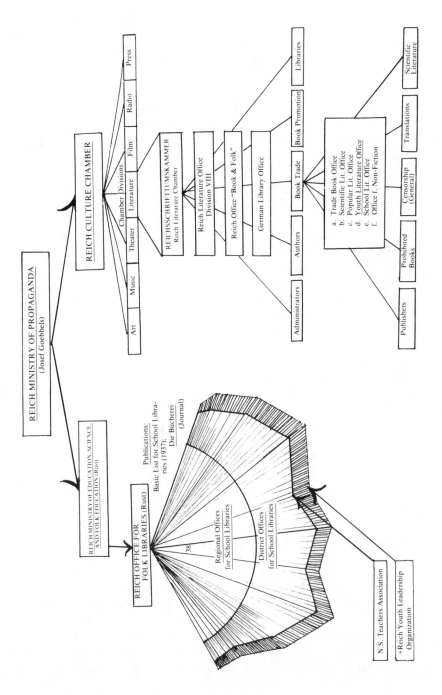

STATE CONTROL OVER CHILDREN'S AND YOUTH LITERATURE

REICH MINISTRY OF PROPAGANDA
(Josef Goebbels)

REICH CULTURE CHAMBER

Chamber Divisions

Art | Music | Theater | Literature | Film | Radio | Press

REICHSSCHRIFTTUMSKAMMER
Reich Literature Chamber

Reich Literature Office
Division VIII

Reich Office "Book & Folk"

German Library Office

Administrators | Authors | Book Trade | Book Promotion | Libraries

a. Trade Book Office
b. Scientific Lit. Office
c. Popular Lit. Office
d. Youth Literature Office
e. School Lit. Office
f. Office f. Non-Fiction

Publishers | Prohibited Books | Censorship (General) | Translations | Scientific Literature

REICH MINISTRY OF EDUCATION, SCIENCE AND FOLK EDUCATION (Rust)

REICH OFFICE FOR FOLK LIBRARIES (Rust)

Publications:
Basic List for School Libraries (1937);
Die Bücherei (Journal)

38

Regional Offices for School Libraries

District Offices for School Libraries

N.S. Teachers Association

+Reich Youth Leadership Organization

tional subdivisions concerned with administrative work, the screening of authors (according to racial origin and attitude toward the Reich), booktrade, book promotion, and library supervision in general. The Tradebook Office included among its six various subdivisions one agency solely concerned with the screening of youth literature.[3] From 1935, Goebbels officially placed Rust in charge of "guiding" all literature used in the libraries and public schools, and Rust then headed 48 regional offices for school libraries and several hundreds of those subordinated to them. Not counting the divisions for which Rust was responsible, the Reich Literature Chamber and its various branches alone supervised the activities of 2,500 publishing houses, 23,000 bookstores, and 3,000 authors (for all of whom membership in the Reich Literature Chamber was mandatory if they wished to publish their works). It screened about 20,000 books annually that were newly published and 1,000,000 books per year that circulated in trade.[4]

From the beginning, Alfred Rosenberg was in a rivalry position to Goebbels. In 1933, Rosenberg was placed in charge of the Reich Office for the Promotion of German Literature that was subordinated to the authority of the Party. In short known as the *Reichsstelle*, it included among its members, in addition to Bäumler, Johst, Langenbucher, Schlösser, and Urban, also Hagemeyer and Wismann, both of whom were also members of the State Censorship Office. In fact, Wismann was President of the Reich Literature Office, Division VIII, which gave Goebbels the idea of controlling Rosenberg's policies through this connection.[5] The show of power led to some friction which Rosenberg settled to his advantage when in 1934 Hitler gave him the authority to control the culture and ideology of the Third Reich and bestowed upon him the imposing title of "Deputy of the *Führer* for the Control of the Total Spiritual and Ideological Leadership of the National Socialist Party."[6] As the Party's chief ideologist, Rosenberg concentrated his major efforts on the promotion of "desirable" literature. Whereas Goebbels became known for his "black lists," Rosenberg made a name for himself with his "white lists" that had a great influence on Rust's library offices and the State censors of literature. The apparatus which he developed to carry out his own spiritual and ideological leadership as he saw it, involved 32 state offices, 55 district offices and between 800 to 1,000 censors. In addition, he controlled the censorship and book promotion activities of the Reich Youth Leadership Organization, the National Socialist Teachers Association, and the Party Control Office under Bouhler. During the initial years there were some overlapping structures of censorship even within the various Party divisions; but as of 1937 Rosenberg managed to bring every branch and division of all offices within his domain of power, by making them responsible to the so-called *Zentrallektorat* (Central Office) that worked under his direct supervision within the *Reichsstelle* or Main Office of Literature.[7]

His "white lists" were many, but best known among them was the *Gutachten-*

anzeiger (*Review Indicator*), which he published periodically as a supplement to the journal *Die Bücherkunde* (*Book News*). In 1933 alone, 2,000 books were reviewed here by his office, and by 1939 the annual book review figure had risen to 4,250. All of the books reviewed were grouped in accordance with the Nazis' understanding of "Volkish literature" in regard to regional and historical novels, war literature, folklore (German and Nordic Germanic) and such nonfiction topics as "Early History," "Law," "The Science of Defense," "Geopolitics," and "Economics."[8] Under each one of the last three mentioned categories a great number of folklore works were included, as the Nazis considered folklore and Germandom the key concepts for securing the newly won territories in Eastern Europe. Further, there were categories pertaining to folk festivals and rituals related to Nordic Germanic traditions—a subject of which Rosenberg was so fond that he dedicated a special branch of his office to their promotion.

Besides, there was another substantial book list, the *N.S.-Bibliographie* (*National Socialist Bibliography*), which was issued by Bouhler's office, the Party Control Commission. It was less exhaustive than the *Gutachtenanzeiger* but also served as a guide for book acquisitions in the initial stages of the Nazi Regime.[9]

This division of power was responsible for the fact that the censorship of children's literature in the Third Reich proceeded in spurts and with lapses, as well as with certain inconsistencies, although the speed with which both Goebbels and Rosenberg set into motion these gigantic bureaucratic machineries for the supervision of literature at all levels is, nevertheless, baffling. From 1933 to 1935 the division of power remained vague, and it was not really until 1937 that both State and Party authorities emerged in a well organized and coordinated form to take care of all facets of children's literature with which children came into contact.

As a first measure of organized control, the Reich Youth Leadership Organization in Berlin founded the Reich Youth Library as a "model" library for German children. Actually, it was developed from a well balanced existing library collection containing 12,000 children's books of five centuries. The Reich Youth Leadership Organization "screened" its contents in accordance with "Volkish criteria" and restocked the empty spaces with books of the "desirable" kind. It then employed several hundreds of readers who, on the basis of the Library's holdings and new acquisitions, periodically would publish a list of "valuable and necessary works" considered conducive to the spirit of German folk education. Reportedly, the Reich Literature Chamber consulted this list, and so did Rosenberg's Main Office of Literature, even before either one of them was well enough organized to develop their own screening commission. Beginning with 1934, the Reich Youth Library began publishing its first "black lists," too, but these were not as binding as those issued by Goebbels.[10]

From the Reich Youth Library and its staff of readers developed the first

PARTY CONTROL
OVER CHILDREN'S AND YOUTH LITERATURE
(Alfred Rosenberg)

PARTY CONTROL OFFICE
(Philip Bouhler)

Publication:
N.S. Bibliography

Readers, Antholo-
gies, Pedagogical
Literature

Calendars, Encyclo-
pedias, Disserta-
tions

Main Office of Literature (Hans Schemm)
(incl. control of youth literature,
folklore, festivals, early history, etc.)

NATIONAL SOCIALIST TEACHERS ASS'N
Bayreuth Headquarters

REICH DIVISION FOR YOUTH LITERATURE
(Rothemund)

DIETRICH ECKART LIBRARY
Publication: Jugendschriften-
Warte

District
Divisions

41 Regional
Divisions

300,000 Mediators for Youth Literature

Lists for School Libraries (Ed. Min. Rust)

Mothers' Service
Organization

N.S. Women's
Organization

Public Schools
(Since 1937 also Private Schools)

Hitler Schools
N.S. Institutes

Youth Organi-
zations

Nordic
Society

REICH YOUTH LEADERSHIP
ORGANIZATION
Berlin Headquarters

Culture Office
Main Office of
Literature
(or Reich Literature
Office)

Publications:
Buch der Jugend
Wille und Macht

(REICH YOUTH LIBRARY)
(Lectures, Exhi-
bits, Early Censor-
ship)

censorship office for youth literature, "Culture Office: Main Office of Literature." Its first two directors were Wolfgang Brockmeier and Fritz Helke, both of whom were well known writers for the Hitler Youth. They were succeeded by Rainer Schlösser, former editor of the National Socialist journal *Völkischer Beobachter* which already in the twenties had advocated the "fight for Germandom." According to Schlösser, it was the main task of his office "to provide a creative stimulus to the members of the Reich Youth Leadership Organization, to give advice, wherever necessary, and to lead young people effectively toward service for the German folk community."[11] Periodically, this office published recommended book lists in the Hitler Youth journal *Wille und Macht* (*Will and Power*), and also in various journals issued by the League of German Girls. Jointly with the National Socialist Teachers Association it sponsored the authoritative bibliographical guide published under the title: *Das Buch der Jugend* (*The Book of Youth*), which the editors of the *Jugendschriften-Warte* in 1937 called "an indispensable guide for the new orientation of German children's literature." Next to a listing of about 600 titles of recommended books, the guide also included under the heading "We Reject" a listing of works not recommended.[12]

In the meanwhile, the National Socialist Teachers Association took the initiative to develop a complex censorship structure of its own. Within the span of several months after Hitler came to power, it managed to build up a gigantic apparatus for the control of children's literature at all levels that remained unmatched in its complexity and efficiency of work throughout the Nazi period. By May, 1933, it had founded the Reich Division for Youth Literature in Bayreuth, which under the leadership of Rothemund after 1935 became better known as the Evaluation Office for Youth Literature. This Office consisted of its headquarters in Bayreuth, 41 regional offices, and several hundred district offices that employed a total of 300,000 censors.[13]

This structure was not altogether a new one. Whereas the Reich Youth Office heavily leaned upon the former youth library in Berlin, the National Socialist Teachers Association utilized the already existing branches and subdivisions of the former Children's Literature Association that was formally dissolved by the Party in April, 1933. Further, it took over its professional journal, the *Jugendschriften-Warte*, in June, 1933, although it was not until January, 1935 that the editors of the journal formally acknowledged their intent to implement the National Socialist ideological guidelines within the context of its publications. This period of time corresponded with that needed by Rosenberg to assert his authority in practice. Whereas from 1933 to 1935 teachers were relatively free in adding their own interpretations to the Party line,[14] the screws were tightened by the time Rothemund became head of the Bayreuth Office. He was directly responsible to Hans Schemm, then Director of the National Socialist Teachers Association, and Schemm, in his turn, had to report to Rosenberg. Henceforth, the *Jugendschriften-Warte* became its major mouthpiece, and through its pages the Ministry of Education, too, announced its policies pertaining to children's literature in the school curriculum and in the school libraries. Rothemund defined the responsibilities of his office as follows:

1. To work toward the education of all members of the National Socialist Teachers Association in the spirit of National Socialism.
2. To support the government and the *Führer's* will.
3. To cooperate in regard to the examination and censorship of all German children's books.[15]

All German educators, from kindergarten level through the high schools, had to join the National Socialist Teachers Association, regardless of whether they were formal members of the Party or not. Also, they were forced to take the loyalty oath to Adolf Hitler, if they wished to remain in their profession. The Association itself was held responsible to implement the Party's ideological guidelines and policies. The request for ideological conformity was an order, and those who did not wish to abide by it, or whose racial background or personal philosophy made them "unfit" for the "New Order," were asked to resign.[16] Only a few took the risk of resigning voluntarily. What happened to the Hamburg Chapter of the formerly free Teachers Association is typical of what happened elsewhere in Germany. In a memo to his colleagues, Chairman Wilhelm Fronemann simply addressed his fellow teachers as follows: "There is no other solution. . . As of May 24, 1933, the Hamburg Chapter of Youth Literature has submitted to the *Gleichschaltung* and the new constitution."[17] The first agenda following this announcement already included such practical issues as the organizational basis of censorship, methods of new book acquisitions, book evaluations, publications, etc., but they did not touch on items pertaining to the ethical question of freedom. Discussions of such matters were out of order under the totalitarian regime. Consequently, there was no dissenting vote and no abstention when this Chapter, along with all the others, formally joined the National Socialist Teachers Association on June 7, 1933 during the Magdeburg Conference.[18]

Rothemund tried his best to cooperate with the Reich Youth Leadership Organization and its various censors, and later he also aided Reich Minister Rust in screening the folk and school libraries.[19] Yet, cooperation between Party and State agencies was difficult to maintain as the rivalries between Goebbels and Rosenberg increased after the Bayreuth Office began to prove its efficiency and independent thinking. Both the Reich Literature Chamber and Reich Minister Rust had filed complaints with Goebbels that the Bayreuth Office was interfering in their realms of censorship and control. In response to these complaints, and partially to make his own show of power, Goebbels issued a decree in 1935, according to which State and Party control over children's literature was to be clearly divided. He made Rust solely responsible for all

matters pertaining to school libraries, and he named Bouhler as the sole authority over all censorship questions pertaining to school textbooks, anthologies,
readers, dictionaries and encyclopedias.[20] As Rust belonged to the domain of
the State and Bouhler to that of the Party, he pretended to have done a "fair
job" in dividing the responsibilities evenly between both authorities. In this
process, however, he had failed to mention Rosenberg, Schemm, Rothemund,
and others, thus ignoring altogether the bulk of the censorship work that had
been carried out by the various agents of the National Socialist Teachers Association. Rosenberg took this omission as an insult. In 1937, he issued a decree
from his own office, according to which he personally became the sole authority
over all matters relating to children's literature. Even though this still did not
give Rosenberg power over the school libraries and the reading curriculum of
the public schools, it helped him in tightening controls within the Party censorship agencies and to retain the final word over all censorship questions within
the Party's realm of authority.[21]

In general, the reigns of censorship were tightened after 1937, when the Civil
Service Act required all state employees (including teachers) to become "the
executors of the will of the Party-supported State."[22] It was in the same year
that Rust issued his first "Basic Lists" of recommended books for the school
libraries and that the first unified reading textbook for the various grade levels
was issued under the title of *Reichslesebuch* (Reich Reader). At about this time,
the school curricula, too, underwent thorough reform in view of the new ideological orientation, which especially affected the reading plans from elementary
school through high school levels.

Thus, the implementation of censorship followed the path of "divide and
rule." By cleverly playing Party and State authorities against each other, Hitler
actually stimulated the censorship policies by the sense of rivalry that he created
between them. Even though certain ambiguities in his division of responsibilities created loopholes and inconsistencies, it generally strengthened the censorship procedure, as Rosenberg and Goebbels frequently doubled their efforts to
exceed each other in their rivalrous positions.[23]

Within the span of four years, Party and State authorities managed to develop the most complex and sophisticated censorship apparatus for controlling
children's literature that Germany had ever experienced in her entire history. By
the end of the thirties, Hitler still tightened the various mechanisms of control
to the effect that Goebbels and Rosenberg were forced to join their forces in
carrying out the tasks of censorship.

In the final analysis, however, it was left to the initiative of teachers and
librarians to remove the unwanted books from the shelves and to replace them
with the approved Volkish literature. Even though both the removal and the
re-ordering of books were censored activities, the definition of the regulations
still contained certain ambiguities that permitted them here and there to cir-
cumvent some instructions so as to follow their personal tastes—although

within some broader limitations. It was considered a crime, for example, to retain books by Jewish authors, but it did not always catch a censor's eye if a book of German religious legends still occupied a modest place, even though it should have been removed along with the rest of "alien" literature.

In the course of World War II and the general turmoil of events resulting from the war situation, the censorship measures were not as thoroughly implemented as had been planned. When in 1940 Goebbels took stock of the situation, he found that it left much to be desired. In a letter to the directors of the various censorship offices who belonged to the domain of the Reich Literature Chamber, he issued another order that immediate action should be taken to remove from circulation all the books that had been left in the libraries due to an "oversight." In addition, he added to his decree a typewritten list of newly censored books that encompassed 169 pages. Among the works mentioned he included a special category of books entitled "Harmful Books for Young People under the Age of Eighteen," which also emcompassed a number of works for younger readers. As a further indication that he was serious, he included an 11-page listing of publishers whose production had been stopped by the State, since they had failed to implement the censorship regulations and policies in accordance with the letter of the law. To frighten off those who might have dared to deviate from the regulations in the future, he threatened to impose heavy fines upon offenders.[24] The very existence of such a document reveals that, on the whole, the censorship system still was far from being perfect at that time. On the other hand, it also indicated that controls were tightened out of proportion to the degree by which the regulations had been disobeyed, and that censorship evolved more and more as a threat to all who had to do with books.

While the Nazis did not reach their utopian goal of controlling every aspect of German cultural life, they made substantial progress toward it, and to the very end they still planned on reaching a perfect control over society, to the point that every book published and read would serve only the interest of the National Socialist state.

NOTES

1. "Guttentagsche Sammlung deutscher Reichsgesetze" Nr. 225. In Walter Ihde, ed., *Das Recht der Reichskulturkammer* (Berlin, Walter de Gruyter & Co., 1943), pp. 30-35.

2. *Ibid.*, p. 256.

3. Dietrich Strothmann, *Nationalsozialistische Literaturpolitik; Ein Beitrag zur Publizistik im Dritten Reich* (Bonn, Bouvier, 1965), pp. 27-30.

4. *Ibid.*, pp. 30-33. See also: Richard Grunberger, *The Twelve-Year Reich: A Social History of Nazi Germany, 1933-45.* (New York, Holt, Rinehart and Winston, 1971), p. 361.

5. Strothmann, pp. 36-42.

6. In German, Rosenberg's title was: "*Beauftragter des Führers für die Überwachung der gesamten geistigen und weltanschaulichen Leitung der N.S.D.A.P.*"—a title which he signed in full after his name on every document. See also: Walter A. Behrendsohn, *Die humanistische Front. Eine Einführung in die deutsche Emigranten Literatur.* Vol. I (1933-1939) (Zurich, Europa Verlag, 1946), pp. 41-42. Rosenberg's Main Office had at its disposal between 800 and 1,000 censors.

7. Rosenberg's office was called successively *Hauptamt Schrifttum, Amt Für Schrifttumspflege*, and the *Rosenberg Schriftstelle*. See Franz Theodor Hart, *Alfred Rosenberg: Der Mann und sein Werk* (Munich, Lehmanns Verlag, 1939), pp. 94-100.

8. See, for example, *Gutachtenanzeiger der Bücherkunde* (February 39 - January 40) Microfilm. *Institut für Zeitgeschichte*, Munich. On the average, the *Gutachtenanzeiger* carried about 3,500 book reviews annually. Some of these were very brief and usually concluded with one of the following labels: "positive," "negative," "of limited interest," "irrelevant," "out-dated, yet conditionally approved," "positive, yet only conditionally approved," or "negative, yet conditionally approved." See also Behrendson, pp. 20-21. The *National Socialist Bibliography* was more limited in its scope, yet it shared a similar goal by "leading to an understanding of the political fight for National Socialism." Strothmann, p. 246.

9. Strothmann, pp. 47-56.

10. The Library had been developed under the leadership of Karl Hobrecker. After 1933, it was called *Reichsjugendbibliothek*. Review articles by its "lectors" on children's books were published periodically in the *Jugendschriften-Warte*.

11. Rainer Schlösser, "Über das Wirken der Jugend im Kulturleben" *Völkischer Beobachter* (March, 1937), 87, and Rainer Schlösser, "Es wird Ordnung im Schrifttum," *Völkischer Beobachter* (July, 1938), 188-195). The office was first called: *Kulturamt der Reichsjugendführung: Hauptamt Literatur* and then was re-named *Hauptreferat Schrifttum*.

12. *Reichsverwaltung des N.S. Lehrerbundes und Reichsjugendführung in der Reichsstelle zur Förderung des deutschen Schrifttums* (Administrative Office of the National Socialist Teachers Association and the Reich Youth Leadership Organization within the Reich Office for the Promotion of German Literature), eds., *Das Buch der Jugend, 1936-1937; Mit Grundliste für Schülerbüchereien* (Berlin, Verlag der N.S.D.A.P., 1937). See "Advertisement" in *Jugendschriften-Warte* 43/1 (January, 1938).

13. Strothmann, p. 50, and Peter Aley, *Jugendliteratur im Dritten Reich:*

Dokumente und Kommentare (Hamburg, Verlag für Buchmarktforschung, 1969), pp. 6-13.

14. Strothmann, pp. 56-62.

15. Eduard Rothemund, "NSLB und *Jugendschriften-Warte*" *Jugendschriften-Warte* 40, 1 (January, 1935), 1 and Eduard Rothemund, "Das Jugendbuch in der deutschen Schule" in Bernhard Payr and Hans Georg Otto, eds., *Das deutsche Jugendbuch* (Munich, Deutscher Volksverlag, 1942). This work was co-sponsored by the Reich Youth Leadership Organization and the National Socialist Teachers Association (Bayreuth Office).

16. William L. Shirer, *The Rise and Fall of the Third Reich: A History of Nazi Germany* (New York, Simon and Schuster, 1960), p. 249 and Aley, pp. 6-13.

17. Fronemann, "Rundschreiben Nr. 4," cited by Aley, p. 8.

18. At the Magdeburg Conference the *Vereinigte Deutsche Prüfungsausschüsse für Jugendschriften* and the former *Deutscher Lehrerbund* were integrated into the National Socialist Teachers Association, which meant that they were formally dissolved in their independent and liberal status. See also Friedrich Sammer, "Entstehung und Entwicklung des NSLB" in Nationalsozialistischer Lehrerbund, ed., *Jahrbuch 1935* (Munich, Fichte Verlag, 1935), pp. 259-267. Sammer emphasized that during the transition period the concept of the folk community helped teachers to adjust to the new trends.

19. Aley, pp. 19-26.

20. Strothmann, pp. 42-47.

21. *Ibid.*, pp. 56-62. Also Aley, pp. 19-20.

22. Shirer, p. 257.

23. Reinhart Bollmus, *Das Amt Rosenberg und seine Gegner; Zum Machtkampf im nationalsozialistischen Herrschaftssystem* (Stuttgart, Deutsche Verlagsanstalt, 1970). See the introduction and Chapter I.

24. *Liste des schädlichen und unerwünschten Schrifttums, 1938-1940 (Nur für den Dienstgebrauch)* (For Official Use Only) (pamphlet). (Munich, Eher Verlag, 1940). Documents Collection, Hoover Institution on War, Revolution, and Peace, Stanford, California.

15

Folklore and Curricular Reforms

The Nazis realized that in order to achieve maximum effectiveness in their ideological teaching through children's books, they would have to engage not only censors but also the teachers in the public schools, for it was by them that most children were guided in their first reading experiences.

When Bernhard Rust was appointed to Reich Minister of Science, Education, and Folk Culture in 1934, he made it known to German educators that all schools should give priority to the teaching of National Socialist values, and that in this process they should give primary attention to Nordic Germanic folklore.[1] Initially, his hands were tied in implementing a planned school reform along "Volkish" lines, as Bouhler was still in charge of supervising all textbooks for the public schools.[2] Thus it was not until 1938 that his laws actually came into effect.

In the meanwhile, the National Socialist Teachers Association generally supported Rust's philosophy of education which was shared by Krieck, Schemm, Rosenberg and others.[3] Journals such as *Deutsches Bildungswesen, Jugendschriften-Warte, Die Volksschule*, and *Zeitschrift für Deutsche Bildung* published many articles about the need for using Nordic Germanic folklore in the school curriculum. Leading in this regard was *Deutsches Bildungswesen* which first printed a formal "Appeal" to all teachers, urging them to help restore German children's faith in the virtues of their ancestors by devoting more time to the myths and sagas of the Germanic North.[4]

Rust felt that such "appeals" were not enough. In 1934, he continued to complain about the failure of the public schools to give sufficient attention to "the living knowledge about Germania, racial science, family studies, the concepts of home, fate, and fatherland, the evaluation of literary and historical periods, and the new function of literature."[5] At that time, a practical reinforcement of "Volkish" thought was still lacking in the public schools. Bouhler was assigned the task of investigating the public school situation in view of

247

ideological themes,[6] but this in itself was not sufficient to keep track of how teachers actually interpreted literature and other subjects in the classrooms, especially since uniform and mandatory guidelines for the German Reich as a whole were not yet available.

Rust approached his assignment step by step. First, he tightened the control by limiting the admissions quota for Jewish children to 1.5 per cent, while sending the rest to Jewish private schools.[7] Then he spelled out more clearly that German schools were for German children only, and that German children were the very future of the German "fight and fate community." Since the very future of the Third Reich depended on children's loyalty and dedication to the "cause," he thought that it was also the schools' responsibility to strengthen their attitudes toward the nation, and not merely to transmit information. Knowledge itself meant nothing if it did not lead children to become better followers under the new regime.

> The new school has the responsibility to form the National Socialist man. The National Socialist movement thus has to get rid of the previous educational goal that used to pursue the concept of a liberal education. We are now facing the task of having to respond to the educational challenge in a new way, namely by replacing the old ideal of the "learned individual" by the new ideal of the real individual. In this attempt, we are guided by the belief that the human being is determined by his blood and historical fate. For the first time, we have found a unifying basis for an ideal that grows out of the order of the fighting folk community and some realistic tasks.[8]

The school reform at first only affected selected individual subjects, while the teaching of the other subjects followed only some general guidelines. One of the first targets of an official reform was the subject of history, for which the Ministry of Education issued uniform and mandatory rules as early as 1933. In 1935, Rust laid out official guidelines for two new required subjects, namely hereditary studies and racial science.

Beginning with April, 1937, uniform curricular guidelines were issued for the elementary schools, according to which all subjects were to be aligned with the official Party objectives. In January, 1938, the secondary schools also underwent a rigorous reform movement which, in this case, affected not only the subjects themselves but the very structure of the curriculum. In addition to the older *Gymnasium* for boys which was patterned upon humanistic ideals and had a rather demanding academic orientation, Rust introduced two alternative options, namely the *Aufbauschule* (development school) and the *Oberschule*. Boys and girls were taught separately within each type of school. In general, these schools placed a much greater emphasis on physical education and practical subjects than the previous *Gymnasium*, although they retained the teaching of foreign languages, with the exception of Greek. Most important in the new orientation, however, was the ideological emphasis in the subjects themselves, regardless of their nature.[9]

It was precisely the "practical" orientation of the Nazis' school reform that betrayed the impact of their ideology upon the German public schools. To be "practical," in their interpretation, meant that knowledge was subordinated to ideological goals. The Nazis not only considered learning itself as "impractical" as pure research if it did not fit the needs of the folk community, but they also thought that it was selfish, unpatriotic, and very suspicious. If it had been up to Hitler alone, he might have abolished all subjects other than the "basics."[10]

With his school reform of 1938, Reich Education Minister Rust introduced a new interdisciplinary approach to studies that mainly affected the subjects of German language and literature, history, prehistory, racial science, and geopolitics. At the center of these studies he placed Nordic Germanic folklore, in order to supply that "unifying factor" which he considered the vital link between the life and thought of the Nordic Germanic ancestors and the goals of the National Socialist ideology.[11]

As a method, the interdisciplinary approach itself was not a new one, for it had already been applied successfully during the Weimar Republic. Especially at the elementary school level, integrative studies had been used to aid the individual child in the learning process while strengthening the motivational factor. Moreover, the secondary schools had encouraged interdisciplinary studies, mainly in order to promote free discussions so as to stimulate the students' examination of various views on a given subject. Reich Education Minister Rust, however, identified his approach with neither one of these, as he pursued ideological objectives that were unrelated to pedagogical goals in a free society. Ironically, his approach brought about a narrowing rather than a widening of perspectives, as it imposed a "unified" world view on every subject, thus making no allowance for differing opinions. As time progressed, the Nazis' concept of interdisciplinary studies diverged more and more from apparently similar approaches that had been tried in the past. The subject of folklore studies itself received much attention in this process, although the emphasis remained confined to the Nordic Germanic traditions, as the Nazis consciously excluded the study of folklore of other cultures, including that related to Christian traditions.

In the Weimar Republic, too, Nordic Germanic folklore had received much attention in the public school curriculum, especially in literature classes. The main difference was that in those days the government had not interfered by enforcing a specific interpretation upon the folklore materials, and that comparative studies and Christian traditions, too, had been considered valuable aspects of the curriculum.

The curricular reform now also linked German language classes to the "resources" of Germanic folklore. Teachers were asked to trace German family

THE REFORMED SCHOOL CURRICULUM:
RUST'S CONCEPT OF INTERDISCIPLINARY STUDIES

THE GOAL:
    NATIONAL SOCIALIST INDOCTRINATION

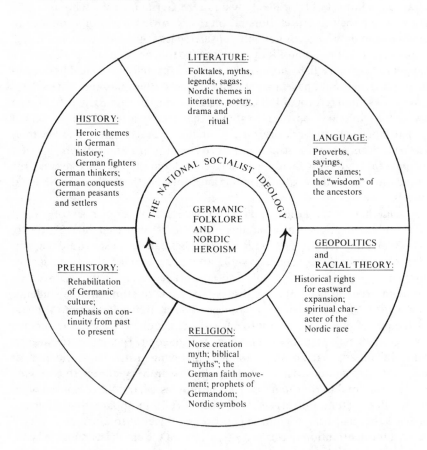

HISTORY:
Heroic themes
in German
history;
German fighters
German thinkers;
German conquests
German peasants
and settlers

LITERATURE:
Folktales, myths,
legends, sagas;
Nordic themes in
literature, poetry,
drama and
ritual

LANGUAGE:
Proverbs,
sayings,
place names;
the "wisdom" of
the ancestors

THE NATIONAL SOCIALIST IDEOLOGY

GERMANIC
FOLKLORE
AND
NORDIC
HEROISM

PREHISTORY:
Rehabilitation
of Germanic
culture;
emphasis on con-
tinuity from past
to present

RELIGION:
Norse creation
myth; biblical
"myths"; the
German faith move-
ment; prophets of
Germandom;
Nordic symbols

GEOPOLITICS
and
RACIAL THEORY:
Historical rights
for eastward
expansion;
spiritual char-
acter of the
Nordic race

SUBJECTS ONLY INDIRECTLY
AFFECTED BY THE FOLKLORE EMPHASIS:
Physical Education
Biology
Geography
Art
Crafts
Music
    (Physics, chemistry
    and foreign languages
    lay outside of this
    scheme.)

and place names back to Germanic "roots," and to use the myths and sagas of the North in order to identify the "Nordic wisdom" of the forefathers that supposedly still survived in peasant proverbs and folk sayings. Further, they were urged to study Icelandic, Norwegian, Danish, and even Gothic, so as to come closer to the original flavor of the "old languages" in which the myths and legends had been recorded. Such a course of preparation was strongly recommended even for kindergarten teachers.[12] In spite of the "Germanization" effort that teachers were expected to pursue in German classes, which involved a systematic replacement of all foreign words by equivalent German expressions (even to the degree that if these did not exist they had to be newly coined), the Nazis were not hostile to the study of foreign languages. Nevertheless, they did change their priorities by giving more attention to English than to French. This was partially due to practical considerations, but probably also because English was well recognized as a "sister language" within the Germanic language branch.

In history and prehistory classes, the Nazis established a new link with racial science, geopolitics, and geography, but also with German literature and Nordic Germanic folklore. History studies usually would begin with prehistory (which was sometimes offered as a separate subject), and then move to trace the heroic character of the German nation in its most glorious moments. The emphasis would be selective, focusing on great warriors, kings, and peasants throughout, but also on German thinkers, writers, and social reformers whose ideas could be associated with the National Socialist movement.[13] Such an exclusive concern with everything German and Germanic implied a conscious neglect of international and comparative studies.

Obligatory guidelines for history classes had been issued by the Ministry of Education in 1933, and Rust's school reform act of 1938 reaffirmed the general direction which appeared in various official handbooks since that time. Rödiger's book on *Geschichte: Ziel, Stoff und Weg (History: Goal, Materials and Message)*, for example, strongly supported an interdisciplinary approach to history to be supported mainly by the study of folklore and literature. He explained the need for such an approach on the basis that it would make history teaching more "concrete" if references were made to Norse mythology, the sagas, and selected German literature and poetry. Children would get more emotionally involved in the subject and would identify more with the "spirit" of history, rather than being bored by cut and dry facts. Essentially, however, the context of Rödiger's book makes it clear that he was less concerned with the motivational factor than with ideological values. The introduction to the work reveals the Nazis' reasons for the new folklore emphasis: "In arranging the material and methods of this subject, attention has been given to those values of the past that are useful to the present and which may lead us to a new unity. Every detail fits into the great goal of political education . . . "[14]

In racial science, teachers were urged to establish a link not only with biology, but also with prehistory and Nordic Germanic folklore. To teach children from an ideological point of view, the Nazis felt that it was not sufficient to instruct them merely in certain facts based on hereditary laws. In order to safeguard the desired value judgment, they drew upon early Germanic history and selected folklore studies, as they considered these subjects helpful for developing in young people the "right attitude" toward the spiritual values of the Nordic race.

In geopolitics, too, folklore and prehistory played a considerable role. Although officially, teachers could rely here on the theories of Karl Haushofer and others, while explaining Germany's "need" for expansion on the basis of its geographical and political "middle position" in Europe, there still remained the question of ethics. Folklore and early history came in handy at this point to justify Germany's drive eastward on the basis of so-called "historical" rights based on earlier claims by the Germanic tribes. Also, the new ideological interpretation of Norse mythology and the sagas helped the Nazis to justify what today we would consider aggressive actions in regard to territorial conquests and new German peasant settlements in the "living space" areas of Eastern Europe.[15]

Religion was another subject affected by interdisciplinary studies involving Germanic folklore. Although Rust did not mention it specifically in the school reform act of 1938, it continued to be taught in the public schools under the name of *Glaubenslehre* (faith education). No longer were teachers bound to the New Testament. Official plans included side by side with the "Jesus religion" the study of the Norse creation myth, Goethe's nature religion, the peculiar anti-semitic "faith" of Paul de Lagarde and Chamberlain, and the "German faith movement." The subject emphasized a religion without dogma, which pursued the goal of glorifying God as reflected in the rise of the German nation. An official curriculum guide issued by the National Socialist Teachers Association for Westphalia in 1940 stated the new purpose of religious education as follows:

> As Germans, we have the right to listen to the revelations of God among our own people. This gives us a great advantage over other nations. We are vitally opposed to the tendency of labelling the religious views of our forefathers, or of our present German faith movement, as a kind of paganism. Only pharisees could have invented such a label.
>
> We do not intend to revive the cult of Wodan (Odin), nor are we out to revive another traditional religion. We do believe, however, that the Norse creation myth can illustrate for our students just as vividly as the Jewish one, the origin and growing importance of God, for the ethics of the ancient Germanic people were at least as significant in so-called "pagan" times as they were in the days of the Jewish people who condemned their most esteemed prophets to solitude.[16]

By setting off the "solitary" prophets of the Bible against the community worship prevailing among Germanic tribes, the National Socialist Teachers Association tried to establish a link between the Germanic religion and the desired community ethics of National Socialism.

The inspiration for such thoughts came from Bergmann's "German faith movement" in the twenties, which had proclaimed the rise of "the original Christ without sorrow" serving not the individual but the fatherland.[17] At least temporarily, the Nazis found it convenient to use this emphasis in order to strengthen children's faith in the German folk community and the *Führer*.

On the whole, religious instruction had been on the decline in the public schools since 1935, when it was reduced to an average of one hour per week. The customary weekly prayer meetings in Catholic regions of Germany then were replaced by festivals and rituals in the Nordic and National Socialist style. In addition, the Hitler Youth Organization exercised pressure on students to drop the subject of religion voluntarily. By the mid-thirties, the bulk of Catholic schools had been converted into interdenominational schools, and according to Rust's school reform act of 1938, they were forced to conform to the new curricular guides if they wished to continue their existence. Judging by this circumstantial evidence, it appears that the subject of "faith education" was introduced as a temporary measure, with a view toward phasing out religion as a subject entirely. On the surface, it could still appear as if National Socialism was not opposed to religion, yet in reality it corroded religious education from within. The reformed religious studies had little left to remind children of the universal message of Christ.[18]

The implementation of the Nazis' folklore emphasis was most evident in the literature plans for various grade levels. These had been issued in the thirties (with minor variations) by the *Jugendschriften-Warte*, under the sponsorship of the National Socialist Teachers Association. Rust's school reform added nothing essentially new to these plans, although they called for a more rigorous reinforcement of the curricular outline. In 1937 Löffler published the first graded literature plan in accordance with National Socialist requirements. At first glance, it looked rather conventional, with its strong emphasis on German and Nordic Germanic folklore throughout the grades, however a closer examination revealed the omission of what used to be customarily taught in the public schools. In the previous years these had included representative works of world literature in translation, folklore of different cultures, and German religious folklore—to cite just a few examples. Missing were also all works written by Jewish authors, along with others that had been cited on the "black lists."[19]

The plan encompassed major genres and works to be studied in literature classes from grades 1 through 10. For the lower elementary grades it listed simple folk and fairy tales, along with animal and nature stories, and nursery rhymes. For the middle grades the folktale emphasis continued, but added were also fables, regional tales, nature stories, heroic ballads and selected short sto-

READING PLAN FOR GRADES 1 THROUGH 10
1937

Grade Levels	Prose Literature				Poetry	General Literature
1.	Fairy Tales	Folktales with a Simple Moral		Simple Animal Folktales	Nursery Rhymes Counting Rhymes Riddles	
2.		Tales with a Fairy Tale Mood and Character			Children's Sermons Children's Songs Children's Poems	
3.	Humorous Folktales	More Complex Folktales Tales with a Fairy Tale Mood and Character			Animal Poems Tales about Nature Story Poems with Heroic Characters	
4.	Anecdotes Short Stories	Folktales Fables	Regional Legends	Fables Animal Stories		
5.	Chapbooks	Literary Fairy Tales	Folk Legends	Animal Epics	Folk Songs (with Narratives)	Historical Tales
6.		Folktale-Novellas of the Folk Books	Short Hero Tales		Historical Poems Simple Nature Stories	Simple Historical Narratives

				Contemporary History (Narratives)
7.	Older Novellas Older Novels	The Newer Writers	Heroic Epics		Travel Tales / Stories about Inventors and Explorers
8.	Stories, Novellas and Novels of the Newer Writers	Hero Songs in Prose Form	Introduction to Mythology	National Socialist Poetry / The New Ballads	
9.		Icelandic Prose The Sagas		Ballads from the Edda	Biographies
10.				Lyrical Poetry	The Political Literature of National Socialism

ries. For the upper elementary grades there were hero tales in a retold form, legends, and historical tales. Children were to be made acquainted with some of the newer writings based in part on German folklore. The junior high school age group (grades 7 and 8) according to this plan received at this point their first introduction to the heroic epics of the Germanic North, as well as to nineteenth century novels and novellas (peasant and saga novels), and narratives concerned with contemporary themes. High school students would have to tackle the *Edda* and the sagas (in German translation), and besides, the ideological and political literature aimed at the general reader, such as Rosenberg's *Mythos* or Hitler's *Mein Kampf*.

The plan gives evidence that the Nazis were serious about implementing the folklore emphasis in the curriculum even prior to Rust's school reform. Further, it shows that teachers persisted in the need for recognizing grade levels in children's literature, in spite of Party pressures to the contrary. Finally, it indicates that the strictly ideological literature was not forced upon younger children in the public schools, although this was the case in the more fanatically oriented Hitler Youth Organization. Throughout the grades, however, the plan was consistent with the goals of the Hitler Youth Organization in pursuing ethnocentric objectives and neglecting the classics of children's literature that originated in other cultures.

The curricular plan for the seventh grade literature class in one of the newer *Aufbauschulen* initiated by Rust's school reforms may serve as an example of the exclusive nationalistic perspective prevalent in the public schools. It was issued for the district of Westphalia in 1940 by the National Socialist Teachers Association,[20] and in a direct line it led children from Nordic Germanic myths and sagas to the regional literature of the nineteenth century. The heroic theme provided the link between the Germanic past and each one of the given units, in which only relevant German characters were in the focus of attention, be it Henry the Lion, Hans Sachs, Albrecht Dürer, Martin Luther, or Schiller's Wallenstein. Through such units as "The Germanic Hero as a Christian Knight," "The Heroic Merchant," "Spiritual Men, Fighters, and Searchers of God," to "German Men in Times of Trouble" students were made to read German literature of several centuries from an idealized nationalistic perspective. The final unit for this grade bore the title "The Beauty of the German Landscape," and, evidently, tried to fulfill the curricular goal of developing in children a love of home and country—just as we have observed in the school readers. The National Socialist literature of the political-ideological type was again reserved for the higher grades, which affirms the pattern that had been established earlier.[21]

The literature plan for the twelfth grade seemed to indicate another direction. One half of the school year was to be devoted to the "Nordic Heritage," but the other half to the "Classical Heritage." Would this imply that the Nazis con-

1940
THE GERMAN YOUTH SCHOOL
LITERATURE PLAN FOR THE 7TH GRADE

I.   Heroic Times: Myths and Sagas of the North

II.   Fight for the Forefathers' Heritage:
Widukind and Charlemagne; Westphalic legends; saga collections by W. Jansen and J.W. Weber; the legends of Charlemagne and Roland.

III.   The Germanic Hero as a Christian Knight:
Henry the Lion; Barbarossa; Konradin; (myths and legends related to all three); Parsifal and Lohengrin; legends and ballads about the knights; Walther von der Vogelweide; knights of the German order; decadent knighthood and the soil-conscious peasantry (*Meier Helmbrecht*).

IV.   The Heroic Merchant:
Hanseatic men (W. Jensen); German artisans; Nuremberg and its Masters; Hans Sachs; Albrecht Dürer.

V.   Spiritual Men, Fighters and Searchers of God:
Martin Luther; the German chapbook of Dr. Faustus.

VI.   German Men in Times of Trouble:
Ballads of the Mercenaries;
Schiller's *Wallenstein*;
Bartels' *Die Dittmarscher*;
Löns' *Der Wehrwolf*;
The Thirty Years War in German literature.

VII.   The Beauty of the German Landscape:
Annette von Droste-Hülshoff;
Storm
Raabe
Stifter
Löns
Keller
Rosegger

tinued to pursue a liberal education after all, in spite of the general school reform?

A closer examination of the reasons given for the inclusion of such a study, however, reveals that the Nazis remained consistent with their ideological demands even in regard to Aeschylus, Sophocles, and Euripides. Following is a listing of some of the works intended to be studied within a new ideological context:

Prometheus: The Nordic Faustian concept:
a man of action.

Oedipus: A tragedy without the concept of guilt.

Euminides: Blood revenge: protection of the Nordic soul in the religion of Apollo—a stark contrast to Asiatic influences.

Medea: Jason's Viking excursion against the Amazons; a battle of the races.

The Birds
and
The Wasps: Fight against decadent democracy, its corruption and ideology.[22]

In accordance with this outline, the Greek heroes bear a striking similarity with the Nordic Germanic heroes. Not only does Jason's quest for the Golden Fleece become a "Viking Excursion," but even Prometheus and Oedipus show a strange resemblance to Odin, as the Nazis portrayed him in his "Faustian" quest that supposedly favored "action" above contemplation. Further, the concepts of blood revenge and the fight against corruption resemble the Nazis' call for war in the name of honor and racial purity. The "Nordic soul" of Apollo clearly reflects the influence of Rosenberg's *Mythos*. It appears, then, that Greek drama was taught and yet, that it was transformed into something else.

The Nazis' emphasis on Nordic Germanic folklore was also evident in such Party-sponsored schools as the *Nationalsozialistische Erziehungsanstalten* (National Socialist Educational Institutes), the *Adolf Hitler Schulen* (Adolf Hitler Schools), and the *Ordensburgen* (Order Castles). The last one was reserved for older youths, yet the other two accepted boys of a younger age group as well. On the surface, all three of these types of institutions resembled the cadet schools and the old-fashioned boarding schools, yet their curricula were designed to emphasize character training in the "Norseman's style" and a perfect adjustment to National Socialist values. Classical languages and literatures had vanished from the lesson plans, although history, prehistory, racial theory, geopolitics, folklore, and Volkish literature still played a leading role, next to the all important subjects of physical education and biology. In general, these curricula placed less emphasis on literature than the public schools, as they were crowded with required outdoor activities and practical projects, such as crafts. The students' weekends were often taken up with camping and hiking trips, and

Hitler, Heß, Himmler, Hierl!
Hitler, Heß, Himmler, Hierl! H
Hitler, Heß, Himmler, Hierl! Heil
Hitler, Heß, Himmler, Hierl! Heil
Hitler, Heß, Himmler, Hierl! Heil
Hitler, Heß, Himmler, Hierl! Heil

Junker, Immelmann, Jäger. J
Junker, Immelmann, Jäger. Ju
Junker, Immelmann, Jäger. Ju
Junker, Immelmann, Jäger Ju
Juker, Immelmann, Jäger Ju
Juker, Immelmann, Jäger Ju

Kampfflieger, Kameraden, Kiel
Kampfflieger, Kameraden, Kiel
Kampfflieger, Kameraden, Kiel
Kampfflieger, Kameraden, Kiel

Plate 60
A Page from the Penmanship Notebook of an Eighth Grader

A CALL FOR COMMUNITY INVOLVEMENT:
WINTER AID PROJECT 1936/37

Plate 61a
"Have your Children Take These Important Scraps to School!"

also with a number of rituals, in which folklore, Volkish literature, and the new symbolic poetry were used in oral recitations and dramatic performances.[23]

The folklore emphasis in the Nazis' school system also affected the universities. Among the newer university courses introduced early in the thirties were such titles as "Folk and State," "Family and Heritage," "Mores, Customs, and Folk Prophecies," and "Folk Customs and Folk Beliefs." In most of these courses interdisciplinary approaches were favored that linked traditional folklore studies with the subjects of philology, prehistory, race theory, and geopolitics. At the University of Berlin, Professor Boehm became the first professor of *Volkssoziologie* (Volkish sociology)—a subject that was closely linked with *Raumplanung* (area science) that concerned itself with the Nazis' expansionist policies in Eastern Europe.[24]

Through their school reforms, the Nazis planned not only to unify the Ger-

Plate 61b
"A Renewed Oath of Loyalty to the Third Reich"

man school curriculum but to impose upon it a uniform ideological orientation. In this process, children's book editions of Norse mythology, the sagas, German legends and folktales gained much attention in a number of subjects, not only in literature classes. Nevertheless, the emphasis remained selective and politically biased. In the final analysis, the new interdisciplinary approach to studies was designed to achieve greater control over the thoughts and attitudes of children, and simultaneously, to eliminate the last remnants of a liberal education in which Christian and universal human values still prevailed. The new "folk education" of Nazism served only the glory of the German nation, and to this end all other goals were to be subordinated.

NOTES

1. *Nationalsozialistischer Lehrerbund* (National Socialist Teachers Association), ed., "Aufruf des N.S.L.B. zur Pflege germanisch-deutschen Schrifttums" *Deutsches Bildungswesen* 10 (October, 1933), 317-322. The "Appeal" was issued jointly by Hans Schemm and the Ministry of Education.

2. Consult George Frederick Kneller, *The Educational Philosophy of National Socialism* (New Haven, Yale University Press, 1941), pp. 140-149. For a more comprehensive discussion of the issues involved consult also: Hans Günther Assel, *Die Perversion der Politischen Pädagogik* (Munich, Ehrenwirt Verlag, 1969).

3. Ernst Krieck, "Reform der Lehrerbildung in Schule und Erziehung im Dritten Reich," in Nationalsozialistischer Lehrerbund, ed., *Jahrbuch, 1935* (Berlin, Verlag der N.S.D.A.P., 1935), pp. 309-312. Also: Ernst Krieck, *Dichtung und Erziehung* (Leipzing, Armanenverlag, 1933), and Alfred Beck, *Erziehung im Grossdeutschen Reich* (Dortmund, W. Druwell Verlag, 1936).

4. *Nationalsozialistischer Lehrerbund*, ed., "Aufruf."

5. *Ibid.* Also: Rust, der Reichs-und Preussische Minister für Wissenschaft, Erziehung und Volksbildung (The Reich-and Prussian Minister of Science, Education, and Folk Education); "Erziehung und Unterricht in der höheren Schule; Grundlagen" *Hamburger Lehrer-Zeitung* (June 29, 1936), 130-132.

6. Dietrich Strothmann, *Nationalsozialistische Literaturpolitik* (Bonn, Bouvier, 1960), pp. 41-43; 52-58. Also: Rudolf Benze, *Erziehung im Dritten Reich* (Frankfurt, Diesterweg Verlag, 1941), pp. 13-58.

7. Erika Mann, *Schools for Barbarians: Education under the Nazis* (New York, Modern Age Books, 1939), p. 51. Mann also mentioned that by 1937 about 97% of all teachers were members of the National Socialist Teachers Association. Further, it is known that in 1937 all boys from the age of ten and up had to become members of the Hitler Youth Organization, and that simultaneously, all private associations for young people were dissolved. These facts undoubtedly had a bearing upon the more uniform implementation of the school reform a year later.

8. Rust, "Erziehung und Unterricht . . . ", 52.

9. Otto Graf zu Rantzau, *Das Reichsministerium für Wissenschaft, Erziehung und Volksbildung* (Berlin, Industrieverlag Spaethe und Linde, 1939), pp. 24-27. See also: Ernst Krieck, *Nationalsozialistische Erziehung* (Series: *Grundlagen, Aufbau und Wirtschaftsordnung des nationalsozialistischen Staates*) (Berlin, Industrieverlag, Spaethe und Linde, 1939). Both sources referred to the new structure of the educational reform, but also to the need for an ideological conformity of all subjects to the National Socialist and "Nordic" view of life. Also: Charlotte Engelmann, *German Education and Re-Education* (New York,

International Universities Press, 1945) and Richard Grunberger, *The 12-Year Reich: A Social History of Nazi Germany 1933-1945* (New York, Holt, Rinehart and Winston, 1972), pp. 283-285.

10. Adolf Hitler, *Mein Kampf* (Munich, Eher Verlag, 1933), pp. 420; 464-465. See also: H. R. Trevor-Roper, *Hitler's Secret Conversations, 1941-1944* (New York, Signet Books, 1953), pp. 343-345. Not only did he think very little of the study of foreign languages, but he also confessed that in his youth the reading of novels had always annoyed him. In general, he thought that most of what was taught in the elementary and secondary schools was a waste of time. See p. 625.

11. Rust, "Erziehung und Unterricht . . . ", 130.

12. This point was frequently made in articles dealing with the uses and interpretations of Norse mythology, yet since most of these were written with a view toward secondary education, for which teacher preparation in any event followed more rigorous philological and language requirements, it was not unusual to see it emphasized. What was new was the recommendation of such studies for kindergarten teachers who generally had a very limited literature and language background. See, for example, Marianne Günzel and Harriet Schneider, *Buch und Erziehung: Jugendschrifttumskunde* (Leipzig, Klinkhardt, 1943), pp. 74-75.

13. Ernst Dobers and Kurt Higelke, *Rassenpolitische Unterrichtspraxis* (Leipzig, Julius Klinkhardt, 1940). Each subject is discussed here in relation to the new National Socialist requirements. See also Rantzau for a clear analysis of the various subjects required in the *Aufbauschulen* and *Oberschulen*.

14. Wilhelm Rödiger, *Geschichte, Ziel, Stoff und Weg* (Leipzig, Klinkhardt, 1934) pp. 1-4. (Series: *Völkisches Lehrgut*). For a critical review of this work consult *Friends of Europe Publications*, No. 41 (London, The Holy Sea, 1938), pp. 1-36, and Karl Ferdinand Werner, *Das NS Geschichtsbild und die deutsche Geschichtswissenschaft* (Stuttgart, Kohlhammer Verlag, 1967). Both Mann and Kneller dedicate a chapter each to the teaching of history and prehistory in the German public schools. Also: Rudolf Limmer, "Geschichte, Sagen- und Märchenunterricht" *Deutsches Bildungswesen* (July, 1933), 105-108.

15. Kneller, p. 178. Also: Otto Schmidt, *Volkstumsarbeit als politische Aufgabe* (Berlin, Zentralverlag der N.S.D.A.P., 1937), pp. 92-115. See Dr. Karl Haushofer, "Die geopolitische Lage Deutschlands" in Carl Lange and Ernst Adolf Dryer, eds., *Deutscher Geist: Kulturdokumente der Gegenwart* (Leipzig, Voigtländer-Verlag, 1933), pp. 79-88.

16. Nationalsozialistischer Lehrerbund, *Die deutsche Jugendschule: Sechsjährige Höhere Schule. Ein Erziehungs-und Unterrichtsplan des Nationalsozialistischen Lehrerbundes Gau Westfalen-Süd* (Bielefeld, Verlag Velhagen und Klasing, 1940).

17. Ernst Bergmann, *Deutschland, das Bildungsland der Menschheit* (Breslau, Hirt Verlag, 1933). The German faith movement had existed since 1908,

but under the National Socialist influence it was changed from a Nordic religious movement into a political cult. Hans Jochen Gamm, *Der braune Kult: Das Dritte Reich und seine Ersatzreligion* (Series: *Beiträge zur politischen Bildung*) (Hamburg, Rütten und Loening, 1962), pp. 76-82.

18. Mann, pp. 85-94. Also: Rolf Eilers, *Die nationalsozialistische Schulpolitik; Eine Studie zur Funktion der Erziehung im nationalsozialistischen Staat* (Cologne, Westdeutscher Verlag, 1963), pp. 19-20, and Georg L. Mosse, *The Crisis of German Ideology: The Intellectual Origins of the Third Reich* (New York, Grosset and Dunlap, 1964), pp. 312-331.

19. Ernst Löffler, "Klassenlesestoffe" *Jugendschriften-Warte* 42, 7 (July, 1937), 46-52. Part II of this essay appeared in the same journal 42, 8 (August, 1937), 51-58. For parallel views consult: Die Schriftleitung (editors), "Stimmen zum Märchen und Sagenunterricht" *Deutsches Bildungswesen* 38, 12 (December, 1933), 357, and Richard Seyfert, "Der Einbau der volkstümlichen Bildung in die national-politische Volkserziehung" *Deutsches Bildungswesen* (Aug./Sept., 1933), 165-169, and Richard Seyfert, "Heimat-und Volkskunde als Grundlage volkhafter Bildung" *Deutsches Bildungswesen* 38, 6 (June, 1933), 24-38.

20. Nationalsozialistischer Lehrerbund, *Die deutsche Jugendschule*, Introduction.

21. *Ibid.* See chart.

22. *Ibid.* See chart.

23. Gamm, pp. 76-82. Also: David Schoenbaum, *Hitler's Social Revolution: Class and Status in Nazi Germany, 1933-1939* (New York, Doubleday, 1966). Consult also the various Nordic rites and ideals on which the ethics of these schools were based in "Auswahl und Auslese für Adolf Hitler Schulen; Bordesholm, Gauschulungsburg" (November 27, 1944), N.S.D.A.P. Gauleitung Schleswig-Holstein, Rundschreiben No. 5/45. *Document No. R 1121*. Institut für Zeitgeschichte, Munich.

24. Ihor Kamenetsky, *Secret Nazi Plans for Eastern Europe: A Study of Lebensraum Policies* (New York, Bookman Associates, 1961), pp. 49-82, and Christa Kamenetsky, "Folklore as a Political Tool in Nazi Germany" *Journal of American Folklore* 85, 337 (July/September, 1972), 221-235.

16

New Directions for School Libraries

The burning of library books and the local library raids in 1933 represented only the first steps toward censorship in an era in which books were considered to be of primary importance in the ideological re-orientation of an entire nation. Now, there arose not only the question of what to order in place of the books that had been removed, but also, of how to coordinate book purchases throughout the country in the interest of German folk education. Various steps were involved in such a process. First, the "cleansing" measures would have to be carried out in accordance with national guidelines on a continuing basis. Secondly, Volkish literature would have to be identified and reorganized around attractive topics, which meant a systematic analysis and rearrangement of the remaining holdings, centrally controlled book purchases, and well organized promotional activities that would help to disseminate Volkish literature among the young readers as well as their older peers and the adult population. In addition, the Nazis realized that some of the public libraries (now called folk libraries) were not only understocked but poorly housed, and that in some areas of Germany school libraries did not even exist at all. New libraries needed to be built and others had to be physically extended.

Such a vast enterprise demanded not only persistence as well as financial support, but patience too. As in the case of the school reforms, the implementation of the various library plans proceeded step by step. Between 1933 and 1935 the Prussian Office for Folk Libraries and the Reich Ministry of Education issued several decrees, so as to align book acquisitions with the demands of the National Socialist ideology.[1] In 1935, Reich Education Minister Rust placed teachers in charge of their local school libraries, hoping that they would exercise "self-censorship" in regard to the holdings of their libraries.[2] He then activated the National Socialist Teachers Association and the 300,000 censors drafted from their own ranks and the former Children's Literature Association, so as to check up on the teachers' "cleansing" procedures and book orders.[3] By the end of the year, he had managed to establish systematically an inventory of the entire holdings of the 25,000 libraries in Germany.[4] At that time, the removal of undesirable literature no longer was as arbitrary as it had been in 1933 but generally followed the guidelines of Goebbels' "black lists," whereas new acquisitions were made in accordance with Rosenberg's "white lists." However, also the lists published periodically in the *Jugendschriften-Warte* and various journals of the Hitler Youth Organization served as a general point of orientation to those in charge of making the distinction between Volkish and un-Volkish literature.[5]

Nevertheless, the existence of several guidelines and variations in the wording of the decrees, here and there caused some confusions and inconsistencies to occur, especially when it came to some individual titles in religious folk literature. A book on the religious legends of Bavaria, for example, might be classified as "Volkish literature" by some censors who felt that it was a work based on German folk traditions of a certain region. However, it might be classified as "un-Volkish literature" by others who considered it primarily as a work based on "folk-alien" Christian traditions. Consequently, the work might be retained in some libraries and discarded in others. In 1936, Reich Education Minister Rust tried to eliminate such confusions by issuing an additional decree, according to which all religious books had to be removed from the school and folk libraries. Simultaneously, he ordered all of the religious libraries to restrict their holdings exclusively to religious literature.[6] In this way he wanted to make sure that the religious libraries would not give shelter to some of the "undesirable" literature discarded by the school and folk libraries. Further, he prohibited mutual loans between the religious libraries and the other libraries.

From Rust's point of view, the school library situation was still far from being perfect, even two years later when he issued the first "Basic Lists" for the acquisition of new library books. Nevertheless, the teachers were their own best censors, for in 1937 they openly endorsed Rust's censorship decree on behalf of the removal of the last remaining "undesirable" books.[7] This was the same crucial year when the *Reichslesebuch* was introduced, when the official school reforms began, and when membership in the Hitler Youth became mandatory. At that time, membership in the National Socialist Teachers Association had become mandatory, too, and the teachers had no way of expressing their open dissent without taking a severe personal risk.[8]

The Nazis' total scheming in regard to the school and folk libraries may be best understood if we first of all consider their material accomplishments within the first five-year span of their rule. The library reforms were not insignificant, as the following "progress report" may show that was issued by the Reich Ministry of Education in 1938. It proudly recorded:

1. The establishment of uniform guidelines for the development and extension of folk libraries.
2. The founding of the Central Reich Office for Folk Libraries.
3. The founding of 43 state offices for folk libraries.

4. The reorganization and founding of 5,000 folk libraries.

5. The founding of new libraries at a rate of 1,500 per year.

6. The compilation and distribution of basic book lists for all folk libraries.

7. The cooperation of folk libraries with the Hitler Youth Organization on behalf of youth libraries.[9]

To these accomplishments would have to be added the astounding figure of 55,000 school libraries which the Reich Ministry of Education founded between the years 1937 and 1941.[10] Most of them were relatively small and did not even have an open-shelf system, but they cannot be overlooked as markers of the Nazis' "cultural guidance" through children's literature.

One of the reasons why the Nazis placed such a great emphasis on the physical extension of folk and school libraries was because they considered them new centers of culture for the entire population. At various times Rust made it clear that folk education was reaching out beyond the walls of the school building, and that the school libraries would have to pursue an open-door policy for everyone interested in reading. He even abolished the bookmobiles that used to visit the smaller towns and villages periodically, in order to ensure that the local people would really make better use of the school libraries.[11]

The greatest task which the Nazis faced in regard to a reorganization of school and folk libraries was to make selections among the older and newer works of literature that would correspond with the basic principles of National Socialist folk education. The first systematic attempt along these lines was made by the National Socialist Teachers Association. In national workshops and conferences it began to publish recommended book lists for young readers early in the thirties, and also began to issue file cards which individual subscribers and schools would receive along with the *Jugendschriften-Warte*. All of these were intended to bring greater uniformity into the pattern of book acquisitions throughout the country.

In this attempt, the National Socialist Teachers Association was aided considerably by Joseph Prestel's work, *Die Schülerbücherei (The School Library)* which was published in 1933.[12] Prestel had designed the new library book acquisition plan in full consciousness of the Nazis' demand for Volkish literature, following a line of continuity from the Nordic Germanic heroic past to the present. The plan encompassed six broad topics which, at first sight, seemed to follow a rather neutral trend. A closer look at the subtitles under which individual book titles were listed, however, revealed a clear ideological orientation corresponding in every respect to the Party's new requirements. Under the general topic of "Our Literary Heritage," for example, he focused exclusively on the Nordic Germanic and German folk tradition while ignoring the folk heritage of other lands. Further, there were some works by German regional writers of the late nineteenth century, and a total of only four "world classics," of which

Die Reichswaltung des NSLB.
die Reichsjugendführung und die Reichsstelle zur Förderung des deutschen Schrifttums sind die Herausgeber des amtlichen
Verzeichnisses

Das Buch der Jugend
1936/37

über 600 Titel, 34 Bilder

Preis 20 Pfennig

Mit Grundliste für Schülerbüchereien

Unentbehrlich für die Neugestaltung des
deutschen Jugendschrifttums!

Verlag des Jugendschriftenverzeichnisses „Das Buch der
Jugend" (Franckh=Thienemann) Stuttgart, Postfach 498

Plate 62
THE BOOK OF YOUTH
OFFICIAL BIBLIOGRAPHY WITH RECOMMENDED "BASIC BOOK LIST"
FOR SCHOOL LIBRARIES

PRESTEL'S SCHOOL LIBRARY PLAN
1933

I. Our Literary Heritage
    A. Folktales
    B. Sagas; Legends; Norse Myths
    C. Hero Tales; Nordic Heroes and the *Nibelungen Epic*
    D. Traditional Merry Tales; Folk Theater; Adventure
    E. Folk Writers (local color); Brentano, Hebel, Gotthelf, Mörike, Storm, Rosegger, etc.
    F. Children's Books Around the World: *Robinson Crusoe,* the *Leatherstocking Tales; Arabian Nights* (Selections); *Nils Holgersson*

II. German History Reflected in Stories and Tales
    A. Prehistory
    B. Germanic History
    C. Cities of the Middle Ages
    D. The Peasantry
    E. Dangerous Exposure of Border Areas; Eastern Territories; The Rhine Area
    F. Wars of Liberation
    G. Colonies; Conquest and Defense
    H. World War I
    I. The National Socialist Movement
    J. Recent Experiences: Biographies and Memoirs

III. Literature of Home and Around the World
    A. Stories of German Regions   E. The Sea and Navigation
    B. German Customs   F. Adventure Stories
    C. Travel Books   G. Great Explorers
    D. Animal Stories   H. Germans in Other Lands

IV. Poetry
    A. Nursery Rhymes; Traditional Verse
    B. Fables
    C. Nonsense Verse
    D. Poetry Anthologies
    E. Ballad Collections
    F. Folk Song Collections
    G. Choral Readings and Song Collections for National Socialist Festivities, such as Labor Day, Mother's Day, Thanksgiving Day, and Christmas

V. Visual Aids

VI. Crafts and Hobbies; Dictionaries

Robinson Crusoe was in any event mainly used in the Germanized edition by Campe. *The Adventures of Nils Holgersson* by Lagerlöf belonged to the "acceptable" Swedish tradition which the Nazis promoted like their own, and there remained as exceptions to the rule only Cooper's *Leatherstocking Tales* which the Nazis considered on the same level as the "heroic" Karl May books, and the *Arabian Nights.*

The second broader topic, too, emphasized only works within the German and Nordic Germanic spheres of interest, be it in relation to prehistory or history, to the peasantry, the wars of liberation, World War I, or the National Socialist movement. Of particular ideological value here was the subtopic dealing with the so-called "dangerous exposure in the border areas, eastern areas, and the Rhine area," as it listed a number of children's books—among them regional folklore of an apparently neutral character—that were supposed to call to the attention of librarians and educators the need for making children aware of the defense of Germandom abroad. In the library programs, these books were to be used in the spirit of emphasizing German solidarity wherever there was "German blood."[13]

To a neutral observer, the third broader topic in Prestel's plan, entitled "Home and the World," again might appear to be very similar to what we might wish to include in our library plans today. The subtopics, however, clearly betrayed that in this case, too, the Nazis' view of the world was limited to German interest in Germans abroad, be it in connection with German colonists, German explorers, or German travellers. Finally, the poetry section, possibly even more so than the other topics, showed the more recent interest in National Socialist poets who had composed choral readings and poems, as well as general stage directions for National Socialist festivals and rituals.

Next to Prestel's plan, Maurer's book, *Jugend und Buch im Neuen Reich (Youth and Books in the New Reich)*[14] helped the Association in its initial work, and as both of these and others basically followed the Nazis' Volkish orientation, Reich Education Minister Rust had a relatively easy job in composing his so-called "Basic List" in 1937, which bore the title: *Grundliste für Schülerbüchereien der Volksschulen (Basic List for Elementary School Libraries).* Even though the *Volksschule* at that time encompassed the first four years of the elementary school and four additional years, Rust included in his list only ten titles suitable for younger children. All of the others were for older children, and the bulk (about seventy-six) were for youth and adults. This seemingly unequal distribution of titles may be explained by the fact that Rust intended them also to be used by the local population. Besides, he mentioned in his preface to the "Basic List" that he expected every school library in Germany to supplement the list. His own listing of books was suggestive rather than mandatory, but essentially, it represented the equivalent of the "core" in the *Reich Reader*, as it focused upon themes that were common to all Germans, in the past and in the present.

RUST'S 'BASIC LIST' FOR 1937

I.   German Folklore: Legends, Folktales, Anecdotes
II.   From the Dawn of History: Nordic Heroes
III.   German Wars
IV.   German Heroism (Sacrifices; Great Leaders)
V.   The Memory of World War I.
VI.   Colonies: Germans Around the World
VII.   Nature and Home
VIII.   Youth Marches for Germany
IX.   Happy Youth
X.   Adventure Stories
XI.   Books About Aviation
XII.   The World of Work
XIII.   Crafts and Hobbies[15]

Rust demanded that in addition to these "core" books, the school libraries should purchase works that were based on regional folklore and local color. These would then represent the equivalent to the "home parts," of the *Reichslesebuch*, whereas the 120 titles listed made up the "core part" of the school library. He stated that in essence, the major headings of the plan should be respected, along with the rationale behind them.[16]

By examining the listing of works more closely, we may get a clearer picture of the types of books actually approved by the Party as "core" reading material. Under "German Folklore" there were the folktales of the Brothers Grimm, of Bechstein and Musäus, but also the fairy tales of Hans Christian Andersen. Further, there were the German folk legends of the Brothers Grimm, *Deutsche Sagen (German Legends)*, along with those pertaining to *Rübezahl, Reineke Fox, Merry Tyll*, and *Munchhausen*. The section on early history complemented the folklore listing by adding Weber's *Asgard* and *Dietrich von Bern*, Schalk's *Meisterbuch deutscher Götter- und Heldensagen (Master Book of German Myths and Hero Tales)*, and Severin Rüttgers' *Nordische Heldensagen (Nordic Hero Tales)*. Besides, there were the hero tales of Walthari and Hildegund, next to hunting and warrior stories based on the saga literature. The Nordic Germanic pattern continued in the following grouping of books listed under the heading of "German Wars," which, among others, included the "Nordic" novels of Will Vesper and Gustav Freytag.

The sections on "German Wars" and on "German Heroism" both focused solely on the German experience. Different from Prestel's listing, however, was the inclusion of books on National Socialist leaders under "German Heroes." Four out of ten among these dealt with Adolf Hitler, namely Stiehler's *Die Geschichte von Adolf Hitler (The Story of Adolf Hitler)*, Beier-Lindhardt's *Das Buch vom Führer für die deutsche Jugend (The Book About the Führer for*

German Youth), Hoffmann's *Jugend um Hitler (Youth Surrounding Hitler)*, and by the same author *Hitler wie ihn keiner kennt (Hitler as Nobody Knows Him)*. Such a grouping placed Hitler as a "descendent of the Nordic heroes" in the same rank as Frederick the Great, Hindenburg, Wessel, Schlageter, and Göring. Hitler's *Mein Kampf*, (abridged edition) was listed under the section of "Youth Marches for Germany," along with Schenzinger's *Der Hitlerjunge Quex (The Hitler Youth Named Quex)* and various books about the German League of Girls, the new army, the navy, and the airforce. The section on "The World of Work" was also strongly oriented toward political-ideological themes, and included books about the Reich Workers' Service and various community projects in which comradeship, discipline, and work were presented with a halo of glory. Axmann's *Olympia der Arbeit (The Olympics of Work)* and Pinette-Decker's *Männer, Land und Spaten (Men, Land, and Spades)* showed the new direction of the Reich Workers' Service in regard to cultivating the land, also in the east. Books of this nature had not been available when Prestel published his work, and they represented an up-dated attempt to raise children and youth in the spirit of National Socialism. The same is true for a number of works listed under the section of "Unforgettable Colonies— Germans in the World," where only the title of Müller-Hennig's *Wolgakinder (The Volga Children)* corresponded with the earlier works cited in the library plan by Prestel.

The only books on Rust's "Basic List" with a childlike appeal were two works by Hermann Löns under the section "Home and Nature," as well as those titles by Rosegger, Hamsun, Götz, and Sapper. We should also mention the humorous illustrated stories of Wilhelm Busch and Defoe's *Robinson Crusoe*.

Rust went on to add two supplementary "Basic Lists" in 1939 and in 1941 respectively.[17] Both of these were intended to list more works for younger children, as this category of books had been somewhat neglected in the listing of 1937, and as some complaints on this account had been voiced in the *Jugendschriften-Warte* and *Die Bücherei*.[18] Rust addressed himself to this issue positively, but the works which he marked as suitable for the eight to ten year olds predominantly showed a Volkish-political orientation, too, even though they were written in a simple style. They included Adler's *Unsere Luftwaffe in Polen (Our Airforce in Poland)*, Kohl's *Wir fliegen gegen England (We are Flying against England)* Utermann's *Panzer nach vorn! (Tanks to the Front)*, and the "true story" of a submarine officer, entitled *U-Boot Fahrer von heute (Submarine Raiders of Today)*. The 1941 list in general showed an increase in the war book category, although folklore was still as strongly represented as before. With the exception of two additional works by Spyri (continuations of the *Heidi* books), no other classics were added to the list.[19]

In the meanwhile, the National Socialist Teachers Association continued under the pressure from the Reich Education Ministry to compile book lists for secondary schools that would match the spirit of Rust's "Basic Lists." In this

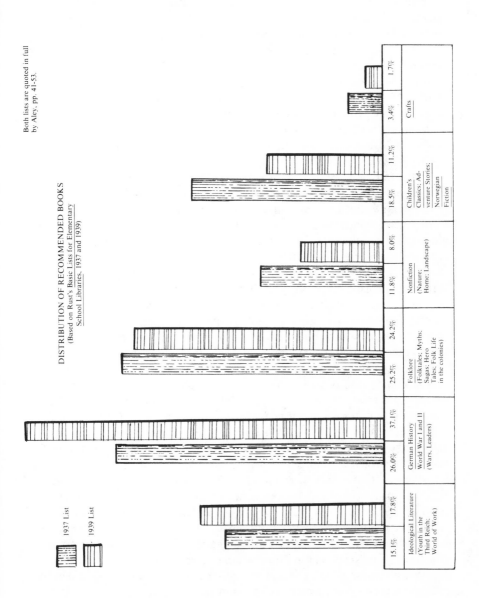

Both lists are quoted in full
by Aley, pp. 41-53.

DISTRIBUTION OF RECOMMENDED BOOKS
(Based on Rust's Basic Lists for Elementary
School Libraries, 1937 and 1939)

1937 List

1939 List

Ideological Literature (Youth in the Third Reich; World of Work)	German History World War I and II (Wars, Leaders)	Folklore (Folktales; Myths; Sagas; Hero Tales; Folk Life in the colonies)	Nonfiction (Nature; Home; Landscape)	Children's Classics; Adventure Stories; Norwegian Fiction	Crafts	
15.1%	26.0%	25.2%	11.8%	18.5%	3.4%	
17.8%	37.1%	24.2%	8.0%	11.2%		1.7%

attempt they went to even greater lengths than Rust himself by including works that had no bearing upon children's and youth literature at all, namely the unabridged editions of Hitler's *Mein Kampf*, Rosenberg's *Der Mythus des zwanzigsten Jahrhunderts (The Mythos of the Twentieth Century)*, Georg Usadel's *Zucht und Ordnung; Grundlagen einer nationalsozialistischen Ethik (Discipline and Order: The Basis of National Socialist Ethics)* and Baldur von Schirach's *Die Hitler-Jugend: Idee und Gestaltung (The Hitler Youth: Idea and Structure)*. In addition, they listed for inclusion the anti-semitic writings of Bartels, Chamberlain, de Lagarde, H.F. Günther, and von Treitschke. Many listings in the folklore area, too, were partially geared toward adult readers. This applied particularly to the twenty-six volumes of the *Thule* collection (Icelandic sagas), and to Weigel's monumental work *Runen und Sinnbilder (Runes and Symbols)*.[20]

Rust's strong emphasis on German and Nordic Germanic folklore had a notable impact on book acquisition patterns in the following years. A library report from Frankfurt (Oder) indicates that several thousand titles were purchased in accordance with Rust's guidelines, and that among these, 6,000 works alone fell under the category of German and Nordic Germanic folklore. Only the war books remained still more numerous.[21] The libraries of Königsberg, too, reported a similar progress, while expressing their gratitude for generous state support. Since 1933, they had purchased a total of 1,5 million new books, of which most had been bought after Rust had published his "Basic Lists."[22]

Very instrumental in getting children and youth to read the Volkish literature were the various promotional activities sponsored by German school and folk libraries around the country. The Dietrich Eckart Library—the model library of the National Socialist Teachers Association—organized lectures, discussions, and exhibits, so as to attract young readers and to set an example for the other libraries. Beginning in 1934, it also donated duplicate copies of every single children's book purchased by the Library to ten school libraries located in the German border areas. As the newly acquired books corresponded basically to the criteria of Volkish literature, the Association hoped by their influence to strengthen the concept of Germandom abroad and to fight off all "alien influences." In an effort to remind children at home of their "brothers and sisters abroad," the Dietrich Eckart Library also sponsored essay contests for them on such topics as "The German Fate and Fight Community," "The Greater German Reich," or "German Folkdom." Contest rules and announcement of book awards usually would be made through the children's journal *Hilf-Mit*.[23] The Reich Youth Library in Berlin sponsored not only lectures but also poetry readings on behalf of the newer poets, among which Balder von Schirach's verse creations received top attention.[24]

Sometimes both libraries would jointly arrange for some large-scale book exhibits featuring the approved literature. As a rule, teachers and Hitler Youth leaders would take children to such exhibits as part of their regular program activities. This may explain why in some cases record numbers of visitors were recorded exceeding 6,000 visitors per exhibit. Door prizes and lottery tickets added a touch of excitement to such events, and winners would usually be presented with a copy of Hitler's *Mein Kampf,* Rosenberg's *Mythus*, or Schenzinger's *Hitlerjunge Quex*.[25]

In larger towns, the Ministry of Education opened a large number of so-called "reading halls" for children in the folk libraries which had programs and exhibits of their own. Following is a listing of topics for three so-called "discussion afternoons" which librarians were expected to conduct with the approved literature:

  I. *The Soldier: Duty and Honor*
       (Readings from Littmann, Franck, and Hans Grimm.)
 II. *German Regional Humor: The Prussian Spirit*
       (Readings from Hebel, Thoma, Winckler, and Kleist.)
III. *National Socialism in Austria*
       (Readings from children's books pertaining to the experience of the Hitler Youth.)[26]

It was understood that the librarians in charge of such programs would read selections from the works listed and then channel the discussions into the "right direction."

Another common practice which librarians used to promote the approved literature among children and youth was to make available certain "package deal" arrangements. They would group together larger bundles of books, ranging from 100 to 200 titles, among which they mixed some more difficult ideological-political literature that had a very low circulation, and then would make the whole package available on a group loan basis for reduced library fees. This made it convenient for leaders from the Hitler Youth Organization to loan books for their troops on a monthly basis.[27] Also, since librarians as well as the troop leaders periodically had to give account of their activities, both could reap the credit for having promoted the works of Hitler, Rosenberg, or von Schirach, for example. Whether or not the children actually ended up selecting these titles from the package as a whole was a different matter.

According to the Nazis' own statistics, children and youth responded positively to the various measures which Party and State had taken to promote reading. The Reich Office for Folk Libraries issued a statement in 1938, indicating that, on the whole, both the folk libraries and the school libraries had done an effective job, for not only did children check out more books than ever before, but also the general population had begun to make active use of their facilities, especially among the rural population.[28] A 1938 report from the Düsseldorf libraries indicated a similar development as it noted an increase of the general circulation of books since 1935, and particularly an increase of up to

Plates 63a and 63b
An Open-Shelf Library in Posen

40% in regard to book loans to children in the rural districts of Düsseldorf. On the average, children between the ages of ten and fourteen checked out more books from the folk libraries than youth between the ages of fourteen and eighteen.[29]

Some official statistics of that time pertaining to the books borrowed from the Frankfurt folk libraries, indicate a similar increase as far as children and youth were concerned. In the Bockenheim Library in 1935, boys and girls between the ages of seven and sixteen on the average borrowed 18.6% in relation to books borrowed by adults.[30] A parallel survey conducted at the Niederrad Library in Frankfurt showed a slightly higher percentage, namely 22% for the same year.[31] In both libraries boys checked out substantially more books than did girls (about ten times more in Bockenheim and six times more in Niederrad). Five years later, boys checked out 35% of the total amount of books in circulation in all of Frankfurt's folk libraries, and for girls the figure had increased to 11%. The average increase of all books borrowed by boys and girls combined amounted to 26.8% in comparison with the average figure in 1934–35. Girls now had a slightly greater share in it, but still less than one-fourth.[32] It appears from this survey that boys between the ages of ten and fourteen years of age made the most frequent use of the folk libraries—a finding which corresponds to that of the Düsseldorf survey.

A library exhibit poster of 1940 gave a visual expression of the growing number of visitors to the Frankfurt libraries among the members of the Hitler Youth Organization.[33] It may be argued, of course, that since membership in this Organization was already mandatory at the time, probably all boys were counted in this chart, regardless of whether they came to the libraries individually or in groups, or even if their troup leaders just checked out books for them in "package deal" arrangements. Nevertheless, it basically does correspond with the statistical findings indicated above, as well as in regard to the girls' growing interest in library books. Both according to this chart and the statistics, boys between the ages of ten and fourteen read more books than the older Hitler Youth. Girls in general read less than boys, although in this case, the older girls reportedly read more than the younger ones.

We would still have to consider a few other factors that contributed to a growing reading trend among the younger population in the Third Reich. First, there were the customary home library book collections which German children always had cherished but which now received a special stimulus because the Hitler Youth Organization formally supported them. Baldur von Schirach once addressed a group of the Hitler Youth as follows:

It is not enough to read books—one has to own them. This request is not at all a fantastic one, for today in Germany we print most of the works of world literature in editions that every citizen can afford to purchase. Whoever says he cannot afford to buy books, acts stupidly and dishon-

PERCENTAGE OF BOOKS BORROWED BY CHILDREN AND YOUTH IN RELATION TO THOSE BORROWED BY ADULTS

FOLK LIBRARIES IN DÜSSELDORF

Sex and Age	1935 City Libraries	1938 City	1938 Industrial Part of City	1938 Rural Areas Adj. City	1938 Average	INCREASE 1935-1938
Boys & Girls 7-14	10.5	23.0	37.7	55.0	38.3	27.8
Boys & Girls 14-18	10.6	18.3	18.2	18.2	18.2	7.6
Average	21.1	41.3	55.9	73.2	56.5	35.4

FOLK LIBRARIES IN FRANKFURT a. MAIN

Sex and Age	1934/35 Bockenheim Library	1934/35 Niederrad Library	1934/35 Average			1939/40 All City Libraries	1939/40 Average	INCREASE 1934/35 —1939/40
Boys 7-16	13.2	18.3	16.0	Boys	10-14	25	17.5	19.0
					14-18	10		
Girls 7-16	1.2	4.0	2.6	Girls	10-14	9	5.5	5.9
					14-18	2		
	14.9	22.3	18.6			46		26.8

estly. For the same amount of money which he might spend on a pack of cigarettes or a glass of beer, he might well acquire the most valuable spiritual treasures on earth.[34]

The question remains, of course, if young people continued to buy for themselves or their friends the kinds of books that their older peers had enjoyed in pre-Nazi days, or if their definition of a "good book" had already been influenced by the Nazis' conception of Volkish literature. At any rate, children and youth did not confine themselves to the books available to them through the folk and school libraries but had the option of buying their own books, or to ask for some of their "favorites" prior to such gift-giving occasions as birthdays, Christmas, Easter, and other holidays. To give books as personal gifts was and still is a very popular custom among German children and adults.

Another factor that is less easily captured in statistics and officially printed

"OUR YOUTH IN THE FRANKFURT FOLK LIBRARIES"
1939/1940

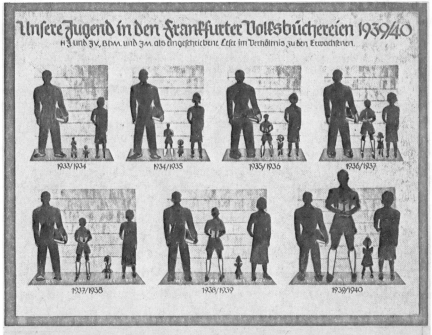

Display Chart from the Exhibit "Youth and Book" 1940
Source: *Die Bücherei* (April, 1940) 441.

policies is that regarding the influence of the church libraries. Even though the church youth organizations were formally abolished in 1939, the churches still maintained their libraries. Among others, the *Borromäus-Verein*, a Catholic league, was in charge of 6,000 religious libraries throughout Germany, and between 1933 and 1944 loaned a total of 3.4 million books to German families;[35] while all of the Catholic folk libraries circulated 140 million books during that time. Reportedly, there was an increasing demand for religious literature in Germany early in the forties,[36] which may have affected a number of children in their interests as well.

If we were to judge the Nazis' accomplishments in regard to library extensions and services solely in quantitative terms, we would have to amit some stunning results, for never before had there been so many books made available to young people than during the Nazi period, and never before did children check out so many books from the libraries.

And yet, such accomplishments cannot be measured in quantitative terms alone. In the first place, the various and continuing book purges in the library deprived young readers of many choices pertaining to world classics, the German literary heritage outside of "Volkish literature," and works about other races and other cultures in general. Secondly, the book promotion policies and activities sponsored by the school and folk libraries were designed to manipulate their interests by channelling them into areas of ideological concern to the Party. Consequently, children were faced with a narrower choice of books than ever before.

To what degree did such policies influence children's book choices and reading tastes? According to a Secret Service report of 1939, the general mood of the public inside of Germany was very receptive to the "well structured" cultural programs carried on by Party and State authorities.[37] Were children, too, affected by this mood, and did they begin to internalize the values which teachers, librarians, and youth leaders tried to promote through children's literature?

The following analysis is intended to throw some light on the question of which books children actually did check out from the libraries, which ones they liked best and why, and which ones they owned and hoped to possess. Such an investigation may give us some additional insights into the various questions raised throughout this chapter.

NOTES

1. The National Socialist Teachers Association made reference to some very early decrees in "Aufruf des N.S.L.B. zur Pflege germanischen Schrifttums" *Deutsches Bildungswesen* 10 (October, 1933) 317-322. See also "Rust-Verordnung" *Die Bücherei* (June, 1934) 12.

2. Ernst Löffler, "Die Schülerbüchereiarbeit" *Jugendschriften-Warte* 42, 2 (February, 1937), 9-12, and Anton Eisenreich, "Jugendbuchverlag, Jugendbuch und Jugendbuchkritik" in Bernhard Payr and Hans-Georg Otto, eds., *Das deutsche Jugendbuch: 4 Vorträge gehalten auf einer Jugendbuch-Arbeitswoche in Bayreuth* (Munich, Deutscher Volksverlag, 1942), pp. 20-23. See also Eduard Rothemund, "Das Jugendbuch in der deutschen Schule" *Ibid.*, pp. 77-79.

3. Reichsverwaltung des Nationalsozialistischen Lehrerbundes, eds., *Die Schülerbücherei* (Leipzig, Dürr, 1939), pp. 151-158.

4. Eduard Rothemund, "Die Neuordnung des Schülerbüchereiwesens und die deutsche Erzieherschaft" *Jugendschriften-Warte* 42, 4 (April, 1938), 128-132.

5. Of particular usefulness in this connection were Hans Maurer, *Jugend*

und Buch im Neuen Reich (Leipzig, Seemanns Verlag, 1934) and Rosenberg's numerous "white lists" (of which he published 38 major ones). These would usually include selected "Volkish literature" for all ages under such titles as "War," "German History," "Prehistory," "National Socialism and Ideology," "Demography," "Race, Folklore, and the Science of Defense," etc. See also; Reichsstelle zur Förderung des deutschen Schrifttums: Reichsschrifttumspflege im Reichsüberwachungsamt der NSDAP, eds., *Die hundert ersten Bücher für nationalsozialistische Büchereien* (Munich, Zentralverlag der N.S.D.A.P., Franz Eher, Nachf., 1940), and (published by the same office) *Sechshundert Bücher für nationalsozialistische Büchereien* (Munich, Zentralverlag der N.S.D.A.P., Franz Eher, Nachf., 1940).

6. Hans Müller, ed., *Katholische Kirche und Nationalsozialismus* (*DTV Dokumente*) (Documents Collection) (Munich, Deutscher Taschenbuchverlag G.m.b.H. & Co., 1965). Particularly relevant to the role of religious schools and youth groups during the early thirties are the following documents: No. 38, "Aus dem Protokoll der Konferenz der Diozesenverwaltung in Berlin vom 25. und 26. April, 1933, pp. 116-131; No. 142, pp. 336-337; No. 132, pp. 318-320.

7. The *Jugendschriften-Warte* carried a number of articles in 1937 that were full of praise for Rust's decree. Two years later, the National Socialist Teachers Association published its own comprehensive listing of library books that was based on Rust's library lists, but also on additional recommended works corresponding to Rosenberg's "white lists" and Maurer's book. See Reichsverwaltung des Nationalsozialistischen Lehrerbundes, eds., *Die Schülerbücherei* (Leipzig, Dürr, 1939). On behalf of Rust's "Basic Lists" consult pp. 151-158.

8. Richard Grunberger, *The Twelve-Year Reich: A Social History of Nazi Germany 1933-1945* (New York, Holt, Rinehart, and Winston, 1971), pp. 275-279.

9. Rothemund, pp. 128-132. Also: Graf zu Rantzau, *Das Erziehungsministerium für Wissenschaft, Erziehung und Volksbildung: Volksbücherei und Bildungswesen* (Berlin, Junker und Dünnhaupt, 1935), p. 28.

10. "Volksbücherei Etats" *Jugendschriften-Warte* 44, 6 (June, 1939), 95, and "Lagebericht über den Stand der Schülerbüchereien im Gau Baden, Feb. 1, 1939" *Jugendschriften-Warte* 44, 6 (June, 1939), 95.

11. Dietrich Strothmann, *Nationalsozialistische Literaturpolitik* (Bonn, Bouvier, 1968), pp. 151-152.

12. Joseph Prestel, *Die Schülerbücherei: Ein Führer zum guten Buch* (Series: *Praxis* IV) (Munich, Schulwissenschaftlicher Verlag, 1933). Recommended for use in the public schools and for teacher preparation were also Prestel's works *Volkhafte Dichtung: Besinnungen und Durchblicke* (Series: *Völkisches Lehrgut: Schriftenreihe zur Neugestaltung des Volksschulunterrichts*, ed. by K. Higelke) (Leipzig, Klinkhardt, 1935), and *Im Geleite der Geschichte: Aus deutschem Erzählgut: Lesebuch für den Schulgebrauch* (Reader)

(Munich, Oldenbourg, 1937). In the preface to the last mentioned work Prestel expressed the "Volkish" spirit of his reading selections by the following statement: "Folktales, sagas, and heroic tales are related to each other like the *Führer* and the German people . . . " pp. i-ii.

13. *Ibid.*, Introduction.

14. Rothemund, pp. 151-158.

15. Reichsstelle für volkstümliches Büchereiwesen, eds., *Grundliste für Schülerbüchereien der Volksschule* (Berlin, Verlag der N.S.D.A.P., 1937). In particular, see Rust's introduction to the list. He marked his list in accordance with four broad age group definitions: I. Folktale Age, II. Robinson Crusoe Age, III. Viking Age, IV. Age of Maturity. The first or "Folktale Age" group received the least attention. For a complete listing of individual titles consult Peter Aley, *Jugendliteratur im Dritten Reich: Dokumente und Kommentare* (Hamburg, Verlag für Buchmarktforschung, 1969), pp. 41-48.

16. Rust, *Ibid.*, introduction.

17. Reichsverwaltung, *Die Schülerbücherei*. Rust ordered in 1939 that if there were still some remaining religious titles in the school libraries, in spite of his previous decrees ordering their removal, they should be removed instantly and donated to the scrap paper collection. By no means should teachers just place them in a closet or store-room. See pp. 112-113.

18. Aley, p. 49. The complete document is cited here.

19. *Ibid.*

20. Reichsverwaltung, *Die Schülerbücherei*, p. 88. See also Strothmann, p. 152.

21. Franz Schriewer, "Leistungszahlen der Schülerbüchereien" *Jugendschriften-Warte* 43, 7 (July, 1938), 49-51. Schriewer commented that on the average, children read about 18 books per year (national statistics). Also Franz Schriewer, *Das Schülerbüchereiwesen der Volksschule in Leistungszahlen (Eine buchpolitische Untersuchung über seine Lage und Möglichkeit auf Grund von Ermittlungen im Reg. Bez. Frankfurt/Oder, für das Jahr 1936/37) 1* (Leipzig, Einkaufshaus für Büchereien, 1938), and by the same author: "Das Schülerbüchereiwesen im Rahmen des gesamten volkstümlichen Büchereiwesens" *Jugendschriften-Warte* 42, 6 (June, 1937), 47.

22. "Volksbücherei-Etats," 6. and Franz Schriewer, "Das Büchereiwesen einer Landschaft: 1934-1938" cited by Eisenreich in Payr, ed., p. 26.

23. Various announcements on behalf of the "Hans Schemm Prize" issued by the Dietrich Eckart Library were published periodically in the *Jugendschriften-Warte*. The *Hilf-Mit* children's journal was published as a supplement to the teachers' journal *Die Volksschule*.

24. The Reich Youth Library in Berlin served as the first censorship office for the Reich Youth Leadership Organization. See the chapter on Censorship.

25. "N.S.L.B. Berichte: Ausstellungen" *Jugendschriften-Warte* 44, 8 (August, 1939), 125.

26. Erik Wilkens, "Vorlesestunden für die Hitler-Jugend: Bericht aus der Praxis der Gruppenausleihe, Stadtbücherei Frankfurt/Oder" *Die Bücherei*, 3, 7-8 (July/August, 1936), 351-355. On behalf of related promotional activities consult also Rothemund, p. 77; Liselotte Bastian, "Schrifttumspolitische Führungsarbeit der HJ" *Bücherkunde* (October, 1943), 243; Irene Graebsch, "Jugendbücherei und Kinderlesehalle" *Die Bücherei* 3, 7-8 (July/August, 1936), 357-367. According to Rothemund, every major city had five reading rooms attached to the folk libraries—a number that he thought was insufficient in comparison with the ratio of about 100 school libraries for every major city, including the surrounding smaller towns. Promotional activities in the folk libraries thus were somewhat handicapped by a lack of space to work with children. The closed shelf system still persisted in most cases.

27. Wilkens, pp. 351-355.

28. Schriewer, "Leistungszahlen . . . " 30.

29. Schriewer, *Das Schülerbüchereiwesen*. Introduction. See also Dr. Wunder, cited by Eisenreich, p. 28, and "Volksbücherei Etats," 95.

30. "Lagebericht über den Stand der Schülerbüchereien . . . ," 95.

31. *Ibid.* The Niederrad Library had an experimental open shelf system, which may account for the higher number of books checked out here, in comparison with the Bockenheim Library.

32. "Unsere Jugend in den Frankfurter Volksbüchereien 1939-1940: HJ und JV, BDM and JM als eingeschriebene Leser im Verhältnis zu den Erwachsenen" *Die Bücherei* (April, 1940), 441. The chart makes reference only to the official names assigned to the various age groups by the Hitler Youth and the League of German Girls respectively. HJ = *Hitlerjugend* (Hitler Youth: 14–18 years of age); JV = *Jungvolk* (Young Folk: 10–14 years of age); BDM = *Bund Deutscher Mädel* (League of German Girls: 14–18 years of age); JM = *Jungmädel* (Young Girls: 10–12 years of age).

33. *Ibid.*

34. Baldur von Schirach, "Das Buch—Dein Freund" in Reichsjugendführung, Presse und Propagandadienst, eds., *Jahrbuch der H.J. 1939* (Berlin, Verlag der N.S.D.A.P., 1939), p. 45.

35. Aley, pp. 217-218. See also: Günter Levy, *The Catholic Church in Nazi Germany* New York, McGraw Hill, 1964).

36. Grunberger, pp. 360-361.

37. Heinz Boberach, ed., *Meldungen aus dem Reich: Auswahl aus den geheimen Lageberichten des Reichssicherheitsdienstes der SS, 1937-1944* (Neuried and Berlin, Luchterhand, 1965), p. 10. See also: William Sheridan Allen, *The Nazi Seizure of Power: The Experience of a Single German Town, 1930-1935* (Chicago, Quadrangle Books, 1965), pp. 277-287.

17

Children's Reading Interests

Were the Nazis successful in promoting Volkish literature among children and youth through educational reforms and library activities of various kinds? This question is an intriguing one, as it promises to give us some insight into the ultimate success of the Nazis' scheming, as far as children's literature was concerned.

The following analysis attempts to establish children's reading interests during the Third Reich by using several approaches to the topic. The first of these will endeavor to examine what books children actually read in the libraries, or which ones they checked out. The second approach will consider children's own votes on behalf of their favorites among the books which they read or hoped to read in the near future. The third approach will lead us to examine the types of books that children owned in their home library collections, and a final investigation will explore the question of who influenced them in the book selection process.

The data used in this study are based on surveys which teachers and librarians conducted during the Nazi period in Germany. These involve a wide range of settings and samplings: some of them polled only one age group of one sex in one particular school, whereas others sent out questionnaires to as many as 3,000 students of various ages and both sexes in several school and library districts. Not only the formats but also the points of view differed in these questionnaires. Nevertheless, the variety of survey types actually does provide us with a more vivid as well as a more accurate picture of what children actually preferred to read in Hitler's Germany, and to what extent they responded to the Nazis' cultural policy, than do mere quantitative studies.

The earliest survey which we have available for our analysis pertained to the year 1933, when a public school teacher, F. Geister, interviewed 60 boys between the ages of eleven and fifteen years, to determine which types of books they liked best.[1] The results showed that all of the boys ranked adventure stories at the very top. Whereas the younger boys favored folktales and the Nordic sagas, the older ones reserved second place for historical novels and short fiction. The fourteen to fifteen year old boys still gave folktales and sagas the fifth and sixth places, and further listed among their favorite reading material religious stories and poetry. All of the later surveys that we examined for the purposes of this study revealed that religious literature was no longer mentioned at all, most likely because Reich Education Minister Rust increasingly urged teachers and librarians to remove books of this nature from the school and folk libraries to which the surveys were confined.

In 1934/35, two folk libraries at Frankfurt kept track of the kinds of books which children between the ages of six and sixteen had most frequently checked out.[2] The analysis indicated that both boys and girls favored fiction above all other genres. Girls read fiction almost exclusively (88%), whereas boys also showed an inclination toward history and biography. Out of the four genres listed, political literature received the lowest score with only 3.5% for boys and 1.1% for girls. The very fact that it was mentioned, however, revealed the didactic intent of the censors who were now consciously trying to interest young people not only in the native folk heritage but also in the literature pertaining to the Third Reich.

During the following years, mounting Party pressures and a tightened net of censorship activities led to a more active promotion of Volkish literature at all levels. Between 1935 and 1937, the Pedagogical Institute at Leipzig conducted a survey based on a title count of all books which children had checked out for reading during 100 afternoons in the reading hall.[3] Of the total of 2,784 readers, most were boys, predominantly of the age group between ten and fourteen. Since in the chart listed below, both sexes were grouped together, we will have to keep in mind that boys made up 71.5% of the readers who would therefore have read the bulk of the books. About one-third of these readers belonged to the younger age group of six to ten, which may partially explain why so many of them selected picture books. On the other hand, the comments accompanying the survey indicated that the "picture posters" were included in the genre of picture books, among which many of the more recent ones depicted scenes related to modern technology that were of interest to older boys, too.

1935 - 1937
SURVEY OF BOOKS READ BY CHILDREN DURING
100 READING AFTERNOONS
(LEIPZIG)

Genre	Number of Books Read or Borrowed	Percent
Picture Books	1,247	24.5
Folktales	924	18.1
Children's Stories	888	17.4
Adventure Stories	561	11.0

SURVEY OF BOOKS - *Continued*

Genre	Number of Books Read or Borrowed	Percent
Humorous Stories	510	10.0
War Literature	376	7.4
Sagas	187	3.7
National Socialist Literature	132	2.6
Nature Stories	89	1.7
Technology & Crafts	76	1.5
Historical Tales and Novels	49	1.0
Poetry and Nonsense Verse	26	0.5
Short Stories; Novellas	17	0.3
Fables	15	0.3
Total:	5,097	100.0 [4]

After the picture books, the children gave the highest rating still to folktales, and then to the sagas—a survey result that may indicate how the children's natural interest in folk literature coincided with the Party's efforts in promoting it. A librarian in another town in Germany at that time commented how this particular reading interest indeed pleased the authorities:

The reason why we have reserved so much space in our youth libraries for folktales and sagas, may be partially explained by the fact that there is such a great demand for such works, especially among our youngest readers, and partially, because it corresponds to our policy of cultivating German folklore. It is self-evident that in selecting such works, we examine them carefully in regard to the quality of language and their flawlessness of style. So far, we have given special attention to regional and local collections of legends that appeal to the younger readers. However, since the Hitler Youth Organization, too, has consciously tried to revive an interest in folktales and sagas among its members, many older children, too, are now reading in this area . . . [5]

Whereas the children in the reading hall in Leipzig had checked out a total of 21.8% (about one-fourth) of all books in the area of folktales and sagas, they also showed a slowly growing interest in political literature and war literature, for both genres combined made up about 10% of all the books they read. Even though that figure still fell short of the Party's expectations at that time, it represented a remarkable progress over the low percentages of books checked out in the equivalent genre in Frankfurt a few years earlier.

Another survey which Uhlig conducted in 1937[6] among children of all grades attending a *Volksschule* (Folk School), indicated that folktales still ranked relatively high on the list of favorite books, although girls tended to like them about twice as much as boys. Boys listed as their most favorite reading adventure stories, followed by stories about the Third Reich and books about war. Girls liked fiction best of all. Within this genre, they gave priority to the girls' books, and then to novels and in general. Obviously, they did not care too much for political or war literature of any kind.

Uhlig still administered a third survey at a secondary school for girls (*Oberschule*)[7] in which customarily more emphasis was placed on literary education. On the basis of his findings, he came to the conclusion that even though the girls were all a little older here (5th through 12th grade), they expressed an even stronger liking for German folktales and the Nordic sagas than the younger girls at the *Volksschule* had indicated. At the same time, they showed only a minor inclination to read the old-fashioned girls' books but favored fiction in general. Simultaneously, he noted among them a greater interest in literature pertaining to the Third Reich. All of these differences Uhlig ascribed to the more pronounced efforts of teachers to educate the girls in the "more enlightened" spirit of the new regime. He commended them for having done a good job of raising the girls with a "new sense of reality" that no longer admitted the artificial world of the girls' books to which the younger girls at the *Volksschule* were still addicted in their reading habits. It is worth noting that Uhlig considered the reading of folktales and sagas in no way contradictory to an education aiming at "a sense of reality."

At a Berlin library in 1937, Ilse Kattenstidt polled 1,000 children between the ages of six and sixteen, in trying to determine what book they would place as "Number One" on their Christmas gift list.[8] Overwhelmingly, the children voted for a volume of folktales or "stories" (260 votes combined for boys and girls). Kattenstedt obviously was pleased with this result, as it seemed to correspond to some major goals of the book promotion policy which librarians had pursued with teachers during the past years. The next highest vote on the list, however, did cause her some embarrassment. She admitted that the girls still clung to the old-fashioned girls' books, particularly to the *Nesthäkchen (Little Nest Hook)* series, whereas the boys stubbornly persisted in reading Karl May's adventure stories about the American Indians. "It is a significant fact that children still show a predominant interest in older books," she commented. "Is this because their parents have transmitted to them their own wishes and preferences, or are these books so genuine and childlike in their appeal that the newer books simply cannot take their place?"[9] She speculated that both of these reasons might have a bearing upon children's book choices, although she made it clear that in her view, such choices were nothing less than "an error in taste." It might be excusable if they were still fond of Busch's *Max and Moritz* or Hoffmann's *Struwwelpeter*, but neither *Little Nest Hook* nor the Karl May books really could be considered to have much literary value.

The following chart indicates how the children actually voted. In some cases, they referred to the specific title of a book which they hoped to receive as a gift; in others they merely mentioned a genre in which they were generally interested.

BOOKS WHICH CHILDREN HOPED TO RECEIVE AS GIFTS UNDER THE CHRISTMAS TREE IN DECEMBER, 1936

The Frequency With Which a Title or Series was Mentioned	Books Desired by Boys	Books Desired by Girls
3	*The Red U* *The Chase of the Emden* Books about Aviation *My Brother Horst*	Andersen's *Fairy Tales* *Dr. Doolittle* *Without a Home* *Nils Holgersson*
3	Robber Tales *Rolf Torring's Adventures* Books about ships *S-Curve at Remberg* *Verdun* *Two Boys in the Navy*	*Robinson Crusoe* *Tomboy* War books
4	Stories by Wilhelm Busch *The Hindenburg* Books about the navy *Rübezahl* *Trapper Tales* *Arabian Nights* *Till Eulenspiegel*	*The Red Fighter Bomber* *Friedel Starmatz* *Inge Must Go into the World* *Girl on Duty* *My Brother Horst* *Little Rose* Animal stories *Till Eulenspiegel* *Udet*
5	*Book about the Führer* *Adventures at Sea* Books about soldiers *Submarine U 9*	Stories by Wilhelm Busch *Gisel and Ursel* *Easter Bunny* *Rosel* *Arabian Nights*

Continued: The Frequency With Which a Title or Series was Mentioned	Books Desired by Boys	Books Desired by Girls
6	Adventure stories *The New Universe* *Baron von Münchhausen*	*Family Pepperling*
8	*German Legends*	*Pommerle* *Bibi* Karl May books
9	*Auerbach's Calendar* *The Red Fighter Bomber* *Sea Devil* Animal stories *Father and Son*	*Auerbach's Calendar* *The Little Hitler Girl* *Little Golden Head* (Series) *Inge Wessel* *Proud Girl Gerda*
11	War books *Leatherstocking Tales* *Robinson Crusoe*	*Professor's Twins* *Struwwelpeter*
12	————	*German Legends* *The Hitler Youth Named Quex* *Mein Kampf*
13	Grimms' *Household Tales* *The Hitler Youth Named Quex* Busch's *Max and Moritz* Books about World War I	————
15	*Battle of Skagerrak*	————
19	Books about American Indians	*Heidi*
22	*Mein Kampf* (Hitler)	[10]
58	Books by Karl May	————
60	————	*Nesthäkchen (Little Nest Hook)*
100-160	Folktales	Folktales

For reasons of consistency, we have included in the above chart the 58 votes for the works of Karl May, the 60 votes for *Little Nest Hook*, and the extremely high votes of 100 and 160 for German folktales by boys and girls respectively.

Kattenstidt mentioned these votes in her article only but did not include them in the chart. It is possible that the chart entries, ending with the twenty-two votes for *Mein Kampf*, were supposed to create the illusion that the educational efforts of the librarians had been successful, so as to hide the embarrassing fact that the Karl May books and the old-fashioned girls' book series had still received more votes than Adolf Hitler himself. It is also possible, of course, that the editors of the *Jugendschriften-Warte* made such an adjustment within the context of their normal censorship routine.[11]

With all the emphasis which the National Socialist Teachers Association placed on a revival of German folktales and Nordic Germanic folklore, it is not surprising that both boys and girls developed a great interest in their native folk heritage. Neither is it unexpected that girls should have begun to take an interest in the newer books representing young heroines of the Third Reich, such as *The Little Hitler Girl, Inge Wessel, Proud Girl Gerda*, and *Gisel and Ursel*, for all of them did not merely preach an abstract ideology but were characterized by active plots—even though their characters remained as unconvincing as those of the old-fashioned girls' book series. Somewhat unusual, however, is the survey result indicating that the girls gave twelve votes to Hitler's *Mein Kampf*. Obviously, girls had begun to share with the boys an interest in Karl May, the *German Legends, Robinson Crusoe, The Hitler Youth Named Quex* and others, yet we may wonder if they knew what they were up to when they asked Santa Claus to place Hitler's book under the Christmas tree.[12] The same holds true for the boys' votes on this behalf, for it is questionable if twenty-two of them really intended to read a book that even the most loyal followers of Hitler found difficult to digest from cover to cover, and which was not even read in an abridged form within the school curriculum. We may assume that either the boys and girls tried to please their librarian by naming it, or that the librarian or the editors of the journal hoped to please the censorship authorities by listing some fictitious votes for this work.

In general, the survey indicates that Volkish literature in its various forms had made a certain impression upon children. Their interest in folklore had gained some strength, and so had their votes for the newer works presenting characters within the National Socialist setting. Eleven boys and three girls had asked for books about war, and in addition, a number of boys did intend to read more books about the *Führer*, German soldiers, and submarines in the near future. Still, it appeared to have escaped the librarian's notice that the boys had not only given fifty-eight votes for Karl May's books, but also nineteen votes for "books about American Indians" in general and eleven votes for Cooper's *Leatherstocking Tales*, which would make a total of eighty-eight votes for the genre of adventure stories dealing with American Indians. The girls, too, not only read *Little Nest Hook* but also the *Little Golden Head* series, and the old-fashioned book *Professor's Twins*, next to Johanna Spyri's *Heidi*.

What the survey tells us is that German children at this time still clung to their favorite books that their mothers and fathers had enjoyed long before the Nazis came to power. Further, it reveals that in regard to folklore and regional literature the Nazis' folk education program obviously coincided with the children's natural inclinations, for it seems they responded positively to the increased exposure to German folktales, sagas, and legends. The newer literature, too, gradually had taken root, although not yet at the expense of the old favorites among the classic adventure stories. The very fact, however, that neither boys nor girls asked for stories from or about other cultures may mean that they did not even miss what the censors had taken away from them in the libraries.[13]

As late as 1941, the librarian Ella Manz observed that, unfortunately, girls were still addicted to the old-fashioned girls' books and also owned many volumes of these series which they eagerly traded with their friends.[14] In conducting a survey with a class of sixth graders in an attempt to discover what books they actually kept at home on their private library shelves, she discovered with some bewilderment that ten continued to list the *Little Nest Hook* series among them, even though the author, Else Ury, had been condemned as a Jewish writer. The series of *Little Golden Head* had moved up on the list, along with other series of old-fashioned girls' books, and only some individual titles reflected the new literary and cultural policy of the Third Reich. She had a difficult time in reconciling this "saccharine-sweet" interest with the girls' newly discovered favorite, the Karl May books; yet she wrote that she would prefer it a hundred times over if girls would read the American Indian adventure stories instead of escaping with a "lingering sentimentality" into the dream world of the old-fashioned girls' books that had nothing whatever to offer in preparing girls for the challenge of present-day life.

THE HOME LIBRARY COLLECTIONS:
BOOKS OWNED BY SIXTH GRADERS IN 1941

Number of Books Owned *or* Number of Series Owned. (Each series was listed only once.)	Author of a Series and/or Book Title
45	Magda Trott, *Little Golden Head* (Series)
34	Johanna Spyri, *Heidi*
14	Agnes Sapper (Series)
14	Josephine Siebe (Series)
12	Karl May (Series)
10	Else Ury, *Little Nest Hook* (Series)
5	Von Rhoden, *Little Block Head* (Series)
5	Steup, *Wiete Wants to Go to Africa*
5	Heinze-Hoferichter, *Friedel Starmatz*
1	Müller-Hennig, *The Volga Children*

THE HOME LIBRARY COLLECTIONS - Continued

Number of Books Owned *or* Number of Series Owned. (Each series was listed only once.)	Author of a Series and/or Book Title
1	Hollesch, *The Black Horse*
1	Hamsun, *The Langerrud Children*
1	Rothmund, *A Child Searches for His Mother*
1	Müller, *Ursel and Her Girls*
1	W. Bauer, *Gertie Looks for a Job*
1	Lagerlöf, *Tales About My Youth*
1	Gieloss, S., *When Mother Was a Child*
1	Fischer, *Jutta's Year of Duty*[15]

We would have to multiply the number of books in each series by about twelve, wrote Manz, to estimate how many of these works were owned by the sixth graders, for no child was allowed to list the author of a given book more than once.

A librarian in Aachen suggested that more should be done to motivate girls to read newer works of fiction, such as *Kamerad Schwester* (*Nurse, Our Comrade*) or *Das Soldatentum der Schwester Cläre* (*The Soldier Spirit of Nurse Clare*), so as to wean them from their old-fashioned favorites.[16] She had personally tried to introduce girls to some of the newer works, as well as to the newer journals, and the attempt had been successful. The same was true in regard to boys. Given the right motivation and introduction, they, too, would gradually move away from the Karl May books toward such works as Matthiessen's *Rotes U* (*The Red U*) and Weidemann's *Jungzug 2* (*Young Track No. 2*).

Judging by the various library reports that we have analyzed in the previous chapter, this type of motivation was systematically applied by teachers and librarians in connection with reading and discussion afternoons, book exhibits, and other activities. The time span from 1933 to 1941 was probably not long enough to indicate more dramatic results from such book promotion efforts, but as the Nazis considered folk education as an on-going process, they were determined to continue their Volkish book policy.

In the meanwhile, the only results which teachers and librarians reported with pride were those pertaining to the children's growing interest in German and Nordic Germanic folklore editions, yet they consistently apologized for their own failure in weaning them from their "un-Volkish" favorites.

In the late thirties Uhlig conducted a survey among 700 girls between the ages of fourteen and sixteen, in order to establish to what extent the various organizational efforts of Party and State on behalf of children's books had had an impact on their reading choices.[17] The questionnaire results basically confirmed the trends which we have established so far. It turned out that the girls gave their highest vote to their personal friend, whom they obviously trusted most in terms of advising them of a good book to read. The private influence sphere, consisting of friends, parents, brothers and sisters, as well as acquaintances, at that time still had a greater impact on their book choices than the public influence sphere, consisting of teachers, librarians, youth leaders, book exhibits organized by the Hitler Youth, radio, and church. Among the public advisors, however, teachers and school librarians still received a higher vote than parents. Uhlig proudly commented on these results: "This response proves that the advice of professional persons (teachers and librarians) is still in demand by young people. The influences of teachers are not lost after all, and are still the most significant ones among the public advisors." The very tone of this statement betrayed that Uhlig did not take the stronger influences of teachers and librarians for granted, although it pleased him very much to learn that they were still leading in the race with the more radical Hitler Youth Organization and their book promotion activities.

The survey also indicated that the churches supposedly had only very minor influences on the girls' book choices. Uhlig preferred not to comment on these figures, and since he failed to provide additional data pertaining to the girls' church affiliations, it is difficult to establish if they reflect an honest response to the situation or not. It is possible that the girls ascribed their reading of religious literature (if any) to the influences of their friends and parents, too, but it is still more likely that they did not wish to betray the church's influences on their reading choices, for fear of being ostricized by the authorities or their peers.[18] It was already common practice at that time to ridicule boys and girls who on Sunday mornings preferred to follow the "Black Frocks" to church instead of dutifully attending the meetings and activities sponsored during the same hours by their troop leaders. Further, the possibility exists that the girls were asked to refer to their book choices only in regard to those which they selected from the school libraries and folk libraries, and since these libraries, upon the order of Rust, had already been "cleansed" of most of the religious books, they may not have had a good reason to respond positively to the survey question. In addition, whatever advice the churches may have to children, most likely did not support their reading of Volkish literature as Party and State authorities understood it, nor would the church have supported the children's private reading interests in American Indian adventure stories and the old-fashioned girls' books which teachers still tolerated to some degree, even though they were not very happy about them either.

The various surveys pertaining to children's reading interests have shown that the Nazis' control system was still marked by certain "imperfections." This was fortunate for German children at the time, for in the perfect society as the

Nazis envisioned it, no child would have been allowed to read anything except the books exactly prescribed by the authorities. Neither would it have been permitted to read even the German folktales merely for the sake of enjoyment. As it was, many teachers and librarians at the time still did not follow their "ultimate duty" of attaching ideological interpretations to every book that children chose to read on their own, and no cases have been reported where they would force children to "cleanse" their home libraries, too, of the undesirable literature. In spite of their numerous complaints, they were still much more tolerant toward children's book choices than one might have expected in a totalitarian state.

On the other hand, we cannot minimize the growing impact which the newer books had on children. Increased censorship activities toward the end of the thirties, and the coordination of reading textbooks, curricular reforms, and library re-organizations further contributed to the implementation of folk education at all levels of society, and simultaneously, toward an increased conformity in children's book choices and reading trends.

In the early forties, some children still managed to use books as an escape into their private dream worlds. One librarian observed that children read more folktales than ever before because it helped them to forget the harsh reality on the outside. Interrupted school schedules, rationed food supplies, and sleepless nights in the bomb shelters had made it more urgent for them than ever to find a quiet retreat in a world of enchantment. She also referred to the case of an older youth who just one day after the city had been devastated by a heavy bomb attack, had calmly withdrawn to a library corner to read Wilhelm Raabe's *Chronik der Sperlingsgasse* (*The Chronicle of Sparrow's Lane*), thus searching for consolation in a nineteenth century novel.[19]

Observations such as these do not belie the Nazis' design for the future to turn every child's private reading experience into a lesson on race and Volkish propaganda, for there were indications enough that they hoped to make progress in that direction. The children's journal *Hilf Mit*, for example, printed a story involving two boys of the Hitler Youth Organization who had done what was ideally expected of every child marching under the banner of the swastika flag: systematically, they had taken an inventory of the contents of their parents' book cases at home, to establish which of the books should have already been removed a long time ago. They had then confronted their parents with a list of "un-Volkish literature" and had successfully induced them to donate the corresponding items to the Hitler Youth's scrap paper collection.[20]

In view of such projected trends, it is not difficult to imagine what might have happened to children's reading interests if the Third Reich had lasted a few decades longer than it did. Certainly it was not in the interest of the Party that children still read folktales and novels for very personal reasons rather than for the sake of strengthening the racial doctrine of Nazi propaganda.

NOTES

1. F. Geister, "Jungen urteilen über Jugendschriften" *Jugendschriften-Warte* 38, 11 (November, 1933), 81-83.
2. For more detailed statistical data consult *Die Bücherei* (March, 1935), 400-402.
3. Marianne Günzel and Harriet Schneider, *Buch und Erziehung: Jugendschrifttumskunde* (Leipzig, Klinkhardt, 1937), p. 126.
4. *Ibid.*
5. Irene Graebsch, "Jugendbücherei und Kinderlesehalle" *Die Bücherei* 3, 7-8 (July/Aug., 1936), 357-367.
6. Dr. Friedrich Uhlig, "Was liest unsere Jugend" *Jugendschriften-Warte* 42, 5 (May, 1937), 33-35.
7. *Ibid.*
8. Ilse Kattenstidt, "Was unsere Kinder lesen möchten" *Jugendschriften-Warte* 42, 10 (October, 1937), 65.
9. *Ibid.*, 69.
10. *Ibid.*
11. Basically, with the exception of the reference to *Mein Kampf*, Kattenstidt's survey appears to have been an honest one, as it did not attempt to paint an artificial picture of success but—at least in the article—admitted certain shortcomings in children's literary interests. This cannot always be said about the statistics cited by librarians and teachers during the Third Reich, some of which, from the outset, limited the survey questions to political literature and war literature only, as if other genres in children's literature simply did not exist. See, for example, statistics cited in *Die Bücherei* (June, 1942), 286. Another survey began with a teacher's preconceived notion that girls liked to read love stories more than anything else. He then let them chose among the genres of humorous stories, folktales, legends, sagas, and love stories, while ignoring realistic fiction, adventure stories, and other genres. As expected, the results then inevitably confirmed his original prejudice. *Die Erziehung* 17, 6 (June, 1942), 113.
12. See Dietrich Strothmann, *Nationalsozialistische Literaturpolitik: Ein Beitrag zur Publizistik im Dritten Reich* (Bonn, Bouvier, 1968), p. 376.
13. In a survey of what books children actually had received as gifts under the Christmas tree, a teacher counted, among others, 9 series of Ury's *Little Nest Hook*, 6 series of Trott's *Little Golden Head*, 7 volumes of Spyri's *Heidi*, and a number of other girls' book series by Sapper, Michaelis, and von Rhoden. There were also a number of folktale collections and Romantic fairy tales by Brentano, a work on Norse mythology and hero tales, and the *Arabian Nights*.

Only 3 books, however, reflected Volkish literature with political inclinations, namely *The Volga Children* (the theme of Germandom abroad), *Inge Wessel* (the League of German Girls) and *Youth About Hitler*. "Bücher zu Weihnachten in einer Sexta" *Jugendschriften-Warte* 47, 7-8 (July/August, 1942), 52.

14. Ella Manz, "Gedanken zum Lesegut heranwachsender Mädchen" *Jugendschriften-Warte* 47, 7-8 (July/Aug., 1942), 49-52.

15. *Ibid.*

16. Elfriede Bister, "Was wird am liebsten gelesen?" *Jugendschriften-Warte* 48, 9 (October, 1943), 62-64. See also Eva Kaulfers, "Was wird am liebsten gelesen?" *Jugendschriften-Warte* 48, 8 (October, 1943), 64-66. Heiderich came to the conclusion that girls were reading too many "undesirable" books, merely because there were not enough of the newer books available for them, and that this was so because "women in general lack the necessary creative originality of men to write a truly good book. . . " A statement like this shows how far some librarians had come to accept the Nazis' definition of the woman's role in society as one that received its ultimate meaning from the "three k's: *Kinder, Kirche* and *Küche*" (children, church, and kitchen). See Hiltraut Heiderich, "Das Mädelbuch in der Jugendarbeit der Volksbüchereien: Was liest das Mädel?" *Jugendschriften-Warte* 47, 7-8 (July/August, 1942), 52-56. Heiderich did not deny, however, that some women of previous decades and centuries had written some good books after all that still deserved attention. Thus, she recommended for girls in particular not only a number of the newer girls' books within the National Socialist setting, but also the works of such women writers as Agnes Miegel, Marie von Ebner-Eschenbach, and Annette von Droste-Hülshoff.

17. Uhlig, 39.

18. George Frederick Kneller, *The Educational Philosophy of National Socialism* (New Haven, Yale University Press, 1941), pp. 184-204. Also: Erika Mann, *Schools for Barbarians: Education under the Nazis* (New York, Modern Age Books, pp. 85-94 and pp. 111-123.

19. Erika Gerlach, "Westdeutsche Jugend 1942: Leserkundliche Betrachtungen einer Volksbibliothekarin" *Die Bücherei* 11, 1-3 (Jan./March, 1944), 61. See also: Peter Aley, *Jugendliteratur im Dritten Reich: Dokumente und Kommentare* (Hamburg, Verlag für Buchmarktforschung, 1967), pp. 208-209.

20. *Hilf Mit* 43 (1936/37), 43. Aley, p. 213.

18

Publishing Trends

The Nazis' plans regarding German folk education are also well reflected in the book production trends during the Third Reich. Even more so than their curricular reforms and their school library reforms, they mirror some different although related approaches taken by the National Socialist Teachers Association on the one hand and the Reich Youth Leadership Organization on the other. At the same time, they give evidence of the existence of certain "loopholes" in the Nazis' censorship system which may explain at least partially why German children still got away with reading some of their old-time favorites.

Early in 1933, Hans Schemm, President of the National Socialist Teachers Association, announced that the Association would do its very best to issue several series of paperback editions that followed the leading ideas of Volkish literature for children and youth.[1] Joseph Prestel, too, in his early library reorganization plan, recommended strongly that paperbacks should be made available to young people, both for classroom use and for their private reading, so as to strengthen German folk education along ideological lines. Among others, he suggested that the schools make use of some already existing series of inexpensive literature that had been initiated in the twenties.[2]

It was not until 1936, however, that such publication plans were actually realized on a large scale. Proudly, the Association announced the paperback publication of 134 individual titles under the following general categories corresponding to the basic concepts of German folk education through literature that was meant to "cultivate the memory of the forefathers and to promote the German national consciousness":

"GERMAN CHARACTER AND FATE"
PAPERBACK SERIES FOR CHILDREN AND YOUTH
1936

1. Thule (Icelandic Sagas)
2. German Hero Tales
3. Folk Legends and Regional Legends

4. German Chapbooks and Tales about Medieval Knights
5. German Jests and Fables
6. German Folktales
7. Germanic-German Prehistory and Early History
8. One Thousand Years of the German "Middle Ages"
9. From Wittenberg to Tauroggen
10. The Second Reich of the Germans
11. World War I and Versailles
12. Battle, Victory, and the Building of National Socialism
13. Studies of Epochs and Historical Periods; Surveys
14. The German People; German Leaders
15. Autobiographies; Memoirs of Great Germans[3]

The titles of these series betrayed the Association's attempt to correlate the works with the new folklore orientation of the core curriculum in the public schools, and simultaneously, also to strengthen the basic concepts emphasized in the reading textbooks. None of these series, with the exception of some change in the titles, actually was a new one. Under the leadership of Rüttgers, Wolgast and others, 44 series had already been initiated for young people after World War I, and by 1933, they had increased to 212.[4] What remained had been more strictly adjusted to the Volkish demands of the National Socialist ideology, and bore the general title of *Deutsches Wesen und Schicksal* (*German Character and Fate*), in which a number of publishing houses participated.

The Nazis' strong emphasis on folklore and regional literature of the nineteenth century, initially made it relatively easy for publishers to adjust their publications to this trend, as many of them had produced such works already in great quantity during the twenties. It seems that they preferred re-publishing older works to publishing the works of newer writers, not only because it was more economic to do so, but also, because less risk was involved.[5] The market was established for German and Nordic Germanic folklore, as much as for the peasant and historical novel, all of which were now promoted not only among adults but also among children and youth. Such leading publishing houses like the Diederichs Verlag in Jena, for example, would issue an abundance of folklore collections with new prefaces, while making them available to the general public in relatively inexpensive editions.[6] In 1936, it issued Genzmer's monumental "folk edition" of the Icelandic sagas, entitled *Thule*, in 10,000 copies—a work, as the reviewers appraised it, that was ideally suited for "our *fighting youth* . . . to lead us to the roots of our own character . . . our Volkish existence . . . the spirit of our German history and the German future."[7] In the same year, it published, apparently in response to the great demand, three folklore series and eight collections and anthologies related to German and Nordic Germanic folklore.[8]

A parallel development could be observed in regard to the proliferation of

BOOKS FOR GERMAN YOUTH

Pamphlet No. 20

THE LIVING SPACE OF THE GERMAN *VOLK*

Map of
"Greater Germany"

All of Germany it Shall Be!

"Take care that our *Volk* will draw its strength from the soil of our home in Europe. Never believe that the Reich is safe, unless for the decades to come it can provide every single citizen with his own piece of land. Never forget that the most sacred right on earth is the right to own your land!"

(Our *Führer*'s words in *Mein Kampf*)

peasant novels and historical novels, most of which were reprinted from earlier editions during the early thirties. Never before had so many peasant novels flooded the market.[9]

Both the folklore trend and the peasant novel trend corresponded to the Nazis' demand for Volkish literature, but they only represented its relatively conservative aspect. Baldur von Schirach and Rainer Schlösser complained on behalf of the Reich Youth Leadership Organization that such works were not sufficient to raise German youth in the spirit of the National Socialist ideology. Urgently needed were more books about the National Socialist leadership, the new heroes, and the new folk community.[10] By 1937, the literary critic Hellmuth Langenbucher felt that "the really good book" that was still lacking should show an interest in themes affecting the present time, such as the settlement policy, the new peasantry, workers, artisans, and even the field of sports.[11]

Children's books dealing with National Socialist themes had been published since 1933, but they did not appeal strongly enough to the children's imagination to tease them away from the Karl May books and the girls' book series. Of sixty new paperbacks published by the Eher Verlag right after the Nazis' seizure of power, for example, the first group of books dealt with such German leaders as Hitler, Hindenburg, Göring, Goebbels, von Schirach, and even the "Iron Chancellor," Bismarck. More popular with young readers was the series on "German Heroes," as it included some booklets on the fate of Leo Schlageter and Horst Wessel, and also on such nineteenth century "freedom fighters" as Theodor Körner and Ernst Moritz Arndt.[12] Early in the thirties a total of thirty-four publishers participated in the production of books about the *Führer* alone. Most of these works, too, were constantly recommended for inclusion in the school libraries and the reading program in the public schools, although most of them lacked vitality and the power of conviction. Among the better known works were such titles as *Das Volk ehrt Hitler* (*The Folk Honors Hitler*), *Jugend um Hitler* (*Youth Around Hitler*), *Hitler in den Bergen* (*Hitler in the Mountains*), and *Hitler wie ihn keiner kennt* (*Hitler; What Nobody Knows About Him*). These were issued in editions of between 70,000 and 100,000 copies.[13]

It was only toward the end of the thirties that some publishers began to turn from the Nazis' conservative trends increasingly toward newer works of fiction for children and youth. For girls, the Schneider Verlag, among others, began to publish a number of works that appealed to their interests, as they showed young heroines in a contemporary setting. For boys, the new trends really set in only after 1939 when the first war booklets were issued in large quantities. In quantitative terms, the war booklets surpassed all other publications during the forties, although their quality left much to be desired.[14] What made both the newer girls' books and the war booklets so popular was less their ideological message than their active plots; yet in terms of characterization and thematic development they projected stereotypes that did not leave a lasting impression on children's minds.

In an attempt to "up-date" the publishing program for young people, the Reich Youth Leadership Organization initiated its own publications. Among these were Baldur von Schirach's own anthology of poetry, entitled *Die Fahne der Verfolgten* (*The Flag of the Persecuted Ones*) and his bestseller, *Die Hitlerjugend—Idee und Gestalt* (*The Hitler Youth: Idea and Structure*). Besides, the Organization would publish its own yearbooks, journals, and series on a regular basis, in an attempt to promote more vigorously the principles of the National Socialist ideology.[15] The yearbooks of the Hitler Youth Organization and the League of German Girls respectively became the "modern almanacs" for progressive youth raised in the spirit of an excessive national pride and a pronounced hatred and contempt for other cultures and "alien races." German and Nordic Germanic folklore, too, were included in these volumes, but to a much lesser degree than in the works promoted by the National Socialist Teachers Association. Such poetry anthologies as *Junges Volk* (*Young Folk*) and *Vom wehrhaften Geist* (*About the Spirit of Defense*) still reflected to some degree the defiant spirit of the Nordic Germanic ancestor, but much more so of the "fighter league" of young National Socialists. Books of choral readings and National Socialist celebrations, including Christmas celebrations, were all geared toward the mass rallies of the "young team."[16]

There was a continuing struggle among the members of the National Socialist Teachers Association and the members of the Reich Youth Leadership Organization on behalf of what trends the publishers should follow: the Volkish conservative ones or the more modern radical ones. As more of the newer works became available and as the Reich Youth Leadership Organization's membership increased in its membership and power,[17] more pressure was placed on publishers to follow their line of thinking. Since, in addition, there was a growing paper shortage, on which basis the Reich Culture Chamber had passed a new law on paper distribution, it became increasingly risky for publishers to walk the easier road by reprinting older approved literature only.[18] Under mounting pressures, they began to respond more and more to the requests from the quarters of the Reich Youth Leadership Organization. As a result, many new works were published in the field of children's and youth literature during the early forties that clearly betrayed the didactic political message of National Socialism.

In terms of real production numbers, this change in emphasis was not very evident, as the actual number of books published for children and youth remained relatively stable between 1935 and 1941, encompassing on the average 1,477 books per year.[19] The picture looks very different, however, if we consider the number of re-publications in comparison with that of the newer publications. Whereas during the early years of the Nazi Regime the re-editions had outweighed all other ones, the situation was reversed during the war. By 1941, 75% of all children's literature represented the newer works, whereas the number of re-editions had shrunk to 25%.[20] The National Socialist Teachers Association did not consider this a welcome trend, and officially voiced a complaint against such a "craving for new books," which, in their view, was not at all in the best interest of German folk education.[21] Such a difference in viewpoints clearly illustrates how much the National Socialist Teachers Association considered traditional German and Nordic Germanic folklore, along with selected older works of German literature, an indispensable part of German folk education.

The book production figures in regard to children's literature during the Third Reich were not always consistent, simply because different sets of statistics used conflicting definitions for this genre. In most cases, they lumped together fiction and nonfiction for children from kindergarten age through eighteen, but in some cases, they ignored the Volkish literature recommended by the Hitler Youth if it was also read by adults. Here and there, even textbooks and anthologies were counted, too, which made the figures particularly confusing after the bulk of them was issued in 1937.[22] In 1937, the *Jugendschriften-Warte* reported that children's literature shared in the general increase of German book production that had occurred since 1933. National statistics for the year 1942 indicated that in relation to books published for adults, children's literature comprised 22%, or roughly a quarter of the entire German book production.[23] This was an increase of 16.2% in comparison with the figure cited for 1937.[24] The editors of the *Börsenblatt (Stockmarket Journal)* commented that, in reality, this increase might still be greater than indicated, as most of the older Hitler Youth had been trained to read many of the same works as adults, in addition to youth literature.[25]

The increasing demand for Volkish literature that would expose children to current political dimensions of the Third Reich indeed had an impact on general book production, for many of the titles originally printed for adults were placed in school and folk libraries for children and general use. A case in point was Hitler's *Mein Kampf* which was distributed to every library in the country and of which free copies even given away to children as "door prizes" during youth book exhibits. Between 1933 and 1936, 1 million copies of this work were printed, and by 1940 it had reached the 6 million mark.[26] Relatively high production figures were also reached by *The Hitler Youth Named Quex* with 140,000 copies and *Horst Wessel*, with 150,000 copies during a two year period.[27]

There were some other works, however, that were neither strongly recommended by Party and State authorities, nor expressly forbidden, which still maintained higher production numbers than the last two mentioned works. Leading was Richard Voss' novel, *Zwei Menschen (Two Human Beings)*, which was issued in an edition of 860,000 copies. Next came Waldemar Bonsels' children's book *Die Biene Maja (The Bee Maja)* which had originally been published in 1912. The print ran 650,000 copies—of a book which did not appear on any one of Rust's "Basic Lists" for the school libraries and which formally had no place in the schools' literature curriculum either. Ludwig Ganghofer's *Schloss Hubertus (Castle Hubertus)* came in third place, and it was followed by the works of Felix Dahn, Rudolf Herzog, Paul Keller, Rudolf G. Binding, Hermann Löns, Rainer Maria Rilke, Felicitas Rose, and Walter Flex. Dahn, Keller and Löns were officially recommended to children in connection with the late nineteenth century historical and regional novels, yet this was not true for Rilke, whose works were officially condemned by the Nazis as much as Wiechert's were. Nevertheless, it turned out that both authors remained very popular in Germany.[28]

The Nazis had formally outlawed Bonsels' works, with the exception of *The Bee Maja* and two other works; they must have frowned upon discovering that it was actually published during their reign and that more than four times as many copies of it were printed than of their highly advertised *The Hitler Youth Named Quex.* The publishers obviously followed the rule that anything would be permissible if it were not specifically prohibited by law, particularly if it promised to bring good business. Why the authorities did not object to the huge editions of the work we may deduct from their general criteria of Volkish literature. It was a fantasy, but with its emphasis on nature viewed through the animating spirit of the imagination, it came to resemble a German folktale in many respects. Perhaps it was still more important to the censors that it ranked high in regard to some values deemed useful within German community life. Close to the end of the work there is a scene in which the Queen gently places her arms around Bee Maja's neck, telling her how much she has appreciated her loyalty toward home and country. "Now we, too, will be loyal to you," she said. "In the future, you will stay by my side to help me in all matters regarding the state."[29]

Bonsels could not have anticipated Hitler's emphasis on being loyal followers and serving the folk community, yet, most likely, the German censors would have banished this work along with other "useless fantasies," had they not perceived in it a potentially effective tool for German folk education.

During the German Writers' Convention in Weimar in 1942, Reich Propaganda Minister Goebbels optimistically announced that the promotion of Volkish literature had been a success. As usual, however, he did not define his terms, and thus, we do not know if he had in mind the promotion of the more conservative Nazi literature, Nordic Germanic folklore, or the more radical political literature that had been published in recent years. Judging by our analysis of trends, the National Socialist Teachers Association would have liked to see a continued stronger emphasis on folklore and older works of folk literature, whereas the Reich Youth Leadership Organization would have preferred more literature with a political bent. Of the two organizations, the Teachers Association was most concerned with the poor literary quality of the newer

DIE BIENE MAJA

UND IHRE ABENTEUER

Plate 65
Even Without the Party's Official Support, *The Bee Maja* Remained a Bestseller

works. Once this quality improved, however, it appeared that they seemed to have had little objection to books with an overt political message for youth.

The prevailing trends indicate that the Nazis actively supported the new ideological direction of children's literature by sponsoring, simultaneously with the school and library reforms, a publications program that reflected the major aspects of the National Socialist ideology. These publications were not only intended as supplementary aids in classroom instruction, but also as literature to be used as instructional material in ideological training camps and in summer camps of the Hitler Youth Organization. Ultimately, the Nazi authorities hoped that children would be induced to purchase the new paperback series for their own home library collections and thus replace their old "favorites" forever. Undoubtedly, they believed with Goebbels that the day would come when German children would read no books other than those specifically approved for the educational goals of the National Socialist movement.

NOTES

1. "Aufruf des N.S.L.B. zur Pflege germanischen Schrifttums" *Deutsches Bildungswesen* 10 (October, 1933), 245-247. The "Appeal" was signed by Hans Schemm, among others.

2. Joseph Prestel, *Besinnungen und Durchblicke* (Leipzig, Klinkhardt, 1935), p. 36. Prestel was already urging teachers to make use of the following series of books in the context of literature classes: *Deutsche Jugendbücher* (later called *Hellgenbücher; Aus deutschem Schrifttum; Kranzbücherei; Deutsches Gut; Hirts Deutsche Sammlung; Schaffsteins Blaue Bändchen; Schaffsteins Grüne Bändchen; Reclambändchen; Deutsche Folge; Insel Bücherei; Münchner Jugendbücher*. Several titles in these series had begun to reflect the Volkish trend initiated during the twenties.

3. The announcement on behalf of the series was made in the following article: N.S.L.B. (National Socialist Teachers Association), "Aufruf" *Hamburger Lehrerzeitung* 43 (October 30, 1937), 456. The individual series of paperback editions published under the general topic of *Deutsches Wesen und Schicksal* appeared under such series titles as *Dürrs Sammlung deutscher Sagen; Aus Deutschlands Werden; Hilf-Mit Schriftenreihe,* and *Deutsches Volk—Deutsche Heimat.* Under the first two series titles alone, twelve works (each in several volumes) were dedicated to German and Nordic Germanic folklore and German history. In addition, the following series generally promoted among young readers had a strong bearing upon Nordic Germanic folklore: *Deutsches Ahnenerbe; Erbe und Verpflichtung; Isländergeschichten; Volk und Führer.* Some of the more contemporary series for young people were *Der*

junge Staat; Deutscher Wille, Schriften für die deutsche Jugend; Vom Weltkrieg zur nationalen Erhebung; Deutschland ist erwacht. Dietrich Strothmann, *Nationalsozialistische Literaturpolitik; Ein Beitraq zur Publizistik im Dritten Reich* (Bonn, Bouvier, 1963), p. 414.

4. Strothmann, pp. 414-415.

5. Georg Lukács, *Die Zerstörung der Vernunft* (Berlin, 1955), pp. 515-555.

6. *Ibid.* For a listing of "Volkish" authors, journals, and publishing houses consult Kurt P. Tauber, *Beyond Eagle and Swastika; German Nationalism since 1945* (Middleton, Connecticut, 1967), pp. 621-632 (Vol. I). Also, consult Gerhard Schönfelder, "Vierzig Jahre Eugen Diederichs Verlag und das deutsche Jugendschrifttum 1896-1936" *Jugendschriften-Warte* 43, 6 (June, 1936) 391-394.

7. Schönfelder, 391.

8. The Eugen Diederichs Verlag published in 1936 the following anthologies and series for young people that were dedicated to German and Nordic Germanic folklore: *Deutsche Stammeskunde; Märchenbände; Germanisches Märchenbuch; Rätselbuch; Sprichwörterbuch; Bauernregeln und Schwänke; Tierfabeln; Bücher vom Jahreslauf; Von Spiel und Brauchtum; Deutsche Volksbücher; Bluncks Geschichten von der Niederelbe; Deutsche Volkheit; Deutsche Reihe; Thule* (26 vols.).

9. Peter Aley, *Jugendliteratur im Dritten Reich: Dokumente und Kommentare* (Hamburg, Verlag für Buchmarktforschung, 1969), pp. 218-220. With reference to the surge of peasant novels consult in particular H. Boeschenstein, *The German Novel, 1939-1945* (Toronto, Toronto University Press, 1949), Introduction, and Rolf Geissler, *Dekadenz und Heroismus; Zeitroman und völkisch-nationalsozialistische Literaturkritik* (Stuttgart, Deutsche Verlagsanstalt, 1964, pp. 140-165. Boeschenstein and others noted, however, that the newer peasant novels no longer emphasized the peaceful and idyllic countryside but the peasant-warrior mood of the Nordic sagas.

10. Strothmann, p. 397. The complaint was voiced primarily by Schlösser and von Schirach. For a new trend in the peasant literature of the Third Reich that tried to adjust to National Socialist demands, consult Herbert Bake, "Der kulturpolitische Auftrag der bäuerlichen Dichtung" *Bücherkunde* 5, 11 (November, 1944), 130.

11. Hellmuth Langenbucher, "Das schöngeistige Buch im Jahre 1938: Ergebnisse, Überlegungen, Wünsche" *Bücherkunde* 4, 6 (June, 1939), 188.

12. Karl Riha, "Massenliteratur im Dritten Reich" in Horst Denkler and Karl Prümm, eds., *Die deutsche Literatur im Dritten Reich; Themen, Traditionen, Wirkungen* (Stuttgart, Reclam, 1976), p. 291. See also Strothmann, p. 361. Strothmann indicated that in 1941 the total book production amounted to 341 million copies, of which 59 million copies alone encompassed war and politics. Children's literature made up about 44.5 million, and school books 32 million. A substantial number of the war books may have been claimed by

children and youth as well, since age group criteria were not usually observed in this genre.

13. Strothmann, pp. 408-413.

14. *Ibid.* For comments on the booklets consult Riha, pp. 296-297. Also: M. Sturm, "Die Kriegsbücherei der deutschen Jugend" *Jugendschriften-Warte* 47, 11/12 (Nov., Dec., 1942), 91. Sturm refers here to the new series, the *Kriegsbücherei*, which had been initiated by the Reich Youth Organization in cooperation with the Supreme Command of the German Army, in order to counteract the so-called *Kitsch* of the popular war booklets that, in some variations, had equally strongly appealed to German youth during World War I.

15. Strothmann, pp. 49-50. Liselotte Bastian, "Schrifttumspolitische Führungsarbeit der H. J." *Bücherkunde* 7, 10 (October, 1943), 249; Langenbucher, "Das schöngeistige Buch . . . ," 188. The most prominent yearbooks and anthologies published by the Reich Youth Leadership Organization for young people were: *Jungen—Eure Welt; Jahrbuch der Hitler-Jugend; Mädel—Eure Welt; Jahrbuch des B.D.M.; Wir Folgen: Jahrbuch; Die Junge Mannschaft; Jahrbuch der Hitlerjugend; Junges Volk* (song book); *Vom wehrhaften Geist* (war poetry); *Unbekannte österreichische Gedichte* (Austrian poems); *Weihnachtsbuch der Jugend* (series).

16. This series was published by the Eher Verlag under the title: *Weihnachtsbuch der Jugend*, and each year at Christmas time was issued under a new subtitle, none of which had a bearing upon Christmas. Among them were E.W. Möller's *Der Führer* and Beumelberg's *Sperrfeuer um Deutschland*. See also Bastian, 249.

17. See Richard Grunberger, *The Twelve-Year Reich; A Social History of Nazi Germany 1933-1945* (New York, Holt, Rinehart, Winston, 1971), pp. 267-284.

18. Aley, pp. 218-219.

19. Strothmann, p. 360.

20. *Ibid.*

21. Reginald Phelps, "Die Autoren des Eher Verlags" *Deutsche Rundschau* 1, 81 (1955), 32.

22. Such was the case with the figures cited above for the year 1941, as they included textbooks and anthologies.

23. Strothmann, in viewing the children's book production in relation to the total book production, came up with the following figures: In 1936, children's books made up 7.2%; in 1937, the production had declined to 5.8%, but in 1941 it had increased to a high of 22.0%. See also: "Das Jugendbuch in der Jahresstatistik des deutschen Buchhandels 1937" *Jugendschriften-Warte* 43, 2 (February, 1938), 397, and Ludwig Schönrock, "Die deutsche Buchproduktion 1938" *Jugendschriften-Warte* 44, 5 (May, 1939); *Börsenblatt für den deutschen Buchhandel* 60 (March, 1939), 9. Also: Strothmann, p. 360.

24. *Ibid.*

25. *Ibid.*

26. The book was indeed a kind of "Party badge" for show and propaganda. Hitler himself had declared it to be "out-dated," while he admitted that it was difficult to read. See Albert Speer, *Erinnerungen* (Berlin, Propyläen Verlag, 1970), p. 511.

27. Strothmann, p. 276. Also: Renate Jaroslawski and Rüdiger Steinlein, "Die politische Jugendschrift: Zur Theorie und Praxis faschistischer deutscher Jugendliteratur" Denkler and Prümm, pp. 325-326. In the case of *The Hitler Youth Named Quex*, the film based on the novel helped to popularize the book also among younger boys and girls.

28. Bonsels' name had appeared on Goebbels' "black lists" between 1937 and 1941, although an exception was made for *The Bee Maja*. Strothmann, pp. 247-249. Another discrepancy of a more pronounced nature occurred in regard to Wiechert's works. Wiechert headed the list of authors condemned by the censors, yet his works were printed during the Third Reich in a total of 1,165,000 copies. Strothmann, p. 379.

29. Waldemar Bonsels, *Die Biene Maja und ihre Abenteuer* (Stuttgart, Deutsche Verlagsanstalt, 1949), pp. 185-186.

Conclusion

The Nazis subjected children's literature to the same Volkish policy through which they hoped to control every aspect of German cultural life. The scope and conception of their censorship exceeded everything that Germany had ever experienced in the past. By institutionalizing didacticism, and by aligning it with the National Socialist ideology, they set the stage for indoctrinating children systematically by means of children's literature and folk education. Within this context, they also used children's drama, festivals, and Volkish rituals to enhance the emotional impact of their message.

Censorship took on a more uniform pattern in the late thirties when Reich Education Minister Rust introduced the *Reich Reader* on a nation-wide basis, along with major curricular reforms and more definite guidelines for a reorganization of the school libraries. It derived its major orientation from values in part from the German and Nordic Germanic folk heritage, but also from the racial-political views of the Nazi ideology. At that time too, Goebbels and Rosenberg cooperated more closely with each other in spite of persisting rivalries between them, as did the Hitler Youth Organization and the National Socialist Teachers Association. The first years of World War II brought with them certain setbacks in the enforcement of the censorship policy, but the authorities did their best to counteract these trends by introducing even stricter measures than before. As they hoped to bring the system to perfection only in the future, it did not discourage them in the least to see that the system was still marred by certain inconsistencies.

One of the most deplorable aspects of the Nazis' censorship procedures was their willful distortion of the German and Nordic Germanic folk heritage. For the sake of enhancing the "Nordic" world view within the context of ideological objectives, the Nazis would select from it whatever concepts they felt were best suited to teach children certain desirable attitudes toward the German folk state and the *Führer*. Such a forced comparison between the Nordic Germanic past and the present not only gave children a distorted view of the values of their native heritage, but it conveyed to them also a misleading idea about the applicability of pagan ethics to a society of the twentieth century. If Thor indeed used to be the Norse god of the settlers, why should he now become a god of aggressive German "colonists" in their drive eastward? If Balder indeed was the god of the sun, why should he emerge as a symbol of Hitler himself, and his scheme to be victorious over all nations in Europe?

In the Nazis' approach to myths and folktales the sun never set, but continued to rise. Even where all traditions pointed to the full cycle of life involving both light and darkness, the Nazis would ignore in their "symbolic" interpretation of folklore all that reminded of doomsday and death. This attitude also characterized their approach to the saga literature and to literature in general. In the saga heroes they saw men who fought defiantly and courageously, and who in the end were always victorious because they never resigned themselves to their fate. If a hero died in battle, his fame would rise as gloriously as the sun itself, and his tribe would still survive and thrive on his honor. To march proudly toward the future and never to know inner defeat: this was one of the Nazis' educational goals for children and youth—next to loyalty and complete dedication to the folk community. In regard to literary criticism the "symbolic" interpretation implied that in every respect authors were obliged to give a "positive" portrayal of German life and thought. Ironically, the type of "realism" such as the Nazis promoted it, in children's literature, too, did not mean a literary concern with the "realities" of life as it is generally understood, but with the "ideal reality" of the German folk community of the future.

As a result of this selective approach based on ethnocentric and Volkish-racial criteria, German children were deprived of a substantial number of classics and folktales from other countries. German children had still enjoyed such works during the Weimar Republic and earlier, partially due to the international attitude of the former Children's Literature Association. During the twenties, the trends had begun to change in favor of a national orientation of children's literature; but the Nazis became exclusive in their concern with books belonging to the German and Nordic Germanic sphere of culture and tradition, while they ruthlessly removed and destroyed books pertaining to "alien" cultures. The few works in translation from other countries that they did retain, they remodelled through re-editions or re-interpretations to the point where their main protagonists looked like Nordic Germanic heroes in disguise. In their censorship procedure, the Nazis also rejected a great number of German literary titles, merely because they supposedly did not "fit" into the German folk education program. Among others, this applied to some literary Romantic fairy tales which they labelled as "too subjective," or "too gloomy and unhealthy," as well as to most of the German religious legends whose ethics they considered "alien" to the German folk spirit itself.

One of the most serious implications of the Nazis' utilitarian approach to children's literature was that it fostered values that were consistent with paganism and Volkish-racial thought. Their policy of omission in itself betrayed that they rejected the values that Germany had shared over several centuries with the Western humanitarian and Christian tradition. In principle, the Nazis were opposed to the idea that contemplation may at times be superior to action; that might is not always right; that there exists the possibility of a peaceful existence among nations; that there are univeral human values, outside of the German and Nordic Germanic sphere of culture, too; that love is better than revenge; that those who are weak and retarded need our help; that the individual has inalienable rights, regardless of race, creed, or religion—and also outside of his "bonds" with the German folk community.

The newer works of fiction for children and youth that were published during the Third Reich reflected this new paganism in the contemporary setting. Even though the protagonists in these novels were mostly idealistic, they were also fanatic and ethnocentric, and with an unquestioning obedience would do anything in the name of the German folk community. While the male characters usually portrayed in one form or another the fight for German nationhood, the female characters were generally depicted as "loyal followers" in such roles as nurses or auxiliaries in military camps, or as helpers in factories, on the farms or in the household. Even as loving mothers they seemed to have borne children only out of a sense of duty to the fatherland.

Some of the shortcomings of the censorship system became particularly evident in regard to the popular Karl May novels and the old-fashioned girls' books. These works and others that were widely read did not meet the Nazis' Volkish criteria, and yet, the publishers supported them and the authorities tolerated them, at least for the time being. The real implications of the Nazis' censorship as a whole, however, should not be estimated in view of what was actually accomplished during the Twelve-Year Reich, but from the perspective of what the Nazis still hoped to accomplish in the future, for only from that angle it is possible to perceive the direction into which the totalitarian regime was moving.

Underlying all of the Nazis' censorship activites were long-range educational plans based on the Volkish ideology. Even though Party and State officials frequently quarrelled, they persistently agreed to the basic concepts of these plans, whereby children were meant to be adjusted and "programmed" to contribute to the efficient operation of the totalitarian state. To children's literature and Nordic Germanic folklore they assigned a definite role in this context. Ultimately, children's literature was no longer meant to benefit the individual child but only the "folk community" and the state. Outside of this goal, neither children nor books were thought to have a purpose and justification for existence.

Bibliography

LIST OF SOURCES CONSULTED

I. PRIMARY SOURCES

A. *Unpublished Documents and Dissertations*

Auswahl und Auslese für Adolf Hitler Schulen. Bordesholm, Gauschulungs-burg, Nov. 27, 1935. N.S.D.A.P., Gauleitung Schleswig-Holstein. Rund-schreiben No. 5/45. (Circular Letter). 2nd folder. Institut für Zeitgeschichte, Munich. Document No. *R1121.*

Friedrichs—R.F.S.S. Reichsführer für die Schutzstaffel, "Sonnenwende" (ver-traulich!) (The report contains the Nazis' official views on solstice celebra-tions and other Volkish festivals). Institut für Zeitgeschichte, Munich. Document No. *FA 131.*

Gauleiter Schleswig-Holstein. "Rundbrief" (Report, including circular letter pertaining to the youth initiation ceremonies of the Party in the district of Schleswig-Holstein). Institut für Zeitgeschichte, Munich, Document No. 1121/1122.

German Youth Movement Collection, Box 956. Archives, Hoover Institution on War, Revolution and Peace, Stanford, California:

"Die Artamanen" (typescript), Folder 3, pp. 60-64.

Kayser, Friedrich, "Wandervogel: Idee und Wirklichkeit; Gedanken einer Selbstdarstellung der deutschen Jugendbewegung" (typescript). Sender Frei-es Berlin, June 23, 1962, 11:05 p.m.

Sontheimer, Kurt, "Das Reich der Unpolitischen; Die Jugendbewegung vor 1933" Südwestfunk—Jugendfunk. October 18, 1961. U.K.W., 10 p.m. (typescript).

Schmidt-Zittel, Herbert, "W.V. Heidelberg: Ein Dokumentarbericht, 1920." No. 3-8245, Folder 4.

Hartmann, Hans, "*Heil* und *heilig* im nordischen Altertum Eine wortkundliche Untersuchung" (Dissertation, University of Göttingen, 1941).

Himmler, Heinrich, "Heldische Forderungen" in "Himmler vor den Führern der 13. S.S. Freiwilligen der Gebirgsdivision, 11. Januar 1944." Institut für Zeitgeschichte, Munich. Document No. M.A. 316 4842-62. (See pp. 9 and 10 for the speech).

_____, "Rede des Reichsführers der SS, Reichsinnenminister Himmler, auf der Tagung der R.P.A. Leiter am 28. Januar 1944." Institut für Zeitgeschichte, Munich. Document No. *MA 316 4732-4820.* (Speech: pp. 72-73).

_____, "Rede des Reichsführers der SS vor den niederländischen SS-Führern der Waffen-SS, anlässlich der erstmaligen Verleihung der Leistungsrune October 3, 1944" (Speech in reference to the "Runic Achievement Award"). Institut für Zeitgeschichte, Munich, Document No. *MA 316 4827-4829.*

_____, "Rede Himmlers vor Generälen im Platterhof" Institut für Zeitgeschichte, Munich. Document No. *MA 316 4888-4959.*

Krebs, Albert, Dr. "Das Märchen der Romantik" (Denkschrift). Institut für Zeitgeschichte, Munich. Document No. MA 144/2 B&S Schnellhefter, Akt II, 4171-4240. Handwritten document. Accompanied by typescript and a personal letter of Krebs to the Party Headquarters. *Microfilm T84, Roll 5, 4168-4240.*

"Liste des schädlichen und unerwünschten Schrifttums" (Geheimsache!). December, 1938. Classified by title in the documents drawer, general library. Hoover Institution on War, Revolution and Peace, Stanford, California.

Ministerialerlass UIIC6767: "Zentralblatt für die gesamte Unterrichtsverwaltung, September 13, 1933." See Dobers and Higelke, p. 194.

National Socialism, *Documents Collection TS National Socialism* No. 467, Archives, Hoover Institution on War, Revolution and Peace, Stanford, California. (Seven folders).

"Einfluss der H.J. auf die Jugend" (typescript, anonymous).

"Schönschreiben 1943" (Penmanship 1943) Document. Archives, Hoover Institution on War, Revolution and Peace, Stanford. German Education Collection.

"Aufsätze" (School Essays)

"Wie ich die H.J. sah und erlebte" (typescript).

Der Reichsführer der SS, Heinrich Himmler, "SS-Befehl, Berlin, October 26, 1937. Institut für Zeitgeschichte, Munich, Document No. *MA 330-4063-4065.*

Schemm, Hans, Bayrisches Staatsministerium für Unterricht und Kultur. Abschrift zu *No. 5162/No. V58852.* Munich December 19, 1933. "Betreff: Volksbüchereiwesen" (signed by Schemm). Institut für Jugendbuchforschung, Frankfurt, Main. Cited by Aley, Documents Collection.

Stabsbefehl 36/37 (June 19, 1937) "Betrifft: Sommersonnenwendfeier" (Signed: Reichsführer der SS, SS Hauptscharführer, and Jost, SS-Oberführer. Only Jost's signature is attached). Institut für Zeitgeschichte, Munich, Document No. *MA 330-4008.*

Stanford University History Department Faculty, "Seminar on the Intellectual Origin of National Socialism, October 7, 1963" (typescript). Stanford.

Hoover Institution on War, Revolution and Peace. Catalogued as document, general catalogue, as listed.

"Undatierter Plan der Reichsführung der SS zur Erschliessung des Germanen-Erbes," (1937). Koblenz, Bundesarchiv. Document No. NS 19/320. Cited by Bollmus.

B. *Published Documents and Government Publications (unsigned)*

Amt für Schrifttumspflege bei den Beauftragten des für die Überwachung der gesamten geistigen Arbeit und weltanschaulichen Schulung und Erziehung der N.S.D.A.P., ed., *Gutachtenanzeiger der Bücherkunde* 1939/1940. (Available in the documents collection of the Institut für Zeitgeschichte, Munich).

————. *Die hundert ersten Bücher für nationalsozialistische Büchereien.* Munich, Verlag der N.S.D.A.P., 1934.

————, sowie die Reichsstelle zur Förderung des deutschen Schrifttums und des Reichsbundes für Deutsche Vorgeschichte. *Deutsche Vorzeit; Ein beratendes Bücherverzeichnis* (Institut für Leser-und Schrifttumskunde). Leipzig, Dürr, 1933.

Nationalsozialistische Kulturgemeinde Kraft durch Freude. Amt Feierabend, Abteilung Volkstum und Brauchtum, eds., *Sommersonnenwende; Texte und Feiern im Jahresring.* Berlin, Verlag der N.S.D.A.P., 1937).

Nationalsozialistischer Lehrerbund, ed., *Die deutsche Jugendschule; Sechsjährige höhere Schule. Ein Erziehungs- und Unterrichtsplan des nationalsozialistischen Lehrerbundes.* Gau Westfalen-Süd. Bielefeld, Velhagen & Klasing, 1941.

————, *Erziehung zur Volksgemeinschaft.* Berlin, H.A. Braun, 1939.

————. *Jahrbuch 1935.* Munich, Fichte Verlag, 1935.

Reichsverwaltung des N.S.L.B., die Reichsjugendführung und die Reichsstelle zur Förderung des deutschen Schrifttums, eds., *Das Buch der Jugend; Mit Grundliste für Schülerbüchereien.* Berlin, Verlag der N.S.D.A.P., 1939-1941.)

Nationalsozialistischer Lehrerbund, ed., *Meine Ahnen.* Bayreuth, Gauverlag Bayreuth Ostmark G.m.b.H., 1934. (Recommended by the Bavarian Cultural Minister.)

————. *Die Schülerbücherei.* Leipzig, Dürr Verlag, 1939.

Reichsjugendführung, ed., *Das deutsche Jahr; Feiern der jungen Nation.* Munich, Zentralverlag der N.S.D.A.P., 1939.

Reichsjugendführung der N.S.D.A.P., *Freude, Zucht, Glaube; Handbuch für die kulturelle Arbeit im Lager.* Potsdam Voggenreiter Verlag, 1937.

————. *Die Jugend des Führers Adolf Hitler; Bilderbuch über die grossdeutsche Jugend.* Berlin/Leipzig, Reichsjugendführung, 1942.

_____. *Nationalsozialistischer Jugendpressedienst; Amtlicher Pressedienst der Reichsjugendführung* der N.S.D.A.P, "Wichtige Mitteilung: Hitlerjugend in Gotha, 30. 12. 32-4. 1. 33," Blatt 9, Juli, 1932.

_____. *Sommerlager- und Heimatabendmaterial für die Schulungs- und Kulturarbeit.* Berlin, Zentralverlag der N.S.D.A.P., 1941.

Reichsjugendführung, Gebiet Sachsen, *H.J. erlebt Deutschland.* Leipzig, B. G. Teubner Verlag, 1935.

Reichsjugendführung, Presse- und Propagandadienst, ed., *Jahrbuch der Hitlerjugend* (1935-1941). (6 vols.) Berlin, Verlag der N.S.D.A.P., 1935-1941.

Reichspropagandaleitung der N.S.D.A.P., *Deutsche Kriegsweihnacht 1941.* Berlin, Verlag der N.S.D.A.P., 1941.

_____. *Grundschullagen für die Reichsthemen der N.S.D.A.P.* Leipzig, Teubner, 1941.

Reichsstelle für volkstümliches Büchereiwesen, ed., *Grundliste für Schülerbüchereien.* Berlin, Verlag der N.S.D.A.P., 1937.

Reichsstelle zur Förderung des deutschen Schrifttums, *Büchergutachtenanzeiger.* Berlin, Verlag der N.S.D.A.P., 1939-1941.

_____, and Reichüberwachungsamt der N.S.D.A.P., *Die hundert ersten Bücher für nationalsozialistische Büchereien.* Berlin, Verlag der N.S.D.A.P., 1935.

_____, *Die sechshundert ersten Bücher für nationalsozialistische Büchereien.* Berlin, Verlag der N.S.D.A.P., 1936.

Schutzstaffel (SS), *Germanische Leithefte.* Potsdam, Voggenreiter, 1940.

Reichsstelle für das Volksbüchereiwesen, *Deutsche Büchereien; Eine Bildauswahl.* Leipzig, Einkaufshaus für Büchereien, 1943.

C. *Published Document Collections*

Anger, Walter, *Das Dritte Reich in Dokumenten.* Frankfurt, Europäische Verlagsanstalt, 1957.

Aley, Peter, *Jugendliteratur im Dritten Reich. Dokumente und Kommentare.* Hamburg, Verlag für Buchmarktforschung, 1965.

Boberach, Heinz, ed., *Meldungen aus dem Reich. Auswahl aus den geheimen Lageberichten des Sicherheitsdienstes der SS 1939-1944.* Berlin, Luchterhand Verlag, 1963.

Braunbuch: Kriegs- und Naziverbrechen in der Bundesrepublik: Staat, Wirtschaft, Verwaltung, Armee, Justiz, Wissenschaft. Berlin, Staatsverlag der Deutschen Demokratischen Republik, 1965.

Domarus, Max, *Hitler; Reden und Proklamationen, 1932-1944.* Würzburg, Jahn Verlag, 1962.

Mosse, Georg, *Nazi Culture: Intellectual, Cultural and Social Life in the Third Reich.* New York, Grosset and Dunlap, 1964.

Leiser, Erwin, *Nazi Cinema.* New York, Collier Books, 1974.

Richter, Dieter, *Das politische Kinderbuch: Eine aktuelle historische Dokumentation.* Ed. by Hildegard Brenner, Vol. 5. Darmstadt, Luchterhand Verlag, 1973.

Seraphim, Hans Günther, ed., *Alfred Rosenberg; Das politische Tagebuch, 1934-1935 und 1939-1940.* Munich, Deutscher Taschenbuchverlag, 1964.

Wulf, Josef, ed., *Kunst im Dritten Reich: Eine Dokumentation.* Gütersloh, Sigbert Mohn Verlag, 1966.

————. *Literatur im Dritten Reich: Eine Dokumentation.* Gütersloh, Sigbert Mohn Verlag, 1965.

————. *Theater und Film im Dritten Reich: Eine Dokumentation.* Gütersloh, Sigbert Mohn Verlag, 1965.

D.   *Children's Literature Anthologies (including Readers and Diaries): A Selective Listing.*

Baumann, Hans, ed., *Um Feuer und Fahne; Verse für Fest und Feier.* Potsdam, Voggenreiter, 1939.

Böhme, Kurt, *Deutsches Brauchtum; Ein Führer durch die jahreszeitlichen Volksfeste.* Potsdam, Voggenreiter, 1935.

Breuer, Hubert, ed., *Die völkische Schulfeier*, 3rd ed. Bochum, Schulwissenschaftliche Verlagsanstalt, 1940.

Carp, Emma, *Feste mit Kindern. Ein Buch für Familie, Kinderheim, Jugendgruppe und Schule.* Ravensburg, Maier Verlag, 1940.

Deutschland, gesund in seinem Stamm und Rasse. (Series: *Deutscher Wille; Schriften für die deutsche Jugend*). Bochum, Verlags- und Lehrmittelanstalt, F. Kamp, 1941.

Deutsches Lesebuch für Volksschulen. Frankfurt, Diesterweg, 1936.

Die deutsche Schulfeier, Heft 11, 1938. (Issued by the Reichsverwaltung des N.S. Lehrerbundes, Bayreuth). Bayreuth, 1938.

Deutsches Volkstum, deutsche Sonnenwende, Heft 13. Bochum, Schulwissenschaftliche Verlagsanstalt, 1939.

Deutscher Wille; Schriften für die deutsche Jugend. Bochum, Verlags- und Lehrmittel-Anstalt, Ferdinand Kamp, 1939.

Dörner, Klaus, ed., *Das deutsche Jahr; Feiern der jungen Nation.* Munich, Zentralverlag der N.S.D.A.P., Franz Eher Nachf., 1939.

————. *Der schwarze Turm; Aus dem Tagebuch eines Jungvolkführers.* Potsdam, Voggenreiter, 1939.

Das ewige Deutschland; Ein deutsches Lesebuch für die achte Klasse. Frankfurt, Diesterweg, 1941.

Fabian, Albert and Otto Loslehner, eds., *Heldengeist im Heldenlied; Eine Einführung in die Edda und andere altdeutsche Dichtungen für die Jugend des Dritten Reiches.* Breslau, Handel, 1934. Schriftenreihe zu Deutschlands Erneuerung.

Findeisen, Kurt Arnold, *Braune Kameraden.* Dresden, O. & R. Becker, Nachf., 1934.

Finder, Ernst, ed. (Leiter des Presse- und Propagandaamtes der Reichsjugendführung), *Die junge Kameradschaft* Berlin, Verlag Zeitgeschichte, 1935.

Granzow, Klaus, ed, *Tagebuch eines Hitlerjungen.* Bremen Carl Schünemann Verlag, 1965.

Haarer, Johanna, ed., *Mutter, erzähl von Adolf Hitler. Ein Buch zum Vorlesen, Nacherzählen und Selbstlesen für kleine und grosse Kinder.* Berlin, Lehmann, 1939.

Hackeberg, Friedrich und Bernhard Schwarz, eds., *Das ewige Deutschland. Ein deutsches Lesebuch für die achte Klasse.* Frankfurt, Verlag Diesterweg, 1941.

Brüder Grimms Kindermärchen, ill. by Paul Henz. Stuttgart, R. Thienemann, 1941. (317,000 - 321,000 copies published).

Das Hilf-Mit-Buch, 3 vols. Edited by the Reichsverwaltung des N.S. Lehrerbundes, and based on selections from the children's journal *Hilf Mit.* Berlin, H.A. Braun, 1939.

Buch der Heimat, with a preface by Heinrich Himmler. (anthology of Christmas stories and poems). Berlin, Verlag der N.S.D.A.P., 1944/45.

Hirts deutsches Lesebuch. Danzig, Hirt Verlag, 1935.

Hirts deutsches Lesebuch für Jungen. Breslau, Ferdinand Hirt Verlag, 1939.

Hobrecker, Karl, ed., *Lieder und Bilder für Kinder; Volksmund und Volkskunst aus der Zeit Ludwig Richters.* (with illustrations by Richter, Schwind, Kaulbach, Bürkner, et al.). Bielefeld, Velhagen und Klasing, 1944.

Klauss, Hermann, *Feierstunden in der deutschen Schule.* Stuttgart, Franck'sche Verlagsbuchhandlung, 1941.

Krebs, Albert, Dr., ed., *Zum Vorlesen.* Hamburg, Hanseatische Verlagsanstalt, 1936.

Kriegsbücherei der deutschen Jugend. (Series). Berlin, Steiniger Verlag, 1941.

Lesebuch zur Deutschen Geistesgeschichte. Berlin, Junker und Dünnhaupt, 1935.

Lukas, Oskar, *Das deutsche Mädel; Ein Buch der Einkehr.* Leipzig, Adam Kraft Verlag, 1936.

Mehden, Heilwig, v.d., ed., *Vor allem eins, mein Kind. Was deutsche Mädchen und Knaben zur Kaiserzeit gelesen haben.* Hamburg, Hoffmann und Campe, 1972.

Mein erstes Buch. Dortmund, 1937.

Mondt, Gerhardt, *Herbert Norkus; Das Tagebuch der Kameradschaft* (Introduction by Baldur von Schirach). Beusselkietz, Verlagsanstalt, 1940.

Munske, Hilde, ed., *Mädel im Dritten Reich.* Berlin, Freiheitsverlag, 1935.

Neuer deutscher Jugendfreund. Zur Unterhaltung und Belehrung der Jugend, vol. 87. Leipzig, Schmidt und Spring Verlag, 1936. (The journal was founded by Franz Hoffmann in the 1880, and like the *Jugendschriften-Warte,* it was edited under the direction of the Party since 1933.

——. *Sonderausgabe: Jungdeutschland.* Leipzig, Wigandsche Buchdruckerei, 1942.

Obrig, Ilse, ed., *Familie Fröhlichs Wunderbuch: Reime, Spiele, Rätsel und Lieder für Mütter und Kinder gesammelt.* Leipzig, Hirt, 1936.

Oppenberg, Ferdinand, ed., *Schwert und Pflug; Eine Feierabendfolge.* Hamburg, Hanseatische Verlagsanstalt, 1937.

Pastenaci, Kurt, ed., *Volksgeschichte der Germanen.* Berlin, Junge Generation, 1935.

Pixberg, Hermann, ed., *Deutsche Göttersagen.* Berlin, Jugendzeitschriftenverlag, 1933 (Series: Die Schule im Dritten Reich, No. 12.)

Plenz, Karl Dr., ed., *Ich hörte ein Heldenlied singen und sagen.* Breslau, Ferdinand Hirt Verlag, 1938. (Published under the sponsorship of the Parteiamtliche Prüfungskommission zum Schutze des N.S. Schrifttums).

Prestel, Josef, ed., *Im Geleite der Geschichte; Aus deutschem Erzählgut. Lesebuch für den Schulgebrauch.* Munich, Verlag Oldenbourg, 1937.

Ramlow, Gerhard, Dr., ed., *Deutsche Jungen auf Fahrt.* Berlin, Rudolf Heussen G.m.b.H., 1939.

Reichardt, K., ed., *Thule: Sagas von altgermanischen Bauern,* 24 vols. Jena, Diederichs Verlag, 1933-35.

Seemann-Segnitz, Erna, ed., *Des deutschen Mädels Sagenbuch; Germanische Frauengestalten.* Ill. by B. Arndt. Berlin Hensius & Co., Verlagsgesellschaft, m. b. H., 1934.

Seidenfaden, Theodor, ed., *Das deutsche Schicksalsbuch* 2 vols. Freiburg i. Brsg., Herder Verlag, 1936.

Vocano-Bohlmann, Erna von, ed., *Das Märchenjahr,* 2 vols. Potsdam, Voggenreiter, 1941.

——, *Jugend im Jahresring.* Potsdam, Voggenreiter, 1933.

Von deutscher Art. Ein Lesebuch für höhere Schulen, Parts I-VI. Frankfurt, Verlag Otto Salle, 1939-40.

Von Drinnern und Draussen. Heimatfibel für die deutsche Jugend. Frankfurt, Diesterweg, 1942.

Wagenführ, H., ed., *Gefolgschaft; Erzählungen, Berichte Quellendarstellun-*

gen, Gesetze und Sprüche über den Kampf der germanischen Helden und ihrer Gefolgschaft. Hamburg, Hanseatische Verlagsanstalt, n.d.

_____, *Gefolgschaft: Der germanische Kampfbund. Eine nach Quellen veranstaltete Sammlung guter Erzählungen germanischen Geistes und germanischen Schicksals.* Hamburg, Hanseatische Verlagsanstalt, 1934.

Weber, Leopold, *Asgard; Die Götterwelt unserer Ahnen.* Stuttgart, Thienemann, 1920.

_____, *Midgart; Die Heldensagen des Nordlandes* Stuttgart, J.F. Steinkopf, 1941.

_____, *Unsere Heldensagen.* Munich, R. Oldenbourg 1936 (Vom Bayerischen Staatsministerium für Unterricht und Kultur mit Verfügung vom 5.9. 36, Nr. VIII 4222888 genehmigt.) (issued in 31,000 - 40,000 copies).

Wir reiten 'gen Tag (Series: *Bücher der jungen Nation*) Munich, Zentralverlag der N.S.D.A.P., 1937).

Wolf, Erich, ed., *Germanisches Märchenbuch.* Ill. by Tamara Ramsay. Jena, Diederichs, 1935.

E. *Individual Children's Books*

As the works consulted are very numerous, only text and footnote references have been indicated in the appropriate chapters. The genres covered in this study are fiction, fantasy, picture book, legend, folktale, saga, mythology, poetry, drama, and nonfiction.

II. SECONDARY SOURCES

A. *Books*

Ackermann, Josef, *Himmler als Ideologe.* Nach Tagebüchern, stenographischen Notizen, Briefen und Reden. Göttingen, Musterschmidt, 1970.

Adolph, Walter, *Hirtenamt und Hitler-Diktatur*, 2nd ed. Berlin, Morus Verlag, 1965.

Allen, William Sheridan, ed. and tr., *The Infamy of Nazism; The Memoirs of Ex-Gauleiter Albert Krebs, 1923-1933.* New York, New Viewpoints, 1976.

_____. *The Nazi Seizure of Power. The Experiences of a Single German Town, 1930-1935.* Chicago, Quadrangle, 1965.

Anderson, Theodore, *The Problem of Icelandic Saga Origins. A Historical Survey.* New Haven, Yale University Press, 1964.

Arendt, Hannah, *The Origins of Totalitarianism.* New York, Harcourt, Brace, 1951.

Assel, Hans-Günther, *Die Perversion der politischen Pädagogik im Nationalsozialismus.* Schriften der Pädagogischen Hochschulen Bayerns. Munich, Ehrenwirth Verlag, 1969.

Atkins, Henry C., *German Literature Through Nazi Eyes*. London, Methuen, 1941.

Aurich, Ernst, *Drei Stücke über nationalsozialistische Weltanschauung*. Stuttgart, Kohlhammer, 1932.

———. *Neue Schulgestaltung aus nationalsozialistischem Denken*. Kulturpolitische Schriftenreihe, Heft 4, Stuttgart, Kohlhammer, 1933.

Bach, Adolf, *Deutsche Volkskunde. Ihre Wege, Ergebnisse und Aufgaben. Eine Einführung*. Leipzig, Koehler und Amelang, 1937.

Baetke, Walter, *Kinderleben und Kindererziehung im alten Norden*. (Nach den Isländersagas). Berlin, Junker und Dünnhaupt, 1936.

———. *Nordischer Schicksalsglaube*. Göttingen, Von Hoechst und Ruprecht, 1944.

Bang, Ilse, *Die Entwicklung der deutschen Märchenillustration*. Munich, F. Bruckmann, 1944.

Barsam, Richard Meran, *Triumph of the Will*. Bloomington, Indiana University Press, 1975.

Bartels, Adolf, *Jüdische Herkunft und Literaturwissenschaft*. Leipzig, H. Haessel Verlag, 1925.

Bäumler, Alfred, *Nietzsche, der Philosoph und Politiker*. Leipzig, A. Kroner, 1930.

Bauer, Fritz, *Die Wurzeln des faschistischen und nationalfaschistischen Handelns*. Frankfurt, Europäische Verlagsanstalt, 1965.

———. *Politik und Erziehung*. Berlin, Junker und Dünnhaupt, 1940.

Beck, Friedrich Alfred, *Die Erziehung im Dritten Reich*. Dortmund, W. Crüwell Verlag, 1936.

Behrendson, Walter, A., *Die Humanistische Front. Eine Einführung in die deutsche Emigranten-Literatur*, 2 vols., Zürich, Europa Verlag, 1946.

Von Beit, Hedwig, *Das Märchen*. München, Franke Verlag, 1937.

Beier-Lindhardt, ed., *Das Buch vom Führer für die deutsche Jugend*. Oldenburg, Stalling, 1933.

Bendiscioli, Mario, *The New Racial Paganism*. London, The Holy Sea, 1939.

Benfer, Heinrich, *Schundkampf und literarische Jugendpflege*. Langensalza, Beltz, 1933.

Bennewitz, Gert, *Die geistige Wehrerziehung der deutschen Jugend*. (Series: Schriften für Politik und Auslandskunde.) Berlin, Junker und Dünnhaupt, 1940.

Benze, Rudolf, *Erziehung im Grossdeutschen Reich*. Frankfurt a.M., Verlag Moritz Diesterweg, 1941.

Benzing, Richard, Dr. med., *Grundlagen der körperlichen und geistigen Erziehung des Kleinkindes im nationalsozialistischen Kindergarten*. Schriftenreihe des N.S.V. Berlin, Zentralverlag der N.S.D.A.P. Franz Eher, Nachf., 1941.

Bergmann, Ernst, *Deutschland, das Bildungsland der Menschheit*. Breslau, Hirt Verlag, 1933.

Bettelheim, Bruno, *The Uses of Enchantment: The Meaning and Importance of Fairy Tales*. New York, Vintage Books, 1977.

Bischoff, Ralph, F., *Nazi Conquest through German Culture*. Cambridge, Mass., Harvard University Press, 1942.

Blüher, Hans, *Wandervogel. Geschichte einer Jugendbewegung*. 4th ed. Berlin, Weise, 1919.

Blunck, Barthold and Ernst Adolf Dreyer, eds., *Deutsche Weihnacht: Die Gabe deutscher Dichter*. Leipzig, Adolf Klein Verlag, 1942.

Blunck, Hans Friedrich, *Die nordische Welt. Geschichte, Wesen und Bedeutung der nordischen Völker*. Berlin, Propyläen Verlag, 1937.

Boehm, Max Hildebert, *R. H. Riehl, Die Volkskunde als Wissenschaft*. Tübingen, 1935.

_____. *Volkskunde*. Berlin, Weidmannsche Verlagsanstalt, 1937.

_____. *Volkstheorie und Volkstumspolitik der Gegenwart*. Berlin, Junker und Dünnhaupt, 1935.

Boehme, Kurt, *Die deutsche Volksseele in den Kinderdichtungen*. Berlin, Verlag der NSDAP., 1939.

Bönner, Karl H. *Deutschlands Jugend und das Erbe ihrer Väter. Wie skeptisch ist die junge Generation*? Bergisch-Gladbach, Gustav Lübbe Verlag, 1967.

Boeschenstein, H., *The German Novel, 1939-45*. Toronto, University of Toronto Press, 1949.

Bollmus, Reinhard, *Das Amt Rosenberg und seine Gegner. Zum Machtkampf im nationalsozialistischen Herrschaftssystem*. Stuttgart, Deutsche Verlagsanstalt, 1970. (Publication of the Institut für Zeitgeschichte, Munich.)

Bonus, Alfred, *Vom neuen Mythos*. Jena, Diederichs, 1911.

Bossenbrook, William T. *The German Mind*. Detroit, Wayne State University Press, 1961.

Boyke, Gustav, *Erziehung durch das Schrifttum. Neue Wege der Jugendführung im Deutschunterricht*. Frankfurt, Diesterweg, 1941.

Bracher, Karl Dietrich, *Die deutsche Diktatur: Entstehung, Struktur, Folgen des Nationalsozialismus*. Cologne and Berlin, Kiepenheuer, & Witsch, 1969.

Bracher, Karl Dietrich, Wolfgang Sauer und Gerhard Schulz, *Die nationalsozialistische Machtergreifung. Studien zur Errichtung des totalitären Herrschaftssystems in Deutschland, 1930-34*. Cologne, Opladen, Westdeutscher Verlag, 1962.

Brady, A. Robert, *The Spirit and Structure of German Fascism*. New York, Howard Fertig, 1965.

Brandenburg, H.C., *Die Geschichte der H.J.* Cologne, Kiepenheuer & Witsch, 1968.

Brennecke, Fritz, *Vom deutschen Volk und seinem Lebensraum. Handbuch der Hitlerjugend.* Munich, Eher, 1937.

Brenner, Hildegard, *Die Kunstpolitik des Nationalsozialismus.* Hamburg, Rowohlt, 1963.

Broszat, Martin, *Der Nationalsozialismus; Weltanschauung, Programm und Wirklichkeit.* Schriftenreihe der Niedersächsischen Landeszentrale für Politische Bildung. Zeitgeschichte Heft No. 8. Stuttgart, Deutsche Verlagsanstalt, 1960.

Buchheim, Hans, *Das Dritte Reich. Grundlagen und politische Entwicklung.* Munich, Koesel, 1958.

————. *Glaubenskrise im Dritten Reich. Grundlagen und politische Entwicklung.* Munich, 1960. Stuttgart, 1953. (Veröffentlichung des Instituts für Zeitgeschichte, Munich).

Burg, Paul, *Neue Geschichte für Jedermann; Von König Heinrich dem Vogelsteller bis zum Volkskanzler Adolf Hitler.* Leipzig, Adolf Klein Verlag, 1934.

Burke, Kenneth, *Die Rhetorik in Hitlers 'Mein Kampf' und andere Essays zur Strategie der Überredung.* Frankfurt, Isar Verlag, 1967.

Butler, Rohan D., *The Roots of National Socialism 1783-1933.* New York, Dutton, 1942.

Cassirer, Ernst, *Vom Mythos des Staates.* Zurich, Europa Verlag, 1949.

Cecil, Robert, *The Myth of the Master Race: Alfred Rosenberg and Nazi Ideology.* London, Methuen, 1972.

Childs, Harwood, tr., *The Nazi Primer. Official Handbook for the Schooling of Hitler Youth.* New York, Harper and Brothers, 1938.

Clauss, Ludwig Ferdinand, *Deutsche Grösse.* Stuttgart, Kohlhammer, 1944.

————, *Die nordische Seele.* Munich, Lehmanns Verlag, 1940.

Dahmen, Hans, *Die nationale Idee von Herder bis Hitler.* Cologne, Hermann Schaffstein Verlag, 1934.

Daitz, Werner (Reichsamtsleiter), *Das Reich als europäischer Ordnungsgedanke* (Series: Nationale Wirschaftsordnung und Grossraumwirtschaft). Pamphlet. Berlin, Verlag der N.S.D.A.P., Franz Eher, Nachf., 1940/41.

Darré, Walter, *Das Bauerntum als Lebensquelle der nordischen Rasse.* Munich, Eher Verlag, 1932.

————. *Blut und Boden.* (Series: Grundlagen, Aufbau und Wirtschaftsordnung des N.S. Staates). Berlin, Industrieverlag, Spaethe & Linde, 1936.

Darton, Harvey, *Children's Books in England: Five Centuries of Social Life.* Cambridge, At the University Press, 1932.

Das deutsche Jugendbuch. Munich, Deutscher Volksverlag, 1942.

Davidson, Ellis, *Gods and Myths of Northern Europe*. Baltimore, Penguin, 1966.

_____, *Scandinavian Mythology*. Toronto, Paul Hamlyn, 1970.

Denkler, Horst and Kurt Prümm, eds., *Die deutsche Literatur im Dritten Reich*. Stuttgart, Reclam, 1976.

Dilg, Karl, *Die deutsche Bauernsage in der Schule*. Leipzig, Otto Harrassowitz, 1935.

Dobers, Ernst and Kurt Higelke, eds., *Rassenpolitische Unterrichtspraxis. Der Rassengedanke in der Unterrichtsgestaltung der Volksschulfächer*. Leipzig, Klinkhardt, 1940.

Doderer, Klaus, ed., *Das Bilderbuch in Deutschland von den Anfängen bis zur Gegenwart*. Weinheim, Beltz Verlag, 1973.

Dreyer, Adolf, *Deutsche Kultur im Neuen Reich*. Berlin, Schlieffen Verlag, 1934.

Dyrenfurth-Graebsch, Irene, *Geschichte der deutschen Jugendbuchforschung*. Hamburg, Stubenrauch, 1951.

Eilemann, Johannes, *Deutsche Seele, deutscher Mensch, deutsche Kultur und Nationalsozialismus*. Leipzig, Teubner, 1933.

Eilers, Rolf, *Die nationalsozialistische Schulpolitik. Eine Einführung zur Funktion der Erziehung im totalitären Staat*. Cologne, Opladen, Westdeutscher Verlag, 1963.

Emmerich, Wolfgang, *Zur Kritik der Volkstumsideologie*. Frankfurt, Suhrkamp Verlag, 1971.

Engelmann, Susanne Charlotte, *German Education and Re-Education*. New York, International University Press, 1942.

Engl, Hans, *Die Kinderlesehalle: Ein pädagogisches Problem*. Munich, Ernst Reinhardt, 1932.

Ernst, Franz, *Mythos und Politik*, (Wilhelmshavener Vorträge. Schriftenreihe der Nordwestdeutschen Universitätsgesellschaft) Heft 31. Wilhelmshaven, 1969.

Fechter, Paul, *Geschichte der deutschen Literatur*. Gütersloh, Bertelsmann, 1954.

Feder, Gottfried, *Das Programm der N.S.D.A.P. und seine weltanschaulichen Grundgedanken*. Munich, Eher Verlag, 1932.

Feldmann, Burton and Robert D. Richardson, *The Rise of Modern Mythology: 1680-1860*. Bloomington, Indiana University Press, 1972.

Fergusson, Francis, *The Idea of a Theater*. Garden City, Doubleday, 1953.

Flake, Otto, *Die Deutschen. Aufsätze zur Literatur und Zeitgeschichte*. Hamburg, Tütten & Loening, 1963.

Fleischhack, Kurt, *Wege zum Wissen. Buch—Buchhandel—Bibliothek: Schrif-

tenverzeichnis, 5th ed. Leipzig, Verlag des Börsenvereins der deutschen Buchhändler, 1944.

Flitner, Andreas, ed., *Deutsches Geistesleben und Nationalsozialismus*. Tübingen, Rainer Wunderlich Verlag, 1964.

Fraezer, James Sir, *The New Golden Bough*, ed. by Gaster. New York, Anchor, 1968.

Freisler, Ronald, Dr. jur. (Präsident des Volksgerichtshofes), *Das Reichsdenken des jungen Europa*. Berlin, Verlag der N.S.D.A.P., 1943.

Frick, Werner and Arthur Gütt, *Nordisches Gedankengut im Dritten Reich*. Munich, Lehmanns Verlag, 1937.

Friends of Europe Publications (Series). London, The Holy Sea, 1936.

Fronemann, Wilhelm, *Das Erbe Wolgasts*. Langensalza, Beltz Verlag, 1927.

Führer, Maria, *Nordgermanische Götterüberlieferung und deutsches Volkstum. 80 Märchen der Gebrüder Grimm vom Mythus her beleuchtet*. Munich, Neuer Filser Verlag, 1938.

Gamm, Hans Jochen, *Der braune Kult. Das Dritte Reich und seine Ersatzreligion*. Hamburg, Rütten & Loening, 1962.

———. *Führung und Verführung*. Munich, Ehrenwirt, 1964.

Gauss, Paul, ed., *Das Buch vom deutschen Volkstum*. Leipzig, Teubner, 1935.

Gehl, Walter, *Ruhm und Ehre bei den Nordgermanen*. Berlin, Junker und Dünnhaupt, 1937.

Geissler, Rolf, *Dekadenz und Heroismus. Zeitroman und völkisch-nationalsozialistische Literaturkritik*. Stuttgart, Deutsche Verlagsanstalt, 1964.

Gerstner, Hermann, *Die Brüder Grimm*. Gerabonn, Hohenloher Verlag, 1970.

Glaser, Hermann, *Spiesser-Ideologie. Von der Zerstörung des deutschen Geistes im 19. und 20. Jahrhunderts*. Freiburg, Rombach, 1964 (2nd ed.).

Graebsch, Irene, *Geschichte des deutschen Jugendbuches*. Leipzig, O. Harrassowitz, 1942. (This edition contains a section on children's literature under Nazism omitted in the later edition published under the name of Dyrenfurth-Graebsch.)

Granzow, Klaus, *Tagebuch eines Hitlerjungen 1943 - 1945*. Bremen, Carl Schünemann, 1965.

Gray, Ronald, *The German Tradition in Literature*. Cambridge, Harvard University Press, 1965.

Grimm, Jacob, *Teutonic Mythology*, ed. by J.S. Stallybrass. New York, Dover Publications, 1966.

Grimm, Jacob and Wilhelm, *Kinder- und Hausmärchen*, Grosse Ausgabe. Vol. I. Göttingen, Dietrichsche Buchhandlung, 1852.

Gruchmann, Lothar, *Nationalsozialistische Grossraumordnung. Die Kon-*

struktion einer deutschen Monroe Doctrine. Stuttgart, Deutsche Verlagsanstalt, 1962.

Grunberger, Richard, *The Twelve-Year Reich. A Social History of Nazi Germany, 1933-1945*. New York, Holt, Rinehart and Winston, 1971.

Guardini, Romano, *Der Heilbringer im Mythos. Offenbarung und Politik*. Stuttgart, Klett Verlag, 1949.

Günther, Hans F.K., *Der nordische Gedanke unter den Deutschen*. Munich, Lehmanns Verlag, 1927.

————. *Ritter, Tod und Teufel. Der heldische Gedanke*. Munich, Lehmanns Verlag, 1924.

Günzel, Marianne, Dr. and Harriet Schneider, *Buch und Erziehung. Jugendschrifttumskunde. Grundrisse der Erziehung*. Leipzig, Klinkhardt, 1943.

Haas, Gerhard, ed., *Kinder- und Jugendliteratur. Zur Typologie und Funktion einer literarischen Gattung*. Stuttgart, Reclam, 1976.

Hagemann, Walter, *Publizistik im Dritten Reich. Ein Beitrag zur Methodik der Massenführung*. Hamburg, Verlag für Buchmarktforschung, 1948.

Hagemeyer, Hans, *Der neue Mensch. Neue Aufgaben des Schrifttums und Mittlertums*. (Series: Schriftenreihe zur nationalpolitischen Erziehung, No. 220). (Leipzig, Eichblatt Verlag, Max Zedler, 1934).

Hamersky, Werner, *Göttliche Vorsehung im Lied und Gedicht der nationalsozialistischen Publizistik*. Hamburg, Verlag für Buchmarktforschung, 1960.

Harder, Hermann, *Das germanische Erbe in der deutschen Dichtung. Ein Überblick*. Potsdam, Voggenreiter, 1939.

Hart, Franz Theodor, *Alfred Rosenberg. Der Mann und sein Werk*. Munich, Lehmanns Verlag, 1939.

Hartmut, Gunter, *Deutsche Weihnachten, Brauchtum und Feiergestaltung*. 3rd ed. Halle, Teut Verlag, 1937.

Harthorne, Edward Y., Jr., *The German Universities and National Socialism*. London, Allen & Unwin, 1937.

Hasubek, Peter, *Das deutsche Lesebuch in der Zeit des Nationalsozialismus. Ein Beitrag zur Literaturpädagogik zwischen 1933 und 1945*. Hannover, Hermann Schroedel Verlag, 1972.

Heiber, Helmut, ed., *The Early Goebbels Diaries, 1925-1926*. New York, Frederick A. Praeger, 1962.

Heinrich, Johanna, *Du und Dein Kind. Flugschriften zur nordischen Glaubensbewegung*. Leipzig, Adolf Klein Verlag, 1936. (pamphlet).

Heiseler, Bernt von, ed., *Goethe: Gesammelte Werke*. Vol. VI. Gütersloh Bertelsmann Verlag, 1954.

Helbing, Lothar, *Der dritte Humanismus*. 3rd ed. Berlin, Stubenrauch, 1935.

Heller, Frederick, *Deutsche Erziehung im neuen Staat.* Langensalza, Beltz, 1939.

Herder, Johann Gottfried, *Herders Sämmtliche Werke*, ed. by Bernhard Suphan. Berlin, Weidmannsche Buchhandlung, 1894.

Herpel, Martin, *Germanische Religion.* Berlin, Junker und Dünnhaupt, 1934.

————, *Hermann Schwarz und der nordische Gedanke.* Berlin, Junker und Dünnhaupt, 1934.

Hesse, Otto Ernst, *Blunck: Beitrag zur nordischen Renaissance.* Jena, Diederichs, 1939.

Hildebrand, Klaus von, *Reich zum Weltreich: Hitler, N.S.D.A.P. und koloniale Frage 1919-1945.* Munich, Verlag Dokumentation, 1969.

Hillel, Marc, *Lebensborn e.V.: Im Namen der Rasse.* Hamburg. Paul Zsolsnay Verlag, 1975.

Hippler, Fritz, *Staat und Gesellschaft bei Mill, Marx, Lagarde. Ein Beitrag zum ideologischen Denken.*

Hitler, Adolf, *Mein Kampf.* 2 vols., unabridged. Munich, Verlag der N.S.D.A.P., Franz Eher Nachf., 1933.

Hoffmann, Heinrich, *Jugend um Hitler. 120 Bilddokumente aus der Umgebung des Führers.* Berlin, Verlag für Zeitgeschichte, 1940.

Hoffmann, Walter, *Die deutsche Volksbücherei.* Bayreuth, Reichsverwaltung des N.S.L.B., 1934.

Höhne, Heinz, *Der Orden unter dem Totenkopf. Die Geschichte der SS.* Hamburg, Fischer Bücherei, 1969.

Hürlimann, Bettina, *Three Centuries of Children's Books in Europe.* Cleveland, World Publishing Co., 1954.

Ihde, Walter, ed., *Das Recht der Reichskulturkammer.* Berlin, Walter de Gruyter, 1943.

Jahn, Friedrich Ludwig, *Vom deutschen Volkstum.* Jena, Diederichs, 1938.

Jarmen, T.F., *The Rise and Fall of Nazi Germany.* New York, New York University Press, 1955.

Kamenetsky, Ihor, *Secret Nazi Plans for Eastern Europe. A Study of Lebensraum Policies.* New York, Bookman Associates, 1961.

Kessler, Harry Graf, *Aus den Tagebüchern 1918-1937.* Munich, Deutscher Taschenbuch Verlag, G.m.b.H., 1965.

Kindermann, Heinz, ed., *Des deutschen Dichters Sendung in der Gegenwart.* Leipzig, Reclam, 1933.

————. *Dichtung und Volkheit. Grundzüge einer neuen Literaturwissenschaft.* Berlin, Junge Generation, 1937.

Klönne, Arno, *Gegen den Strom. Bericht über den Jugendwiderstand im Dritten Reich.* 2nd ed. Hannover, Norddeutsche Verlagsanstalt, O. Goedel, 1960.

_____. *Hitlerjugend. Die Jugend und ihre Organisation im Dritten Reich.* Hannover, Norddeutsche Verlagsanstalt, O. Goedel, 1957.

Klose, Werner, *Generation im Gleichschritt.* Gütersloh, Sigbert Mohn Verlag, 1964.

_____, *Lebensformen deutscher Jugend; Vom Wandervogel bis zur Popgeneration.* München, Günter Olzog Verlag, 1970.

Kneller, George Frederick, *The Educational Philosophy of National Socialism* New Haven, Yale University Press, 1941.

Köster, H.L., *Geschichte der deutschen Jugendliteratur,* 4th ed. Munich, Pullach, Verlag Dokumentation, 1968.

Kohn, Hans, *The Mind of Germany. The Education of a Nation.* New York, Scribner's, 1960.

_____. *Prophets and People. Nineteenth Century Nationalism.* New York, Macmillan Co., 1946.

Kolbenheyer, Erwin Guido, *Die Bauhütte. Grundzüge einer Metaphysik der Gegenwart.* Munich, Langen-Müller Verlag, 1940.

Krieck, Ernst, *Dichtung und Erziehung.* Leipzig, Armanen-Verlag, 1933.

_____, *Nationalpolitische Erziehung.* Leipzig, Artmanen Verlag, 1933.

_____, *Nationalsozialistische Erziehung.* (Series: *Grundlagen, Aufbau und Wirtschaftsordung des Nationalsozialistischen Staates*). Berlin, Industrieverlag, Spaethe und Linde, 1936.

Alfred, *Geschichte des Alldeutschen Verbandes, 1890-1939.* Wiesbaden, Steiner Verlag, 1956.

Kummer, Bernhard Dr., *Die altgermanische Weltanschauung nach altnordischer Überlieferung* (Vortrag gehalten im Auftrage der Vereinigung der Freunde germanischer Vorgeschichte. Detmold, June 10, 1930). Leipzig, Adolf Klein Verlag, 1930.

_____, *Midgards Untergang. Germanischer Kult und Glaube.* Leipzig, Adolf Klein Verlag, 1937.

_____, *Persönlichkeit und Gemeinschaft. Die germanische Weltanschauung nach altnordischer Überlieferung.* Leipzig, Adolf Klein Verlag, 1937.

Kunze, Horst, *Schatzbehalter alter Kinderbücher.* Hanau, Main, Verlag Werner Dause, 1965.

Lagarde, Paul, *Deutsche Schriften.* Munich, Dürr Verlag, 1924.

Langbehn, Julius, *Rembrandt als Erzieher.* Leipzig, Selbstverlag, 1927. (The first edition was issued anonymously and signed "*Von einem Deutschen*" (By a German).

Lange, Carl and Ernst Adolf Dryer, eds., *Deutscher Geist: Kulturdokumente der Gegenwart.* Berlin, Verlag der N.S.D.A.P. 1944.

Lange, Friedrich, *Deutsche Volksgeschichte, Deutsche Raumgeschichte.* Berlin, Verlag der N.S.D.A.P., 1944.

Laqueur, Walter Z., *Young Germany. A History of the German Youth Movement.* New York, Basic Books, Inc., 1962.

Langenbucher, Hellmuth, *Die deutsche Gegenwartsdichtung. Eine Einführung in das volkhafte Schrifttum unserer Zeit.* Foreword by Heinz Kindermann. Berlin, Junker und Dünnhaupt, 1940.

———, *Nationalsozialistische Dichtung. Einführung und Überblick.* Berlin, Junker und Dünnhaupt, 1934.

———, *Volkhafte Dichtung der Zeit.* Berlin, Junker und Dünnhaupt, 1933.

Langenmaier, Theodor, *Deutsches Schrifttum unserer Zeit.* Bamberg, Büchners Verlag, 1940.

Langer, Norbert, *Die deutsche Dichtung seit dem Weltkrieg, von Paul Ernst bis Hans Baumann.* Leipzig, Adam Kraft Verlag, 1941.

Ledermann, Wilhelm and Josef Prestel, *Die deutsche Sage im Unterricht.* Munich, Oldenbourg Verlag, 1927.

Leers, Heinrich von, *Das alte Wissen und der neue Glaube. Geschichte auf rassischer Grundlage.* Leipzig, Reclam, 1939.

———. *Geschichte auf rassischer Grundlage.* Leipzig, Reclam, 1934.

Leiser, Erwin, *Nazi Cinema.* Translated from the German by Gertrud Mander and David Wilson. New York, Collier Books, 1974.

Lewai, Jenö, *Geheime Reichssache: Papst Pius XII hat nicht geschwiegen.* Cologne, Müngersdorf, 1966.

Lewy, Guenther, *The Catholic Church and Nazi Germany.* New York, McGraw-Hill Book Company, 1964.

Linden, Walter, *Geschichte der deutschen Literatur.* Leipzig, Reclam, 1937.

Lingelbach, Karl Christoph, *Erziehung und Erziehungstheorien im nationalsozialistischen Deutschland.* Weinheim, Beltz Verlag, 1970.

Löbsack, Wilhelm, *Von den Pflichten und Aufgaben des politischen Führers* (Series: Schriften der Adolf-Hitler Schule) Heft 4, 1935.

Loewy, Emil, ed., *Literatur unterm Hakenkreuz. Das Dritte Reich und Seine Dichtung.* Eine Dokumentation. Frankfurt, Europäische Verlagsanstalt, 1966.

Lohrmann, Heinrich Friedrich, *Die altnordische Bauernsage in der deutschen Erziehung.* (Series: Volkhafte Schularbeit) Erfurt, Kurt Stenger Verlag, 1938.

Lorenz, Klemens and Otto Moslehner, *Das deutsche Bauerntum als Rückgrat des deutschen Volkstums in Vergangenheit, Gegenwart und Zukunft.* Für die Jugend von Stadt und Land. Breslau, Handel Verlag, 1934.

Longes, Robert U., *Paul de Lagarde 1827-1891. A Study of Radical Conservatism in Germany.* Cambridge, Harvard University Press, 1962.

Löpelmann, Martin (Ministerialdirektor), *Wege und Ziele der Kindererziehung in unserer Zeit.* Leipzig, Hesse und Becke Verlag, 1936.

Lübbe, Fritz und Professor Heinrich Lohrmann, *Deutsche Dichtung in Vergangenheit und Gegenwart. Ein Führer durch die deutsche Literatur.* 5th ed., Berlin, Carl Mayer Verlag, 1943.

Lüber, Annedore, *Das Gewissen steht auf. 64 Lebensbilder aus dem deutschen Widerstand.* Berlin, Leber, 1963.

Luis, Werner, *Das Bauerntum im grenz- und volksdeutschen Roman der Gegenwart.* Berlin, Verlag der N.S.D.A.P., Franz Eher, Nachfolger, 1940.

Lukács, Georg, *Von Nietzsche zu Hitler: oder der Irrationalismus in der deutschen Politik.* Hamburg, Fischer Verlag, 1966.

_____, *Die Zerstörung der Vernunft.* Berlin, Verlagsanstalt, 1955.

Lukas, Oskar, *Das deutsche Mädel. Ein Buch der Einkehr.* Leipzig, Adam Kraft Verlag, 1936.

Lüthi, Max. *Das Märchen* (Sammlung Metzler). Stuttgart, Metzlersche Verlagsbuchhandlung, 1964.

_____. *Once Upon a Time: On the Nature of Fairy Tales.* Bloomington, Indiana University Press, 1970.

Lützhoff, Jürgen, *Der nordische Gedanke in Deutschland, 1920-1940.* Kieler Historische Studien XIV. Stuttgart, Ernst Klett Verlag, 1971.

Maier, Karl Ernst, ed., *Historische Aspekte der Jugendliteratur.* Stuttgart, Athenäum Verlag, 1974.

Mann, Erika, *Schools for Barbarians. Education under the Nazis.* New York, Modern Age Books, 1939.

Manvell, Roger. *SS Gestapo: Rule by Terror.* New York, Ballantine, 1970.

Maser, Werner, *Frühgeschichte der N.S.D.A.P. Hitlers Weg bis 1929.* Frankfurt, Athenäum Verlag, 1965.

Masur, Gerhardt, *Prophets of Yesterday. Studies in European Culture 1898-1914.* New York, Macmillan Co., 1961.

Mayer, Hans, ed., *Deutsche Literaturkritik im 20. Jahrhundert. Kaiserreich, erster Weltkrieg und Nachkriegszeit.* Stuttgart, Geverts, 1965.

McNamee, Maurice, *Honor and the Epic Hero. A Study of the Shifting Concepts of Magnanimity in Philosophy and Epic Poetry.* New York, Holt, 1960.

Meinecke, Friedrich, *The German Catastrophe; Reflections and Recollections.* Cambridge, Oxford University Press, 1950.

Menzel, Wolfgang, *Die deutsche Literatur* I. Stuttgart, 1828.

Michel, Paul, *Der neue deutsche Erzieher.* Esslingen, W. Schneider Verlag, 1939.

Moeller, Armin, *Die konservative Revolution in Deutschland 1918-1932. Grundriss ihrer Weltanschauungen.* Stuttgart, Vorwerk, 1950.

Mosse, George L., *The Crisis of German Ideology. Ideological Origins of the Third Reich.* New York, Grosset and Dunlap, 1964.

————, *Nazi Culture, Intellectual, Cultural and Social Life in the Third Reich.* Tr. by Salvator Attanasio, et al. New York, Grosset and Dunlap, 1966.

Müller, Hans, ed., *Katholische Kirche und Nationalsozialismus.* Munich, Deutscher Taschenbuchverlag, 1965.

Murray, Henry, ed., *Myth and Mythmaking.* Boston, Beacon Press, 1968.

Muschg, Walter, *Die Zerstörung der deutschen Literatur.* Munich, Paul List Verlag, 1960.

Nadler, Josef, *Literaturgeschichte des Deutschen Volkes.* Berlin, Propyläen Verlag, 1941.

Naess, Arne, et al., *Democracy, Ideology and Objectivity; Studies in the Semantics and Cognitive Analysis of Ideological Controversy.* Oxford, Basil Blackwell, 1956.

Naumann, Hans, *Germanischer Schicksalsglaube.* Jena, Diederichs, 1934.

Neckel, Gustav, *Germanisches Heldentum.* Jena, Diederichs, 1936.

————, *Die Welt der Götter.* Leipzig, Otto Harrassowitz, 1933.

Neese, Gottfried, *Reichsjugendführung* (Series: *Grundlagen, Aufbau und Wirtschaftsordnung des nationalsozialistischen Staates*). Berlin, Industrieverlag, Spaethe und Linde, 1938.

Neurohr, Jean Friedrich, *Der Mythos vom Dritten Reich. Zur Geistesgeschichte des Nationalsozialismus.* Stuttgart, Cotta Verlag, 1957.

Niekisch, Ernst, *Das Reich der niederen Dämonen.* Hamburg, Rowohlt, 1953.

Nietzsche, Friedrich von, *The Birth of Tragedy from the Spirit of Music.* New York, Anchor Press, 1965.

Ninck, Martin, *Götter- und Jenseitsglauben der Germanen.* Jena, Diederichs Verlag, 1934.

————, *Wodan und der germanische Schicksalsglaube.* Jena, Diederichs, 1935.

Nolte, Ernst, *Three Faces of Fascism. Action Française, Italian Fascism, National Socialism.* Munich, Piper Verlag, 1965.

Nordisches Thing. Bremen, Angelsächsischer Verlag, 1933.

Obenauer, Karl Justus, *Das Märchen: Dichtung und Deutung.* Frankfurt a.M., Vittorio Klostermann, 1934.

Otto, Stefan, *Die altnordische Dichtung in der Schule. Einführung und Möglichkeiten der schulischen Behandlung.* Esslingen, a.N., Burgbücherei, 1940.

Pachter, Henry M., *Modern Germany: A Social, Cultural and Political History.* Boulder, Col., Westview Pr., 1978.

Payr, Bernhard, *Das Amt Schrifttumspflege.* Berlin, Junker und Dünnhaupt Verlag, 1941.

Payr, Bernhard and Hans Georg Otto, eds., *Das deutsche Jugendbuch.* (4 Vorträge gehalten auf einer Jugendbuch-Arbeitswoche veranstaltet vom Hauptamt für Schrifttumspflege des Beauftragten des Führers für die Überwachung der gesamten geistigen und weltanschaulichen Schulung und

Erziehung der NSDAP in Verbindung mit dem Hauptamt für Erzieher und der Reichsjugendführung in Bayreuth vom 30. Mai bis 3. Juni 1939. Munich, Deutscher Volksverlag, 1942.

Paetel, K.O., *Jugendbewegung und Politik*. Bad Godesberg, Voggenreiter, 1961.

Peters, Elke, *Nationalistisch-völkische Bildungspolitik in der Weimarer Republik. Deutschkunde und höhere Schule in Preussen*. Weinheim, Beltz, 1972.

Pickering, Samuel F., *John Locke and Children's Books in Eighteenth-Century England*. Knoxville, The University of Tennessee Press, 1981.

Polenzky, Karl, *Deutsche Dichtung im Unterricht*. Berlin, A.W. Zickfeldt, 1938.

Pongs, Hermann, *Im Umbruch der Zeit. Das Romanschaffen der Gegenwart*. Göttingen, Göttinger Verlagsanstalt, 1954.

_____. *Krieg als Volksschicksal im deutschen Schrifttum*. Stuttgart, Metzler, 1934.

Prestel, Joseph, *Dichtung der Gegenwart in der Volksschule*. Leipzig, Klinkhardt, 1938.

_____. *Handbuch zur Jugendliteratur*. Freiburg, i. Breisgau, Herder Verlag, 1933.

_____. *Märchen als Lebensdichtung. Das Werk der Brüder Grimm*. Munich, Max Hueber Verlag, 1938.

_____. *Sage und Volkheit*. Leipzig, Dürrsche Buchhandlung, 1934.

_____. *Die Schülerbücherei. Ein Führer zum guten Buch*. Munich, Schulwissenschaftlicher Verlag, 1933.

_____. *Volkhafte Dichtung. Besinnungen und Durchblicke*. (Series: Völkisches Lehrgut. Schriftenreihe zur Neugestaltung des Volksschulunterrichts). Leipzig, Klinkhardt, 1935.

Pross, Harry, *Literatur und Politik*. Freiburg im Breisgau, Walter Verlag, 1963.

_____. *Vor und nach Hitler. Zur deutschen Sozialpathalogie*. Freiburg, Walter Verlag, 1962.

Rantzau, Otto (Graf zu), Ministerialrat, *Das Reichsministerium für Wissenschaft, Erziehung und Volksbildung* (Schriften der Hochschule für Politik). Berlin, Junker und Dünnhaupt, 1939.

Reiss, H.E., ed., *Political Thought of the German Romantics: 1793-1815*. Oxford, Blackwell, 1955.

Riehl, Wilhelm Heinrich, *Die Naturgeschichte des deutschen Volkes*, ed. by Dr. Hans Naumann and Dr. Rolf Haller. Leipzig, Reclam, 1934.

Rödiger, Wilhelm, *The Teaching of History, Its Purpose, Materials and Methods*. London, St. Stephens House, Friends of Europe Publications, 1939. (Series entitled: Friends of Europe Publications, issued in pamphlet form).

————, *Geschichte, Ziel, Stoff und Weg.* Leipzig, Klinkhardt, 1934.

Roessler, H., *Jugend im Erziehungsfeld. Haltung und Verhalten der deutschen Jugend in der ersten Hälfte des 20. Jahrhunderts, unter besonderer Berücksichtigung der westdeutschen Jugend der Gegenwart.* Düsseldorf, Pädagogischer Verlag, 1959.

Rosenberg, Alfred, *Gestaltung der Idee; Reden und Aufsätze,* 1933-35. Reichstagung der N.S. Kulturgemeinde in Düsseldorf, June 6, 1935. Berlin, Zentralverlag der N.S.D.A.P., 1935.

————. *Der Mythus des 20. Jahrhunderts.* 9th ed. Munich, Eher Verlag, 1943.

————. *Nationalismus, Religion und Kultur.* (Series: Grundlagen, Aufbau und Wirtschaftsordnung des Nationalsozialistischen Staates). Berlin, Verlag der N.S.D.A.P., 1936.

————. *Die neue Mission des Erziehers. Reden des Reichsleiters* Alfred Rosenberg und des Reichsverwalters des N.S. Lehrerbundes, Fritz Wächler, anlässlich der Einweihung der Reichsschule des NSLB in Donndorf bei Bayreuth am 7. Oktober, 1938. Munich, Deutscher Volksverlag, 1939.

————. *Nordische Wiedergeburt.* Berlin, Verlag der N.S.D.A.P., 1935.

————. *Das Parteiprogramm. Wesen, Grunds*ätze und Ziele der N.S.D.A.P. Munich, Eher Verlag, 1943.

Rothfels, Hans, *German Opposition to Hitler.* Translated by Lawrence Wilson. Chicago, Regnery, 1962.

Rüttgers, Severin, *Erweckung des Volkes durch seine Dichtung.* Leipzig, Dürr, 1933.

————. *Deutsche Dichtung in der Volksschule.* Leipzig, Dürrsche Buchhandlung, 1914.

Rust, Bernhard (Reichsminister für Wissenschaft, Erziehung und Volksbildung), *Erziehung und Unterricht in der Volksschule.* Berlin, Verlag der N.S.D.A.P., 1940.

————. *Das nationalsozialistische Deutschland und die Wissenschaft* (Schriften des Reichsinstituts für Geschichte des neuen Deutschland. (Includes also: Ernst Krieck, "Heidelberger Reden"). Hamburg, Hanseatische Verlagsanstalt, 1936.

Saller, Karl, *Die Rassenlehre des Nationalsozialismus in Wissenschaft und Propaganda.* Darmstadt, Progress Verlag, 1961.

Schedler, Melchior, *Kindertheater: Geschichte, Modelle, Projekte.* Frankfurt, Suhrkamp, 1972.

Schirach, Baldur von, *Die Hitler-Jugend: Idee und Gestalt.* Berlin, Verlag Zeitgeschichte, 1934.

————. *Ich glaubte an Hitler.* Hamburg, Mosaik Verlag, 1967.

————. *Revolution der Erziehung. Reden aus den Jahren des Aufbaus.* 2nd ed., Munich, Eher Verlag, 1939.

Schirach, Henriette von, *Der Preis der Herrlichkeit.* Wiebaden, Limes Verlag, 1956.

Schlund, G., *Neugermanisches Heldentum im heutigen Deutschland.* Munich, Eher Verlag, 1924.

Schmidt, Otto, *Volkstumsarbeit als politische Aufgabe.* Berlin, Industrieverlag, 1937.

Schmidt-Henkel, Gerhard, *Mythos und Dichtung. Zur Begriffs- und Stilgeschichte der deutschen Literatur des 19. und 20. Jahrhunderts.* Berlin, Gehen Verlag, 1967.

Schnabel, Reimund (Bannführer), *Das Führerschulungswerk der Hitler-Jugend.* Berlin, Junker und Dünnhaupt, 1938.

Schneider, Hermann, *Die Götter der Germanen.* Tübingen, J.C.B. Mohr, Paul Siebeck, 1938.

Schönbaum, David, *Hitler's Social Revolution, Class and Status in Nazi Germany 1933-1939.* New York, Doubleday, 1966.

Schonauer, Franz, *Deutsche Literatur im Dritten Reich.* Freiburg im Breisgau, Walter Verlag, 1961.

Schoof, Wilhelm, ed., *Unbekannte Briefe der Brüder Grimm. Unter Ausnutzung des Grimmschen Nachlasses.* Bonn, Athenäum, 1960.

Schwan, Alexander, *Politische Philosophie im Denken Heideggers.* Köln, Westdeutscher Verlag, 1965.

Schwarz, Hermann, *Christentum, Nationalismus und deutsche Glaubensbewegung.* Berlin, Verlag der N.S.D.A.P., 1939.

Schriewer, Franz, *Das Schülerbüchereiwesen der Volksschulen in Leistungszahlen.* Leipzig, Einkaufshaus für Büchereien, 1938.

Scott, Walter Sir, *Letters on Demonology and Witchcraft.* Wakefield, Yorkshire, S.R. Publishers, Ltd. Reprint, 1968.

Sebeok, Thomas, ed., *Myth: A Symposium.* Bloomington, Indiana University Press, 1955.

See, Klaus von, *Deutsche Germanen-Ideologie vom Humanismus bis zur Gegenwart.* Berlin, Propyläen Verlag, 1970.

Shafer, Boyd, *Nationalism, Myth and Reality.* New York, Harcourt, Brace & Co., 1955.

Shirer, William L., *The Rise and Fall of Nazi Germany.* New York, Simon and Schuster, 1960.

Sington, Derrick and Arthur Weidenfeld, *The Goebbels Experiment; A Study of the Nazi Propaganda Machine.* New Haven, Yale University Press, 1941.

Sonthheimer, Kurt, *Antidemokratisches Denken in der Weimarer Republik. Die politischen Ideen des deutschen Nationalismus zwischen 1918 und 1933.* Munich, Nymphenburg, 1967. 2nd ed.

Speer, Albert, *Erinnerungen*. Berlin, Propyläen Verlag, 1970.

———, *Spandauer Tagebücher*. Frankfurt, Propyläen Verlag, 1975.

Spiess, Karl von, *Deutsche Volkskunde als Erschliesserin deutscher Kultur*. Berlin, Stubenrauch, 1934.

Spiess, Karl von and Edmund Mudrak, *Deutsche Märchen—Deutsche Welt; Zeugnisse nordischer Weltanschauung in volkstümlicher Überlieferung*. Berlin, Stubenrauch, 1935.

———, *Deutsche Volkskunde als politische Wissenschaft*. Berlin, Stubenrauch, 1938.

Stachura, Peter D., *Nazi Youth in the Weimar Republic*. (Studies in Comparative Politics). Santa Barbara, California, Clio Books, 1975.

Steinitz Fraenzer, Wilhelm v., *Jacob Grimm zur 100. Wiederkehr seines Todestages. (Festschrift)*. Berlin, Akademischer Verlag, 1963.

Stern, Fritz, *The Politics of Cultural Despair. A Study in the Rise of the Germanic Ideology*. Berkeley, University of California Press, 1961.

Stockley, A., *German Literature as Known in England*, 1752-1830. London, Routledge & Sons, 1929.

Strobel, Hans Dr., *Bauernbrauch im Jahreslauf*. Leipzig, Koehler und Amelang, 1940.

———, *Neue Brauchtumskunde*. Leipzig, Koehler und Amelang, 1937.

———, *Volkskundliche Grundlagen der Feiergestaltung*. Leipzig, Verlag Koehler & Amelang, 1938.

Strothmann, Dietrich, *Nationalsozialistische Literaturpolitik. Ein Beitrag zur Publizistik im Dritten Reich*. Bonn, Bouvier, 1960.

Strzgowski, Josef, *Geistige Umkehr; Indogermanische Gegenwartsstreifzüge eines Kunstforschers*. Heidelberg, 1938.

Sturluson, Snorri, *The Prose Edda; Tales from Norse Mythology*. Edited by Young. Berkeley, University of California Press, 1966.

Suren, Hans, *Volkserziehung im Dritten Reich*. Stuttgart, Franck'sche Verlagsbuchhandlung, 1934.

Tauber, Kurt P., *Beyond Eagle and Swastika. German Nationalism since 1945*. 2 vols. Middleton, Connecticut, Wesleyan University Press, 1967.

Tenenbaum, Joseph, *Race and Reich*. New York, Twayne, 1956.

Thiele, Ernst Otto, *Sinnbild und Brauchtum*. Potsdam, Voggenreiter Verlag, 1937.

Tisner, Jens, *Kunstmärchen*. Stuttgart, Metzler, 1977.

Tönnies, Ferdinand, *Gemeinschaft und Gesellschaft; Grundbegriffe der reinen Soziologie*. Berlin, 1926.

Trevor-Roper, H.R., *Hitler's Secret Conversations, 1941-1944*. New York, New American Library, 1961.

Usadel, Georg, *Zucht und Ordnung. Versuch einer nationalsozialistischen Ethik*. Hamburg, Hanseatische Verlagsanstalt, 1935.

Viereck, Peter, *Metapolitics. The Roots of the Nazi Mind*. New York, Capricorn Books, 1961.

Vries, Jan de, *Altnordische Literaturgeschichte*. Berlin, Walther de Gruyter & Co., 1968.

———. *Die geistige Welt der Germanen*. Halle, Saale, E. Niemeyer, 1943.

Wagner, Frank, *Literatur und Kriegskurs. Eine literarische Analyse*. Berlin, Luchterhand Verlag, 1961.

Wagner, Paul, *Die Schülerbücherei in der Volksschule*. Leipzig, Dürr, 1930.

Walzel, Oscar, *German Romanticism*. New York, Putnam's Sons, 1967.

Weinreich, Max, *Hitler's Professors: The Part of Scholarship in Germany's Crimes against the Jewish People*. New York, Yiddish Scientific Institute (YIVO), 1946.

Werner, Karl Ferdinand, *Das N.S. Geschichtsbild und die deutsche Geschichtswissenschaft*. Stuttgart, Kohlhammer, 1967.

Westecker, Wilhelm, *Volksschicksal bestimmt den Wandel der Dichtung*. Berlin, Verlag der N.S.D.A.P., 1942.

Wildner, Adolf, *Die Jugendliteratur*. Reichenberg, Paul Sollers, 1937.

Willrich, Wolfgang, *Säuberung des Kunsttempels. Eine kunstpolitische Kampfschrift zur Gesundung deutscher Kunst im Geiste nordischer Art*. Munich, Lehmanns Verlag, 1937.

Wirth, Hermann, *Aufgang der Menschheit*. Jena, Diederichs, 1928.

———, *Die heilige Urschrift der Menschheit*. 2 vols. Leipzig, Klinkhardt, 1936.

Wolf, A., *Higher Education in Nazi Germany*. London, Methuen, 1944.

Wolff, Ludwig, *Rittertum und Germanentum im Mannestum und Heldenideal*. Marburg, Wegener, 1942.

Wolgast, Heinrich, *Das Elend unserer Jugendliteratur; Beiträge zur künstlerischen Erziehung unserer Jugend*. Hamburg, Selbstverlag, 1950.

———, ed., *Vom Kinderbuch; Gesammelte Aufsätze*. Leipzig, Teubner, 1906.

Ziegler, Matthias, *Die Frau im Märchen*. Leipzig, Koehler und Amelang, 1937.

———, *Volkskunde auf rassischer Grundlage. Voraussetzungen und Aufgaben*. (Series: Deutsche Volkskunde für die Schulungs- und Erziehungsarbeit der N.S.D.A.P.). Munich, Hoheneichen Verlag, 1939.

Ziemer, Gregor, A., *Education for Death. The Making of the Nazis*. New York, Oxford University Press, 1941.

Zimmermann, Karl, *Die geistigen Grundlagen des Nationalsozialismus*. Leipzig, Adolf Klein Verlag, 1935.

Zimmermann, Peter, *Der Bauernroman: Antifeudalismus, Konservatismus, Faschismus*. Stuttgart, Deutsche Verlagsanstalt, 1975.

Zimmermann, Walther, *Nordische Verpflichtung: Beiträge zum nordischen Gedanken* (Im Auftrage der Nordischen Gesellschaft). Berlin, Limpert, 1935.

———. *Nordische Wiedergeburt; Beiträge zum nordischen Gedanken*. Berlin, Limpert, 1935.

Zuckmayer, Carl, *Die Brüder Grimm: Ein deutscher Beitrag zur Humanität*. Frankfurt, Suhrkamp, 1948.

B.   *Periodicals* (Individual articles are listed in the chapter notes.)

The American Political Science Review (quarterly)
Berliner Lokalanzeiger (daily)
Börsenblatt für den deutschen Buchhandel (weekly)
Bremer Nachrichten und Weser-Kurier (daily)
Die Buchbesprechung (monthly)
Die Bücherkunde (monthly)
Deutsche Kultur-Wacht (monthly)
Deutsche Kulturwoche (weekly)
Deutsche Rundschau (monthly)
Deutsche Vierteljahresschrift für Literaturwissenschaft und Geistesgeschichte (quarterly)
Deutsch-Nordische Zeitschrift (monthly)
Deutsches Ahnenerbe (monthly)
Deutsches Bildungswesen (monthly)
Deutsches Geistesleben (monthly)
Deutsches Volkstum (monthly)
Dichtung und Volkstum (formerly: *Euphorion*) (monthly)
Eden (monthly)
Elementary English (quarterly)
Encounter (quarterly)
Freude und Arbeit (weekly)
German International (monthly)
Germanien (monthly)
Germanen-Erbe (monthly)
Hagal (monthly)
Hilf-Mit (monthly)
Hamburger Lehrerzeitung (daily)
Hamburger Nachrichten (daily)
History of the Second World War (illustrated weekly)
The Horn Book Magazine (quarterly)
Journal of American Folklore (quarterly)
Jugendschriften-Warte (monthly)
Jungen—Eure Welt (monthly)
Mädel—Eure Welt (monthly)
Metaphilosophy (quarterly)

Mitteilungsblatt des R.K. d.b.K. (monthly)
Nationalsozialistische Bibliographie (monthly)
Nationalsozialistische Erziehung (monthly)
Nationalsozialistische Monatshefte (monthly)
Die Neue Literatur (quarterly)
Die Neue Gemeinschaft (quarterly)
Parabola: Myth and the Quest for Meaning (quarterly)
Der Spiegel (weekly)
Volk und Rasse (quarterly)
Die Volksschule (monthly)
Völkischer Beobachter (daily)
Völkische Kultur (monthly)
Von deutscher Art in Sprache und Dichtung (quarterly)
Westfälischer Erzieher (monthly)
Wille und Macht (monthly)
Die Zeit (daily)
Zeitschrift für deutsche Bildung (monthly)
Zeitschrift für deutsche Kulturphilosophie (monthly)

Index